interpersonal communication

②

KORY FLOYD

Arizona State University

McGraw Hill — Connect Learn Succeed™

Boston   Burr Ridge, IL   Dubuque, IA   New York   San Francisco   St. Louis
Bangkok   Bogotá   Caracas   Kuala Lumpur   Lisbon   London   Madrid   Mexico City
Milan   Montreal   New Delhi   Santiago   Seoul   Singapore   Sydney   Taipei   Toronto

The McGraw-Hill Companies

Mc Graw Hill

Connect
Learn
Succeed™

Published by McGraw-Hill, an imprint of The McGraw-Hill Companies, Inc., 1221 Avenue of the Americas, New York, NY 10020. Copyright © 2011, 2009. All rights reserved. No part of this publication may be reproduced or distributed in any form or by any means, or stored in a database or retrieval system, without the prior written consent of The McGraw-Hill Companies, Inc., including, but not limited to, in any network or other electronic storage or transmission, or broadcast for distance learning.

This book is printed on acid-free paper.

This book was printed in the United States of America.

2 3 4 5 6 7 8 9 0 RJE/RJE 1 0 9 8 7 6 5 4 3 2

ISBN: 978-0-07-340675-6 (Student's Edition)
MHID: 0-07-340675-9
ISBN: 978-0-07-741005-6 (Instructor's Edition)
MHID: 0-07-74105-X

Sponsoring Editor: *Susan Gouijnstook*
Marketing Manager: *Leslie Oberhuber*
Developmental Editors: *Mikola De Roo and Sylvia Mallory*
Production Editor: *Holly Irish*
Production Service: *The Left Coast Group*
Manuscript Editor: *Jennifer Gordon*
Designer: *Cassandra Chu*
Text and Cover Designer: *Linda Beaupre*
Photo Research: *Jennifer Blankenship*
Buyer: *Tandra Jorgensen*
Media Project Manager: *Mathew Sletten*
Digital Product Manager: *Janet Byrne Smith*
Composition: *10.5/12 Adobe Garamond by Thompson Type*
Printing: *45# Liberty Dull, R. R. Donnelley & Sons/Jefferson City*

Vice President Editorial: *Michael Ryan*
Publisher: *David Patterson*
Editorial Director: *William Glass*
Director of Development: *Rhona Robbin*

Credits: The credits section for this book begins on page C-1 and is considered an extension of the copyright page.

Library of Congress Cataloging-in-Publication Data
Floyd, Kory.
    Interpersonal communication / Kory Floyd. — 2nd ed.
       p. cm.
    ISBN: 978-0-07-340675-6 (Student's Edition)
    MHID: 0-07-340675-9
    1. Interpersonal communication.   I. Title.
BF637.C45F56   2011
153.6—dc23

                                   2011032663

The Internet addresses listed in the text were accurate at the time of publication. The inclusion of a website does not indicate an endorsement by the authors or McGraw-Hill, and McGraw-Hill does not guarantee the accuracy of the information presented at these sites.

www.mhhe.com

For all who labor
to make life better

Name: Kory Floyd

Education: I got my undergraduate degree from Western Washington University, my Masters degree from the University of Washington, and my PhD from the University of Arizona.

Current jobs: Professor, book writer

Favorite job growing up: Singing busboy

Worst childhood memory: Getting sent to the principal's office in third grade. (It's possible I haven't told my parents about that.)

Best childhood memory: The birth of my sister and brother

Hobbies: Playing piano, singing, reading, traveling, playing Wii tennis

Pets: I have a kitty, whose name is Kitty. I also have a family of goldfish in the pond in my back yard.

Favorite recent book: Outliers, by Malcolm Gladwell

Favorite TV show: NCIS (the original one)

Places I love: New Zealand, Starbucks, my parents' house

Dear Readers,

I can still recall how my family reacted when I said I wanted to study communication. *You already know how to communicate,* I remember one relative saying. Communication seemed like common sense to my family members, so they weren't entirely sure why I needed a PhD just to understand it.

As it turns out, a lot of other people feel the way my relatives do. Because each of us communicates in some form nearly every day of our lives, it's hard not to think of communication as completely intuitive.

That is especially true for interpersonal communication, since forming and maintaining relationships with others is such a pervasive human activity. What can we learn from research and formal study that we don't already know from our lived experience? Aren't we all experts in interpersonal communication? Just for the sake of argument, let's say we were. Why, then, do we so often misunderstand each other? Why is our divorce rate as high as it is? How come it seems like women and men speak different languages? How do we explain the popularity of self-help books, relationship counselors, and talk shows? If we're all experts at communicating interpersonally, why is it so challenging so often? Maybe communication isn't as intuitive as one might think.

When I wrote the first edition of *Interpersonal Communication,* my goal was to help students see how interpersonal communication not only affects their relationships but also influences their health, happiness, and quality of life. I wanted to guide students to go beyond commonsense notions about communication and help them see the value of investigating interpersonal processes systematically. I wanted to meet those priorities while speaking to students in a way that interests them and encourages them to use both the content and the cognitive tools to relate theories and concepts to their own experiences.

Our world is changing quickly these days—and so, too, are the ways we communicate. In the last few years, we've seen people use computer-mediated forms of communication in unprecedented ways. Deployed servicemen watch the birth of their children live via Skype. College students organize rallies with less than a day's notice on Twitter. Adults given up for adoption as infants use Facebook to find their biological parents. And despite the growth of these newer platforms, e-mail is far from dead: Most adults in a recent survey said their e-mail load either increased or stayed the same over the past year. Each new technology shrinks our world just a little more, making interpersonal communication skills increasingly valuable. While keeping the original focus on well-being and everyday applications, this new edition of *Interpersonal Communication* helps students build the interpersonal skills they'll need to communicate effectively in today's environments.

Ideally, a good textbook will not only interest and excite students; it will also provide relevant, contemporary, and high-quality support for instructors. *Interpersonal Communication 2/e* offers instructors their own edition of the text, with annotations in the margins, as well as an instructor's website and test bank designed to help make the interpersonal communication course come alive in their classrooms. And instructors and students will benefit from the addition of Connect Interpersonal, a flexible, groundbreaking online learning platform that features LearnSmart, an adaptive diagnostic; hands-on learning activities; quizzes; and a fully integrated e-book. Connect Interpersonal enables instructors to better tailor class time to student needs, and gives students more opportunities than ever for interpersonal skills practice and assessment. I hope you will find the result of these efforts to be a well-integrated package of engaging and contemporary materials for the study of interpersonal communication.

brief contents

contents

4 Interpersonal Perception 107

PART 2 INTERPERSONAL COMMUNICATION SKILLS IN ACTION

5 Language 143

PART 3 DYNAMICS OF INTERPERSONAL RELATIONSHIPS

9 Interpersonal Communication in Friendships and Professional Relationships 277

10 Interpersonal Communication in Romantic and Family Relationships 313

11 Interpersonal Conflict   349

12 Deceptive Communication   381

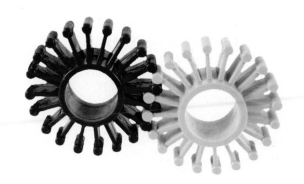

Boxes

Interpersonal Communication: Skills for Real Life

Dr. Kory Floyd wrote his introductory interpersonal communication textbook because he wanted to show students that effective interpersonal communication can improve their lives. The result: *Interpersonal Communication,* a widely praised, comprehensive text that helps students learn principles they can put into action effectively, every day.

This second edition of *Interpersonal Communication* does more than prepare students for class. Reflecting the rapid changes of the world in which today's students live and interact—including the increase in computer-mediated communication platforms—it helps them build vital interpersonal skills and make sound choices—academically, personally, and professionally.

Connect to interpersonal essentials.

What if your students could bridge theory and practice?

The text and digital components of Floyd's *Interpersonal Communication* invite students to go beyond superficial ideas about communication:

Current communication theory, research, and scholarship. Floyd's text presents and investigates the interpersonal process systematically, based on the most current research and scholarship. But most important, it uses story-telling to connect those principles and concepts to students' own experiences.

Critical thinking opportunities abound both in the text and online in Connect Interpersonal, McGraw-Hill's groundbreaking, interactive digital learning platform:

LEARN IT What does it mean to say that self-concepts are partly subjective? Compare and contrast reflected appraisal and social comparison as influences on the development of a self-concept. What are the advantages and disadvantages of being a low self-monitor?

APPLY IT Create a version of Figure 3.1 for yourself. Around the figure in the middle, draw six to eight small images that represent your different selves. Then draw three or four new selves that represent not the person you are but the person you would like to become. Next to each of those ideal selves, write one statement describing something you can do to become more like that ideal self.

REFLECT ON IT How do your friends and relatives affirm and reinforce your perceptions of yourself? If you had to create a time capsule to describe yourself to future generations and could include only five things, what things would you choose? Why?

NEW Section-ending "Learn It/Apply It/Reflect on It" feature expanded to provide more skills practice options. "Learn It" exercises also appear in Connect Interpersonal, offering students numerous ways to review, apply, and reflect on the principles they are studying and making use of every day.

FACT OR fiction

LET IT OUT: DISCLOSURE DOES A BODY GOOD

When you've gone through troubling times, have you ever noticed that you feel better after putting your feelings into words? Some people say they benefit from talking with supportive friends or counselors about their experiences. Others say that even writing about their feelings in a private journal makes them feel better, both mentally and physically. Is that idea fact or fiction?

A large body of research suggests that it's a fact. Multiple experiments by psychologist James Pennebaker and his colleagues have demonstrated that disclosing feelings in writing—particularly feelings related to experiences of trauma—produces measurable benefits in physical and mental health. In a typical study, participants write once a week for 20 minutes at a time over a three-week period about a traumatic event.

neutral topics, such as what they did over the weekend. Pennebaker and his team have found that compared to the control group, participants who disclose about traumatic events experience significant improvements in their mental and physical health, some of which last several months after the experiment has ended. Pennebaker believes that suppressing emotions requires effort that can also impair a person's health. Expressing emotions in words—even in writing—may relieve people of the effort required to suppress their emotions and cause their health to improve as a result.

ASK YOURSELF

- How do you notice that you feel better, if at all, after disclosing your emotions?
- Are you generally more comfortable self-disclosing to members of one sex than to members of the other, or do you feel equally comfortable disclosing to both women and men?

"Fact or Fiction?" boxes in every text chapter and new online "Misconceptions" quizzes in Connect Interpersonal. These valuable elements prompt students to challenge their assumptions about seemingly self-evident communication questions.

Connect to interpersonal competence.

What if your students could think more critically about all their communication choices, face-to-face and online?

assess your SKILLS

PEOPLE, ACTION, CONTENT, TIME: WHAT'S YOUR LISTENING STYLE?

People listen for various reasons—sometimes to learn, sometimes to evaluate, and sometimes to provide empathy. Researchers have identified four distinct styles, each consisting of a different set of attitudes and beliefs about listening. Research suggests that most of us have one primary style that we use the most often. Which of the following styles best describes you?

- *People-oriented style:* This style emphasizes concern for other people's emotions and interests. As the name suggests, someone with a people-oriented style tries to find common interests with others. For instance, when Palik listens to his middle school students, he tries to understand what they are thinking and feeling so that he can relate to them effectively.

- *Action-oriented style:* This style emphasizes organization and precision. An action-oriented listener likes neat, concise, error-free presentations. For example, Monica approves when her interns fill her in on the week's activities in a clear, straightforward way, and gets frustrated when she can't understand them.

Each style has its distinctive strengths and weaknesses, so none is inherently better than the others. If you're primarily a people-oriented listener, for example, you're likely to get to know other people well, but you might not be able to work as efficiently as a time-oriented listener. Action-oriented listeners might do best in majors that emphasize clarity and precision, such as engineering and computer science, whereas content-oriented listeners might prefer majors that involve greater ambiguity and room for debate, such as art and political science.

Regardless of your primary listening style, research demonstrates that we adopt different styles for different situations. For instance, you might prefer a time-oriented style when you're in a rush but a people-oriented style when you're visiting loved ones. Similarly, you might adopt a content-oriented style when listening to your professor give a lecture but an action-oriented style when listening to the evening news.

Sources: Imhof, M. (2004). Who are we as we listen? Individual listening profiles in varying contexts. *International Journal of Listening, 18,* 36–45; Watson, K. W., Barker, L. L., & Weaver, J. B. (1995). The listening styles profile (LSP-16): Development and validation of an instrument to assess four listening styles. *International Journal of Listening, 9,* 1–13.

Skills self-assessment. "Assess Your Skills" features in each textbook chapter and "Skills Self-Assessments" in Connect Interpersonal ask students to evaluate their tendencies and competence at a particular IPC skill.

NEW **Technology, computer-mediated communication (CMC), and IPC.** With embedded technology-related examples in every chapter, as well as up-to-date coverage of social networking, e-mail, texting, IMing, and more, *Interpersonal Communication* explores the implications, opportunities, and challenges individuals encounter as they rely more and more on new technologies for interpersonal communication.

NEW **"Get Connected" feature.** In every chapter, "Get Connected" boxes focus on interpersonal issues that arise within CMC-based platforms—in people's personal lives, in their workplaces, and in online classrooms.

NEW **Online Video Activities in Connect Interpersonal.** High-interest video clips from current pop-culture sources illustrate and test students' understanding of communication concepts.

g@t connected

PEOPLE 2.0: PERCEPTIONS OF AVATARS

When interacting online, many people use avatars as representations of themselves. Although avatars are not "real" people, they signify real people, and so we become accustomed to perceiving them in many of the same ways we perceive the people around us. Including an avatar alongside an e-mail message or chat room posting can make our words seem more personal to others—but how is our avatar *really* being perceived? To find out, communication researchers Kristine Nowak and Christian Rauh had college students evaluate a series of avatars and report on their perceptions. The researchers learned that

- *Avatars should look as human as possible.* Some people create avatars that are based on images of animals or inanimate objects. Nowak and Rauh found, however, that human-looking avatars were perceived to be more credible and more attractive.

- *Avatars should have a defined gender.* Many avatars appear androgynous, meaning that it is difficult to tell whether the avatar is intended to be female or male. According to the research, people prefer interacting with avatars that they perceive as clearly male or female rather than androgynous.

If you create an avatar to use in computer-mediated communication, remember that others will perceive it as a representation of you. Consider the perceptions you want your avatar to create when you're communicating interpersonally, and notice the perceptions you form of others' avatars.

What if your students had an online tool that identified the gaps in their learning and created a personal study plan?

NEW *LearnSmart,* **McGraw-Hill's adaptive learning system for assessing student knowledge of course content and mapping out a personalized study plan for success.** Accessible within Connect Interpersonal, *LearnSmart* uses a series of adaptive questions to pinpoint the concepts students understand— and those they don't. The result is an online tool that helps students learn faster and study more efficiently and that enables instructors to customize classroom lectures and activities to meet their students' needs.

Connect to culture.
What if your students had more insight into the role culture plays in communication?

A strong, integrated emphasis on culture, gender, and diversity throughout the text. In addition to a full chapter on culture and gender and communication, *Interpersonal Communication* weaves coverage of culture and gender throughout the text. The communication priorities and challenges of socially marginalized groups (for example, the elderly, economically disadvantaged individuals, immigrants, sexual minorities, persons with psychological disorders, and those with physical disabilities) are also addressed across chapters.

NEW **Groundbreaking "Dark Side" coverage expanded to a broader "Light Side/Dark Side" lens.** To give students a holistic view of the IPC spectrum, alternating "Communication: Dark Side" and "Communication: Light Side" boxes examine interpersonal communication issues that people commonly experience respectively as either negative or positive. Through this practical feature, students gain insight into how best to navigate various choices and challenges they might encounter in everyday life situations.

communication — dark side

EATING DISORDERS AND THE PRESSURE TO BE ATTRACTIVE

There's little question that being physically attractive is an advantage. Because of the halo effect, we think attractive people are nicer, smarter, friendlier, more honest, and more competent than unattractive people, and we treat them accordingly. From childhood, most of us are taught to prize physical attractiveness. Unfortunately, this emphasis on physical looks can create enormous social and psychological pressures for people to make themselves as attractive as possible.

Because of the pressure to be attractive, and because being attractive often means being thin, an alarming number of people suffer from eating disorders.

The U.S. National Institute of Mental Health identifies two major types of eating disorders: anorexia nervosa and bulimia nervosa. *Anorexia nervosa* derives from the

health problems, including gastrointestinal disorders, clinical depression, and tooth decay (stemming from frequent purging).

Even people without eating disorders can take extreme measures to achieve thinness. Some undergo a procedure called *vertical banded gastroplasty*—better known as stomach stapling—that surgically alters the stomach to restrict food intake so that they will lose weight. A different procedure called *abdominoplasty*—or a tummy tuck—surgically removes excess skin and fat from the abdomen to make a person appear thinner.

FROM ME TO YOU

If you've never had an eating disorder, it might be easy to dismiss anorexia and bulimia as merely a symptom of

NEW **"Know Yourself" activities in Connect Interpersonal.** Students' understanding of the range of views of different communication concepts is enhanced and deepened as they apply those varying perspectives to their own thoughts.

Connect to interpersonal skills.

What if your students had more ways to sharpen their skills?

NEW **"Got Skills?" activities in every chapter.** These all-new boxes serve as a bridge between theory and practice, enabling students to apply IPC concepts to real-world situations.

[APPEALING TO LOGOS]

Use logical arguments to persuade others.

WHAT?

Learn to persuade through the use of logic and reason.

WHY?

To encourage individuals to think or act in a particular way by appealing to their sense of reason, as when you are trying to get someone to end a dangerous practice (such as drinking and driving) or to persuade a person to contribute to a cause you support.

HOW?

1. Select someone you want to persuade and an issue on which you want to persuade the person. For example, suppose you want to persuade your father to pay for your study abroad next summer.

2. In a letter, lay out two specific reasons why the person should do as you suggest. Remember, your goal is to show why your suggested action makes sense. So, be sure to appeal to logic, not emotion.

3. For each reason, give evidence for your claims. For the study-abroad example, you might explain how study abroad helps students get better-paying jobs when they graduate. You might support that claim using information from your school's study-abroad office.

TRY!

1. Write your persuasive letter, but don't send it to the addressee. Rather, share it with a small group in your class or with your instructor, for feedback on ways to make the logic in your arguments more persuasive.

2. Once you have received feedback on your letter, you may either keep it or send it and see if it is persuasive.

CONSIDER: *In what instances is it more persuasive to appeal to reason than to emotion?*

NEW **Digital Learning Solutions that assess and improve students' knowledge.** Connect Interpersonal integrates an interactive e-book with path-breaking online activities and assignments that help students study more effectively and efficiently. This flexible platform also makes the management and grading of assignments easier for instructors. Connect Interpersonal includes the following features:

- *LearnSmart,* an adaptive study tool
- A fully integrated e-book
- Integration with the BlackBoard CMS
- Chapter quizzes
- "Misconceptions" tests
- "Situation Analysis" activities geared to developing students' understanding of communication concepts and applying their learning to realistic scenarios
- Skills self-assessments
- "Know Yourself" exercises prompting students to look at communication concepts from multiple viewpoints
- "Self-Reflection" activities
- Video-based activities

Changes for the Second Edition
Chapter-by-Chapter Changes

CHAPTER 1: ABOUT COMMUNICATION
- New table describing uses of computer-mediated communication
- "Got Skills?" boxes focusing on relational dimensions of communication and on cognitive complexity
- Inclusion of impersonal communication in description of communication types
- New "Fact or Fiction?" box addressing the connection between online communication and happiness
- "Get Connected" feature exploring netiquette

CHAPTER 2: CULTURE AND GENDER
- "Got Skills?" boxes examining cultural norms and expressive talk
- "Get Connected" feature focusing on Facebook culture
- Expanded coverage of cultural influences on gender roles

CHAPTER 3: COMMUNICATION AND THE SELF
- Expanded application of Johari window
- "Got Skills?" boxes focusing on self-fulfilling prophecies and on facework
- "Assess Your Skills" box on managing one's online image
- New "Fact or Fiction?" box probing the health benefits of self-disclosure
- "Get Connected" feature looking at Internet addiction as a component of self-concept

CHAPTER 4: INTERPERSONAL PERCEPTION
- "Get Connected" feature examining perceptions of avatars
- "Communication: Light Side" feature on seeing lovers through rose-colored glasses
- "Got Skills?" boxes on self-serving biases and on direct perception checking

CHAPTER 5: LANGUAGE
- Expanded treatment of loaded language
- Updated table of popular names
- Replacement of social influence strategies with rhetorical strategies for persuasion: ethos, pathos, logos
- New table offering examples of emotional appeals
- "Got Skills?" boxes giving practice on appeals to logos and on I-statements
- "Get Connected" feature focusing on gender and language in blogs
- New "Communication: Light Side" box on websites offering words of comfort to bullying victims

CHAPTER 6: NONVERBAL COMMUNICATION
- "Get Connected" feature on immediacy behaviors in online classrooms
- Streamlined presentation of nonverbal communication functions
- New section on culture, sex, and nonverbal communication
- "Got Skills?" boxes on adapting to sex differences and on generating interpretations for nonverbal behaviors

THE EXPANSION OF FLOYD'S GROUNDBREAKING "DARK SIDE" COVERAGE TO A BROADER "LIGHT SIDE/DARK SIDE" LENS. Floyd's text was the first in its field to devote meaningful coverage to "dark side" interpersonal communication topics. The second edition builds on that "dark side" focus by recognizing that IPC is a spectrum and that it is to students' advantage to understand all the dimensions of interpersonal communication. To this end, "Communication: Dark Side" boxes and "Communication: Light Side" boxes examine one interpersonal communication issue per chapter that people commonly experience as either negative or positive—and, in doing so, give students a foundation for understanding how their own choices impact the way a given interpersonal scenario plays out. Topics include electronic eavesdropping, eating disorders, and deception, as well as positive social connections online and the health benefits of positive emotion.

MORE ON TECHNOLOGY AND COMPUTER-MEDIATED COMMUNICATION (CMC), INCLUDING COVERAGE OF ONLINE EDUCATION. In keeping with Floyd's holistic approach to IPC, the text's CMC-focused content is not limited to its misuses but also includes the positive implications and opportunities CMC presents for better and increased interpersonal communication. In addition to new, integrated CMC coverage of social networking, texting, gaming, e-mailing, and IMing in the text narrative, new "Get Connected" boxes in every chapter focus on interpersonal issues that arise within CMC-based platforms—in people's personal lives, in their workplaces, and in online classrooms. The inclusion of the latter context makes Floyd's *Interpersonal Communication* 2/e the first text to acknowledge the rapid increase in college courses being taught online, with little or no face-to-face contact—including IPC courses.

MORE COVERAGE IN TOPIC AREAS IPC INSTRUCTORS SAY ARE MOST IMPORTANT TO THEM AND MOST CHALLENGING FOR STUDENTS. Added coverage includes

- Extensive new section on communication climate
- New material on Greek and Roman approaches to persuasion, exploring the concepts of ethos, pathos, and logos
- A section on power
- Expanded treatment of appreciative listening
- More consideration of evaluative and non-evaluative feedback types
- Integration of many additional examples from contemporary pop culture and actual world events

FRESH NEW DESIGN, PLUS ORGANIZATIONAL ENHANCEMENTS, FOR ENGAGEMENT, CLARITY, AND EASE OF USE. A vibrant new design showcases the book's many new photographic and other images and makes the text's pedagogy easy to use. At instructors' request, the "Emotion" chapter has been moved from the end of the text to follow Chapter 7, "Listening." To differentiate the functions of the text's chapters, they have been organized into three overarching parts in the table of contents.

ONLINE ACTIVITIES AND TOOLS THAT HELP STUDENTS STUDY MORE EFFECTIVELY—AND MAKE THE MANAGEMENT OF ASSIGNMENTS EASIER FOR INSTRUCTORS. The content of Connect Interpersonal, an innovative online learning platform, includes the following:

- New hands-on learning activities, including chapter quizzes
- Videos
- An adaptive diagnostic
- A fully integrated e-book

Additional Resources for Instructors

NEW **Easier online course management through Connect–Blackboard integration.** Full integration between Connect Interpersonal and the Blackboard CMS features single sign-on capability.

Annotated Instructor's Edition. Written and revised by the author, the AIE features a plethora of marginal notes to help instructors make use of the full range of the text's coverage and activities:

- *Outside of Class* notes present out-of-class activities.
- *Talking Points* provide examples or extensions of a particular point.
- *Focus on Ethics* probes ethical questions on a specific issue.
- *Focus on Scholarship* gives examples of relevant studies or research programs.
- *In Everyday Life* shows how specific concepts can be observed in ordinary interactions.
- *Writing Notes* present suggested short-writing assignments.
- *Media Notes* demonstrate how instructors can use the text's—and other—media tools and resources.

Online Learning Center. *Interpersonal Communication*'s Online Learning Center at **http://www. mhhe.com/ floydipc2e** includes an array of comprehensive resources to aid instructors:

Instructor's Manual. Written and updated by the author, the Instructor's Manual provides chapter outlines, discussion questions, key terms and their definitions, and examples of in-class and out-of-class assignments for every chapter.

Test Bank. The Test Bank, also written and updated by the author, offers multiple-choice questions, true/false questions, short-answer questions, and essay questions for each chapter. The preparation of materials by the book's author ensures that every assignment, test question, key term, and learning objective directly reflects the book's content.

PowerPoints for each chapter, created by the author.

Video clips. *Interpersonal Communication* offers 30 video clips that illustrate core concepts of the text, including such topics as cultural differences, social construction of gender roles, nonverbal communication, listening, conflict, harassment, and self-disclosure.

Tegrity Campus

Tegrity Campus is a service that makes class time available around the clock. It automatically captures every lecture in a searchable format for students to review when they study and complete assignments. With a simple one-click start-and-stop process, you capture all computer screens and corresponding audio. Students replay any part of any class with easy-to-use browser-based viewing on a PC or Mac.

With Tegrity Campus, students quickly recall key moments by using Tegrity Campus's unique search feature. This search helps students efficiently find what they need, when they need it, across an entire semester of class recordings. Help turn all your students' study time into learning moments immediately supported by your lecture.

To learn more about Tegrity, watch a 2-minute Flash demo at **http:// tegritycampus.mhhe.com.**

Visit coursesmart.com to purchase registration codes for this exciting new product.

CourseSmart offers thousands of the most commonly adopted textbooks across hundreds of courses from a wide variety of higher education publishers. It is the only place for faculty to review and compare the full text of a book online, providing immediate access without the environmental impact of requesting a printed exam copy. At CourseSmart, students can save up to 50 percent off the cost of a printed book, reduce their impact on the environment, and gain access to powerful web tools for learning, including full text search, notes and highlighting, and e-mail tools for sharing notes among classmates. Learn more at **http://www.coursesmart.com.**

CREATE, because customization for your course needs matters.

Design your own ideal course materials with McGraw-Hill's Create, **http:// www.mcgrawhillcreate.com!** Rearrange or omit chapters, combine material from other sources, upload your syllabus or any other content you have written to make the perfect resource for your students. Search thousands of leading McGraw-Hill textbooks to find the best content for your students; then arrange it to fit your teaching style. You can even personalize your book's appearance by selecting the cover and adding your name, school, and course information. When you order a Create book, you receive a complimentary review copy. Get a printed copy in 3 to 5 business days or an electronic copy (e-Comp) via e-mail in about an hour. Register today at **http://www .mcgrawhillcreate.com,** and craft your course resources to match the way you teach.

Contributors

I am most grateful to have had exceptional, astute groups of instructors across the country who served as reviewers and offered insights and suggestions that improved *Interpersonal Communication,* Second Edition, immeasurably:

MANUSCRIPT REVIEWERS

Courtney Allen, *University of Florida*
Amy Arellano, *Kansas City, Kansas, Community College*
Jacob Arndt, *Kalamazoo Valley Community College*
Suzanne Atkin, *Portland State University*
Cameron Basquiat, *College of Southern Nevada*
Carol L. Benton, *University of Central Missouri*
Leah E. Bryant, *DePaul University*
Nanci Burk, *Glendale Community College*
Jack Byer, *Bucks County Community College*
Judy Carter, *Amarillo College*
Donetta Cooper, *Ivy Tech Community College*
Tasha Davis, *Austin Community College–Northridge*
Jennifer Del Quadro, *Northampton Community College*
Donna Ditton, *Ivy Tech Community College*
Jean Dolan, *Bucks County Community College*
Katrina M. Eicher, *Kentucky Community & Technical College*
Jodi Gaete, *Suffolk County Community College*
Colleen Garside, *Weber State University*
Jill Gibson, *Amarillo College*
Ava Good, *San Jacinto College*
Stacy Gresell, *Lone Star College CyFair*
Neva Kay Gronert, *Arapahoe Community College*
Anneliese M. Harper, *Scottsdale Community College*
Tina M. Harris, *University of Georgia*
Terry Helmick, *Johnson County Community College*
John Hyatt, *Trident Technical College*
Jacob Isaacs, *Ivy Tech Community College–Lafayette*
Jacqueline Luongo, *Johnson County Community College*
Jessica Moore, *North Carolina State University*
Mark Morman, *Baylor University*
Thomas Morra, *Northern Virginia Community College*
David Moss, *Mt. San Jacinto College*
Susan Olson, *Mesa Community College*
Lisa M. Orick-Martinez, *Central New Mexico Community College*
Daniel Paulnock, *Saint Paul College*
Amber Reinhardt, *University of Missouri–St. Louis*
Sarah Riley, *University of Kentucky*
Barbara Rochon, *Bay de Noc Community College*

Paul Schrodt, *Texas Christian University*
Alan Shiller, *Southern Illinois University, Edwardsville*
Jamie Stech, *Iowa Western Community College*
Brigit K. Talkington, *George Mason University*
Calvin L. Troup, *Duquesne University*
Joseph M. Valenzano III, *University of Dayton*
Aimee Zadak, *Nova Southeastern University*
Lori Zakel, *Sinclair Community College*
Kent Zimmerman, *Sinclair Community College*

CONNECT CONTRIBUTORS

Courtney Allen, *University of Florida*
Leah E. Bryant, lead subject matter expert, *DePaul University*
Nanci Burk, *Glendale Community College*
Stacy Gresell, *Lone Star College CyFair*
Jacqueline Luongo, *Johnson County Community College*

DIGITAL SURVEY REVIEWERS

Courtney Allen, *University of Florida*
Cameron Basquiat, *College of Southern Nevada*
Jack Byer, *Bucks County Community College*
Jean Dolan, *Bucks County Community College*
Tina M. Harris, *University of Georgia*
Jacqueline Luongo, *Johnson County Community College*
Thomas Morra, *Northern Virginia Community College*
Susan Olson, *Mesa Community College*
Amy Poteet, *Ashland Community & Technical College, Kentucky*
Amber Reinhardt, *University of Missouri–St. Louis*
Alan Shiller, *Southern Illinois University, Edwardsville*
Jamie Stech, *Iowa Western Community College*

DESIGN REVIEWERS

Hilary Altman, *Merritt College*
Amy Arellano, *Kansas City, Kansas, Community College*
Jacob Arndt, *Kalamazoo Valley Community College*
Jack Byer, *Bucks County Community College*
Donna Ditton, *Ivy Tech Community College–Northeast Indiana*
James C. Duncan, *Ivy Tech Community College–Central Indiana*
Nicole Juranek, *Iowa Western Community College*
Steven King, *Ivy Tech Community College–Southern Indiana*
Brian Lempke, *University of Phoenix*
Richard Morales, *Sinclair Community College*
Jorge Mota, *San Jacinto College*
Joanne Tucker, *Dutchess Community College*

# Acknowledgments

One of my favorite parts about writing books is that so many people play key roles in helping a new book come together. This one was no exception, and it's my pleasure to thank those whose contributions and support are responsible for the book you are now reading.

First and foremost, my sincere gratitude goes to everyone at McGraw-Hill Higher Education. They are a true joy to work with and to know. Steve Debow, Mike Ryan, Rhona Robbin, Leslie Oberhuber, Mika De Roo, Susan Gouijnstook, David Patterson, Jamie Daron, and Elena Mackawgy have been a constant source of inspiration, energy, humor, and warmth, and I value immensely my relationship with each of them. Special thanks also to production editor Holly Irish and to Cassandra Chu and her design team for their exceptional creativity, as well as to digital product manager Janet Byrne Smith and media project manager Mathew Sletten for their capable work on Connect.

Sylvia Mallory is as good as development editors get. She has offered countless hours to the task of making this book as fresh and interesting as possible, and she has done so with an extraordinary measure of grace. Every page of this book is better because of her involvement, and I cannot thank her enough.

I also want to express enthusiastic thanks to the entire sales team at McGraw-Hill Higher Education. Those are the professionals who visit your campus and make sure students and instructors have everything they need to succeed in the classroom. It's a demanding and sometimes thankless job, but the McGraw-Hill representatives are truly dedicated to your success, and I appreciate all they do.

Finally, I will always be grateful for the support of my family and friends. The more I learn about interpersonal communication, the more appreciative I become of the people who accept, value, challenge, and love me. You know who you are, and I thank you.

1 About Communication

COMMUNICATION CAN PRESERVE A LIFE

The A&E television series *Intervention* chronicles stories of young adults who face serious health risks because of their addictions to alcohol, drugs, or gambling; problems with eating disorders; or practice of unprotected sex. Each episode includes a real-life intervention, a structured conversation in which an addict's family and friends try to talk the person into getting professional help. Such was the case with Brooks, a 21-year-old who became addicted to drugs after an automobile accident left him paralyzed from the waist down. When his family intervened, his younger brother Chace pleaded with Brooks to enter a treatment facility:

> Brooks, I have seen your drug addiction affect your life negatively in the following ways. By destroying the close relationship that you and I once had. You sleep all day and party all night. It is not all right for me to keep enabling you to live like this. I can only support your life if you are willing to help yourself. Will you go to treatment today?

As a result of his family's communication, Brooks began rehabilitation. Although his recovery was long and painful, he became sober in December 2006. For Brooks and his family, therefore, communication had a positive—perhaps even life-saving—effect.

It is nearly impossible to overestimate the importance of our close relationships. Our friends can make us laugh, keep us sane, and pick us up when we're feeling down. Our romantic partners can make us feel as though we're the only person in the world who matters. And, on occasion, our relatives can give us the tough love necessary to preserve our well-being, as Brooks's brother did for him. At the same time, relationships can be profoundly challenging. Sometimes even our closest friends can get under our skin. Sometimes our family members aren't completely honest with us. Sometimes we don't quite know how to reach out to others when they need our help.

It's pretty remarkable that human relationships can be the source of such joy and such heartache. What makes the difference between a relationship that's going well and one that's going poorly? One of the biggest factors is how we communicate. Had Chace not had the courage to confront his brother about his addiction, Brooks may never have been persuaded to become sober.

 # 1 Why We Communicate

Asking why we communicate may seem about as useful as asking why we breathe. After all, could you imagine your life without communication? We all have times, of course, when we prefer to be alone. Nevertheless, most of us would find it nearly impossible—and very unsatisfying—to go through life without the chance to interact with others. Perhaps that's why we spend so much of our time communicating, whether face-to-face or electronically (see Table 1.1).

You might think that communicating as much as we do would make us all communication experts. In truth, however, we often don't recognize how many communication challenges we face. Learning to overcome those challenges starts with appreciating why we communicate in the first place. As we'll discover in this section, communication touches many aspects of our lives, from our physical and other everyday needs to our experiences with relationships, spirituality, and identity.

Communication Meets Physical Needs

Communication keeps us healthy. Human beings are such inherently social beings that when we are denied the opportunity for

TABLE 1.1

Life Online: Communicating in Cyberspace

18	Number of hours per week the average American spends on the Internet
87	Percentage of American teenagers who sleep with, or next to, their cell phone
357	Number of text messages the average American sends per month
600	Number of tweets sent per second
141,000,000	Number of active blogs online
247,000,000,000	Average number of e-mail messages sent per day

Sources: Nielsen Company; Pew Research Center; Twitterblog; Blogpulse. Statistics are from May 2010.

interaction, our mental and physical health can suffer. That is a major reason why solitary confinement is such a harsh punishment. Several studies have shown that when people are cut off from others for an extended period, their health can quickly deteriorate.[1] Similarly, individuals who feel socially isolated because of poverty, homelessness, mental illness, or obesity can also suffer from a lack of quality interaction with others.[2]

It may sound like an exaggeration to say that we can't survive without human contact, but that statement isn't far from the truth, as a bizarre experiment in the thirteenth century helps to show. German emperor Frederick II wanted to know what language humans would speak naturally if they weren't taught any particular language. To find out, he placed 50 newborns in the care of nurses who were instructed only to feed and bathe them but not to speak to or hold them. The emperor never discovered the answer to his question because all the infants died.[3] That experiment was clearly unethical, meaning that it did not follow established principles that guide people in judging whether something is morally right or wrong. Such an experiment fortunately wouldn't be repeated today. But as touch expert Tiffany Field reports, more recent studies conducted in orphanages and adoption centers have convincingly shown that human interaction, especially touch, is critical for infants' survival and healthy development.[4]

Social interaction keeps adults healthy too. Research shows that people without strong social ties, such as close friendships and family relationships, are more likely to suffer from major ailments, including heart disease and high blood pressure, and to die prematurely than people who have close, satisfying relationships.[5] They are also more likely to suffer from lesser ailments, such as colds, and they often take longer to recover from illnesses or injuries.[6] Communication researchers Chris Segrin and Stacey Passalacqua have even found that loneliness is related to sleep disturbances and stress.[7]

The importance of social interaction is often particularly evident to people who are stigmatized. A **stigma** is a characteristic that discredits a person, causing him or her to be seen as abnormal or undesirable.[8] It isn't the attribute itself that stigmatizes a person, however, but the way that attribute is viewed by others in that person's society. In the United States, for instance, being HIV-positive has been widely stigmatized because of its association with two marginalized populations—gay men and intravenous drug users—even though many individuals with HIV do not belong to either group.[9] U.S. Americans don't tend to stigmatize people with asthma or diabetes or even cancer to the same extent as they do people with HIV, even though those other illnesses can also be serious and even life-threatening.

Stigmatized people might frequently feel like outsiders who "don't fit in" with others. As a result, they may be more likely to suffer the negative physical effects of limited social interaction. Going further, the less social interaction they have, the more they are likely to continue feeling stigmatized. Although not everyone needs the same degree of interaction to stay healthy, communication plays an important role in maintaining human health and well-being.

"Chirp and peep are passé. Now it's all Twitter!"

CartoonStock.com

stigma A characteristic that discredits a person, making him or her be seen as abnormal or undesirable.

Imagine how challenging it would be to communicate if you couldn't speak the language everyone else was using. That is a common experience for many immigrants.

Communication Meets Relational Needs

Besides our physical needs, we have several relational needs, such as needs for companionship and affection, relaxation and escape.[10] We don't necessarily have the same needs in all our relationships—you probably value your friends for somewhat different reasons than you value your relatives, for instance. The bottom line, though, is that we need relationships, and communication is a large part of how we build and keep those relationships.[11]

Think about how many structures in our lives are designed to promote social interaction. Neighborhoods, schools, workplaces, malls, theaters, and restaurants are all social settings in which we interact with people. In addition, the Internet offers innumerable ways of connecting with others, and many people have made new friends—or even met romantic partners—online.[12] Imagine how challenging it would be to form and maintain strong social relationships if you lacked the ability to communicate with people. Human development scholar Rosemary Blieszner has found that this is a common experience for many immigrants, who often struggle to learn the cultural values, as well as the language, of their new environments and may feel lonely or ignored by others in the process.[13]

Some scholars believe our need for relationships is so fundamental that we can hardly get by without them.[14] For example, research has shown that having a rich social life is one of the most powerful predictors of a person's overall happiness.[15] Mere interaction isn't enough, though: Studies show that having *meaningful* conversations leads to happiness, whereas "small talk" is associated with reduced well-being.[16] In the movie *No Strings Attached* (2011), Adam (played by Ashton Kutcher) and Emma (played by Natalie Portman) try to keep their relationship strictly physical and superficial but discover that they need something more meaningful from each other.

According to research by sociologist Norval Glenn and psychologist Charles Weaver, the most important predictor of happiness in life—by far—is marital happiness.[17] Being happily married is more important than income, job status, education, leisure time, or anything else in accounting for how content people are. On the negative side, people in distressed marriages are much more likely to suffer from major depression, and they report being in worse physical health than their happily married counterparts.[18]

The cause-and-effect relationship between marriage and happiness isn't a simple one. It may be that strong marriages promote happiness and well-being, or it may be that happy, healthy people are more likely than others to be married. Whatever the association, personal relationships clearly play an important role in our lives, and communication helps us form and maintain them.

Communication Fills Identity Needs

Are you energetic? Trustworthy? Intelligent? Withdrawn? Each of us can probably come up with a long list of adjectives to describe ourselves, but here's the critical question: How do you *know* you are these things? In other words, how do you form an identity?

How we communicate with others, and how others communicate with us, play a big role in shaping how we see ourselves—whether it's as intelligent, as popular, or as altruistic.

The ways we communicate with others—and the ways others communicate with us—play a major role in shaping how we see ourselves.[19] As you'll learn in Chapter 3, people form their identities partly by comparing themselves with others. If you consider yourself intelligent, for instance, what that really means is that you see yourself as more intelligent than most other people. If you think you're shy, you see most other people as more outgoing than you are. If you think of yourself as attractive, that translates into viewing yourself as better looking than most others.

One way we learn how we compare with others is through our communication with those around us. If people treat you as intelligent, shy, or attractive, you may begin to believe you have those characteristics. In other words, those qualities will become part of how you view yourself. As you'll see in Chapter 3, your identity develops over your lifetime, and communication plays a critical role in driving that process. Good communicators also have the ability to emphasize different aspects of their identities in different situations. During a job interview it might be most important for you to portray your organized, efficient side; when you're hanging out with friends, you might emphasize your fun-loving nature and sense of humor.

Besides expressing personal identity, communication also helps us express our cultural identity. As you'll discover in the next chapter, culture includes the symbols, beliefs, practices, and languages that distinguish groups of people. The ways you speak, dress, gesture, and entertain yourself all reflect the cultural values you hold dear.

Communication Meets Spiritual Needs

An important aspect of identity for many people in many cultures is their spirituality. Spirituality includes the principles valued in life ("I value loyalty" or "I value equal treatment for all people"). It also encompasses people's morals, or their notions about right and wrong ("It's never okay to steal, regardless of the circumstances" or "I would lie to save a life, because life is more important than honesty"). Finally, spirituality involves people's beliefs about the meaning of life, which often include personal philosophies, an awe of nature, a belief in a higher purpose, and religious faith and practices ("I believe in God" or "I believe I will reap what I sow in life").

A 2010 survey of more than 112,000 U.S. college students found that many students consider some form of spirituality to be an important part of their identity.[20] Almost half of those surveyed said they consider integrating spirituality into their

Communication lets people express their faith and spirituality.

lives to be very important or essential. For those in the study, spirituality didn't necessarily include formal religion; over 68 percent believed that people can grow spiritually without being religious. For people who include spirituality as a part of their identity, communication provides a means of expressing and sharing spiritual ideas and practices with one another.

Communication Serves Instrumental Needs

instrumental needs
Practical, everyday needs.

Finally, people communicate to meet their practical, everyday needs. Researchers refer to those needs as **instrumental needs.** Instrumental needs include short-term tasks such as ordering a drink in a restaurant, scheduling a haircut on the telephone, filling out a rebate card, and raising one's hand to speak in class. They also include longer-term goals such as getting a job and earning a promotion. Those communicative behaviors may not always contribute much to our health, our relationships, our identity, or our spirituality. Each behavior is valuable, however, because it serves a need that helps us get through our daily lives.

AT A GLANCE

FIVE NEEDS SERVED BY COMMUNICATION

Physical Needs	Communication helps us maintain physical and mental well-being.
Relational Needs	Communication helps us form social and personal relationships.
Identity Needs	Communication helps us decide who we are and who we want to be.
Spiritual Needs	Communication lets us share our beliefs and values with others.
Instrumental Needs	Communication helps us accomplish many day-to-day tasks.

Meeting instrumental needs is important for two reasons. The first reason is simply that we have many instrumental needs. In fact, most of the communication you engage in on a day-to-day basis is probably mundane and routine—not heavy, emotionally charged conversation but instrumental interaction such as talking to professors about assignments or taking orders from customers at work. The second reason satisfying instrumental needs is so important is that many of them—such as buying groceries at the store and ordering clothes online—have to be met before other needs—such as maintaining quality relationships and finding career fulfillment—become relevant.[21]

LEARN IT How is communication related to our physical well-being? What relational needs does communication help us fill? In what ways do communication behaviors meet our identity needs? How does communication help us express spirituality? What are some of the instrumental needs served by communication?

APPLY IT Describe in a short paragraph how, in a recent conversation, your communication behavior contributed to your physical, relational, identity, spiritual, and instrumental needs. Which need or needs took precedence? Why?

REFLECT ON IT Can you identify ways in which your own communication meets your relational or spiritual needs? Do you communicate for any reasons that are not discussed in this section?

2 The Nature of Communication

In the television comedy *The Big Bang Theory,* Sheldon Cooper is a theoretical physicist at Caltech. With two doctoral degrees and an IQ of 187, Cooper qualifies as a genius. Yet despite his intellect and professional accomplishments, Cooper is socially inept. He is childish and self-centered, and he rarely realizes how his lack of communication skills affects other people. How could someone so smart—and someone who has communicated practically every day he has been alive—be such a poor communicator?

In one way or another, you, too, have communicated daily since birth, so you may be wondering what you could possibly have left to learn about communication. In fact, researchers still have many questions about how we communicate, how we make sense of one another's behaviors, and what effects communication has on our lives and our relationships.

We begin this section by looking at different ways to understand the communication process. Next, we'll examine some important characteristics of communication, and we'll consider various ways to think about communication in social interaction. Finally, we'll tackle some common communication myths.

Three Models of Human Communication

How would you describe the process of communicating? It's not as easy as it might seem, and even researchers have answered that question in different ways. A formal description of a process such as communication is called a **model.** In this section we'll look at three models developed by communication scholars: the action, interaction, and transaction models. These models represent the evolution of how communication researchers have defined and described communication over the years.

model A formal description of a process.

source The originator of a thought or an idea.

encode To put an idea into language or gesture.

message Verbal and non-verbal elements of communication to which people give meaning.

channel A pathway through which messages are conveyed.

decode To interpret or give meaning to a message.

receiver The party who interprets a message.

noise Anything that interferes with the encoding or decoding of a message.

COMMUNICATION AS ACTION.   In the action model, we think of communication as a one-way process. Let's say you want to leave work early one day to attend a parent–teacher conference at your daughter's school, and you're getting ready to ask your supervisor for permission. As illustrated in Figure 1.1, the action model starts with a **source**—you—who comes up with a thought or an idea you wish to communicate.

To convey the idea that you'd like to leave early, you must **encode** it; that is, you must put your idea into the form of language or a gesture that your supervisor can understand. Through that process, you create a **message,** which consists of the verbal and/or nonverbal elements of communication to which people give meaning. In this example, your message might be the question "Would it be all right if I leave work a little early today?"

According to the action model, you then send your message through a communication **channel,** a type of pathway. You might pose your question to your supervisor face-to-face. Alternatively, you might send your question by e-mail, through a text message, or by phoning your supervisor. Those are all channels of communication. Your supervisor acts as the **receiver** of the message—the person who will **decode** or interpret it.

During the communication process, there is also likely to be some **noise,** which is anything that interferes with a receiver's ability to attend to your message. The major types of noise are physical noise (such as background conversation in the room or static on the telephone line), psychological noise (such as other concerns your supervisor is dealing with that day), and physiological noise (such as fatigue or hunger). Experiencing any of those forms of noise could prevent your supervisor from paying full attention to your question.

Noise also interferes with the ability to interpret a message accurately. Decoding a message doesn't necessarily mean we have understood what the speaker is trying to say. Physical, psychological, and physiological noise can all cause us to misunderstand someone's words, which may prompt the person to say "That's not what I meant."

You can see that the action model is very linear: A source sends a message through some channel to a receiver, and noise interferes with the message somehow. Many people talk and think about the communication process in this linear manner. For example, when you ask someone "Did you get my message?" you are implying that communication is a one-way process. The problem is that human communication is rarely that simple. It is usually more of a back-and-forth exchange than a one-way process—more similar to tennis than to bowling. Over time, this criticism of the action model of communication gave rise to an updated model known as the interaction model.

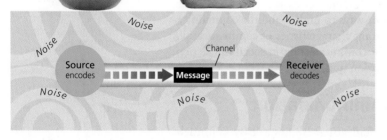

FIGURE 1.1 The Action Model In the action model of communication, a sender encodes a message and conveys it through a communication channel for a receiver to decode. Leaving someone a voice mail message illustrates the one-way process of the action model.

COMMUNICATION AS INTERACTION. The interaction model, depicted in Figure 1.2, takes up where the action model leaves off. It includes all the same elements: source, message, channel, receiver, noise, encoding, and decoding. However, it differs from the action model in two basic ways. First, it recognizes that communication is a two-way process. Second, it adds two elements to the mix: feedback and context.

If you've studied physics, you know that every action has a reaction. That rule also applies to communication. Let's say you're telling your friend Julio about a person you find attractive at the hospital where you volunteer. As you relate your story, Julio probably nods and says "uh-huh" to show you he's listening (or maybe he yawns because he worked late the night before). He might also ask you questions about how you met the person or tell you that he or she sounds nice. In other words, Julio reacts to your story by giving you **feedback,** or various verbal and nonverbal responses to your message. In that way, Julio is not just a passive receiver of your message. Instead, he is actively involved in creating your conversation.

Now let's imagine you're sharing your story with Julio while you're having coffee in a crowded employee cafe. Would you tell your story any differently if you were alone? How about if you were in a classroom at school? What if your parents were in the same room?

All those situations are part of the **context,** or the environment that you're in. That environment includes both the physical and the psychological context. The physical context is where you are physically interacting with each other. In contrast, the psychological context involves factors that influence your state of mind, such as how formal the situation is, how much privacy you have, and how emotionally charged the situation is. According to the interaction model, we

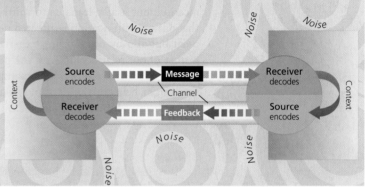

FIGURE 1.2 The Interaction Model The interaction model of communication explains that our messages are shaped by the feedback we receive from others and by the context in which we are interacting. Here we see speakers paying attention to their friends' feedback and communicating in a way that is appropriate for a public restaurant.

take context into account when we engage in conversation. That is, we realize that what is appropriate in some contexts may be inappropriate in others, so we adapt our behaviors accordingly.

By taking account of feedback and context, the interaction model presents the communication process more realistically than the action model does. In the case of your telling Julio about your new romantic interest, for instance, your story and Julio's feedback would probably be affected by where you were speaking, how many other people could overhear you (if any), and whether those people were co-workers, classmates, family members, or strangers.

Although the interaction model is more realistic than the action model, it still has limitations. One drawback is that it doesn't represent how complex communication can be. Often during conversations, it seems as though two people are sending and receiving information simultaneously rather than simply communicating back and forth one message at a time. The interaction model doesn't quite account for that process, however. To understand that aspect of communication, we turn to the transaction model, currently the most complete and widely used of the three models we examine in this chapter.

feedback Verbal and nonverbal responses to a message.

context The physical or psychological environment in which communication occurs.

COMMUNICATION AS TRANSACTION.   Unlike the action and interaction models, the transaction model of communication, illustrated in Figure 1.3, doesn't distinguish between the roles of source and receiver. Nor does it represent communication as a series of messages going back and forth. Rather, it maintains that both people in a conversation are simultaneously sources and receivers. In addition, it argues that the conversation flows in both directions at the same time.

To understand the transaction model, imagine you're a medical technician at a community clinic and you're explaining to an elderly patient how to apply a prescription cream to his skin. You notice a confused—perhaps even worried—look on his face. According to the interaction model, those facial expressions constitute feedback to your message. In contrast, the transaction model recognizes that you will interpret those expressions as messages in and of themselves, making the patient a source and you a receiver. Note that this process occurs while you are giving the patient instructions. In other words, you are both sending messages to and receiving messages from the other at the same time.

Not only does the transaction model better reflect the complex nature of communication, but it also leads us to think about context a little more broadly. It suggests that our communication is affected not only by the physical or psychological environment but also by our culture, experience, gender, and social class—and even by the history of our relationship with the person to whom we're talking.

Let's go back to our previous example. If you have a history with the elderly patient, you might help him understand your directions by referring to products you have prescribed for him in the past.

If he isn't a native English speaker, you might have to demonstrate the use of the cream rather than just describing it verbally. If he comes from a very different socioeconomic class from yours, you might be taking it for granted that he can afford the medication. Sometimes it is hard to consider all the ways these aspects of context might affect how we communicate. According to the transaction model, however, they are always with us.

ASSESSING THE MODELS.   Clearly, researchers have many different ways of understanding the communication process. Instead of debating which model is right, it is more helpful to look at the useful ideas each model offers. When we do so, we find that each model fits certain situations better than others.

For instance, sending a text message to your professor is a good example of the action model. You're the source, and you convey your message through a written channel to a receiver (your professor). Noise includes any difficulty your professor experiences in opening up the message or in understanding its intent because of the language you have used.

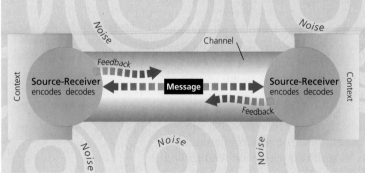

FIGURE 1.3 The Transaction Model The transaction model recognizes that both people in a conversation are simultaneously senders and receivers. The doctor encodes messages that her patient decodes, but the patient also encodes messages for the doctor to decode.

A good example of the interaction model occurs when you submit a report at your job, and the co-workers on your team give written comments on your recommendations. You (the source) have conveyed your message through your report, and your co-workers (the receivers) provide written feedback within the context of the activity. Noise in this example includes any difficulties either you or your co-workers experience in understanding what the other has said.

With respect to the transaction model, we've seen that most conversations are good examples of the model because both parties are sending and receiving messages simultaneously. That process occurs, for instance, when you strike up a conversation with someone while standing in an airport security line. You might make small talk about where each of you is traveling that day or how annoying but necessary the screening process is. As you do so, each of you is sending verbal and nonverbal messages to the other and is simultaneously receiving and interpreting such messages from the other. Your conversation is affected by the context, in that you may be communicating only to pass the time until one of you goes through screening. It is also affected by noise, including the sound of the screeners' instructions.

Each model, then, is useful in some situations but not in others. The action model is too simplistic to describe a face-to-face conversation, but when you're just leaving a note for someone, it describes the situation quite well. As you come across examples of different communication situations in this book, you might ask yourself how well each model reflects them.

Keep in mind that these communication models were developed over time. As scholars came to appreciate the limitations of the action model, they developed the interaction model to take its place. Likewise, the shortcomings of the interaction model gave rise to the transaction model, which many researchers consider the most comprehensive description of communication. As our understanding of communication continues to grow, researchers will likely develop new models that will represent the communication process even more accurately.

Now that we've looked at different ways of modeling the communication process, let's consider some of communication's most important characteristics.

Six Characteristics of Communication

Describing the communication process requires more than just mapping out how it takes place. We also need to catalog its important features.

COMMUNICATION RELIES ON MULTIPLE CHANNELS. In how many different ways do people communicate with one another? Facial expressions convey how a person is feeling. Someone's gestures and tone of voice help others interpret his or her messages. Touch can signal feelings such as affection and aggression. Even a person's clothing and physical appearance communicate messages about that individual to others.

Some situations are **channel-rich contexts,** meaning that they involve many different communication channels at once. In face-to-face conversations, for instance, you can pay attention to your partners' words, see their expressions and gestures, hear their tone of voice, and feel them touch you. Because you experience multiple communication channels at once, you can evaluate the information you receive from all the channels simultaneously. Other situations are **channel-lean contexts,** with a smaller number of channels.[22] Text messaging, for example, relies almost entirely on text, so we don't experience a person's voice or gestures. As a consequence, we may pay more attention to that person's words.

channel-rich context
A communication context involving many channels at once.

channel-lean context
A communication context involving few channels at once.

Some interpersonal communication contexts are channel-rich, such as a face-to-face conversation between friends. Other interpersonal communication contexts are channel-lean, such as sending and receiving text messages.

COMMUNICATION PASSES THROUGH PERCEPTUAL FILTERS. Anything you put through a filter—such as air, water, or light—comes out a little different from how it went in. The same thing happens when we communicate: What one person says is not always exactly what the other person hears. We all "filter" incoming communication through our perceptions, experiences, biases, and beliefs.[23]

Let's say you're listening to a senator speak on television. The way you process and make sense of the speech probably depends on how much you agree with the senator's ideas or whether you belong to the same political party. Two people with contrasting political viewpoints may listen to the same speech but hear something very different. I may hear a set of logical, well-thought-out ideas, whereas you may hear nothing but lies and empty promises.

Perceptual filters can also influence how people understand their own words. In an episode of the television show *Friends,* Rachel (played by Jennifer Aniston) and her boyfriend Ross (played by David Schwimmer) have a big fight and decide to go "on a break" from their relationship. They quickly learn that they perceive the meaning of being "on a break" quite differently. To Rachel, it simply means not seeing each other for a while but keeping their relationship intact. To Ross, being on a break means his relationship with Rachel is over. Thus, in the wake of their conflict, Ross has sex with someone else. Rachel feels completely betrayed when she finds out. As a result, she

Perceptual filters affect how we make sense of communication. In an episode of Modern Family, Claire encourages Hayley not to marry someone who's immature. Claire is implying that Hayley should be less serious with her boyfriend, but Hayley thinks that Claire is referencing her own marriage and signaling an intention to divorce.

and Ross end their relationship officially. It is important to note that Ross and Rachel agreed that they were "on a break" when Ross slept with someone else, but they had very different perceptions of what the expression meant.

Many aspects of our lives can influence our perception of communication. Whether we're aware of it or not, our ethnic and cultural background, gender, religious beliefs, socioeconomic status, intelligence and education, level of physical attractiveness, and experiences with illness, disease, and death can all act as filters, coloring the way we see the world and the way we make sense of communication. You might listen sympathetically to someone describing her experiences of homelessness based on those and other characteristics. In contrast, other people might blame that person for her homelessness because they have different perceptual filters than you do.

PEOPLE GIVE COMMUNICATION ITS MEANING. When we write or speak, we choose our words deliberately so we can say what we mean. Where does that meaning come from? By itself, a word has no meaning; it's just a sound or a set of marks on a piece of paper or a monitor. A word is a **symbol,** or a representation of an idea, but the word itself isn't the idea or the meaning. The meaning of words—and many other forms of communication—comes from the people and groups who use them.

> **symbol** A representation of an idea.

Almost all language is arbitrary in the sense that words mean whatever groups of people decide they mean. As a result, we can't assume that other people understand the meanings we intend to communicate just because we ourselves understand what we mean. For instance, what is a mouse? If you had asked that question 40 years ago, the obvious answer would have been a small rodent that likes cheese and is chased by cats. Today, however, many people know a mouse as a pointing device for navigating on a computer screen. As another example, what is a robot? In the United States, it's a humanlike machine that performs mechanical tasks. In South Africa, it's a traffic light.

Those are just two examples of how the meaning of a word depends on who is using it and how meanings can vary over time and across cultures. How do you define each of the following words? What other meanings might they have, depending on who is using them?

pot	crack
flat	gay
cell	biscuit

You might know that in some countries a flat is an apartment and a biscuit is a cookie. How have the meanings of words such as *pot, cell, crack,* and *gay* changed in U.S. society over time?

COMMUNICATION HAS LITERAL MEANINGS AND RELATIONAL IMPLICATIONS. Nearly every verbal statement has a **content dimension,** which consists of the literal information being communicated about the subject of the message.[24] When you say to your friend, "I'm kind of down today," the content dimension of your message is that you're feeling unhappy, bored, or depressed. When your roommate says, "We're out of detergent again," the content dimension of the message is that you have no detergent left.

> **content dimension** Literal information that is communicated by a message.

There's more to messages than their literal content, though. Many messages also carry signals about the nature of the relationship in which they're shared. Those signals make up the **relational dimension** of the message. For example, by telling your

> **relational dimension** Signals about the relationship in which a message is being communicated.

[RELATIONAL DIMENSION OF COMMUNICATION]

The relational dimension of messages is important—learn how to recognize it.

WHAT?

Identify the relational dimension of a statement.

WHY?

To understand the unspoken message(s) that a person may be trying to convey to you—that is, the relationship-based signals beyond statements, such as "I feel like a failure" and "The landlord called to remind us that our rent is late."

HOW?

1. Consider the statement from the sender's point of view.

2. Formulate a guess as to what the speaker is trying to convey to you about your relationship.

3. Check your interpretation.

TRY!

Your roommate wakes you to say, "It's snowing, and the driveway isn't shoveled." Based on your relationship with the roommate, what different messages might he or she be sending you?

CONSIDER: *What role do tone and manner play in your roommate's message?*

---

friend you're feeling down, you may also be sending the message "I feel comfortable enough with you to share my feelings," or you may be signaling "I want you to help me feel better." Likewise, you might interpret your roommate's statement that you're out of detergent as also saying "I'm sure you're aware of this, but I'm just reminding you," or you might take it as meaning "I'm irritated that you never replace household items when they are empty." Even though these messages were never spoken, we often infer meanings about our relationships from the tone and manner in which the statements are made.

Check out the "Got Skills?" box for suggestions on how to identify the relational dimension of interpersonal messages. As you come across the "Got Skills?" features in this book, you'll find practical advice for applying the principles of interpersonal communication in your own life.

One way in which people distinguish between content and relational dimensions is through **metacommunication,** which is communication about communication. Let's say that Ethan asks his stepdad Daniel to read over his senior thesis before Ethan submits it to his undergraduate advisor. Daniel reads the manuscript and marks it up with critical comments such as "this argument isn't convincing," "awkward wording," and "I can't tell what you're trying to say." After reading Daniel's comments, Ethan is crushed.

> **Daniel:** I thought you wanted my feedback. I was just trying to help you make your thesis better; that's what you asked for. Why are you taking my comments so personally?
>
> **Ethan:** It's not so much what you said, it's how you said it.

By focusing his attention on Ethan's request for feedback, Daniel is attending to the content dimension of their conversation. He can't understand why Ethan is upset, because Ethan had asked him for his feedback. To Ethan, however, Daniel's comments were overly harsh and insensitive, and they made him think that Daniel didn't care about his feelings. Therefore, Ethan's focus is on the relational dimension of their

⊰ metacommunication
Communication about communication.

conversation. To highlight that distinction, Ethan metacommunicates with Daniel by explaining that his hurt feelings were not caused by what Daniel said but by the way in which he said it. That phrase conveys Ethan's thoughts about his communication with Daniel; thus, it is metacommunicative.

COMMUNICATION SENDS A MESSAGE, WHETHER INTENTIONAL OR UNINTENTIONAL.

Much of what we communicate to others is deliberate. When you set up a job interview, for instance, you do so intentionally, having thought about why you want the job and how you will respond to the interviewer's questions. Very rarely do you schedule an interview by accident.

You might, however, communicate a number of other things without meaning to. For example, have you ever tried hard to stay awake in an important meeting? Despite your efforts to look engaged and interested, you might not have been aware that your slouched posture and droopy eyelids were signaling the fatigue you were feeling, perhaps after a long day of working at a part-time job and attending several classes. In that instance, your behavior was sending unintentional messages.

Your behavior sends messages, whether intentional or not. What message is this person's behavior sending?

Communication scholars have debated for many years whether unintentional messages should qualify as communication. Some researchers believe that only deliberate, intentional messages are a part of communication and that if you don't intend to communicate, then you aren't communicating.[25] Others subscribe to the belief that "you cannot not communicate," meaning absolutely everything you do has communicative value.[26]

My own position lies somewhere in between. Although I don't believe every possible behavior is a form of communication, neither do I think behaviors must be intentional to have communicative value.[27] I would suggest that even unintended messages—such as the ones you might have expressed while trying to stay awake during a meeting—are forms of communication because they still convey meaning.[28] Many aspects of appearance illustrate that effect. For instance, seeing someone in a wheelchair probably leads you to different conclusions than seeing someone in a white lab coat or an orange prison jumpsuit, yet those messages might not be intentional on that person's part.

COMMUNICATION IS GOVERNED BY RULES.

Rules tell us what behaviors are required, preferred, or prohibited in various social contexts.[29] Some rules for communication are **explicit rules,** meaning that someone has clearly articulated them. Perhaps your parents used to say, "Don't talk with your mouth full." Your college or university may have explicit rules banning hate speech at campus events or in school publications. These are examples of explicit communication rules because they express direct expectations for communicative behavior.

explicit rule A rule about behavior that has been clearly articulated.

A lack of explicit communication rules can be problematic at the start of new relationships. In the movie *I Love You, Man* (2009), newly engaged Peter Klaven (played by Paul Rudd) discovers that he doesn't have enough male friends to compose his wedding party. While searching for some new pals, he finds that forming male friend-ships can be confusing because of a lack of rules. After meeting a prospective friend, Peter is nervous about calling him because he isn't sure of what's expected. He expresses his frustrations in a conversation with his brother Robbie (played by Andy Samberg):

Peter: I can't just call him.

Robbie: Why are you being such a chicken? He gave you his card; it's an open invitation.

Peter: I hate this. There's no rules for male friendships.

Robbie: What are you freaking out about? You went out with those other guys.

Peter: I'm really nervous about this one.

Robbie: 'Cause you really like him.

In this scene, Peter expresses his concerns about the lack of explicit rules for form-ing male friendships, and Robbie clarifies the rule that receiving someone's business card is an "open invitation" to call that person. However, many communication rules are **implicit rules**—rules that almost everyone in a certain social group knows and follows, even though no one has formally articulated and expressed them.

In North American cultures, for instance, there are implicit rules about riding in an elevator, such as "Don't get on if it's already full" and "Don't make eye contact with others while you're riding." There are also implicit rules about lining up while you're waiting for something, including "Maintain an orderly line" and "Don't cut ahead of someone else." Most people seem to know and accept those rules, even though they usually aren't posted anywhere—they're just part of everyone's cultural knowledge. Because they're implicit, though, they are likely to vary more from person to person than explicit rules do. For example, some people believe it's an implicit rule that you shouldn't talk on your cell phone while in a crowded environment, whereas other people don't see that behavior as inappropriate.

Now that we know more about the basic characteristics of communication, let's take a look at some common beliefs about communication that are not as valid as they might seem.

implicit rule A rule about behavior that has not been clearly articulated but is nonetheless understood.

Dispelling Some Communication Myths

Perhaps because communication is such an essential part of life, people have many different ideas about it. Some of these notions are not very accurate. In this section we'll probe five common communication myths—in the process, honing our ability to separate fact from fiction.

MYTH #1: EVERYONE IS AN EXPERT IN COMMUNICATION. People com-municate constantly, so it's easy to believe that just about everyone is an expert in communication. Indeed, in a nationwide survey of U.S. American adults conducted by the National Communication Association, fully 91 percent of participants rated their communication skills as above average.[30] It's important to remember, though, that having *experience* with something is not the same as having *expertise* in it. Many people drive, but that doesn't make them expert drivers. Many people have children, but that doesn't make them experts at parenting. Experience can be invaluable, but expertise requires the development of knowledge and ability that goes beyond per-sonal experience. Thus, experts in driving, parenting, or communication have train-ing in those areas and a level of understanding that most people who drive, parent, or communicate do not have.

MYTH #2: COMMUNICATION WILL SOLVE ANY PROBLEM. The classic Paul Newman movie *Cool Hand Luke* (1967) features a prison warden who has his own special way of dealing with inmates. Whenever things go wrong, he says, "What we've got here is a failure to communicate," after which he beats a particular inmate unconscious and sends him to solitary confinement. Sometimes it seems as though we could solve almost any problem, especially in our relationships, if only we could communicate better. It's easy to blame a lack of communication when things go wrong. The fact is, however, that poor communication isn't the cause of every problem.[31]

On his television talk show *Dr. Phil,* psychologist Phil McGraw often counsels couples encountering difficulties in their relationships. Suppose that Matt and Belinda appear on *Dr. Phil* complaining that they have been drifting apart for some time. Belinda feels they need to communicate better to save their relationship. However, Matt states very clearly that his feelings have changed and that he is no longer in love with Belinda. Will communication solve this couple's marital problems? No—but it will probably cause Belinda to realize that their relationship is already over. We must be careful not to assume that better communication can resolve any problem we might face in our relationships.

MYTH #3: COMMUNICATION CAN BREAK DOWN. Just as we sometimes blame our problems on a lack of communication, many of us also point to a "breakdown in communication" as the root of problems. When a married couple divorces, the spouses may say it was a breakdown in communication that led to their relational difficulties.

The metaphor of a communication breakdown makes intuitive sense. After all, our progress on a trip is halted if our car breaks down, so it's easy to think that our progress in other endeavors is halted because our communication has broken down. The fact is that communication isn't a mechanical object like a car, a computer, or an iPad. Instead, it's a process that unfolds between and among people over time.

It may be easy to blame a breakdown in communication for problems we face in personal relationships. What's really happening in these situations is that we are no longer communicating *effectively*. In other words, the problem lies not with communication itself but with the way we're using it. That is one reason why learning about communication—as you are doing in this class—can be so beneficial.

MYTH #4: COMMUNICATION IS INHERENTLY GOOD. Watch or listen to almost any talk show and you'll hear people say they no longer communicate with their romantic partners, parents, or others who are important to them. "Sure, we talk all the time," someone might say, "but we don't really communicate anymore." Reflected in that statement is the idea that *talking* means just producing words, but *communicating* means sharing meaning with another person in an open, supportive, and inherently positive manner.[32]

Thinking that communication is inherently good is similar to thinking that money is inherently good. Sometimes money can be put to a positive use, such as providing a home for your family or donating to a worthy charity. At other times it can be used negatively, such as in providing funding for a terrorist group or squandering a hard-earned paycheck on online gambling. In either case, it isn't the money itself that's good or bad—it's how it is used.

CELL PHONES AND STRESSED-OUT FAMILIES

Interpersonal communication has many positive aspects, but it isn't all rosy. At times, we also have to deal with negative feelings and events. We can therefore say that communication has both a "light side" and a "dark side," and it's to our advantage to understand both. In the "Communication: Light Side" and "Communication: Dark Side" boxes in this book, we will examine interpersonal communication issues that people commonly experience, respectively, as positive or negative. In this instance, we'll talk about stress, a dark side matter.

Cell phones are so common these days that some people can't imagine life without them. Like other communication technologies, cell phones have certainly made it easier for people to keep in touch. You can get in touch with people by cell phone—and they can reach you—from just about anywhere.

One downside of being so easy to reach is that keeping work life and family life separate can be difficult. A dad might find himself reassuring the babysitter while he's running a staff meeting. A mom might have to take a call from an irate customer while she's watching her daughter's soccer game. Such examples led sociologist Noelle Chesley to wonder whether cell phone use has affected how happy people are with their lives and how satisfied they are with their families.

Using data collected from more than 1,300 working adults, Chesley determined that the more people used cell phones, the less happy they were, the less satisfied they were with their families, and the more likely they were to say their work lives "spilled over" into their family lives. Some of those patterns were particularly true for women, whereas others were equally true for both sexes. Chesley thinks that electronic devices such as cell phones can blur the boundaries between people's personal and professional lives, making it tougher for them to concentrate on their families when they're away from work.

In some of the text boxes in this book, I will include a personal hint about improving your interpersonal communication. These additions will be called "From Me to You," and here's the first:

FROM ME TO YOU

When spending time with people you care about, put your cell phone away. If it rings, let the caller leave a message. Unless you are expecting a specific and urgent call, don't allow your cell phone to determine where you spend your energy and attention. Instead, give your energy and attention to the person you're with, and let that person know that he or she is more important to you than your phone.

Source: Chesley, N. (2005). Blurring boundaries? Linking technology use, spillover, individual distress, and family satisfaction. *Journal of Marriage and Family, 67*, 1237–1248.

We can make the same observation regarding communication. We can use communication for positive purposes, such as expressing love for our parents and providing comfort to a grieving friend. We can also use it for negative purposes, such as intimidating and deceiving people. In fact, one common communication behavior—talking on cell phones—has been linked to stress in families, as "Communication: Dark Side" explains.

MYTH #5: MORE COMMUNICATION IS ALWAYS BETTER. Lorenzo thinks that in cases when others don't agree with him, the issue is that they just don't understand him. In those situations, he talks on and on, figuring that others will eventually see things his way if he simply gives them enough information. Perhaps you know someone like Lorenzo. Is it really the case that more communication always produces a better outcome?

When people have genuine disagreements, more talk doesn't always help. In some cases, increasing communication can just lead to frustration and anger. A 2007 study of consultations between doctors and patients found that the more doctors talked, the more likely they were to get off-track and forget about the patients' problems, a pattern that can translate into worse care for the patient.[33]

Sometimes it seems that the less said, the better. The *effectiveness* of our communication—rather than the *amount* of communication—is often what matters. That fact explains why learning to be a competent communicator is so advantageous.

LEARN IT What are the primary differences among the action, interaction, and transaction models of communication? What does it mean to say that communication has literal and relational implications? What is the difference between having experience and having expertise?

APPLY IT Talk with a friend or a classmate about a topic that is very important to you. Experiment with talking less and caring less about getting your point across than you usually would. What happens when you talk less than you normally would? How do the transactional features of the conversation change? Document your findings in a one-page report.

REFLECT ON IT What are some implicit communication rules that you can recall? Why do you suppose we so often think communication can solve any problem?

3 How We Communicate Interpersonally

Communication takes place in many contexts. Sometimes it involves one person talking to a large audience, as when the president gives a speech on TV or a journalist writes an article for a magazine. At other times it involves a small group of people communicating with one another, as in a college seminar, a team of surgeons in an operating room, or a football huddle. Communication occurs in families, in business organizations, in political institutions, in schools, and through the media. And, as you are probably aware, it often differs from one context to another. For example, few of us would talk to a grandparent in the same way we would address a TV reporter or a group of customers.

We communicate in many ways, so how do we know whether we're communicating interpersonally? In this section, we'll look at what makes communication interpersonal, and we'll consider how interpersonal communication—relative to other forms of communication—is unique in terms of its effects on people and their relationships.

Characteristics of Interpersonal Communication

In the movie *Eat Pray Love* (2010), Elizabeth Gilbert (played by Julia Roberts) realizes she is dissatisfied with her life and undertakes a year-long trip across three cultures to find meaning. Along her journey, she befriends a Texan named Richard (played by

In the 2010 film Eat Pray Love, *Elizabeth Gilbert (played by Julia Roberts) discovers the uniqueness of interpersonal communication.*

Richard Jenkins) at an ashram—a religious community—in India. Their friendship gives them the opportunity to talk about their lives, share their struggles, and support each another emotionally. There is something about their conversations that Elizabeth finds more comforting and more engaging than many of the interactions she'd become used to in her home life. Without necessarily realizing it, Elizabeth is taking note of the uniqueness of interpersonal communication.

Interpersonal communication consists of communication that occurs between two people within the context of their relationship and that, as it evolves, helps them to negotiate and define their relationship. The content of an interpersonal conversation is sometimes highly intimate, as when two romantic partners discuss the details of a sensitive health issue that one of them is experiencing. Interpersonal conversations can also focus on more mundane, impersonal content, as when the same romantic partners talk about what they need to buy at the grocery store. The content of yet other interpersonal conversations falls somewhere along the continuum between intimate and mundane topics. Each of those conversations is interpersonal, however, to the extent that it helps two people negotiate and define their relationships.

Interpersonal communication is different from many other forms of communication. To understand how, let's survey some of its most important characteristics.

INTERPERSONAL COMMUNICATION OCCURS BETWEEN TWO PEOPLE. The word *interpersonal* means "between people," and interpersonal communication involves interaction between two people at once. If only one person is involved—as when you talk to yourself—that is **intrapersonal communication.** Intrapersonal communication is important because it often affects how we relate to others; how often, for instance, do you rehearse a conversation in your mind before talking with someone?

There are other forms of communication, too. Communication that is being transmitted to large numbers of people is known as **mass communication.** Communication that occurs in small groups of three or more people, as in a family, on a committee, or in a support group, is called **small group communication.**

interpersonal communication Communication that occurs between two people within the context of their relationship and that, as it evolves, helps them to negotiate and define their relationship.

intrapersonal communication Communication with oneself.

mass communication Communication from one source to a large audience.

small group communication Communication occurring within small groups of three or more people.

Most research on interpersonal communication, however, focuses on interaction within a **dyad,** a pair of people. Two people can communicate face-to-face, over the telephone, by text message, on Skype, or in many other ways.

dyad A pair of people.

INTERPERSONAL COMMUNICATION OCCURS WITHIN A RELATIONSHIP.

People who communicate interpersonally share some sort of relationship. To some people, the word *relationship* implies an intimate bond, such as the union between spouses or romantic partners. However, the truth is that we have relationships with many different people. Some relationships, such as those with relatives or close friends, tend to be close significant relationships that may last for many years. Others, such as those with classmates, acquaintances, and co-workers, may not be as close and may last only as long as people live or work near one another.

In general, we communicate with each person on the basis of the expectations we have for that relationship. For instance, we might reveal private information, such as news about a family member's marital problems or serious health issues, to a friend but not to a co-worker, because we expect a friendship to be a closer relationship.

Much of our day-to-day communication is *impersonal,* meaning that it focuses on a task rather than on a relationship. Ordering coffee, calling a tech support line, and e-mailing a public official with a complaint are all examples of communication that helps you accomplish a task but does not necessarily help you build or maintain a relationship with others.

INTERPERSONAL COMMUNICATION EVOLVES WITHIN RELATIONSHIPS.

Long-distance friends sometimes say that when they see each other, they pick up their conversation right where they left off, as if no time had passed. Interpersonal communication in those friendships—and in all relationships—unfolds over time as people get to know one another better and have new experiences. In fact, people in long-term relationships can often recall how their communication has changed over the course of their relationship.[34]

In the early stages of a romantic relationship, for instance, individuals may spend hours at a time talking and disclosing facts about their life, such as where they grew up and what their career goals are. As they get to know each other better, their communication might become more instrumental, focusing on tasks such as where they're going to spend the holidays and who's going to make a dinner reservation, instead of sharing deep disclosures. They might even start to experience conflict. In any case, interpersonal communication is something that occurs over time. It's not a one-shot deal but something that is continually evolving within relationships.

INTERPERSONAL COMMUNICATION NEGOTIATES AND DEFINES RELA-TIONSHIPS.

Every relationship has its own identity. When you think about all your friends, for example, you can probably group them into friendship types, such as very close friends, casual friends, work friends, and school friends. Within every group, each friendship is probably a little different from the others.

How does each relationship get its own personality? The answer is that you negotiate the relationship over time using interpersonal communication. The way you talk to people you know, the topics you talk (or don't talk) about, and the kinds of nonverbal behaviors you use all help to define the kind of relationship you have with each person. You can also use interpersonal communication to change the nature of a relationship, as when friends disclose feelings of romantic interest in each other.

So, what makes communication interpersonal? Interpersonal communication evolves over time between people in some type of dyadic relationship and helps to define the nature of their relationship. You might notice we haven't said anything about how intimate the communication is. Some people think interpersonal communication means only sharing secrets and other private information, but that isn't the case. It includes *all* communication behaviors, verbal as well as nonverbal, that unfold over time to form and maintain relationships, whether those relationships are casual or intimate.

Let's turn to some of the reasons why interpersonal communication can be so important.

Why Interpersonal Communication Matters

You can probably think of many reasons why interpersonal communication is important to you. For example, you practice it almost every day, you use it to maintain your current relationships and form new relationships, and you find it engaging and enjoyable. The many reasons why interpersonal communication matters to people fall in three general categories: pervasiveness, relational benefits, and health benefits.

INTERPERSONAL COMMUNICATION IS PERVASIVE.   We all have relationships, so we all engage in interpersonal communication. For most of us, interpersonal communication is as much a part of everyday life as sleeping or eating or putting on clothes. Sometimes we take part in face-to-face interpersonal communication with the people with whom we live or work. At other times interpersonal communication takes place over the telephone, such as when we talk to relatives or friends we don't see regularly. At still other times we communicate interpersonally via electronically mediated channels, as when we share text messages or tweets with people in our social circles. No matter how we do it, nearly everyone engages in some form of interpersonal communication almost every day.

INTERPERSONAL COMMUNICATION CAN IMPROVE OUR RELATIONSHIPS.
We've seen that not every problem in relationships can be traced back to communication. Nevertheless, many relationship problems do stem from poor communication. In fact, in a nationwide survey conducted by the National Communication Association, respondents indicated that a "lack of effective communication" is the number one reason why relationships, including marriages, end.[35] Therefore, improving our interpersonal communication skills will also help us to improve our relationships. Significantly, this observation is true for far more than intimate relationships. Indeed, research shows that effective interpersonal communication can improve a wide range of relationships, including those between and among friends, physicians and patients, parents and children, and businesspeople and customers.[36]

CartoonStock.com

"But, sweety, why don't you just read my blog like everyone else?"

INTERPERSONAL COMMUNICATION CAN IMPROVE OUR HEALTH.
As we saw earlier in this chapter, we communicate partly to meet our physical needs for social contact. Close personal relationships are very important to our health. Several studies have shown, for example, that married people live longer, healthier, and more satisfying lives than individuals who are single, divorced, or widowed.[37] According to research by developmental psychologist Diane Jones, even having close friendships and other supportive relationships helps us manage stress and stay healthy.[38]

Interpersonal communication doesn't have to be face-to-face to benefit us. As the "Fact or Fiction?" box explains, a 2010 study of over 35,000 people from around the world found that the ability to interact with others online was significantly related to mental health, happiness, and well-being. Importantly,

THE INTERNET MAKES US HAPPIER

You're likely to encounter a number of intuitive findings as you study interpersonal communication, and your own intuition is probably right most of the time. The occasional failure of intuition is one reason why the systematic study of communication is so useful. In the "Fact or Fiction?" box in each chapter, we'll take a look at some common ideas about communication to determine whether they're as true as we might think they are.

For instance, the Internet is such an important means of communication that you might think your well-being would suffer if you didn't have access. Is that notion fact or fiction? Research indicates that it's a fact.

A British research team recently examined data from a survey of over 35,000 adults from around the world. The researchers asked participants about their ability to access the Internet to communicate with others. They also measured participants' life satisfaction, which encompasses their happiness and mental well-being. The team's analyses found a direct relationship between life satisfaction and the ability to communicate online.

Participants' age didn't matter—older adults benefited as much as younger adults did. Notably, however, the benefits of Internet communication were greater for people with lower incomes and less education. They were also greater for women than men, particularly in developing nations. Those findings led the researchers to speculate that access to online communication empowers people to form relationships, share ideas, and get information that their life circumstances might otherwise inhibit.

ASK YOURSELF

- Why do you think women might benefit more than men from access to online communication?
- Besides life satisfaction, what other physical and/or mental health benefits might computer-mediated communication enhance?

Source: Trajectory Partnership. (2010, May). *The information dividend: Can IT make you "happier"?* London: Author.

access to interpersonal interaction via computer-mediated communication benefited people regardless of their age and was particularly positive for women, for individuals with little education, and for those without financial means.

LEARN IT What are the features of communication that determine whether it is interpersonal? How and why is interpersonal communication important for health?

APPLY IT Using the Internet to help you, look up a friend you've lost touch with and make contact with that person again. Even if you don't communicate with long-term friends often, they are worth holding onto because of the history and the good times you have shared with them.

REFLECT ON IT In what ways do your close relationships improve your life? What are some of the challenges involved in maintaining those relationships?

4 Building Your Communication Competence

No one is born a competent communicator. Rather, as with driving a car, playing a musical instrument, or writing a computer program, communicating competently requires skills that we have to learn and practice. That doesn't mean nature doesn't give some people a head start. Research shows that some of our communication traits—for example, how sociable, aggressive, or shy we are—are partly determined by our genes.[39] No matter which traits we're born with, though, we still have to learn how to communicate competently.

What Communicating Competently Involves

Think about five people you consider to be really good communicators. Who's on your list? Any of your friends or relatives? Teachers? Co-workers? Politicians or celebrities? Yourself? You probably recognize that identifying good communicators means first asking yourself what a good communicator is. Most scholars seem to agree that **communication competence** means communicating in ways that are effective and appropriate in a given situation.[40]

COMMUNICATING EFFECTIVELY. Effectiveness describes how well your communication achieves its goals.[41] Suppose that you want to persuade your neighbor to donate money to a shelter for abused animals. There are many ways to achieve that goal. You could explain how much the shelter needs the money and identify how many services it provides to animals in need. You could offer to do yard work in exchange for your neighbor's donation. You could even recite the times when you have donated to causes that were important to your neighbor.

Your choice of strategy may depend in part on what other goals you are trying to achieve at the same time. If maintaining a good relationship with your neighbor is also important to you, then asking politely may be the most effective course of action. If all you want is the money, however, and your neighbor's feelings are unimportant to you, then making your neighbor feel obligated to donate may help you achieve your goal, even though it may not be as ethical.

The point is that no single communication strategy will be effective in all situations. Because you will often pursue more than one goal at a time, being an effective communicator means using behaviors that meet all the goals you have in the specific context in which you have them.

COMMUNICATING APPROPRIATELY. Besides being effective, competent communication should also be appropriate. That means attending to the rules and expectations that apply in a social situation. Recall that communication is governed by rules. A competent communicator takes those rules into account when deciding how to act. For instance, when you bump into an acquaintance and he asks, "How are you?" it's appropriate to say, "Fine, how are you?" in return. The acquaintance probably isn't expecting a long, detailed description of how your day is going, so if you launch into one, he may find that response inappropriate.

Similarly, it's appropriate in most classrooms to raise your hand and wait to be called on before speaking, so it would be inappropriate in those cases to blurt out your words. Different rules of appropriate behavior apply in an online course, as the "Get Connected" box details.

Communicating appropriately can be especially challenging when you're interacting with people from other cultures. Because many communication rules are culture-specific, what might be perfectly appropriate in one culture could be seen as inappropriate or even offensive in another.[42] For example, if you're visiting a Canadian household and your hosts offer you food, it's appropriate to accept the food if you're hungry. In many Japanese households, however, it is inappropriate to accept the food even if you're hungry, until you decline it twice and your hosts offer it a third time.

communication competence Communicating in ways that are effective and appropriate for a given situation.

g@t connected

NETIQUETTE AS APPROPRIATE COMMUNICATION

At some point during your college career, you may take one or more of your courses online. Observing the rules of appropriate online communication—known as *netiquette*—is important for maintaining a constructive learning environment. In a study of online classes, researcher Dianne Conrad found that students most often observed the following rules of netiquette:

■ *Be nice.* Communicate politely and respectfully by choosing your words carefully.

■ *Conduct conflict privately.* If you experience conflict with another student, don't engage it in a public forum. Rather, e-mail the person and work out your differences in private.

■ *Show support.* Watch out for "orphan postings," messages from other students that don't generate any responses. Help others feel supported by offering your thoughts on their postings.

■ *Use silence to reduce negativity.* When someone communicates negatively, don't make the situation worse by responding in kind. Rather, stay silent until the negativity dies down.

Source: Conrad, D. (2002). Inhibition, integrity, and etiquette among online learners: The art of niceness. *Distance Education, 23,* 197–212.

Even within a specific culture, expectations for appropriate communication can vary according to the social situation. For example, behavior that's appropriate at home might not be appropriate at work, and vice versa. Moreover, behavior that's appropriate for a powerful person is not necessarily appropriate for less powerful individuals. For that reason it might not be out of line for your boss to arrive late for a meeting, though engaging in the same behavior yourself would be inappropriate.

Communication competence, then, implies both effectiveness and appropriateness. Note that those are aspects of communication, not aspects of people. Thus, the next question we need to consider is whether competent communicators share common characteristics.

Characteristics of Competent Communicators

Look again at your list of five competent communicators. What do they have in common? Competence itself is situation-specific, so what works in one context may not work in another. However, good communicators tend to have certain characteristics that help them behave competently in most situations.

SELF-AWARENESS.   Good communicators are aware of their own behavior and its effects on others.[43] Researchers call this awareness **self-monitoring.** People who are high self-monitors pay close attention to the way they look, sound, and act in social situations. In contrast, people who are low self-monitors often seem oblivious to both their own behaviors and other people's reactions to them. For instance, you may know someone who never seems to notice that he dominates the conversation or someone who seems unaware that she speaks louder than anyone around her.

self-monitoring Awareness of one's behavior and how it affects others.

Self-monitoring usually makes people more competent communicators because it enables them to see how their behavior fits or doesn't fit in a given social setting. In addition, high self-monitors often have high levels of social and emotional intelligence, qualities that allow them to understand people's social behaviors and emotions accurately.[44]

ADAPTABILITY. It's one thing to be aware of your own behavior; it's quite another to be able to adapt it to different situations. Competent communicators are able to assess what is going to be appropriate and effective in a given context and then modify their behaviors accordingly.[45] That ability is important because what works in one situation might be ineffective in another.

Part of delivering a good speech, for instance, is being aware of the audience and adapting your behavior to your listeners. A competent communicator would speak differently to a group of senior executives than to a group of new hires, because what works with one audience would probably not work with the other.

empathy The ability to think and feel as others do.

EMPATHY. Good communicators practice **empathy,** the ability to be "other-oriented" and understand other people's thoughts and feelings.[46] When people say "Put yourself in my shoes," they are asking you to consider a situation from their perspective rather than your own. Empathy is an important skill because people often think and feel differently than you do about the same situation.

For example, suppose you want to ask your boss for a one-week extension on an assignment. You might think, "What's the big deal? It's only a week." To your boss, though, the extension might mean that she would be unable to complete her work in time for her family vacation. If the situation were reversed, how would you feel? An empathic person would consider the situation from the boss's perspective and then choose his or her behaviors accordingly.

People who don't practice empathy tend to assume everyone thinks and feels the same way they do, and they risk creating problems when that assumption isn't accurate. How empathic are you? Take the quiz in "Assess Your Skills" to find out.

Empathy is a particular challenge for individuals with disorders such as autism and Asperger's syndrome. Both conditions impair a person's ability to interpret other people's nonverbal behaviors. For instance, you may have little difficulty judging when a friend is being sarcastic, because you infer his intent from his facial expressions and tone of voice. For people with these disorders, however, nonverbal signals may not be as evident, and so understanding and adopting another person's perspective may be challenging.

COGNITIVE COMPLEXITY. Let's say you see your friend Tony coming toward you in the hallway. You smile and get ready to say hi, but he walks right by as if you're not even there. Several possibilities for Tony's behavior might come to mind. Maybe he's

Do you believe this woman is practicing appropriate communication behavior? Why or why not?

HOW EMPATHIC ARE YOU?

One of the ways to improve your communication ability is to think about how you communicate now. Each "Assess Your Skills" box will help you do so by presenting a self-assessment of a communication skill or tendency. For instance, we have seen that empathy is one of the characteristics of competent communicators. How empathic are you? Read each of the following statements, and indicate how much it describes you by assigning a number between 1 ("not at all") and 7 ("very much").

1. _____ It makes me sad to see a lonely stranger in a group.
2. _____ I become nervous if others around me seem nervous.
3. _____ I tend to get emotionally involved with a friend's problems.
4. _____ Sometimes the words of a love song can move me deeply.
5. _____ The people around me have a great influence on my moods.
6. _____ Seeing people cry upsets me.
7. _____ I get very angry when I see someone being ill-treated.
8. _____ I cannot continue to feel okay if people around me are depressed.
9. _____ I am very upset when I see an animal in pain.
10. _____ It upsets me to see helpless elderly people.

When you're finished, add up your scores and write the total on this line: _____ The ranges below will help you see how empathic you are.

- 10–25: Empathy is a skill you can work on, as you are doing in this class.
- 26–55: You are moderately empathic, with a good ability to understand others' emotions. Continued practice will strengthen that skill
- 56–70: You are highly empathic, which makes your interpersonal communication more effective.

Your score on this quiz—and on all of the quizzes in this book—reflects only how you see yourself at this time. If your score surprises you, take the quiz again later in the course to see how studying interpersonal communication may have changed your assessment of your communication abilities.

Source: Items adapted from Mehrabian, A., & Epstein, N. (1972). A measure of emotional empathy. *Journal of Personality, 40,* 525–543.

mad at you. Maybe he was concentrating on something and didn't notice you. Maybe he did smile at you and you didn't see it. The ability to consider a variety of explanations and to understand a given situation in multiple ways is called **cognitive complexity.** Cognitive complexity is a valuable skill because it keeps you from jumping to the wrong conclusion and responding inappropriately.[47]

cognitive complexity The ability to understand a given situation in multiple ways.

Someone with little cognitive complexity might feel slighted by Tony's behavior and might therefore ignore him the next time they meet. In contrast, someone with more cognitive complexity would remember that behaviors do not always mean what we think they mean. That person would be more open-minded, considering several possible interpretations of Tony's actions. The "Got Skills?" box provides guidance for increasing your own cognitive complexity.

[COGNITIVE COMPLEXITY]

Consider various ways of understanding another person's communication.

WHAT?

Formulate multiple explanations for a person's behavior.

WHY?

To avoid jumping to an inaccurate conclusion about the meaning of a behavior, such as concluding that you are not going to get the pay raise you hoped for because your manager criticized some aspects of a big project you worked hard to complete on time.

HOW?

1. Remind yourself that your explanation for the behavior is only one possible explanation.

2. Consider other aspects of the person, the environment, or the situation that might have caused the behavior.

3. Formulate additional, even competing, explanations for the behavior.

TRY!

You worked on the early stages of a successful fundraiser, and the project's leader doesn't include you when publicly acknowledging the fundraising team. What are at least three different explanations for this apparent oversight?

CONSIDER: *Delaying your response will force you to weigh the merits of competing explanations for the individual's behavior.*

---

ethics A code of morality or a set of ideas about what is right.

ETHICS. Finally, competent communicators are ethical communicators. **Ethics** guides us in judging whether something is morally right or wrong. Ethical communication, then, generally dictates treating people fairly, communicating honestly, and avoiding immoral or unethical behavior. That can be easier said than done, because people often have very different ideas about right and wrong. What may be morally justified to one person or one culture may be considered unethical to another.

Ethical considerations are often particularly important when we're engaged in compliance-gaining strategies—that is, trying to change the way another person thinks or behaves. Looking back at a previous example, is it ethical to try making your neighbor feel obligated to contribute to the animal shelter? To some people, that compliance-gaining strategy might seem manipulative and potentially unfair, because it may give the neighbor little choice but to make the donation. Depending on how badly the shelter needs the money, however, or how your neighbor has treated you in the past, you might not consider that strategy unethical, even if others do. Competent communicators are aware that people's ideas about ethics vary. However, they are also aware of their own ethical beliefs, and they communicate in ways that are consistent with those beliefs.

AT A GLANCE

FIVE CHARACTERISTICS OF COMPETENT COMMUNICATORS

Self-Awareness	Awareness of how your behavior is affecting others
Adaptability	Ability to modify your behaviors as the situation demands
Empathy	Skill at identifying and feeling what others around you are feeling
Cognitive Complexity	Ability to understand a given situation in multiple ways
Ethics	Guidelines in judging whether something is morally right or morally wrong

Take one last look at your list of five good communicators. Are they generally aware of their own behaviors and able to adapt those behaviors to different contexts? Can they adopt other people's perspectives on things and consider various ways of explaining situations? Do they behave ethically? Those aren't the only things that make someone a competent communicator, but they are among the most important. To the extent that you can develop and practice these skills, you can become better at the process of communication.

Self-awareness was turned on its head in the 2010 movie Inception, *which featured characters affecting one another's dreams.*

LEARN IT What is the difference between effectiveness and appropriateness? How is cognitive complexity defined?

APPLY IT Choose your favorite reality TV show and think about the characters and their communication behaviors. On the basis of what you've learned in this section, how would you rate each character in terms of communication competence? What makes some characters more competent than others? Try to identify specific skills, such as empathy and cognitive complexity, that differentiate the characters from one another. Consider how each person might improve his or her communication competencies.

REFLECT ON IT How would you describe your own level of self-monitoring? Where do your ideas about ethics come from?

MASTER the chapter

1 Why We Communicate (p. 4)

- Communication meets physical needs, such as helping us to stay healthy.
- Communication meets relational needs by helping us form and maintain important relationships.
- Communication fills identity needs by helping us see how others think of us.
- Communication meets spiritual needs by letting us express our beliefs and values.
- Communication serves instrumental needs, such as helping us to schedule a meeting and order a meal.

2 The Nature of Communication (p. 9)

- Through various models, communication scholars have viewed communication as action, as interaction, and most recently as transaction.

- Communication relies on multiple channels, passes through perceptual filters, is given its meaning by the people who use it, has literal and relational implications, sends intentional and unintentional messages, and is governed by rules.

- Five myths about communication are (1) everyone is an expert in communication, (2) communication can solve any problem, (3) communication can break down, (4) communication is inherently good, and (5) more communication is always better.

3 How We Communicate Interpersonally (p. 21)

- Interpersonal communication occurs between two people, evolves over time within their relationship, and helps them to negotiate and define their relationship.
- Interpersonal communication is pervasive, has benefits for our relationships, and has benefits for our health.

4 Building Your Communication Competence (p. 25)

■ Communicating competently means communicating effectively and appropriately.

■ Competent communicators typically have high self-awareness, adaptability, empathy, cognitive complexity, and ethics.

KEY TERMS

channel (p. 10)
channel-lean context (p. 13)
channel-rich context (p. 13)
cognitive complexity (p. 29)
communication competence (p. 26)
content dimension (p. 15)
context (p. 11)
decode (p. 10)
dyad (p. 23)
empathy (p. 28)

encode (p. 10)
ethics (p. 30)
explicit rule (p. 17)
feedback (p. 11)
implicit rule (p. 18)
instrumental needs (p. 8)
interpersonal communication (p. 22)
intrapersonal communication (p. 22)
mass communication (p. 22)
message (p. 10)

metacommunication (p. 16)
model (p. 9)
noise (p. 10)
receiver (p. 10)
relational dimension (p. 15)
self-monitoring (p. 27)
small group communication (p. 22)
source (p. 10)
stigma (p. 5)
symbol (p. 15)

DISCUSSION QUESTIONS

1. In what ways do we negotiate our own identities through communication? How do we do this as individuals? As families? As societies?

2. Suppose your mom says to you, "I love it when you call me." What are some ways you could describe the relational dimension of that message?

3. Implicit communication rules are never taught or verbalized, yet people seem to know and follow them anyway. How do you think we learn implicit rules?

4. Why is it important to communicate ethically, when people often have such different ideas about ethics?

PRACTICE QUIZ

MULTIPLE CHOICE

1. **All of the following are a type of noise that might inhibit communication** *except*
   a. physical noise
   b. psychological noise
   c. psychonormative noise
   d. physiological noise

2. **Ethical communication generally involves**
   a. treating people fairly
   b. honesty in communication
   c. avoiding immoral behavior
   d. all of these

3. **Empathy is best defined as**
   a. feeling sorry for someone else
   b. an ability to identify, feel, and relate to what others are feeling
   c. the ability to keep other people's feelings separated from your feelings
   d. paying attention to how others are evaluating your social skills

4. **An example of a channel-lean communication context would be**
   a. having a face-to-face conversation with your mom
   b. sending a text message to your roommate
   c. taking a long walk with your romantic partner
   d. going deer hunting with your dad and brothers

5. **Research has found that communication with friends and confidants**
   a. decreases a person's physical and mental health
   b. increases a person's self-monitoring skills
   c. increases a person's life expectancy
   d. decreases a person's ability to relate to his or her own family members

FILL IN THE BLANK

6. The tendency to behave in morally correct ways is a characteristic of a/an _____ person.

7. Most people believe that _____ is the number one reason that relationships are ended.

8. The receiver of a message will _____ it, or interpret it.

9. The most contemporary model of human communication is the _____ model.

10. A _____ is a characteristic that discredits a person, making him or her to be seen as abnormal or undesirable.

ANSWERS

Multiple Choice: 1 (c); 2 (d); 3 (b); 4 (b); 5 (c); **Fill in the Blank:** 6 (ethical); 7 (poor communication); 8 (decode); 9 (transaction); 10 (stigma)

RESEARCH LIBRARY

MOVIES

Legally Blonde (comedy; 2001; PG-13)
This movie focuses on a college sorority president, Elle Woods, who decides to attend Harvard Law School to win back the affections of a former boyfriend. In several places, the film illustrates explicit and implicit communication rules. While assisting her law professor in preparation for a murder trial, for instance, Elle discovers that the defendant is a former member of her sorority. After learning the defendant's alibi but promising to keep it secret, she is pressured by her professor and colleagues to disclose it, but she refuses to do so on the grounds that she cannot "break the bonds of sisterhood," which is a rule about keeping confidences among sorority sisters.

Love Actually (comedy; 2003; R)
This British romantic comedy chronicles the week-by-week lives of several characters. A recurring theme is how interpersonal communication negotiates and defines relationships. Many of the characters—particularly Juliet and Mark, Jamie and Aurélia, and David and Natalie—use communication behaviors to define the nature of their relationships. These story lines also illustrate the idea that communication helps people meet their relational needs.

BOOKS AND JOURNAL ARTICLES

Baxter, L. A., & Braithwaite, D. O. (2008). *Engaging theories in interpersonal communication: Multiple perspectives.* Thousand Oaks, CA: Sage.

Buck, R., & Van Lear, C. A. (2002). Verbal and nonverbal communication: Distinguishing symbolic, spontaneous and pseudo-spontaneous nonverbal behavior. *Journal of Communication, 52,* 522–541.

Motley, M. T. (1990). On whether one can(not) not communicate: An examination via traditional communication postulates. *Western Journal of Communication, 54,* 1–20.

Spitzberg, B. H., & Cupach, W. R. (Eds.). (2007). *The dark side of interpersonal communication* (2nd ed.). Mahwah, NJ: Lawrence Erlbaum Associates.

WEBSITES

www.natcom.org/research/Roper/how_americans_communicate.htm
This website reports results from a survey of U.S. American adults about their communication behaviors and perceptions. The survey was commissioned by the National Communication Association, the largest academic association for communication scholars and students in the world.

www.icahdq.org
This is the main website for the International Communication Association, an academic association for communication scholars and students with members from 70 countries.

2 Culture and Gender

WHEN CULTURAL ASSUMPTIONS BACKFIRE

When 14-year-old Santiago Ventura left his home in the Mexican state of Oaxaca for farm work in Oregon, he had no way of foreseeing the problems he would face. After the fatal stabbing of a fellow farm worker at a party, Ventura was questioned by a Spanish-speaking police officer. Ventura spoke neither Spanish nor English, however, but only the native language of the Mixtec Indians. While being questioned, Ventura never made eye contact with the officer, because Mixtec Indians believe it is rude to look people directly in the eye. Due to his poor grasp of Spanish, Ventura simply answered "yes" to all of the officer's questions, leading the officer to presume his guilt. After a trial in which his lawyer forbade him to testify because of his language limitations, Ventura was convicted of murder and sentenced to 10 years to life in prison. Only after five years of protest by immigration advocates and jurors who doubted Ventura's guilt did another judge set aside the verdict, freeing Ventura from his wrongful imprisonment.

Had we been involved in Santiago Ventura's case, many of us would have interpreted his words and behaviors just as the arresting officer did. If we had asked Ventura whether he had committed a crime and he replied "yes" while also avoiding eye contact, most of us would have concluded that he was guilty. As this story illustrates, however, culture acts as a lens through which we make sense of communication behavior. The arresting officer applied his own cultural lens to Ventura's behavior by assuming—incorrectly—that everyone from Mexico speaks Spanish and that a lack of eye contact signifies dishonesty.

Culture isn't the only lens that affects our understanding of communication. Another powerful influence—one that is always with us—is gender. Indeed, many people feel that communicating across genders can be nearly as confusing as communicating across cultures, if not more so. Moreover, culture and gender affect not only how we communicate but also how we interpret and respond to other people's behaviors. Other lenses, such as ethnicity, age, and socioeconomic status, also can influence communication. However, gender and culture shape our behaviors and interpretations in so many ways that it's worth taking an in-depth look at each.

1 Understanding Culture and Communication

Our cultural traditions and beliefs can influence how we make sense of communication behavior even without our realizing it. The officer who questioned Santiago Ventura probably never considered the possibility that he was applying inaccurate cultural assumptions to Ventura's behavior. By the same token, Ventura would have had an enormous advantage if he had understood the officer's cultural beliefs and adapted his behavior accordingly. Each of us is affected by the culture in which we were raised, and we tend to notice other cultures only when they differ from ours. In many people's minds, culture—like an accent—is something that only other people have. Let's begin by understanding in what sense we all have cultural traits and biases.

Defining Culture

We use the term *culture* to mean all sorts of things. Sometimes we connect it to a place, as in "French culture" and "New York culture." Other times we use it to refer to an ethnic or a religious group, as in "African American culture" and "Jewish culture." We also speak of "deaf culture" and "the culture of the rich."

For our purposes, we will define **culture** as the system of learned and shared symbols, language, values, and norms that distinguish one group of people from another. That definition tells us that culture isn't a property of countries or ethnicities or economic classes; rather, it's a property of people. Each of us identifies with one or more groups that have a common culture comprising a shared language, values, beliefs, traditions, and customs. We'll refer to a group of people who share a given culture as a **society.**

culture The system of learned and shared symbols, language, values, and norms that distinguish one group of people from another.

society A group of people who share symbols, language, values, and norms.

DISTINGUISHING BETWEEN IN-GROUPS AND OUT-GROUPS. Researchers use the term **in-group** to refer to a group with whom we identify, and **out-group** to describe a group we see as different from ourselves.[1] If you grew up in the U.S. Midwest, for example, you would probably view other midwesterners as part of your in-group, whereas someone from the Pacific Northwest would not. Similarly, when you are traveling in foreign countries, the residents may perceive you as being from an out-group if you look or sound different from them or behave differently.

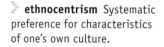

> **in-group** A group of people with whom one identifies.

> **out-group** A group of people with whom one does not identify.

For some people, being perceived as different can be an exciting or intriguing experience. For others, however, that experience can be stress inducing. For example, research shows that immigrants often experience abnormally high stress during their first year in their new homeland.[2] We often refer to that stress as *culture shock,* or the jarring reaction we have when we find ourselves in highly unfamiliar situations. In the film *The Kite Runner* (2007), for instance, Amir and his father are forced to flee Afghanistan after the Soviet invasion in the 1980s, and they relocate in Fremont, California. Amir's father goes from being a wealthy merchant to a gas station attendant, as he and Amir struggle to adapt to an entirely new cultural environment in the United States. Research shows that the stress of culture shock can contribute to illnesses such as high blood pressure, depression, and heart disease.[3]

Some researchers point out that our ability to distinguish between those who are similar to us and those who are different probably helped our ancestors survive by encouraging them to associate with people whose goals and priorities were similar to their own.[4] That tendency endures today, and research shows that many people exhibit strong preferences for individuals and groups they perceive to be like themselves. In other words, people are often more suspicious and less trusting of others whose ethnic, national, and/or cultural backgrounds are different from their own.[5] Researchers use the term **ethnocentrism** to describe the systematic preference for characteristics of one's own culture. That tendency can make it particularly discomforting to live or work someplace where you are considered a minority. In its account of Muslim students studying in the United States, the "Communication: Dark Side" box illustrates that point.

> **ethnocentrism** Systematic preference for characteristics of one's own culture.

Culture shock can be a stressful experience for immigrants, as it was for Amir and his father in The Kite Runner.

communication dark side

CULTURAL INTOLERANCE: DISCRIMINATION AGAINST MUSLIM STUDENTS ON U.S. COLLEGE CAMPUSES

Since the 9/11 attacks and the onset of the U.S. military action in Iraq and Afghanistan, many Muslim students have felt like outsiders at the U.S. colleges and universities they attend. Some receive hostile looks or threatening e-mail messages. Some feel excluded from social events where they once would have felt welcome. And some have been the target of verbal abuse blaming all Muslims for the terrorist actions of a few.

Distinguishing between in-groups and out-groups may be a natural tendency among human beings and other species, but it can lead to erroneous judgments. After 19 Islamic extremists carried out deadly attacks on the United States on September 11, 2001, many U.S. Muslims felt as though they were being treated as terrorists themselves simply because they shared a cultural and religious background with the hijackers. Although the attacks were genuine atrocities, in truth the vast majority of Muslims had nothing to do with them. In fact, many major Islamic organizations explicitly condemned the terrorist strikes. Such discrimination against Muslims shows how, during times of stress or uncertainty, it may be especially easy to make broad generalizations about groups of people. For competent communicators, however, it is vitally important not to condemn an entire group based on the actions of a few individuals.

ASK YOURSELF

- In what ways, if any, have you seen or heard discrimination against Muslims on your campus?
- Why is it so easy to stereotype people, especially during times of stress or uncertainty?

Source: Kerr, M. (2003, February 19). Muslims face discrimination and intolerance. *Stony Brook Statesman*. Retrieved July 29, 2007, from http://wwrn.org/articles/10019/?&section=discrimination

---

The in-group/out-group distinction is a major reason why so many nations struggle with the issue of immigration. Some countries, including Sweden and the United States, have relatively lenient policies that allow many immigration applicants to move to those countries and eventually to become citizens. Other nations have much stricter immigration policies. Denmark, for instance, significantly toughened its immigration policies in 2001, making it harder for foreign-born people to immigrate or become citizens.[6]

How best to manage immigration—and the population of immigrants living in the country illegally—is a controversial issue in the United States. It illustrates the complex and sometimes contentious relationship between in-groups, such as the country's current citizens and residents, and out-groups, such as those who have immigrated or who wish to move to the country.

ACQUIRING A CULTURE. Because cultures and societies vary so much around the world, it might seem that we inherit our culture genetically, the same way we inherit our eye color; but that isn't the case. Rather, culture is learned. Researchers call that learning process *enculturation*. Moreover, culture is not necessarily related to or based on our **ethnicity,** which is our perception of our ancestry or heritage. Nor is culture necessarily tied to our **nationality,** our status as a citizen of a particular country. Culture is determined by who raised us, by where we were raised, and by the symbols, language, values, and norms of that place. For instance, a Cambodian citizen raised in the United States will likely adopt the language and practices common to where she was brought up. Her ethnicity and citizenship are Cambodian, but her culture is American.

ethnicity An individual's perception of his or her ancestry or heritage.

nationality An individual's status as a citizen of a particular country.

g@t connected

FACEBOOK CULTURE

Has the social-networking site Facebook become so large that it should qualify as its own culture? Consider the following:

- Facebook has over 350,000,000 registered users.
- If Facebook were its own country, it would be the third most populous country in the world, after China and India.
- Although Facebook began in the United States, 70 percent of users today are from other countries.
- Facebook is available in 70 different languages.
- More than 3.5 billion pieces of content are shared on Facebook every week.

As we've seen, cultures are characterized by symbols, language, values, and norms. What symbols, terms, values, and norms do you associate with Facebook? What co-cultures does Facebook incorporate?

Source: Osmond, C. (2010, January 30). *The Economist* on social networking. *The Economist,* 3–5.

The Components of Culture

Cultures and societies vary enormously. Imagine a group consisting of people raised in Saudi Arabia, Vietnam, Iceland, Namibia, Paraguay, Israel, and the U.S. Southwest. Not only would the group's members differ in their native languages, but they most likely would also have different religious beliefs and political views, enjoy different sports, prefer different foods, wear different clothing styles, and have varying ideas about education, marriage, money, and sexuality. In fact, it might be harder to identify their similarities than their differences. Yet even people from vastly different societies can share experiences online. Check out the "Get Connected" box to learn more about how people from around the world are linked together through Facebook—creating what is, in a sense, a new mass culture.

Your culture depends not on where you were born but rather on where and by whom you were raised. Although their adopted son Maddox was born in Cambodia, adopted son Pax was born in Vietnam, and adopted daughter Zahara was born in Ethiopia, each child will acquire Angelina Jolie and Brad Pitt's cultural norms, values, symbols, and language.

Values, beliefs, and preferences often vary even among different regions of the same country. For example, native Hawaiians, native Texans, and native New Yorkers might differ considerably in their customs and values, even though they were all raised in the United States. No matter what their differences, though, cultures have some common components, as our definition of culture made clear. Those components include symbols, language, values, and norms.

SYMBOLS. As we saw in Chapter 1, a symbol is something that represents an idea. Words are symbols, and every culture has its own symbols that represent ideas that are vital to that culture. For example, when someone says that something is "as American as baseball and apple pie," he or she is using baseball and apple pie as symbols of U.S. American life. The U.S. flag, the bald eagle, and "The Star-Spangled Banner" are also symbols of the United States. Each society makes use of symbols that carry particular meanings for its members. For instance, the Chinese national anthem, "Yiyongjun Jinxingqu" ("March of the Volunteers"), serves as a symbol of Chinese culture. Similarly, the national anthem "Die Stem van Suid-Afrika" ("The Call of South Africa") symbolizes South African culture.

LANGUAGE. Researchers believe there are about 6,800 languages used in the world today.[7] (And, according to the New York State Comptroller's Office, more languages are spoken in Queens, New York, than in any other city in the world: 138 at last count.)[8] Language allows for written and spoken communication, and it also ensures that cultures and cultural ideas are passed from one generation to the next. Today, Chinese, Spanish, and English—in that order—are the three most commonly spoken languages in the world.[9] Unfortunately, many other languages are in danger of extinction. In fact, researchers believe that at least 10 percent of the world's languages are spoken by fewer than 100 people each.[10] We'll learn more about the use of language in Chapter 5.

VALUES. A culture's values are its standards for judging how good, desirable, or beautiful something is. In short, they're cultural ideas about what ought to be. Sociological research indicates that U.S. culture values ideals such as equal opportunity, material comfort, practicality and efficiency, achievement, democracy, free enterprise, and individual choice.[11] When you travel to other countries, you might find that their cultural values are dramatically different from yours.

U.S. American culture values freedom, opportunity, choice, and material comfort. Those values are epitomized in the media by scenes such as this— where two people are driving a sports car on a spacious open road with the sun on their face and the wind in their hair.

WHAT?

Learn about a cultural norm for politeness in a society that is different from your own.

WHY?

To avoid giving offense when communicating with people from that culture, such as during a cultural pride event or in classroom or on-the-job interactions.

HOW?

1. Think about a friend or an acquaintance who comes from a different society than yours.

2. Use the Internet to research the behavioral norms for politeness that characterize the culture of that person's society.

Focus in particular on the communication behaviors—verbal and nonverbal—that are considered polite or impolite in that culture. The website www.executiveplanet.com provides many such examples.

TRY!

1. In a short report, document what you have learned about the cultural norms of politeness in that society.

2. In your next couple of conversations with your friend or acquaintance, practice those cultural norms of politeness.

CONSIDER: *How has your intercultural communication improved with this exercise?*

NORMS. Finally, norms are rules or expectations that guide people's behavior in a culture. As an example, consider the norms for greeting people. In North American countries people shake hands and say "Nice to meet you." In other cultures it's normal to hug, kiss on both cheeks, or even kiss on the lips. Cultures also vary in their norms for politeness: A behavior that would be considered very polite in one culture may be frowned upon in another. Check out the "Got Skills?" box to learn more about cultural norms.

Cultures and Co-Cultures

When you think about culture as shared language, beliefs, and customs, it may seem as though you belong to many different cultures at once. If you grew up in the United States, for example, then you likely feel a part of the U.S. American culture. At the same time, if you're really into computers, music, or skateboarding, you may notice that the people who share those interests appear to have their own ways of speaking and acting. You may notice, too, that people in your generation have different values and customs than older people—or that different ethnic or religious groups at your school have their own traditions and beliefs. Does each of those groups have a culture of its own? In a manner of speaking, the answer is yes.

DEFINING CO-CULTURES. Within many large cultures, such as those of Italian, Vietnamese, or U.S. American societies, are a host of smaller cultural entities that researchers call co-cultures. **Co-cultures** are groups of people who share values, customs, and norms related to mutual interests or characteristics besides their national citizenship. A co-culture isn't based on the country where we were born or the national society in which we were raised. Instead, it is composed of smaller groups of people with whom we identify.

> **co-cultures** Groups of people who share values, customs, and norms related to mutual interests or characteristics beyond their national citizenship.

Eye contact serves some indispensable functions in the deaf co-culture.

THE BASES OF CO-CULTURES. Some co-cultures are based on shared activities or beliefs. If you're into fly fishing, organic gardening, or political activism, for example, then there are co-cultures for those interests. Similarly, Buddhists have beliefs and traditions that distinguish them from Baptists, regardless of where they grew up.

Some co-cultures reflect differences in mental or physical abilities. For instance, many deaf populations have certain values and customs that differ from those of hearing populations.[12] Even if they don't share the same language, political positions, or religious beliefs, deaf people often share distinctive social customs. For example, whereas many people would be uncomfortable having constant eye contact with another person while talking, deaf people frequently maintain a steady mutual gaze while communicating through sign language. As well, they often make it a point to notify others in the group if they are leaving the room, even if just for a few moments. Because they cannot hear one another call out from another room, that practice helps prevent frantic searches for the person who has left. (Among hearing people, it would be considered annoying at the very least to announce one's every departure.) Sharing those and other customs, then, helps deaf people interact with one another as members of a shared co-culture.[13]

BELONGING TO MULTIPLE CO-CULTURES. Many people identify with several co-cultures at once. You might relate to co-cultures for your age group, ethnicity, religion, sexual orientation, musical tastes, athletic interests, and even your college major. Every one of those groups probably has its own values, beliefs, traditions, customs, and even ways of using language that distinguish it from other groups. Going further, some co-cultures have smaller co-cultures within them. For example, the deaf co-culture comprises people who advocate using only sign language as well as individuals who support the use of cochlear implants, devices that may help a person hear.

Communicating with Cultural Awareness

People with different cultural backgrounds don't just communicate differently; in many cases they also *think* differently. Those differences can present real challenges when people from different cultures interact.

The same thing can happen even when people from different co-cultures communicate. For instance, teenagers and senior citizens may have difficulty getting along because their customs and values are so different. Adolescents often enjoy the most contemporary music and fashions, whereas seniors frequently prefer songs and clothing that they enjoyed as younger adults. Teenagers may value independence and individuality; older people may value loyalty, family, and community.

Young and elderly people might speak the same language, but they don't necessarily use language in the same ways. Young adults may have no problem understanding one another when they talk about blogging and texting, for example, but their grandparents may have no idea what these terms mean. Maybe you've experienced that kind of situation, or perhaps you've seen other co-cultures have difficulty understanding each other, such as Democrats and Republicans, or gay and straight people.

To complicate that problem, people from different cultures (and co-cultures) not only differ in how they think and behave, they're also often unaware of how they differ. For instance, a U.S. college professor might think a Japanese student is being dishonest because the student doesn't look her in the eyes. In the United States that behavior can suggest dishonesty. Within Japanese society, however, it signals respect. If neither the professor nor the student is aware of how the other is likely to interpret the behavior, it's easy to see how a misunderstanding could arise.

Communicating effectively with people from other cultures and co-cultures requires us to be aware of how their behaviors and ways of thinking are likely to differ from our own. Unfortunately, that is easier said than done. Many of us operate on what researchers call a *similarity assumption*—that is, we presume that most people think the same way we do, without asking ourselves whether that's true.[14] In the preceding example, the professor thought the student was being dishonest because she assumed the lack of eye contact had the same meaning for the student that it had for her. The student assumed the professor would interpret his lack of eye contact as a sign of respect, because that's how he understood and intended it.

Questioning your cultural assumptions can be a challenge, because you're probably often unaware that you hold them in the first place. However, it's worth the effort to try, since checking your assumptions when interacting with people of other cultures can make you a more effective communicator.

LEARN IT What is a culture, and how is it different from a society? How do societies use symbols, language, values, and norms to reflect their cultures? What are some examples of co-cultures? What is the similarity assumption, and how does it influence our ability to communicate with cultural awareness?

APPLY IT Choose two of your close friends, and make a list of the co-cultures to which each friend belongs. Include co-cultures for age, ethnicity, disability, religion, and activities or interests if they are relevant. Next to each co-culture that you list, write down one statement about how you think it affects your friend's personality or communication style. What did you learn about each friend by going through this exercise?

REFLECT ON IT With which in-groups do you identify the most strongly? When have you noticed your own cultural awareness being challenged? How did you respond?

2 How Culture Affects Communication

If you've ever had difficulty communicating with someone from a different cultural background, you've experienced the challenge of overcoming cultural differences in communication. Dutch social psychologist Geert Hofstede and American anthropologist Edward T. Hall have pioneered the study of cultures and cultural differences. Their work and that of others suggest that seven cultural differences in particular influence how people interact with one another.

Individualism and Collectivism

individualistic culture
A culture that emphasizes individuality and responsibility to oneself.

One way cultures differ is in how much they emphasize individuals rather than groups. In an **individualistic culture,** people believe that their primary responsibility is to themselves. Children in individualistic cultures are raised hearing messages such as "Be yourself," "You're special," and "There's no one else in the world who's just like you." Those messages emphasize the importance of knowing oneself, being self-sufficient, and being true to what one wants in life.[15] Indeed, the motto in an individualistic culture might be "I gotta be me!" People in individualistic societies also value self-reliance and the idea that people should "pull themselves up by their own bootstraps"—help themselves when they need it—instead of waiting for others to help them. Research shows that the United States, Canada, Great Britain, and Australia are among the world's most individualistic societies.[16]

collectivistic culture
A culture that places greater emphasis on loyalty to the family, workplace, or community than on the needs of the individual.

In contrast, people in a **collectivistic culture** are taught that their primary responsibility is to their families, communities, and employers. Instead of emphasizing the importance of being an individual, collectivistic cultures focus on taking care of the needs of the group. People in collectivistic cultures place a high value on duty and loyalty, and they see themselves not as unique or special but as a part of the groups to which they belong. Among the Kabre of Togo, for instance, people try to give away many of their material possessions to build relationships and benefit their social groups.[17] The motto in a collectivistic culture might be "I am my family and my family is me." Collectivistic cultures include Korea, Japan, and many countries in Africa and Latin America.[18]

How individualistic or collectivistic a culture is can affect communication behavior in several ways. When people in individualistic cultures experience conflict with one another, for instance, they are expected to express it and work toward resolving it. In contrast, as communication scholars Deborah Cai and Edward Fink explain, people in collectivistic cultures are taught to handle disagreements much less directly, to preserve social harmony.[19]

Another difference involves people's comfort level with public speaking. Many people experience anxiety when they have to give a speech, especially those in collectivistic societies, where individuals are taught to blend in rather than to stand out. Being assertive and "standing up for yourself" are valued in individualistic cultures, but they can cause embarrassment or shame for individuals in a collectivistic culture.

Cultural values are often expressed through personal appearance. Among the Maori of New Zealand, tattoos are commonly used to reflect collectivism, their shared sense of heritage and community. When people in the United States sport similar, tribal-style tattoos, it's often to express their individuality rather than their connection to a group or community.

Low- and High-Context Cultures

If you've traveled much, you may have noticed that people's language in various parts of the world differs in how direct and explicit it is. In a **low-context culture,** people are expected to be direct, say what they mean, and not "beat around the bush." Low-context cultures value expressing oneself, sharing personal opinions, and trying to persuade others to see things one's way.[20] The United States is an example of a low-context society, as are Canada, Israel, and most northern European countries.

In contrast, people in a **high-context culture,** such as Korea, the Maori of New Zealand, and Native Americans, are taught to speak much less directly. In those societies, maintaining harmony and avoiding offending people are more important than expressing one's true feelings.[21] As a result, people speak in a less direct, more ambiguous manner and convey much more of their meaning through subtle behaviors and contextual cues such as facial expressions and tone of voice.

One example of how this cultural difference affects communication is the way people handle criticism and disagreement. In a low-context culture, a supervisor might openly reprimand an irresponsible employee to make an example of the person. The supervisor would probably be direct and explicit about the employee's mistakes, the company's expectations for improvement, and the consequences for failing to meet them. In a high-context culture, however, the supervisor probably wouldn't reprimand the employee publicly for fear that it would shame the employee and cause the person to lose face. Criticism in a high-context culture is more likely to take place in private. The supervisor in a high-context culture would also likely use more ambiguous language to convey what the employee was doing wrong instead of confronting the issue directly. To reprimand an employee for repeated absence, for example, the supervisor might point out that responsibility to one's co-workers is important and that letting down the team would be cause for shame. The supervisor may never actually say that the employee's attendance needs to improve. Instead, the employee would be expected to understand that message by listening to the supervisor's words and paying attention to the boss's body language, tone of voice, and facial expressions.

When people from low- and high-context cultures communicate with one another, the potential for misunderstanding is great. Imagine that you have asked two of your friends if they'd like to meet you tomorrow evening for a coffee tasting at a popular bookstore cafe. Your friend Tina, who's from a low-context culture, says, "No, I've got a lot of studying to do, but thanks anyway." Lee, who grew up in a high-context culture, nods his head and says, "That sounds like fun." Thus, you're surprised later when Lee doesn't show up.

How can you account for those different behaviors? The answer is that people raised in high-context cultures are often reluctant to say no—even when they mean no—for fear of causing offense. Another person from Lee's culture might have understood from Lee's facial expression or tone of voice that he didn't intend to go to the coffee tasting with you. Because you grew up in a low-context society, however, you interpreted his answer and head nods to mean he was accepting your invitation.

Low- and High-Power-Distance Cultures

A third way cultures differ from one another is in the degree to which power is evenly distributed. Several characteristics can give someone power, including money or other valuable resources, education, expertise,

> **low-context culture**
> A culture in which verbal communication is expected to be explicit and is often interpreted literally.

> **high-context culture**
> A culture in which verbal communication is often ambiguous, and meaning is drawn from contextual cues, such as facial expressions and tone of voice.

When people from low- and high-context cultures communicate with one another, the potential for misunderstanding is great.

low-power-distance culture A culture in which power is not highly concentrated in specific groups of people.

high-power-distance culture A culture in which much or most of the power is concentrated in a few people, such as royalty or a ruling political party.

age, popularity, talent, intelligence, and experience. In democratic societies, people believe in the value of equality—that all men and women are created equal and that no one person or group should have excessive power. That belief is characteristic of **low-power-distance cultures.** The United States and Canada fall in this category, as do Israel, New Zealand, Denmark, and Austria.[22] People in low-power-distance cultures are raised to believe that even though some individuals are born with more advantages (such as wealth or fame), no one is inherently better than anyone else. That doesn't necessarily mean that people in such cultures *are* treated equally, only that they value the idea that they should be.

In **high-power-distance cultures** power is distributed less evenly. Certain groups, such as the royal family or the ruling political party, have great power, and the average citizen has much less. People in such cultures are taught that certain people or groups deserve to have more power than others and that respecting power is more important than respecting equality. Mexico, Brazil, India, Singapore, and the Philippines are examples of high-power-distance cultures.[23]

Power distance affects many aspects of interpersonal communication. For example, people in low-power-distance cultures usually expect friendships and romantic relationships to be based on love rather than social status. In contrast, people in high-power-distance cultures are expected to choose friends or mates from within their social class.[24]

Another difference involves the way people think about authority. People in low-power-distance cultures are often taught that it is their right—even their responsibility—to question authority. In such cultures it is not uncommon for people to ask "Why?" when their parents or teachers tell them to do something. In contrast, high-power-distance cultures place great emphasis on obedience and respect for those in power. People are taught to obey their parents and teachers without question.[25]

That difference is also seen in the relationships and communication patterns people have with their employers. Workers in low-power-distance cultures value autonomy, the right to make choices about the way they do their jobs, and the ability to have input into decisions that affect them. Such workers might provide their input through union spokespersons or employee satisfaction surveys. In contrast, employees in high-power-distance cultures are used to having little or no say about how to do their jobs. They expect their employers to make the decisions and are more likely to follow those decisions without question.

Saudi Arabia has a high-power-distance culture. Members of the royal family have considerably more power than the average citizen.

Masculine and Feminine Cultures

We usually use the terms *masculine* and *feminine* when referring to people. Hofstede has suggested that we can also apply those terms to cultures.[26] In a highly masculine culture, people tend to cherish traditionally masculine values, such as ambition, achievement, and the acquisition of material goods. They also value sex-specific roles for women and men, preferring that men hold the wage-earning and decision-making positions (such as corporate executive) while women occupy the nurturing positions (such as home-maker). Examples of masculine cultures are Austria, Japan, and Mexico.

In contrast, in a highly feminine culture, people tend to value nurturance, quality of life, and service to others, all of which are stereotypically feminine qualities. They also tend to believe that men's and women's roles should not be strongly differentiated. Compared with masculine cultures, therefore, it would not be as unusual for a man to care for children or a woman to be her family's primary wage earner. Examples of feminine cultures are Sweden, Chile, and the Netherlands.

According to Hofstede's research, the United States has a moderately masculine culture. U.S. Americans tend to value sex-differentiated roles—although not as strongly as Austrians, Japanese, or Mexicans do—and they place a fairly high value on stereotypically masculine qualities such as achievement and the acquisition of resources.[27]

Monochronic and Polychronic Cultures

Cultures also vary with respect to their norms and expectations concerning the use of time. Societies that have a **monochronic** concept of time, such as Swiss, Germans, and most Americans, view time as a commodity. We save time, spend time, fill time, invest time, and waste time as though time were tangible. We treat time as valuable, believe that "time is money," and talk about making time and losing time.[28]

A monochronic orientation toward time influences several social behaviors. Because people in monochronic cultures think of time as valuable, they hate to waste it. Therefore, they expect meetings and classes to start on time (within a minute or so), and when that doesn't happen, they are willing to wait only so long before leaving. They also expect others to show up when they say they will.

In comparison, societies with a **polychronic** orientation—which include Latin America, the Arab part of the Middle East, and much of sub-Saharan Africa—conceive of time as more holistic and fluid and less structured. Instead of treating time as a finite commodity that must be managed properly to avoid being wasted, people in polychronic cultures perceive it more like a never-ending river, flowing infinitely into the future.[29]

Schedules are more fluid and flexible in polychronic than in monochronic cultures. In the polychronic culture of Pakistan, for instance, if you're invited to a wedding that begins at 4:30 P.M. and you arrive at that hour, you will most likely be the first one there. A bank may not open at a specified time—as would be expected in a monochronic society—but whenever the manager decides. People in a polychronic culture do not prioritize efficiency and punctuality. Instead, they attach greater value to the quality of their lives and their relationships with others.

monochronic A concept that treats time as a finite commodity that can be earned, saved, spent, and wasted.

polychronic A concept that treats time as an infinite resource rather than a finite commodity.

Uncertainty Avoidance

People have a natural tendency to avoid unfamiliar and uncomfortable situations. In other words, we dislike uncertainty, and in fact uncertainty causes many of us a good deal of stress.[30] Not all cultures find uncertainty to be equally problematic, however. Cultures vary in what Hofstede called **uncertainty avoidance,** or the extent to which people try to avoid situations that are unstructured, unclear, or unpredictable.[31] Individuals from cultures that are highly uncertainty avoidant are drawn to people and situations that are familiar, and they are relatively unlikely to take risks, for fear of failure. They are also uncomfortable with differences of opinion, and they tend to favor rules and laws that maximize security and reduce ambiguity wherever possible. Argentina, Portugal, and Uruguay are among the most uncertainty avoidant societies.

In contrast, people in uncertainty-accepting cultures are more open to new situations, and they are more accommodating of people and ideas that are different from their own. They take a "live and let live" approach, preferring as few rules as possible that would restrict their behaviors. Societies with cultures that are highly accepting of uncertainty include Hong Kong, Jamaica, and New Zealand. Hofstede has determined that the U.S. society is more accepting than avoidant of uncertainty, but it is closer to the midpoint of the scale than many countries are.

uncertainty avoidance The degree to which people try to avoid situations that are unstructured, unclear, or unpredictable.

Cultural Communication Codes

> **communication codes** Verbal and nonverbal behaviors, such as idioms and gestures, that characterize a culture and distinguish it from other cultures.

Finally, cultures differ from one another in their use of **communication codes,** which are verbal and nonverbal behaviors whose meanings are often understood only by people from the same culture. Three kinds of communication codes—idioms, jargon, and gestures—differ greatly from society to society and can make intercultural communication especially challenging.

IDIOMS.   An idiom is a phrase whose meaning is purely figurative; that is, we cannot understand the meaning by interpreting the words literally. For example, most U.S. adults know the phrase "kicking the bucket" has nothing to do with kicking a bucket. In U.S. American society, that is an idiom that means "to die." Similarly, if something is "a dime a dozen," then it is very common or is nothing special. "Shaking a leg" means hurrying, and "breaking a leg" means having a great performance.

Every society has its own idioms whose meanings are not necessarily obvious to people from other cultures. In Portugal, for instance, a person who "doesn't give one for the box" is someone who can't say or do anything right. In Finland, if something "becomes gingerbread," that means it goes completely wrong. Likewise, if an Australian is "as flash as a rat with a gold tooth," he's very pleased with himself. When we interact with people from other societies, we need to be aware that they may use unfamiliar phrases.[32]

Cultural differences in language use can also make it hard to translate phrases or slogans from one society to the next. The challenge is evident in the following humorous examples of mistranslated signs and advertisements:

- Sign in a Bangkok dry cleaner: "Drop your trousers here for best results!"
- Sign in a Copenhagen airline ticket office: "We take your bags and send them in all directions."
- Sign in a Hong Kong tailor shop: "Ladies may have a fit upstairs."
- Sign in an Acapulco restaurant: "The manager has personally passed all the water served here."
- Sign in a Moscow hotel room: "If this is your first visit to the USSR, you are welcome to it."

JARGON.   A specific form of idiomatic communication that often separates co-cultures is jargon, or language whose technical meaning is understood by people within that co-culture but not necessarily by those outside it. Physicians, for instance, use precise medical terminology to communicate among themselves about medical conditions and treatments. In most cases, that technical jargon is used only with people in the same co-culture. Therefore, although your doctor might tell her nurse that you have "ecchymosis on a distal phalange," she'd probably just tell you that you have a bruise on your fingertip. Similarly, if your dentist orders a "periapical radiograph," he wants an X-ray of the roots of one of your teeth.

Not understanding co-cultural jargon can make you feel like an outsider. You might even get the impression that co-cultures such as doctors and dentists talk the way they do to reinforce their in-group status. However, jargon can serve an important function by allowing people to communicate specifically, efficiently, and accurately.

GESTURES.   Societies also differ a great deal in their use of gestures, which are movements, usually of the hand or the arm, that express ideas. The same gesture can have different meanings from society to society. For instance, U.S. parents sometimes play the game "I've got your nose!" with infants by putting a thumb between the index and middle finger. That gesture means good luck in Brazil, but it is an obscene

SEVEN ASPECTS OF CULTURE

Individualism and Collectivism	Whether a culture emphasizes the needs of the individual or the group
Low and High Context	Whether language is expected to be explicit or subtle
Low- and High-Power Distance	Whether power is widely or narrowly distributed among people
Masculine and Feminine	Whether traditionally masculine or feminine values are promoted
Monochronic and Polychronic	Whether time is seen as a finite commodity or an infinite resource
Uncertainty Avoidance	Whether people welcome or shy away from uncertainty
Communication Codes	How idioms, jargon, and gestures reflect cultural values

gesture in Russia and Indonesia. Similarly, holding up the index and pinky finger while holding down the middle and ring finger is a common gesture for fans of the University of Texas Longhorns. In Italy, however, that gesture is used to suggest that a man's wife has been unfaithful.[33]

The "At a Glance" box summarizes the seven aspects of culture we have surveyed. Keep these dimensions in mind as you communicate cross-culturally, to hone your skill in such interactions.

How sensitive are you to other cultures? Fill out the Intercultural Sensitivity Scale in the "Assess Your Skills" box to find out. If your score is lower than you'd like, remember that the first step to becoming more culturally sensitive is learning as much as you can about what culture is and how cultures vary.

Do you ever feel that men and women don't speak quite the same language? In the next section, we examine several reasons why that may sometimes be the case.

LEARN IT In what ways do people from individualistic and collectivistic cultures differ in their communication behaviors? Do people use more explicit language in high- or low-context cultures? Is power more evenly distributed in a high- or a low-power-distance culture? What makes a culture feminine as opposed to masculine? How do people from monochronic and polychronic cultures differ in their use of time? In what ways does a culture's uncertainty avoidance affect the communication behaviors of its members? Why are idioms and gestures examples of cultural communication codes?

APPLY IT Select a gesture that is commonly used in U.S. American society, such as the thumbs-up or OK sign. Using the Internet, research and document the many different interpretations that gesture has in cultures around the world. This exercise will sharpen your skill as an intercultural communicator by helping you avoid awkwardly misusing that gesture.

REFLECT ON IT How are culture's effects on communication learned and reinforced? What challenges have you experienced when communicating with people from other cultures?

HOW CULTURALLY SENSITIVE ARE YOU?

On the line before each of the following statements, record your level of agreement on a 1–5 scale. Higher numbers mean you agree more, and lower numbers mean you agree less.

1. _____ I enjoy interacting with people from different cultures.
2. _____ I am pretty sure of myself when interacting with people from different cultures.
3. _____ I rarely find it very hard to talk in front of people from different cultures.
4. _____ I like to be with people from different cultures.
5. _____ I respect the values of people from different cultures.
6. _____ I tend to wait before forming an impression of people from different cultures.
7. _____ I am open-minded to people from different cultures.
8. _____ I am very observant when interacting with people from different cultures.
9. _____ I respect the ways people from different cultures behave.
10. _____ I try to obtain as much information as I can when interacting with people from different cultures.

When you're finished, add your scores and write the total on this line: _____. The ranges below will help you assess how culturally sensitive you are.

- 10–25: Cultural sensitivity is a skill you can improve, and the material in this chapter may help.
- 26–35: You are sometimes comfortable in intercultural conversations, but they make you uncomfortable from time to time. Continued practice may improve your ease in communicating interculturally.
- 36–50: You find it relatively easy to interact with people from other cultures.

Source: Chen, G. M., & Starosta, W. J. (2000). The development and validation of the intercultural sensitivity scale. *Human Communication, 3,* 1–14.

3 Understanding Gender and Communication

In the film comedy *She's the Man* (2006), Viola Hastings (played by Amanda Bynes) is a high school soccer player who finds out that the girls' team at her school is being cut. When her request to join the boys' team is rejected, she enrolls in a new high school disguised as her twin brother so that she can play for the boys' team there. During the school year, Viola has to be constantly diligent not to give away her identity as female. That task is complicated on many occasions, such as when she accidentally expresses feminine opinions and then suddenly switches to more masculine views. Although humorous, Viola's situation reflects a very real truth: Gender profoundly influences

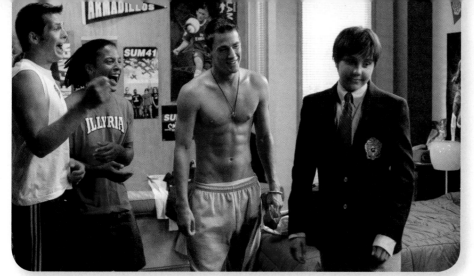

In the movie She's the Man, *Amanda Bynes's character disguises herself as a boy so that she can play high school soccer. Does changing her appearance change her gender?*

how we live our lives. It is a defining feature of our identity, shaping the way we think, look, and communicate. After all, what's the first question you ask about a new baby? "Is it a boy or a girl?"

Although gender is powerful, it is far from simple or straightforward. The concept of gender includes many influences, such as psychological gender roles, biological sex, and sexual orientation. Some interpersonal behaviors are strongly influenced by psychological gender roles, and others are more strongly influenced by biological sex or sexual orientation. In this section, we'll take a look at these components of gender, and we'll critique one of the most common explanations for why communicating across gender lines can be so challenging.

I will use the word *gender* as a broad term encompassing the influences of gender roles, biological sex, and sexual orientation in places where I'm not drawing specific distinctions among those terms. Otherwise, I will use *gender roles* in reference to masculinity, femininity, and androgyny. When addressing the differences between females and males, I'll apply the term *biological sex* (or simply *sex*), and I'll use *sexual orientation* when discussing how one's sexuality influences behavior. See Figure 2.1 for an illustration of how I'm using these various terms.

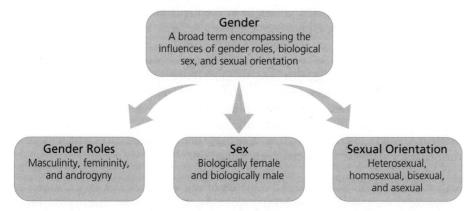

FIGURE 2.1 Diagram Explaining Gender, Biological Sex, and Sexual Orientation
Communication research has examined effects of gender roles, biological sex, and sexual orientation on interpersonal communication behavior.

Films such as Million Dollar Baby *portray female characters engaged in stereotypically masculine activities.*

Gender Roles and Communication

A role is a set of behaviors expected of someone in a particular social position. Expectations for male and female behavior make up a culture's **gender roles,** or norms for how women and men are supposed to act. In the United States, for instance, by tradition men are the breadwinners, and women are the homemakers. Men are supposed to be interested in cars, sports, and guns; women, to like shopping, cooking, and childrearing.[34] That doesn't mean men and women always *have* those interests, only that traditional gender roles suggest that they ought to. Similarly, in many cultures, men are expected to make the decisions and occupy the positions of power, although that is not always the reality.[35]

Such expectations reflect culturally influenced ideas about what it means to be a woman or a man. We can think of gender roles as falling into three specific categories: masculinity, femininity, and androgyny.

THE MASCULINE GENDER ROLE. When used in reference to people rather than cultures, the term **masculinity** refers to the set of gender role expectations a society typically assigns to men, although anyone can have masculine characteristics and communication behavior patterns. Specific masculine qualities might differ from one culture to the next, but the masculine role usually emphasizes strength, competition, independence, sexual aggressiveness, risk taking, logical thinking, and the acquisition of resources. Traditional masculinity also tends to reject weakness, emotional expressiveness, and characteristics or behaviors that resemble those of women.[36] In childhood, masculine behavior includes playing with toy guns and cars and competing in sports, since those activities emphasize strength, dominance, and winning. Masculine behavior in adulthood includes being a leader, being a breadwinner, and focusing more on action than on talk.

Masculinity has good and bad points. For instance, the emphasis on strength and dominance can motivate and enable men to protect themselves and their families against threats. Thinking logically can help solve problems, and being willing to take risks can help someone achieve things he or she didn't believe were possible. At the same time, masculine role expectations can pose problems. For example, the emphasis on independence may keep men from asking for help—such as medical care—when they need it.[37] Focusing on competition and aggression can put men in harm's way and may account for the fact that men are more likely than women to be victims in every type of violent crime except rape.[38] Men are also much more likely than women to commit violent crimes. Further, masculinity emphasizes risk taking; therefore, men are more likely than women to smoke, drink excessively, drink and drive, and fail to use seatbelts and sunscreen, as well as more likely not to exercise, all of which increase their chances of illness, injury, and premature death.[39]

THE FEMININE GENDER ROLE. The set of role expectations a society typically assigns to women is called **femininity,** although this term can characterize either sex.[40] In general, the feminine gender role typically emphasizes empathy and emotional expressiveness; a focus on relationships and on maintaining them; an interest in bearing and raising children; and attentiveness to appearance. Traditional femininity

gender role A set of expectations for appropriate behavior that a culture typically assigns to an individual based on his or her biological sex.

masculinity A gender role, typically assigned to men, that emphasizes strength, dominance, competition, and logical thinking.

femininity A gender role, typically assigned to women, that emphasizes expressive, nurturing behavior.

also emphasizes cooperation and submissiveness and tends to downplay intellectual achievement and career ambition.

Like masculinity, femininity has pros and cons. The focus on caregiving has helped to ensure the survival of countless generations of children and families. The emphasis on empathy and relationships has allowed women to build strong, intimate friendships with one another and to excel at careers that require interpersonal sensitivity, such as teaching and counseling. Emphasizing cooperation instead of competition has probably also helped women to solve interpersonal problems in mutually beneficial ways. However, traditional femininity can also impose limits on the choices and options available to women. In the past, tradition discouraged many women from pursuing their education and achieving their career goals out of the belief that a woman's proper place is in the home. In addition, the emphasis on appearance puts tremendous pressure on women to achieve certain body types. As a result, women are far more likely than men to develop depression and eating disorders.[41] The focus on submissiveness has also made it difficult for some women to leave abusive relationships.[42]

THE ANDROGYNOUS GENDER ROLE. To a large extent, masculinity and femininity are opposing concepts; that is, part of what makes a trait masculine is that it is not feminine, and vice versa. Not everyone is best described as either feminine or masculine, however. Rather, some people seem to have both characteristics. For example, a woman might love children yet be very assertive, logical, and unemotional in her job. Similarly, a man may be strong and independent while still being sensitive and caring deeply and expressively for his friends. **Androgyny** is the term used to describe the combination of masculine and feminine characteristics. When a person strongly identifies with both gender roles, we say that he or she is psychologically androgynous.[43]

androgyny A gender role distinguished by a combination of masculine and feminine characteristics.

Being androgynous does not mean that a person is homosexual or bisexual or that he or she wants to be of the other sex. Instead, it means the person identifies strongly with aspects of both femininity and masculinity. Consequently, an androgynous person is often less concerned about behaving in gender-appropriate ways than someone who is more strongly masculine or feminine.

For instance, an androgynous man probably would not view working as a nurse as a threat to his gender identity. Likewise, an androgynous woman probably would not be uncomfortable serving as her family's primary breadwinner. In 1994, British journalist Mark Simpson coined the term *metrosexual* to refer to a man, usually a heterosexual, who has adopted the more feminine behavior of paying a great deal of attention to his appearance and grooming—and who thus exemplifies an androgynous person.[44]

HOW GENDER VARIES BY TIME AND CULTURE. Gender roles are never set in stone. Like most roles, they change over time, and they vary from culture to culture.

In the United States, for example, images of women and men in the media—including movies, television shows, and advertisements—have changed dramatically within the last several decades. In the 1950s, TV shows such as *Leave It to Beaver* and *Father Knows Best* depicted men, women, and children in gender-specific ways. Fathers were strong, authoritative, and the sole family breadwinners. Mothers were homemakers whose concerns centered on their husbands, children, and housework. Boys were interested in masculine activities, such as fishing and playing with cars, and girls pursued feminine activities, such as playing with dolls and baking cakes. More recent television shows, including *CSI, House,* and *Modern Family,* have portrayed a more flexible femininity and masculinity. Women work outside the home, sometimes in traditionally masculine professions such as surgery and law enforcement, and men express their feelings, even with other men. And in fact, television shows such as *The Good Wife* and *Hawaii Five-O* offer uncharacteristically strong portrayals of female characters.

Gender roles also differ by culture. For example, in nomadic societies, in which people move from place to place to hunt and forage, there is little difference in girls' and boys' upbringing. Everyone's daily tasks are similar—to find food and water—so there is little need to differentiate the roles of girls and boys. In contrast, agricultural societies that rely on farming and herding for their food usually socialize boys and girls very differently, raising girls to care for the children and home and boys to tend to the livestock and crops.[45]

As discussed earlier, culture's influence on gender roles is so strong that researchers label cultures themselves as masculine or feminine. In masculine cultures, roles for women and men are clearly defined and differentiated, and there is little overlap. It would be highly unusual in a masculine culture for a man to be a stay-at-home dad, for instance, because childcare is considered part of the feminine role. Gender roles in feminine cultures are far less differentiated, however, so there is less of an expectation that women and men will behave differently.

There's no question that gender role expectations influence our lives, but being masculine or feminine is not the same thing as being physically male or female. Next, we'll explore the meaning of biological sex, along with its effects on communication behavior.

Biological Sex and Communication

The term *biological sex* refers to being female or male rather than feminine or masculine. Before we examine how biological sex influences communication behavior, let's take a closer look at what biological sex is and how it differs from gender roles.

When you were conceived, you were neither male nor female. About seven weeks later, though, your genes activated your biological sex. Each of us has 23 pairs of chromosomes, which are strands of DNA, in our cells. The 23rd pair is made up of the sex chromosomes that determine whether we're female or male. Human sex chromosomes are called X and Y, and we inherit one from each parent. Mothers supply us with one X chromosome. Fathers give us either a second X or a Y, depending on which one their sperm is carrying. If we get another X, we grow up female. If we get a Y, we become male.

We tend to think of "male" and "female" as the only categories of biological sex, but some people have difficulty fitting into one or the other group. Understanding the diversity in forms of biological sex helps us appreciate why studying sex differences in communication behavior is often more complex than it may first seem. Consider the following:

- Some people experience conflict between the sex they were born into and the sex they feel they should be. For instance, a person may see herself as male even though she was born female. The term *transgendered* describes individuals who experience such conflict.[46] Transgendered people may use hormone therapy or sex-reassignment surgery to bring their physical body in line with their self-image. We often refer to those who have undergone such procedures as *transsexual* individuals.[47]

- Not everyone is born with either XX (female) or XY (male) chromosomes. Women with Turner syndrome, for example, have an X chromosome only (XO), and men with Klinefelter syndrome have an extra X chromosome (XXY). Researchers estimate that about 1 in 1,700 people is born with some type of chromosomal disorder.[48]

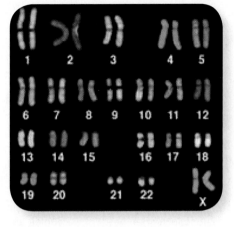

You have 23 pairs of chromosomes in nearly every cell of your body. The 23rd pair determines your biological sex. You are biologically male if this chromosome pair has an X and a Y chromosome. If it has a pair of X chromosomes, as illustrated here, you are biologically female.

- Finally, some people have internal sexual organs that do not match their external appearance. For instance, a child might be born with a penis but have ovaries instead of testicles. Doctors call that condition *intersex,* and it can be caused by delayed physical development or by hormonal problems.[49] People with this condition are often able to lead normal, healthy lives, although questions about their correct biological sex may make it difficult for others in their social environments to accept them.[50]

Like gender roles, biological sex is a fundamental part of a person's identity. No matter the person's biological sex and gender roles, however, interpersonal behavior can also be influenced by a third aspect of gender: sexual orientation.

Sexual Orientation and Communication

Sexual orientation describes the sex or sexes to which an individual is sexually attracted. Scientists disagree over the extent to which sexual orientation is determined genetically (the way biological sex is) versus socially (the way gender roles are). Sexual orientation isn't always considered an aspect of gender, but a growing body of research suggests that it influences communication behavior just as gender roles and biological sex do. We'll look briefly at four patterns of sexual orientation: heterosexuality, homosexuality, bisexuality, and asexuality.

sexual orientation
A characteristic determining the sex or sexes to which someone is sexually attracted.

HETEROSEXUALITY.   **Heterosexuality** refers to being physically and romantically attracted to people of the other sex. Several studies have confirmed that the majority of adults in most societies have experienced mostly heterosexual attraction and have engaged in primarily heterosexual behavior.[51] One possible reason for this tendency is that heterosexual interaction has the potential to support reproduction, whereas other forms of sexual interaction do not. Another reason is that in most cultures, heterosexuality is the most socially approved form of sexuality. Therefore, heterosexual people in those cultures enjoy a level of social support that others often do not.[52]

heterosexuality A sexual orientation characterized by sexual interest in members of the other sex.

HOMOSEXUALITY.   **Homosexuality** refers to romantic and sexual attraction to members of one's own sex. Homosexual males are commonly referred to as "gay," and female homosexuals are typically called "lesbian." Although sexual contact between members of the same sex has been common across cultures and time periods, homosexuality did not become a recognized part of a person's identity until the 1800s.[53] Before that point, it was not uncommon for adults of the same sex to sleep in the same bed or to write love letters to each other; but such behaviors were interpreted as expressions of affection rather than markers of sexual orientation.[54]

Researchers have developed many different theories to explain homosexuality. Some studies have focused on the social influences of parents and other role models,

homosexuality A sexual orientation characterized by sexual interest in members of one's own sex.

FACT OR fiction?

HETEROSEXUAL RELATIONSHIPS ARE MORE STABLE AND SATISFYING THAN GAY AND LESBIAN RELATIONSHIPS

There's a great deal of disagreement these days about whether homosexual adults should be allowed to marry. At present, same-sex marriage is legal in only a few U.S. states. In contrast, 17 states have constitutional provisions banning it. Opponents of same-sex marriage have long claimed that gay and lesbian relationships are less stable and more dysfunctional than heterosexual relationships. Is that true?

At this point the answer appears to be no. In fact, several studies have shown that same-sex romantic relationships are just as stable and satisfying, on average, as opposite-sex relationships. For example, one study matched samples of heterosexual and homosexual men and women who were in serious romantic relationships. After ruling out any differences in the participants' age, education level, ethnicity, and length of relationship, the researchers found no differences between the heterosexual and homosexual samples in how close or satisfying their relationships were.

Those findings do not suggest that all gay and lesbian couples are happy and problem-free. They do indicate, however, that same-sex relationships can be just as stable and satisfying as heterosexual relationships. Whatever your individual beliefs about the morality of homosexual relationships, the argument that they are prone to dysfunction does not stand up to the evidence.

ASK YOURSELF

- Where do you stand on this issue? What type of evidence is the most persuasive to you?

- What do you think contributes to relationship stability and satisfaction?

Source: Kurdek, L. A. (1992). Relationship stability and relationship satisfaction in cohabiting gay and lesbian couples: A prospective longitudinal test of the contextual and interdependence models. *Journal of Social and Personal Relationships, 9,* 125–142.

whereas others have emphasized physiological or genetic differences.[55] According to a national survey conducted by the Centers for Disease Control and Prevention (CDC), 2.3 percent of American men aged 15–44 identified themselves as homosexual, although 6.5 percent reported having had sexual interaction with another man. Similarly, 1.3 percent of American women identified themselves as homosexual, although 11 percent reported having had sexual interaction with another woman.[56]

The question of whether homosexual adults should be allowed to marry or form legal domestic partnerships has been contentious in the United States for some time. The argument against formalizing homosexual romantic relationships often implies that such relationships are inherently less stable than heterosexual marriages. Is that true? Check out the "Fact or Fiction?" box to find out.

bisexuality A sexual orientation characterized by sexual interest in both women and men.

BISEXUALITY. **Bisexuality** refers to having romantic and/or sexual attraction to both women and men. Although bisexuals have some level of attraction to both sexes, they are not necessarily attracted to both sexes equally.[57] Moreover, bisexual people don't usually maintain long-term romantic relationships with members of both sexes. Rather, they often have a romantic relationship with a partner of one sex while engaging in or thinking about sexual interaction with people of the other sex.[58] According to the CDC survey mentioned earlier, 1.8 percent of men and 2.8 percent of women in the United States identify themselves as bisexual.[59]

THREE COMPONENTS OF GENDER

Gender Roles	Psychological orientation toward masculinity, femininity, or androgyny
Biological Sex	Genetic characteristics that distinguish females from males
Sexual Orientation	Sexual attraction toward members of the other sex, the same sex, both sexes, or neither sex

ASEXUALITY. **Asexuality** is used to describe people who have very little interest in sex. This orientation is fairly uncommon. In one British study, for example, only 1 percent of respondents indicated they had never been sexually attracted to anyone.[60] Researchers aren't sure whether asexuality is a disorder or whether it represents another sexual orientation. Asexuality is not the same as *celibacy,* which is the practice of abstaining from sex. In fact, some asexual people do have sex, and most celibate people are not asexual.

> **asexuality** A sexual orientation characterized by a general lack of interest in sex.

A summary of the three primary components of gender appears in the "At a Glance" box.

Some Explanations for Gendered Communication

From time to time, you may feel as though talking with a person of the other sex is like talking to an extraterrestrial. Popular author John Gray captured that sentiment in his book *Men Are from Mars, Women Are from Venus.*[61] According to Gray, "Men and women differ in all areas of their lives. Not only do men and women communicate differently but they think, feel, perceive, react, respond, love, need, and appreciate differently. They almost seem to be from different planets, speaking different languages and needing different nourishment."[62]

Communication experts do not go as far as Gray and claim that men and women might as well be from different planets. Nevertheless, some researchers, including communication scholar Julia Wood and linguist Deborah Tannen, do argue that women and men constitute different *gender cultures,* with each sex being a distinctive culture with its own rules and values.[63] The fundamental difference between the two cultures is that each sex values different components of relationships. Specifically, women are taught to value the communicating of intimacy and emotional support, whereas men are taught to value the sharing of activities.

When Zach and his friend Sergio get together, for instance, their time is likely to revolve around a mutual activity, such as going for a hike or watching car racing on TV, because for them sharing activities is a means of bonding. Sometimes they talk about personal topics, but their conversation is of lesser importance than the shared activity. For Zach's wife Aisha and her friend Thérèse, however, time together is more likely to revolve around conversation. Whatever shared activity they may be doing is often of lesser importance than the conversation itself.

The concept of gender cultures further maintains that when women and men communicate with each other, they each bring their own rules and values to the table. Because these rules and values differ, the result is often *gender clash,* or the experience of each sex not understanding the other.[64] For instance, when Sergio's daughter was undergoing treatment for leukemia, Aisha couldn't understand why Zach didn't invite him over "just to talk" but instead invited him to a baseball game. That action seemed

From time to time, you may feel as though talking with a person of the other sex is like talking to an extraterrestrial.

insensitive to Aisha, who thought Zach should be a better friend to Sergio by getting him to open up about his feelings. As Zach explained, however, going to a ball game and just hanging out with no expectation of a deep conversation was his way of letting Sergio know he cared. He also assured Aisha that Sergio would interpret it that way.

There's little question that communicating across genders can be challenging and that several communicative behaviors appear to be affected by sex, gender roles, and/or sexual orientation. However, some scholars disagree that the sexes constitute different cultures. For example, communication scientists Brant Burleson and Adrianne Kunkel have pointed out that the "different cultures" idea has not been well supported by the data.[65] Several studies have demonstrated that women and men are more similar than different in the forms of communication they value.[66] Indeed, the lack of scientific evidence for the gender cultures idea has led communication researcher Kathryn Dindia to suggest a more modest metaphor for gendered communication: "Men are from North Dakota, women are from South Dakota."[67]

Each of those perspectives—the sexes come from different planets, the sexes represent different cultures, and the sexes are more similar than different—is intuitively appealing in its own way. In fact, it's easy for many of us to see sex differences in communication behavior almost anywhere we look. The fact that many societies make sex differences the focus of jokes and comedic movies and television shows probably adds to our tendency to see sex differences as large and pervasive.

However, just because an idea is intuitive or seems to reflect our personal experience doesn't mean the idea is accurate. That is one reason why scientific research is so important: It allows us to subject our ideas to rigorous scrutiny. The best scientific evidence tells us that sex, gender roles, and sexual orientation all play a part in how people communicate, but not as large a part as we might think. Women and men differ from each other in many ways—as do masculine, feminine, and androgynous people, and heterosexual, homosexual, bisexual, and asexual people. When it comes to communication behavior, however, we are more alike than different. The research tells us that Gray's claim that women and men "differ in all areas of their lives" may be an exaggeration. It is true that our differences are often more apparent to us than our similarities, but the scientific evidence suggests that as communicators, we are not as different as we often think we are.

LEARN IT How do masculinity, femininity, and androgyny compare with one another? In what ways do psychological, genetic, and anatomical differences influence one's biological sex? What is a sexual orientation? What are the principal ways of explaining gendered communication, and how well are those explanations supported by scientific evidence?

APPLY IT In small groups or with your class as a whole, create a discussion board or blog to identify the ways in which masculine and feminine communication behaviors are taught and reinforced in your society. Consider not only the family, the school system, religion, and the media, but other aspects of social life that teach people how to communicate in gender-specific ways.

REFLECT ON IT How do you feel about people whose sexual orientation is different from yours? How do you think those feelings affect your communication with them? What are the biggest challenges you have noticed in male–female communication?

4 How Gender Affects Communication

Clearly, then, our gender roles, biological sex, and sexual orientation all play a part in how we communicate. In this section, we'll look at differences in language (the use of spoken and written words) and nonverbal behavior (the ways we communicate without words) to gain specific insight into how these various aspects of gender affect our interactions with others.

Before we go on, we need to consider two important points. First, even though gender includes the influences of biological sex, gender roles, and sexual orientation, most of the research we'll examine has simply compared the communication behaviors of men and women. As a result, we know quite a bit about sex differences but comparatively little about the effects of gender roles and sexual orientation on communication. Second, although some behaviors differ between the sexes, other behaviors do not. In addition, some sex differences are large, but many others are fairly small. In recent years, several scholars have called for caution when we are looking at sex differences in behavior so that we don't exaggerate them beyond what the evidence supports.[68]

In U.S. American culture, women often practice expressive talk, treating communication as a way to establish closeness.

Gender and Verbal Communication

Research shows that gender influences both the content and the style of our speech. Let's take a close look at three gender effects:

- Expressive and instrumental talk
- Language and power
- Gendered linguistic styles

EXPRESSIVE AND INSTRUMENTAL TALK. Some communication scholars have argued that women and men grow up in different "speech communities," meaning they have different norms and beliefs concerning the purpose of communication.[69] That idea is similar to the gender cultures theory, but it focuses more specifically on differences in speech and communication behaviors. In particular, those researchers believe that women are socialized to practice **expressive talk,** which means they are taught to view communication as the primary way to establish closeness and intimacy in relationships. In contrast, men are taught to practice **instrumental talk,** or to see communication as a means to solve problems and accomplish tasks.[70]

To understand these sex-related differences in communication, consider the following scenario. Shannon has noticed that whenever she talks to her co-worker Max about a problem, he always responds by telling her what she should do to fix it. The following exchange illustrates that point.

> **Shannon:** My boss is totally blaming me for losing one of our biggest accounts—but it's completely his fault! He's the one who never returns the customer's calls and wouldn't let me help last year when one of their shipments was delayed.

expressive talk Verbal communication whose purpose is to express emotions and build relationships.

instrumental talk Verbal communication whose purpose is to solve problems and accomplish tasks.

[EXPRESSIVE TALK]

Learn to use expressive talk when it is appropriate.

WHAT?

Practice speaking for the purpose of expressing emotions and building relationships.

WHY?

To convey to others—such as your close friends or co-workers—that you care about them and what they have to say.

HOW?

1. When someone describes a problem to you, resist thinking of ways to solve the problem.

2. Instead, focus on the emotions the speaker is likely to be experiencing.

3. In your reply, describe how you believe the speaker is feeling.

TRY!

Your friend comes to you complaining about the vandalism in your neighborhood. Respond in a way that expresses your emotions.

CONSIDER: *In what ways does expressive talk benefit relationships?*

Max: You should call your regional manager and tell her what's going on. Show her the paperwork from the order that got delayed so she'll see that you tried to help.

Max's response is a good example of instrumental talk. When Shannon explains her problem, Max views it as a request for help, and he suggests how to make the situation better. Contrast Max's comments with the response Shannon gets when she shares the same problem with her sister Sabrina:

Sabrina: That's so unfair! I'm sorry he's blaming you—you must be so frustrated, especially since it's his fault in the first place.

Sabrina's response is an example of expressive talk. Instead of suggesting how Shannon might solve the problem, Sabrina acknowledges Shannon's feelings and expresses her own unhappiness at Shannon's frustration. According to communication scholars such as Julia Wood, that is a common difference between women and men. That is, for women the purpose of sharing problems is to express one's feelings. From that perspective, a good friend should listen and empathize. For men, though, the purpose of sharing problems is to get advice on how to solve them. From that perspective, a good friend should offer his opinions about what to do.[71] The "Got Skills?" box offers suggestions for improving your expressive talk ability.

How do men and women become socialized into different speech communities? One of the earliest influences seems to be the childhood games they play. If you think back to your own childhood, you probably remember that at an early age most children played only with other children of their same sex and that boys and girls played very different games.[72] Boys' games, such as football and model building, emphasize structure, rules, and competition. Girls' games, such as playing house and jumping rope, emphasize cooperation, sensitivity, and flexibility. One possible result of those patterns is that boys learn to use language to give instructions and share information, and girls learn to use language to express their feelings and to build camaraderie.[73]

With respect to sexual orientation, the common stereotypes of gay men as feminine and lesbians as masculine would suggest that gay men engage in more expressive and less instrumental talk than heterosexual men, whereas lesbians engage in more instrumental and less expressive talk than heterosexual women. Research indicates that both of those predictions are accurate.[74] Importantly, that observation does not mean that gay men talk like women or that lesbian women talk like men. Rather, it suggests only that gay men's speech patterns are more expressive and less instrumental than those of heterosexual men and that lesbian women's speech is more instrumental and less expressive than that of heterosexual women.

LANGUAGE AND POWER. For years, researchers have noticed that men and women talk to each other in a style that reflects how superiors and subordinates talk to each other.[75] Powerful speech behaviors, such as those used by superiors, include talking more, interrupting more frequently, giving more directions, and expressing more opinions. Less powerful speech behaviors, such as those used by subordinates, include asking more questions, using more hedges ("sort of," "might be") and disclaimers ("I could be wrong, but . . ."), and speaking less overall.

In an extensive review of the current research, communication scholars Pam Kalbfleisch and Anita Herold found that on average, American men use more powerful forms of speech than American women.[76] For instance, research indicates that contrary to the stereotype, men are often as talkative as women, as the "Fact or Fiction?" box explains. In fact, men often talk *more* than women do, particularly about impersonal topics such as money and work.[77] Men also interrupt more frequently, give more directions, and express more opinions—all characteristics of powerful speech.[78] In contrast, women's language use is more attentive to others.[79] Compared with men, women ask more questions and use more disclaimers and hedges in their speech.[80]

The following exchange between two colleagues at an advertising firm illustrates more powerful and less powerful forms of communication.

Language is described as more powerful or less powerful based on communication behaviors such as interrupting, giving directions, expressing opinions, asking questions, using disclaimers, and speaking more or speaking less. From the perspective of language and power, how would you characterize the speaking styles of the three judges on American Idol?

> **Emelie:** I don't know if this is a good idea, but I sort of think we should keep the new ad slogans secret until we launch the marketing campaign, don't you?
>
> **Stefan:** Find out what the client wants and then we'll decide. The slogans aren't that great anyway. We need to bring some new account reps in on this project and get some fresh ideas in here.

In this exchange, Emelie starts off with a disclaimer ("I don't know if this is a good idea"); she then hedges her opinion ("I sort of think"); and she concludes with a question that seeks validation from others ("don't you?"). In contrast, Stefan's words are directive ("Find out what the client wants") and opinionated ("The slogans aren't that great"). Also, unlike Emelie, Stefan doesn't end his statement by asking if others agree with him. Their conversation exemplifies less powerful (Emelie) and more powerful (Stefan) forms of speech.

Although the research findings are important, keep in mind two critical points. First, the findings don't apply

WOMEN ARE MORE TALKATIVE THAN MEN

When it comes to sex differences in communication, perhaps the most common stereotype is that women are more talkative than men. Is that idea fact or fiction?

Carefully conducted research tells us that it's fiction. The truth is that women and men speak approximately the same number of words per day: roughly 16,000 on average. The study that identified that finding took place between 1998 and 2005 and involved almost 400 students from universities in the United States and Mexico. Each participant wore a device called an electronically activated recorder, or EAR. The EAR is a digital voice recorder that unobtrusively tracks a person's real-world interactions with others by recording 30-second snippets of sound every 12.5 minutes while the person is awake. The researchers then transcribed each recording and counted the number of words spoken, analyzing them as a function of the percentage of waking time the EAR recorded.

When the researchers compared the results by sex, they found that women and men spoke, on average, 16,215 and 15,669 words per day, respectively. Those totals were not significantly different and thus suggested that the stereotype that women are more talkative than men is more fiction than fact.

ASK YOURSELF

- Why does the stereotype of talkative women persist?
- What other stereotypes about sex and communication do you think may be inaccurate?

Source: Mehl, M. R., Vazire, S., Ramírez-Esparza, N., Slatcher, R. B., & Pennebaker, J. W. (2007). Are women really more talkative than men? *Science, 317,* 82.

equally to every woman and man. There are women who use very powerful styles of speaking and men whose language styles are less powerful. Whenever we compare groups (such as women and men), we're focusing specifically on average differences. Clearly, there can be many individual exceptions to whatever differences we discover. Second, even if a man uses more powerful speech patterns than a woman does, that doesn't necessarily mean that he *is* more powerful. Rather, he is simply using the speech patterns that are typical for men in our society.

A particularly troubling example of the difference between powerful and powerless speech is the use of *linguistic violence,* language that degrades and dehumanizes a group of people.[81] One way the more powerful nature of men's speech is expressed, for instance, is through terms that objectify and degrade women.[82] Using language to put down other people can constitute a type of emotional violence in the same way that hitting can constitute a type of physical violence. Linguistic violence is also frequently directed against homosexual, bisexual, and/or transgendered people. Those communities are frequently *marginalized,* meaning they are subjected to unfair discrimination and prejudice on the basis of their sexual orientation or gender identity.[83]

GENDERED LINGUISTIC STYLES. In addition to gender differences in the purpose (expressive versus instrumental) and the power of speech, research suggests that men and women differ in other aspects of their speech patterns, or *linguistic styles.* For example, women are more likely than men to use second- and third-person pronouns ("we," "they") and to make references to emotions ("hurt," "scared") when they talk. They also use more intensive adverbs, such as describing someone as "really" tall or "so" smart. As well, women speak in longer sentences than men do, on average.[84] Carmen, for example, might describe her new house in this way:

We love our new home! It has a really big yard where the neighborhood children can play, and two very large guestrooms on the ground floor for when we have company. We also have a really nice kitchen, and the master suite is so spacious!

Men's linguistic style makes greater use of self-references ("I" statements) and judgmental adjectives such as "good" or "worthless." Compared with women, men also use more references to quantity, such as informing other people that something "costs $400" or someone "is 6 feet, 8 inches tall." Men are also more likely than women to use location statements ("It's in the back") and incomplete sentences ("Nice job.").[85] For example, Carmen's husband Diego might describe their new home in this way:

The house is great. It's got 2,200 square feet, plus a three-car detached garage. There's about an acre and a half of land. I got a good deal on the mortgage, too. 4.1 percent for 30 years.

In these examples, Carmen uses the pronoun "we" whereas Diego uses the pronoun "I." Carmen also uses intensive adverbs ("really big yard," "very large guestrooms"), whereas Diego makes specific references to quantity ("2,200 square feet," "acre and a half of land"). Carmen's sentences are also longer than Diego's on average, and Diego uses an incomplete sentence ("4.1 percent for 30 years"), whereas Carmen does not. Only a few studies have examined whether those patterns are influenced by sexual orientation, and most of the results indicate that they are not.[86] Whether gender role affects the use of these linguistic styles is still unclear.

Gender and Nonverbal Communication

We use several behaviors that are *nonverbal*—carried out without words—to communicate. Nonverbal behaviors include gestures, facial expressions, tone of voice, and conventions about personal space. To understand how gender affects nonverbal communication, let's look at three specific areas:

- Touch and body movement
- Emotional communication
- Affectionate behavior

TOUCH AND BODY MOVEMENT.   Touch is an important form of nonverbal communication because it can express warmth and intimacy as well as power and dominance (as we'll see in Chapter 6). Many studies have shown that women and men exhibit different patterns of touch behavior. In an analysis of several of these studies, one research team discovered that sex differences in touch depend on whether the touch involves two adults or an adult and a child.[87]

When only adults are interacting, the researchers found that

- Men are more likely to touch women than women are to touch men, unless the touch is occurring as part of a greeting (such as a handshake).
- Other-sex touch is more common than same-sex touch.
- In same-sex pairs, women touch each other more than men do, but that difference is smaller in close friendships than among acquaintances.

In general, these results show that men do more touching than women in other-sex relationships, whereas women do more touching than men in same-sex relationships.

The patterns are quite different when one of the parties is a child:

- Same-sex touch is more common than other-sex touch.
- Women are more likely than men to initiate touch.
- Boys and girls are about equally likely to be touched.

These patterns may also be affected by culture. In feminine cultures, for instance, women and men may behave more similarly than in masculine cultures.

In addition to touch, sex appears to affect other forms of body movement. Compared with women, men use more body movement, prefer a greater amount of personal space around them, and try harder to preserve their personal space when it is violated.[88] Men also use more relaxed body movements. Both men and women appear to be more relaxed in their posture and gesturing when talking to men than to women.[89]

With respect to personal space, however, some evidence suggests that gender role rather than biological sex (or sexual orientation) is the most influential factor. For instance, one experiment found that masculine people (whether male or female) maintained a greater amount of personal distance from others than did feminine people (whether male or female).[90]

EMOTIONAL COMMUNICATION. Common stereotypes would have us believe that women are more emotional than men. We often expect women to cry more than men at sad movies, for instance, and to be more expressive of their feelings for one another than men are. Indeed, a 2001 Gallup poll found that adults in the United States are significantly more likely to use the term *emotional* to describe women than men.[91]

Even if women are more emotional than men, what does that mean, exactly? Does it mean that women experience more emotion than men or just that they're more willing to express the emotions they feel? Going further, if women are more expressive than men, does that difference apply to every kind of emotion or just to certain ones? Let's look at what research tells us about the effects of sex on emotional communication.

To begin with, women generally express more positive emotions—such as happiness and joy—than men do.[92] The most basic behavior we use to communicate positive emotions is smiling, and several studies have found that women smile more than men.[93] Women also use more *affiliation behaviors* than men do. Affiliation behaviors demonstrate feelings of closeness or attachment to someone else. Common affiliation behaviors include eye contact, head nods, pleasant facial expressions, and warm vocal tones.[94] Research even suggests that women are more likely than men to express positive emotions in e-mail messages through the use of "smileys."[95]

When it comes to negative emotions, though, sex differences appear to vary according to which emotion we consider. Some studies have found that men are more likely than women to express anger, but other studies haven't found a difference.[96] Men appear to express jealousy in more intense forms than women do, by engaging in dangerous, aggressive behaviors such as getting drunk, confronting a romantic rival, and becoming sexually involved with someone else.[97] Women are more likely than men to express the emotions of sadness and depression, however.[98]

Do women actually experience more emotion than men, or are they just more likely to express it? In a pair of studies, researchers Ann Kring and Albert Gordon found that although women were more expressive than men, they didn't report actually experiencing any more emotion than men did. Rather, men and women reported experiencing the same amount of emotion. Women simply expressed their emotions more frequently and openly, whereas men were more likely to mask their feelings.[99]

Although most research on gender and emotion has focused on biological sex, some studies have examined the influence of gender roles or sexual orientation. In one study, participants reported on their psychological gender roles. Afterward, they watched film clips that were emotionally arousing while researchers videotaped and subsequently coded their facial expressions. The researchers found that both women and men were more emotionally expressive if they were androgynous than if they were primarily masculine or feminine.[100]

In another experiment, lesbian and gay romantic couples took part in conflict discussions in a laboratory while their facial expressions were video-recorded. The researchers found that compared with gay men, lesbians were more expressive of both positive and negative emotion. This finding suggests that the biological sex difference in expression—meaning that women are more expressive than men—is not really affected by sexual orientation.[101]

AFFECTIONATE BEHAVIOR.   *Affectionate communication* includes those behaviors we use to express our love and appreciation for people we care about. Several studies have shown that women use more nonverbal affection behaviors—such as hugging, kissing, and handholding—than men do.[102] This observation appears to be especially true in same-sex relationships. That is, the sex differences in nonverbal affection behaviors are even greater when women and men are interacting with same-sex friends or relatives than when they are interacting with members of the other sex.[103]

Why are women more affectionate than men? Researchers have offered several explanations. One theory is that because girls receive more affection than boys do, they are more likely to grow up perceiving interpersonal interactions as opportunities for communicating affection.[104] Another explanation is that men are more likely than women to see affectionate communication as a feminine behavior, so they avoid expressing affection out of a fear of appearing feminine.[105] A third possible reason is that the different balances of hormones typically found in men and women make women

People sometimes interpret the same behavior differently depending on the sex of those enacting it. What interpretations would you make of each of these behaviors?

more likely to behave affectionately.[106] Any or all of these factors may play a part in making women more affectionate than men.

Masculinity and femininity are also related to affectionate behavior, although not in the way you might guess. Because affection is often thought of as a "feminine" way of behaving—at least in North American cultures—you might expect that the more feminine people are, the more affectionate they are. Several studies have found this to be the case. The same studies have shown, however, that the more masculine people are, the more affectionate they are.[107] So, it appears that people who score high on both femininity and masculinity are particularly affectionate.

Only a small number of studies have examined the influence of sexual orientation on affectionate communication. One large national U.S. survey reported that both gay men and lesbian women were more expressive of affection and positive emotion within their romantic relationships than were heterosexual spouses with children. They were not more expressive than heterosexual spouses without children or heterosexual unmarried partners, however.[108]

Two other studies looked specifically at affectionate behavior between adult men and their fathers. The results indicated that fathers are most affectionate with heterosexual sons, less affectionate if they are unsure of their sons' sexual orientation, and least affectionate with sons who are homosexual or bisexual.[109]

Considered together, the studies we've reviewed in this section present a complex picture of how gender roles, biological sex, and sexual orientation influence verbal and nonverbal communication behaviors. Sometimes these factors make a difference, other times they don't, and in some cases they matter in unexpected ways, as when masculinity is positively related to affectionate communication. In addition, as we saw earlier, even when we do find differences—for example, women use longer sentences than men, or lesbian women use more instrumental speech than heterosexual women—we must keep in mind that these are *average* differences. Thus, not every woman speaks in longer sentences than every man. Rather, women use longer sentences than men do on average.

We should take care not to exaggerate or oversimplify the influence of gender roles, sex, or sexual orientation on communication behavior. These features often influence how we behave, but they do not affect every aspect of our lives at all times. In addition, our interpersonal interaction is affected by many influences besides the gender role, biological sex, or sexual orientation with which we identify.

LEARN IT What is the difference between expressive and instrumental talk? How do gender roles, biological sex, and sexual orientation influence the experience and expression of emotion?

APPLY IT The next time you talk to an adult of the other sex, pay attention to your language style. Is your speech more instrumental or more expressive? Are you using powerful or powerless speech? Think about the ways your language style influences how effectively you are communicating. Write a paragraph or two documenting your observations.

REFLECT ON IT How would you characterize your verbal and nonverbal behavior? What role do you think your biological sex, gender role, and sexual orientation play in how you communicate with others?

MASTER the chapter

1 Understanding Culture and Communication (p. 36)

■ Culture is the system of learned and shared symbols, language, values, and norms that distinguish one group of people from another.

■ Cultures vary in their symbols, language, values, and norms.

■ Co-cultures are groups of people who share values, customs, and norms related to a mutual interest or characteristic.

■ Communicating with cultural awareness means paying attention to one's own cultural values and biases and remembering that others don't always share them.

2 How Culture Affects Communication (p. 43)

■ Individualistic cultures emphasize the importance of individuality and personal achievement, whereas collectivistic cultures emphasize the needs of the family and community.

■ People in low-context cultures expect language to be direct and explicit; those in high-context cultures rely more on contextual cues to interpret verbal statements.

■ In a low-power-distance culture, power is more equitably distributed among people; in a high-power-distance culture, most of the power is held by relatively few people.

■ Masculine cultures value competition and achievement and maintain largely different expectations for women and men. Feminine cultures value nurturing behavior and do not enforce rigidly different expectations for women and men.

■ Time is considered to be a finite commodity in a monochronic culture; it is considered to be more infinite in a polychronic culture.

■ Cultures vary in their uncertainty avoidance, or their aversion to novelty and uncertainty.

■ Cultures differ in their use of communication codes, such as idioms and gestures, which often have meaning only to people in a given culture.

3 Understanding Gender and Communication (p. 50)

■ Gender roles include masculinity, femininity, and androgyny, the meanings of which evolve over time.

■ Biological sex differentiates men and women but is influenced by psychological, genetic, and anatomical factors.

■ Sexual orientations include heterosexuality, homosexuality, bisexuality, and asexuality.

■ Some writers have argued that women and men communicate as though they come from different planets or at least different cultures. Others have asserted that those metaphors are exaggerations.

4 How Gender Affects Communication (p. 59)

■ Gender influences verbal communication, such as expressive and instrumental talk, power, and linguistic styles.

■ Gender influences nonverbal communication, including touch and body movement, emotional communication, and nonverbal affection.

KEY TERMS

DISCUSSION QUESTIONS

1. Culture is something that we often assume only other people have. What are some of the cultural and co-cultural influences on *your* behavior?

2. The United States is sometimes criticized for being as individualistic as it is. What are some good things about growing up in an individualistic culture? In what ways might growing up in a collectivistic culture be better?

3. Many researchers believe that all behavioral differences between women and men (apart from reproductive behaviors) stem from social influences. Do you think that's true? Can you think of any behavioral differences that might be biological or genetic in origin?

4. Are masculinity and femininity different cultures? What are some reasons to think they are?

PRACTICE QUIZ

MULTIPLE CHOICE

1. **People from the southern United States often say "y'all" when referring to others; however, people from other parts of the United States do not typically use that term. For people from the South, this is an example of**
   a. in-group language use
   b. out-group language use
   c. psychonormative language use
   d. gendered language use

2. **Researchers Ann Kring and Albert Gordon have found that when it comes to sex differences and emotion,**
   a. men and women report expressing equal amounts of emotion
   b. men and women report experiencing equal amounts of emotion
   c. men and women are equally likely to limit or mask their emotional expressions
   d. men and women vary greatly in their emotional experiences

3. **People raised in a/an _____ culture are taught to believe that all people are equal and that no one person or group should have excessive power.**
   a. high-power-distance
   b. low-power-distance
   c. expressive
   d. high-context

4. **The U.S. American phrase "a dime a dozen" is an example of a cultural**
   a. norm
   b. jargon
   c. idiom
   d. tradition

5. **Of the statements below, the best example of expressive talk is**
   a. "If I were you, this is how I would fix your problem."
   b. "I think you and Sally should just break up. I mean, what's the point in hanging on?"
   c. "I love you and I am so thankful for your support during this rough time for me."
   d. "You're crazy! You need to get into therapy and fast!"

FILL IN THE BLANK

6. Within many large cultures are a host of smaller groups of people researchers refer to as _____.

7. The phrase "looking out for number one" is reflective of the _____ cultural viewpoint.

8. People in high- _____ cultures are raised to believe that certain people or groups deserve to have more power than others.

9. The perception of time as holistic, fluid, and unstructured is associated with the _____ orientation toward time.

10. A person who is both highly masculine and highly feminine would be described as _____.

ANSWERS

RESEARCH LIBRARY

MOVIES

Brick Lane (drama; 2007; PG-13)
This film centers on the story of Nazneen, a Bangladeshi resident of London who makes a living by taking in sewing jobs in her home. The story traces the struggles of Nazneen and Chanu, her much older husband, to adapt to English culture. The couple and their two daughters must also deal with anti-Muslim sentiment, especially in the wake of 9/11. As the family's debts mount, Chanu considers moving back to Bangladesh, forcing Nazneen to decide between staying in Britain, where she is romantically involved with a fellow Bangladeshi, and going back to her native land.

Transamerica (drama; 2005; R)
In this indie movie, Bree, a male-to-female transsexual, learns she has an adolescent son who was recently released from jail. The two undertake a cross-country road trip together, visiting family members along the way. The film portrays many of Bree's struggles and triumphs related to her transsexual conversion, illustrating the point that biological sex has psychological, genetic, and anatomical characteristics that are not always aligned.

BOOKS AND JOURNAL ARTICLES

Dindia, K., & Canary, D. J. (Eds.). (2006). *Sex differences and similarities in communication* (2nd ed.). Mahwah, NJ: Lawrence Erlbaum Associates.

Hofstede, G. (2003). *Culture's consequences: Comparing values, behaviors, institutions, and organizations across nations* (2nd ed.). Thousand Oaks, CA: Sage.

McConnell, A. R., & Leibold, J. M. (2001). Relations among the Implicit Association Test, discriminatory behavior, and explicit measures of racial attitudes. *Journal of Experimental Social Psychology, 37,* 435–442.

Moran, R. T., Harris, P. R., & Moran, S. V. (2007). *Managing cultural differences: Global leadership strategies for the 21st century* (7th ed.). Oxford, England: Butterworth-Heinemann.

Wood, J. (2002). A critical response to John Gray's Mars and Venus portrayals of men and women. *Southern Communication Journal, 67,* 201–210.

WEBSITES

www.un.org
This is the principal website of the United Nations, an international organization of 192 countries that works to facilitate human rights, social progress, economic development, and security in societies around the world.

www.trinity.edu/~mkearl/gender.html
This website offers discussion, statistics, and numerous links related to sex and gender equality.

3 Communication and the Self

LIVING MULTIPLE LIVES

The romantic comedy film *Sweet Home Alabama* (2002) is a tale of identity clashes. Reese Witherspoon plays Melanie Smooter, who leaves behind her southern roots to become a successful New York City fashion designer. Upon her engagement to Andrew Hennings—the son of New York's mayor—Melanie announces that she must return to Alabama alone to tell her parents the good news. What Andrew doesn't know is that she is returning to demand a divorce from her childhood boyfriend, Jake Perry, to whom she is still married. When she arrives in Alabama, Melanie discovers the complexity of negotiating two very different selves—one representing her past, the other representing her present.

Many of us have gone through an ordeal like Melanie's—a situation in which two of our selves clash, and we are left feeling uncomfortable and unsure. In her case, there was the Melanie from childhood, steeped in the traditions and values of the rural, conservative South. Then there was the Melanie from adulthood, the high-achieving professional in the urban, progressive North. Early adulthood is a time when many of us try to break away from our childhood self-concepts—our ideas about ourselves— and figure out who we want to be as adults. It's not at all uncommon for individuals, like Melanie, to find their past and their present identities at odds.

1 Understanding the Self: Self-Concept

Interpersonal communication begins with you and your understanding of yourself. Who are you? How do you relate to others? What is the *self* in *myself*? Answering those questions allows you to communicate and form relationships with a solid understanding of who you are and what you have to offer.

In this section we examine the self-concept and consider various influences on its development. We probe how individuals manage their identities in day-to-day life and how communication with others reflects one's self-concept.

What Is a Self-Concept?

Think about the ways you would answer the question "Who am I?" What words would you choose? Which answers would be most important? Each of us has a set of ideas about who we are that isn't influenced by moment-to-moment events (such as "I'm happy right now") but is fairly stable over the course of life (such as "I'm a happy person"). Your **self-concept** is composed of those stable ideas about who you are. It is your **identity,** your understanding of who you are. Self-concepts have three fundamental characteristics: They are multifaceted, partly subjective, and enduring but changeable.

> **self-concept** The set of stable ideas a person has about who he or she is; also known as *identity*.

> **identity** See *self-concept*.

SELF-CONCEPTS ARE MULTIFACETED.   We define ourselves in many ways. Some ways rely on our name: "I'm Michaela"; "I am Bill." Some rely on physical or social categories: "I am a woman"; "I'm Australian." Others speak to our skills or interests: "I'm artistic"; "I'm a good cook." Still others are based on our relationships to other people: "I am an uncle"; "I do volunteer work with homeless children." Finally, some rely on our evaluations of ourselves: "I am an honest person"; "I am an impatient person."

Each of those descriptions taps into one or more parts of a person's self-concept, and in this sense the self-concept is *multifaceted*. Put another way, what we call the self is actually a collection of smaller selves, as Figure 3.1 depicts. If you're female, that's a part of who you are, but it isn't everything you are. If you're Asian, athletic, agnostic, or asthmatic, these may all be parts of your self-concept, but none of these terms defines you completely. All the different ways you would describe yourself are pieces of your overall self-concept.

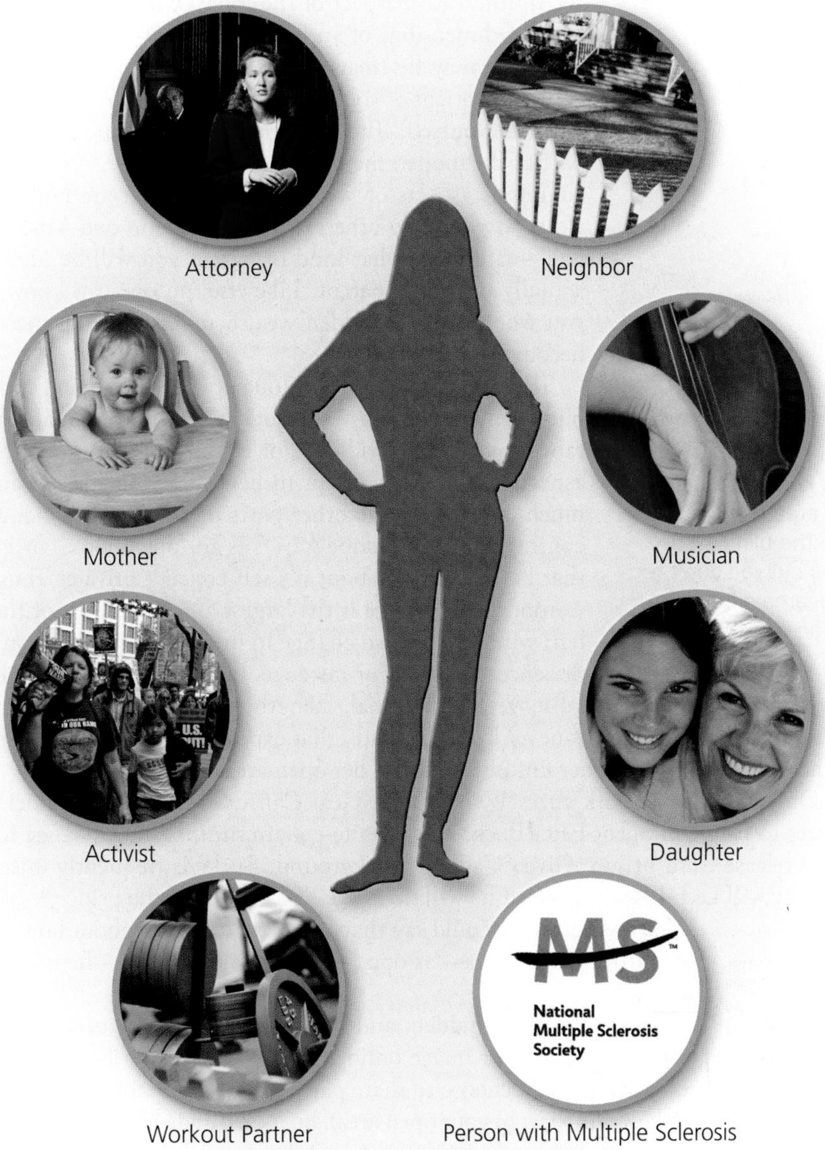
Attorney
Neighbor
Mother
Musician
Activist
Daughter
MS
National
Multiple Sclerosis
Society
Workout Partner
Person with Multiple Sclerosis

FIGURE 3.1 Multiple Selves What we call "the self" is actually a collection of smaller "selves," each representing only one aspect of who a person is.

One way to think about your self-concept is to distinguish between aspects of yourself that are known to others and aspects that are known only to you. In 1955, American psychologists Joseph Luft and Harry Ingham created the **Johari window,** a visual representation of the self as composed of four parts.[1] According to the model (Figure 3.2), the *open area* consists of characteristics that are known both to the self and to others. That probably includes your name, sex, hobbies, and academic major, and other aspects of your self-concept that you are aware of and freely share with others. In contrast, the *hidden area* consists of characteristics that you know about yourself but

Johari window A visual representation of components of the self that are known or unknown to the self and to others.

	Known to Self	Unknown to Self
Known to Others	OPEN	BLIND
Unknown to Others	HIDDEN	UNKNOWN

FIGURE 3.2 The Johari Window In the Johari window, the open area represents what you know and choose to reveal to others, and the hidden area depicts what you know but choose not to reveal. The blind area reflects what others know about you but you don't recognize in yourself, and the unknown area comprises the dimensions of yourself that no one knows.

choose not to reveal to others, such as emotional insecurities or past traumas that you elect to keep hidden.

An innovative aspect of the Johari window is that it recognizes dimensions of an individual's self-concept of which he or she may be unaware. For instance, others might see you as impatient or volatile though you don't recognize those traits in yourself. Those characteristics make up the third part of the model, the *blind area.* Finally, the *unknown area* comprises aspects of your self-concept that are not known either to you or to others. For example, no one—including you—can know what kind of parent you will be until you actually become a parent. Likewise, no one can know how you would handle sudden wealth unless you unexpectedly become wealthy.

These four parts of the Johari window—open, hidden, blind, and unknown—are not necessarily of equal importance for each individual. For example, Raisa keeps many aspects of her self-concept to herself, so her hidden area is much larger than the other parts of her Johari window. In contrast, people describe Aaron as an "open book," meaning that he keeps little about his self-concept private. Thus, for Aaron, the open area is the largest area. The areas of the Johari window can also change in importance as a person's experiences change. For instance, when Denae was diagnosed with terminal cancer, she discovered emotional strength, compassion, and a sense of humor that she and others never knew she had. That experience moved those aspects of her self-concept from her unknown area to her open area.

On the USA Network series *White Collar,* Neal Caffrey is a forger and thief who agrees to help FBI agent Peter Burke catch white-collar criminals in exchange for an early release from prison. Given Caffrey's background, Burke is frequently unsure if Caffrey will keep his word—or if he will lie to the FBI. Applying the principles of the Johari window, we could say that Burke is uncertain about how much of Caffrey's open area—as opposed to his hidden area—he is actually seeing.

Your own open, hidden, and blind areas of the Johari window are also relevant to your image online. When you create a Facebook page, for instance, you choose to share particular information about yourself with others (part of your open area), but you decide to keep some details private (part of your hidden area). Other people's Facebook pages may also contain information about you that you aren't aware of but that others can see (part of your blind area). Because the Internet is so vast, managing your online image can seem like a never-ending task. It's an important skill, though, as the "Assess Your Skills" box emphasizes.

SELF-CONCEPTS ARE PARTLY SUBJECTIVE. Some of the details we know about ourselves are based on objective facts. For instance, I'm 5 feet, 8 inches tall and have brown hair, I was born in Seattle but now live in Phoenix, and I teach at a college for a living. Those aspects of my self-concept are *objective*—they're based on fact and not on someone's opinion. That doesn't mean I have no choice about them. I chose to move to Arizona and get a teaching job, and although I was born with

off the mark.com   by Mark Parisi

facebook

offthemark.com

GOOGLE YOURSELF: MANAGING YOUR ONLINE IMAGE

Creditors, potential employers, and even prospective romantic partners use the Internet to learn about you. Will you like what they find? To assess your online image, type your name in quotation marks into google.com and explore the first dozen websites that the search identifies that are relevant to you (rather than to someone else with your name). Then respond with "true" or "false" to each of the following statements.

1. _____ Nearly everything I saw about myself online was positive.

2. _____ I came across information I wouldn't necessarily want others to have about me.

3. _____ I would be fine knowing that a prospective romantic partner was looking at these websites.

4. _____ I found pictures of myself that I wouldn't be comfortable letting my employer see.

5. _____ Most people would have a positive impression of me after seeing the websites I found.

6. _____ Some of the information I found might make me look irresponsible.

7. _____ I'd feel comfortable letting my parents read the websites I came across.

8. _____ I wouldn't want someone coming across these websites before going out with me.

9. _____ All in all, I feel good about the information and photographs of myself that I found.

10. _____ At least some of what I found online about myself was troubling.

It's best if you answered "true" to the odd-numbered statements and "false" to the even-numbered statements. If any of your answers were otherwise, consider taking steps to alter the online content. If the information or photos that concern you appear on websites over which you have some control—such as your Facebook page and a friend's personal web page—remove the material or make it viewable only by close acquaintances. This may be a particularly important consideration before you go on a job interview or set up a date.

---

brown hair, I could change my hair color if I wanted to. Referring to those personal characteristics as objective simply means that they are factually true.

Many aspects of our self-concept are *subjective* rather than objective. "Subjective" means that they're based on our impressions of ourselves rather than objective facts. Importantly, it's often difficult for us to judge ourselves accurately or objectively.

Sometimes our self-assessments are unreasonably positive. For instance, you might know people who have unrealistic ideas about their intelligence, special talents, or understanding of the world or other people. In one study, the College Board (the company that administers the SAT college entrance examination) asked almost a million U.S. high school seniors to rate their ability to get along with others. *Every single student* in the study responded that he or she was "above average," which is mathematically impossible! Moreover, 60 percent claimed their ability to get along with others was in the top 10 percent, and a whopping 25 percent rated themselves in the top 1 percent, both of which are highly improbable.[2]

In contrast, sometimes our judgments of ourselves are unreasonably negative. That is especially true for people with low self-esteem. Several studies have shown that such people tend to magnify the importance of their failures.[3] They often underestimate their abilities, and when they get negative feedback, such as a bad evaluation at work or a disrespectful remark from someone they know, they are likely to believe that it accurately reflects their self-worth. Several studies have also suggested that people with low self-esteem have a higher-than-average risk of being clinically depressed, a condition that impairs not only an individual's mental and emotional well-being but also physical health and the quality of social relationships.[4]

People with high self-esteem tend to minimize the importance of negative feedback, treating it as a fluke or a random event. We'll look more closely at how self-esteem influences our interpersonal communication behaviors later in the chapter.

SELF-CONCEPTS ARE ENDURING BUT CHANGEABLE. For the most part, the self-concept develops slowly, over a lifetime. As we'll see, many factors affect how our self-concept develops, including biological makeup, how and where we were raised, and the kinds of people with whom we spend our time.

Those and other influences create an understanding of the self that is not easily changed. In fact, several studies have shown that once we develop a self-concept, we tend to seek out others who will confirm it by treating us as we see ourselves.[5] If you're someone with a positive self-concept, for instance, you'll likely associate with friends, co-workers, classmates, and relatives who also have a positive impression of you. In contrast, if your self-concept is negative, you may be more likely to surround yourself with people whose impression of you is also negative.[6] When you associate with people who see you as you see yourself, your self-concept is continually reinforced, and it becomes even more resistant to change.

Self-concepts do change, however, in response to developmental changes and significant life events. As we go through developmental changes in life, for instance, many of us grow to feel more positive or less positive about ourselves. One study reported that between the ages of 14 to 23—a period when changes in self-concept are often the most pronounced—both men and women go through shifts in their level of confidence and self-esteem. Child psychologists Jack Block and Richard Robins found that approximately 80 percent of people experienced either an increase or a decrease in their self-esteem during this period.[7]

Battling cancer or another serious illness can significantly affect a person's self-concept.

People can also undergo changes in their self-concept as a result of a significant life event, such as undergoing a religious conversion or battling a serious illness.[8] After being widowed and losing her job, for instance, Sherry found herself homeless and living in her car. The more she adapted to the routines of homelessness, the more she came to think of herself as homeless and shunned by society—and the more distrustful she became of people she was once close to. Friends and relatives offered their help, but Sherry felt too ashamed to accept it. Over time, she began to prefer the company of other homeless people because she felt she could relate to them more easily.

A healthy self-concept is flexible and can change as life circumstances evolve. That doesn't mean that every significant event changes a person's self-concept, but it does suggest that shifts in a person's self-concept are frequently associated with noteworthy events in his or her developmental stage. Undergoing extensive therapy can also help a person change his or her self-concept, usually for the better. Overall, however, an individual's self-concept generally does not change dramatically over adult life.[9]

How a Self-Concept Develops

None of us is born with a self-concept.[10] In this section, we explore how factors such as personality and biology, culture and gender roles, reflected appraisal, and social comparison help determine who we are.

PERSONALITY AND BIOLOGY.   An important part of your self-concept is your **personality,** the pattern of distinctive ways you tend to think and act across most situations. Are you usually talkative and outgoing, or shy and reserved? Are you a worrier, or happy-go-lucky? Do you tend to be suspicious or trusting of others? Each of those questions relates to a different personality *trait,* a characteristic that describes you in most circumstances. If you have an outgoing personality, for instance, that means you're friendly and talkative most of the time.

> **personality** The pattern of behaviors and ways of thinking that characterize a person.

Some aspects of our personality are undoubtedly affected by where we grow up or how we are raised. Research suggests, however, that biology also plays a role in shaping personality.[11] For instance, several studies have shown that identical twins, who share 100 percent of their genes, are much more similar in their personality than fraternal twins, who share only 50 percent of their genes, the same as regular siblings.[12]

Other research shows that children start displaying certain personality traits early in life, before the effects of culture or upbringing are likely to be influential, and that those traits often remain as the children grow up. Toddlers who act shy around strangers, for example, are likely to continue being shy as adolescents and adults. Although personality is strongly affected by biology, however, with concerted effort many people can change their personality traits if they choose.[13]

CULTURE AND GENDER ROLES.   The way we see ourselves is also strongly affected by the culture in which we grow up and the gender roles we enact. We saw in Chapter 2 that cultures differ from one another in how individualistic they are: Some are highly individualistic, some are highly collectivistic, and some are in the middle. People in highly collectivistic cultures tend to think of their identities as embedded within their families and communities. In other words, they define the self in terms of the groups to which they belong, and they place more emphasis on the group than on the individual. In comparison, people in highly individualistic cultures think of themselves as independent and unique and not as strongly defined by family or communitiy.[14]

Gender also matters when it comes to the self-concept. Recall that gender roles are socially constructed ideas about how women and men should think and behave. Most cultures expect men to exhibit more stereotypically masculine traits, such as assertiveness and self-sufficiency, than women. Conversely, they expect women to exhibit more traits that are stereotypically feminine, such as empathy and emotional expressiveness.

Those observations don't imply that all men are assertive or that all women are emotionally expressive. Rather, they acknowledge general tendencies that can significantly affect the self-concepts that women and men develop. For instance, competition and achievement may be more important to the self-concept of a masculine person, whereas a feminine person may place a greater emphasis on having strong, equitable relationships.

REFLECTED APPRAISAL. As we grow up, one of the ways we figure out who we are is by considering who other people think we are. Perhaps you can recall someone important from your childhood who made you feel especially loved and appreciated. That individual may have been a favorite teacher who encouraged you to pursue your interests or an aunt or uncle who always listened to you talk about your favorite music. It's also possible that you were influenced in negative ways by people who were important to you, such as a callous older sibling who teased you in front of your friends.

Those types of positive or negative messages help us form a mental picture of what others think of us. In turn, that mental picture often affects the image we form of ourselves. The process whereby our self-concept is influenced by how we think other people see us is called **reflected appraisal.** When other people treat us with love and appreciation, we may come to think of ourselves as lovable and worthy. In the same way, when other people tease, ignore, or physically or verbally abuse us, we may perceive ourselves as inadequate or unimportant.

In the early 1900s, sociologist Charles Horton Cooley conceived of what he called the "looking-glass self" to explain how reflected appraisal works. In his model, each of us imagines how we appear to others. For instance, you might believe that others see you as caring and compassionate. Next, we imagine how others evaluate their image of us. For example, if people see care and compassion as positive traits, you would likely imagine they would evaluate you positively. Finally, we develop our self-concept based on those evaluations. For instance, if people seem to think positively of you, then you would think positively of yourself.[16]

In general, the more important someone is to us, the more his or her judgments will affect the way we see ourselves. Parents, friends, teachers, coaches, and others who play a significant role in our lives are usually the ones whose opinions matter the most.[17] As a result, their appraisals often exert more influence on the development of our self-concept than other people's appraisals.

The effects of reflected appraisal aren't confined to childhood. For example, after years of being told by his father that he's "no good," Jerome lacks confidence in his abilities, even though he is highly intelligent. That problem has made it difficult for him to hold down a job for more than a couple of years at a time. He also finds it hard to develop a lasting romantic relationship. Because his father's behavior led him to feel unworthy of love, Jerome has a tough time believing that any romantic partner will ever want to stay with him. As a result, his relationships are fleeting.[18] In Jerome's case, the reflected appraisal he received from his father while growing up shapes his self-concept as a "no good" adult.

SOCIAL COMPARISON. Besides taking note of what other people think of us, we also notice how we compare with the people around us. Maybe you're the least athletic of all your friends. Perhaps you find that you're funnier, better looking, or more musically talented than most of the people with whom you interact. A large part of the way we form a self-concept

> **reflected appraisal** The process whereby a person's self-concept is influenced by his or her beliefs concerning what other people think of the person.

> *Our self-concept is influenced by the way we believe others see us. That process is called reflected appraisal.*

is through this type of **social comparison,** or observation of how we compare with others. Thus, if you're more attractive than most of the people you know, attractiveness is likely to be a part of your self-concept.

social comparison The process of comparing oneself with others.

With social comparison, as with reflected appraisal, some people influence our self-concept more than others. For that reason, a key element in social comparison is the individuals or groups with whom we compare ourselves. The people we use to evaluate our characteristics are called **reference groups.** In most cases, our reference groups are our peers. You're more likely to consider yourself a smart person, for instance, if your reference group consists of your classmates than a group of Nobel Prize winners. Similarly, you'll probably feel wealthier if you compare yourself with your friends than with Facebook's founder Mark Zuckerberg, one of the world's youngest billionaires.

reference groups The groups of people with whom one compares oneself in the process of social comparison.

Those are extreme examples, but research shows that people sometimes pick unreasonable reference groups when they evaluate themselves. Unfortunately, comparing oneself with unreasonable reference groups can be frustrating—and even dangerous. For example, both men and women are likely to develop negative images of their bodies when they compare themselves with movie stars or models. In response, they often put pressure on themselves to achieve an unrealistic body. In some cases this pressure leads to eating disorders, which can be very serious or even life-threatening.[19]

The influences we've just reviewed—personality and biology, culture and gender roles, reflected appraisal, and social comparison—can significantly affect self-concept. Importantly, none of those factors operates on self-concept by itself. Rather, *all* come into play in shaping self-identity.

Awareness and Management of the Self-Concept

Part of being a competent, skilled communicator is being aware of your self-concept and managing its influences on your behavior. Two pathways through which self-concept can shape communicative behavior are self-monitoring and the self-fulfilling prophecy.

SELF-MONITORING. In Chapter 1, we defined self-monitoring as an individual's awareness of how he or she looks and sounds and of how that person's behavior is affecting others. Recall that people on the high end of the self-monitoring scale pay attention to how others are reacting to them, and they have the ability to adjust their communication as needed. Conversely, people on the low end express whatever they are thinking or feeling without paying attention to the impression they're creating.

To understand how self-monitoring operates, imagine that you've fixed up your friends Jin and Katie to go on a blind date. As a high self-monitor, Jin pays a great deal of attention to his clothes and grooming to make sure he looks and smells good. As a low self-monitor, Katie doesn't spend much time thinking about those things. During their date, Jin is aware of what he's saying, so he comes across as nice, easygoing, and funny. Katie, however, says whatever is on her mind without considering what Jin might think. Jin notices if his behavior seems to make Katie uncomfortable, and he adjusts his actions accordingly, whereas Katie doesn't particularly pay attention to what she's doing and how she's affecting Jin.

Self-monitoring certainly has its advantages. High self-monitors tend to be better at making whatever kind of impression they want to make, because they are aware of their behaviors and of others' responses to them. They often find it easier than low self-monitors to put other people at ease in social situations. High self-monitors also tend to be good at figuring out what others are thinking and feeling, an ability that gives

Temple Grandin, who was diagnosed with autism at an early age, learned to deal successfully with the communication challenges posed by the disorder. Today an animal scientist at Colorado State University, she is also an inspiring world-renowned speaker on the topic of autism.

them a clear advantage in many social settings. However, being a high self-monitor also has its drawbacks. Because high self-monitors are constantly aware of themselves and others, they may have a hard time relaxing and "living in the moment." Also, the fact that they can adjust their behaviors to create a certain impression can make it difficult to tell what they are genuinely thinking or feeling. Their motto might be "What you see is what I want you to see."[20]

Being a low self-monitor also has advantages and disadvantages. On the positive side, low self-monitors spend less time and energy thinking about their appearance and behavior, so they are probably more relaxed than high self-monitors in many situations. Indeed, their motto might be "What you see is what you get." In addition, because they are less aware of, or concerned with, the impressions they make, they are often more straightforward communicators—and may even be seen as more genuine and trustworthy. At the same time, however, because low self-monitors are less skilled than high self-monitors in adjusting their behaviors to the demands of the situation, they frequently appear unsophisticated or socially awkward. As a result, they are more likely to make a poor first impression.[21]

Some medical conditions can inhibit self-monitoring ability, including autism, a developmental disorder that impairs a person's capability for social interaction. A 2007 report from the Centers for Disease Control and Prevention found that approximately 1 in 150 U.S. American children has some form of autism.[22] Individuals with autism are often unresponsive to others. They frequently avoid eye contact and have difficulty understanding other people's thoughts and feelings. That obstacle limits their ability to notice how others are reacting to them and to adjust their behaviors accordingly, two hallmarks of self-monitoring. Despite these challenges, however, it is possible for many people with autism to lead relatively independent, productive lives.

SELF-FULFILLING PROPHECY.   Imagine meeting a new co-worker whom you've heard other people describe as painfully shy. Because you don't want to make her uncomfortable, you spend little time talking to her when you meet her, and you don't invite her to join you and your friends for lunch. Consequently, she says little to you all day and eats lunch alone at her desk. You think to yourself, "I guess everyone was right about her; she *is* really shy." Why did your expectation about a shy co-worker come true? Most likely, it's due to a phenomenon called **self-fulfilling prophecy**—a situation in which a prediction causes people to act and communicate in ways that make that prediction come true.

As another example, let's say you volunteer at an afterschool literacy program, and everyone is talking about how much they like the new program director. Because everyone else seems to like him, you expect that you will too. You therefore communicate in a positive, outgoing way when you meet him. You introduce yourself to him in the hallway, and you listen with interest when he tells you about his background. In return, he treats you in a friendly manner. As a result, you do like him! What has happened here is that your expectation ("I will like this person") led you to behave in a certain way (talking in a friendly way toward him; not interrupting him as he talked

self-fulfilling prophecy
An expectation that gives rise to behaviors that cause the expectation to come true.

[SELF-FULFILLING PROPHECY]

Influence others' communication behaviors in positive ways.

WHAT?

Learn to use the self-fulfilling prophecy to your advantage in interpersonal communication.

WHY?

To help make potentially contentious interactions—such as asking an instructor to reconsider the grade he or she gave you on an assignment—more positive.

HOW?

1. Let's say you make an appointment to ask your instructor to reconsider your grade. Before the conversation, repeat to yourself positive messages such as "This instructor will deal with me kindly and fairly" and "He will recognize my intelligence and integrity."

2. Mentally remind yourself of those messages as you engage in the conversation. In every way possible, behave as though those statements are already true.

TRY!

1. With a classmate, friend, or co-worker, role-play a conversation about a *different* difficult interaction. Do not tell the person beforehand of your expectations.

2. Afterward, discuss what went well during the conversation and what would have made it even more positive. Ask the person to identify the behaviors you enacted that contributed to positivity. Identify the ways in which you believe your expectations influenced your partner's behavior.

CONSIDER: *How did having positive expectations about the conversation help to produce positive results?*

---

about himself) that caused your expectation to be fulfilled (he acted friendly toward you, and therefore you liked him).

How do self-fulfilling prophecies affect how we communicate? Sometimes our expectations influence our communication behavior, as when we think it's going to be a bad day and we then have a bad day. Similarly, when we expect our relationships to fail, we behave in ways that sabotage them, and when we expect to be socially rejected, we perceive and react to rejection even when it isn't really there.[23]

Just as our expectations can influence our behavior, so can other people's expectations. In one study, some college men were informed that a certain woman was attracted to them, and other men were told she wasn't. After each man had a conversation with the woman, the researchers found a self-fulfilling prophecy: When the man believed the woman was attracted to him, she was more likely to behave as if she were.[24] The most likely explanation for that outcome is that the men who thought the woman was attracted to them communicated in a friendly, outgoing way toward her, causing her to reciprocate those communication behaviors and thus behave as though she were attracted to them.

Research has shown that other people's expectations cause us to behave in expectancy-confirming ways across a range of situations, including the management of our relationships, our ability to heal from illness, and even our productivity on the job.[25] You can use that information to help generate positive encounters with others, as the "Got Skills?" box illustrates.

There is one very important clarification about self-fulfilling prophecies. For a prophecy to be self-fulfilling, it's not enough that you expect something to happen and then it does. Rather, it has to be your expectation that causes it to happen. To illustrate the point, let's say you expected it to rain yesterday, and it did. That isn't a self-fulfilling prophecy, because your expectation didn't cause the rain—it would have rained whether you thought it would rain or not. In other words, your expectation was fulfilled, but it was not *self*-fulfilled. A self-fulfilling prophecy is one in which the expectation itself causes the behaviors that make it come true.

> **LEARN IT** What does it mean to say that self-concepts are partly subjective? Compare and contrast reflected appraisal and social comparison as influences on the development of a self-concept. What are the advantages and disadvantages of being a low self-monitor?
>
> **APPLY IT** Create a version of Figure 3.1 for yourself. Around the figure in the middle, draw six to eight small images that represent your different selves. Then draw three or four new selves that represent not the person you are but the person you would like to become. Next to each of those ideal selves, write one statement describing something you can do to become more like that ideal self.
>
> **REFLECT ON IT** How do your friends and relatives affirm and reinforce your perceptions of yourself? If you had to create a time capsule to describe yourself to future generations and could include only five things, what things would you choose? Why?

2 Valuing the Self: Self-Esteem

> **self-esteem** One's subjective evaluation of one's value and worth as a person.

The television series *Drop Dead Diva* features an aspiring model who, after being killed in a car crash, returns to life in the body of an overweight lawyer. Initially horrified by the change in her physical appearance, she soon learns to appreciate her increased intelligence and savvy. By learning to value more than just her looks, she gains a level of self-confidence that she lacked in her previous life.

How do *you* feel about *yourself*? Are you satisfied with your looks? Your accomplishments? Your personality? Your relationships? Do you feel confident and proud of who you are? Those questions ask you to think about your **self-esteem,** your subjective evaluation of your value and worth as a person.

Many people have speculated about the value of having high self-esteem, but the research results have been mixed. As we'll see, some behaviors and characteristics do appear to be enhanced by high self-esteem.

Others seem as though they would be, but they really aren't. In this section, we'll look at what it means to have high or low self-esteem, and we'll investigate how characteristics such as sex and culture affect our self-esteem. We'll conclude by focusing on three interpersonal needs that interact with self-esteem to influence the way we communicate with others.

In Drop Dead Diva, *Brooke Elliott's character discovers that self-esteem depends on more than just personal appearance.*

Benefits and Drawbacks of Self-Esteem

Turn on any talk show or browse the self-help aisle of any bookstore and you'll find plenty of discussion about the importance of self-esteem. High self-esteem is often believed to boost academic performance and shield people from stress, whereas low self-esteem is frequently blamed as the underlying cause of juvenile delinquency and antisocial behavior. Such beliefs have led many parents, educators, and government agencies to pay more attention to improving children's self-esteem as a way to help them grow into more successful adults.

Those ideas make good sense in part because they're intuitively appealing. It's easy to believe that if you feel good about yourself, you'll be more successful in school, work, and relationships. Although research shows that high self-esteem does have some important benefits, it also suggests that we might be giving self-esteem more credit than it's due.

SELF-ESTEEM AND SOCIAL BEHAVIOR. Maintaining a positive image of ourselves does appear to have its advantages when it comes to behavior. Compared with people with lower self-esteem, those with higher self-esteem are generally more outgoing and more willing to communicate.[26] After trying and failing at a difficult task, they try harder to accomplish it a second time.[27] They are more comfortable initiating relationships, and they're more likely to believe that their partners' expressions of love and support are genuine.[28] They don't necessarily have more friends than people with lower self-esteem, however. Moreover, when their relationships have problems, they are more likely to end those relationships and seek out new ones.[29]

Several researchers have speculated that lower self-esteem is related to antisocial behavior, especially among adolescents and young adults. They suggest that people who view themselves negatively are more likely to act aggressively toward others, to abuse drugs or alcohol, and to become sexually active at a young age than people with a more positive self-image. The research hasn't supported those ideas, however. In fact, aggressive people tend to have higher self-esteem, not lower.[30] In addition, the evidence suggests that self-esteem is not related to drinking or drug use, at least among teenagers.[31]

A similar scenario occurs with teenage sexuality: Adolescents with higher self-esteem are more prone to be sexually active and to engage in risky sexual behaviors than teens with lower self-esteem.[32] One explanation for those conclusions is that high self-esteem gives some adolescents confidence in their ability to win a fight, attract a sexual partner, or escape the problems of risky sexual behaviors, making them more prone to engage in those types of interactions. In contrast, low self-esteem might lead other adolescents to avoid those situations.

Some research indicates that problems associated with low self-esteem—which include social anxiety, loneliness, and depression—can lead people to use the Internet as a way to escape those troubles. Although it provides a wealth of information, entertainment, and social-networking opportunity, excessive reliance on the Internet as a substitute for interpersonal relationships can be problematic. As the "Get Connected" box details, Internet use can even become addictive for those who turn to it as a means of escaping their social difficulties.[33]

SELF-ESTEEM AND HOW WE SEE OURSELVES AND OTHERS. Research indicates that people who have high self-esteem are happier with their lives than are people with low self-esteem.[34] That finding is true around the world, although there is a stronger relationship between happiness and self-esteem in countries with individualistic cultures—which emphasize the importance of the self—than in others with collectivistic

g@t connected

RECOGNIZE THE SIGNS: INTERNET ADDICTION

Research shows that people with psychosocial problems—including loneliness and low self-esteem—may rely heavily on the Internet as a means to escape those problems. Although spending time online can be a pleasant distraction from everyday stresses, excessive Internet use can turn into an addiction. An addiction is more than just a habit; it's something that is difficult or impossible to control. Internet addiction can damage your interpersonal relationships by diverting your attention from the important people in your life. How can you tell if you're at risk? Watch for the following signs:

- *You lose track of the time you spend online.* You're frequently on the Internet for longer than you realize. You find yourself running late to school, work, or appointments because of time spent online.

- *You have trouble completing tasks at work or home.* You get so busy online that household chores, such as laundry and grocery shopping, don't get done. You sometimes stay late at work to surf the web.

- *You feel isolated from your friends and family.* You start to feel that no one in your face-to-face life understands you the way your online friends do. You skip social engagements to spend time on the Internet.

- *You lie about your Internet use.* You find ways to hide your online activities. You lie to friends, relatives, and colleagues about how much time you spend on the Internet or what you do online.

If you're suffering from Internet addiction, assistance is available. Talk to someone at your school's student counseling center. That person may be able to help you find more productive ways of meeting your emotional and social needs and may work with you to wean your dependence on the Internet as a source of support to your self-esteem.

Source: Center for Internet Addiction and Recovery: www.netaddiction .com.

---

cultures—which emphasize the needs of the group or community (Table 3.1).[35] In addition, people with high self-esteem have a lower risk of depression[36] and an enhanced ability to recognize and manage emotions, a skill researchers call *emotional intelligence.*[37]

In contrast, people who have a poorer image of themselves adopt more negative emotions and ways of looking at and handling situations. They tend to be more judgmental of others than people with higher self-esteem.[38] They're also more likely to speak poorly of others and to express racial prejudices.[39] When others put them down, they often respond by being excessively critical of others, so as to appear more impressive.[40] Some research has also shown that having low self-esteem in childhood is a predictor of having thoughts of suicide[41] and of making suicide attempts[42] in adolescence or young adulthood.

SELF-ESTEEM AND PERFORMANCE.   Much emphasis has been placed on self-esteem in schools and its effects on students' academic performance. Many people have argued that high self-esteem gives students the confidence to work hard in school and achieve academic success. They have also maintained that low self-esteem is often the root cause of poor grades.

Those beliefs have led parents and educators to implement policies to boost students' self-esteem. One fairly common approach has been to reduce or eliminate opportunities for competition among students, particularly competition based on academic achievement. For instance, many schools refuse to publish an honor roll, fearing that recognizing high achievers will diminish the self-esteem of students who didn't earn the grades to qualify. Some schools have gone so far as to eliminate grades.[43] Some

U.S. school districts have even stopped participating in the National Spelling Bee—a national student spelling competition—because only one child in each grade can win in any given year, a tradition that, concerned observers say, might harm other children's self-esteem.[44] Those and similar school policies are based on the notion that competition is problematic because students who don't win will suffer a loss of self-esteem that in turn will impair their academic performance.

The research shows, however, that efforts to protect students' self-esteem have had little effect. In fact, several studies suggest that students' self-esteem has very little association with their academic performance.[45] For instance, some studies have found no correlation between students' self-esteem and their scores on standardized tests.[46] At least one study has shown that attempting to boost students' self-esteem can backfire and cause the students to perform more poorly.[47] That may be because inflating students' self-esteem causes the students to have such a degree of confidence in their natural abilities that they study less than they otherwise would.

Importantly, those conclusions are not true just for students. The evidence suggests that self-esteem is also largely unrelated to performance on the job.[48] Research has shown, for instance, that high self-esteem provides no advantage when performing arithmetic tasks[49] or tasks that require sensitivity to nonverbal behaviors,[50] two common components of many jobs.

TABLE 3.1

The Relationship Between Self-Esteem and Happiness in Various Parts of the World

The higher the number, the more strongly self-esteem is related to happiness in that country.

Country	Self-Esteem/Happiness Relationship
United States	.58
New Zealand	.59
Germany	.50
Spain	.39
Brazil	.36
Jordan	.34
Bangladesh	.16

Note: The countries shown are listed from most individualistic to most collectivistic. As you can see, self-esteem generally has a stronger relationship to happiness in individualistic societies than in collectivistic ones. This relationship is not perfect; for instance, the United States is more individualistic than New Zealand, but the New Zealand correlation is slightly stronger. Rather, the relationship is general. These correlations are averaged for women and men.

Source: Diener, E., & Diener, M. (1995). Cross-cultural correlates of life satisfaction and self-esteem. *Journal of Personality and Social Psychology, 68*, 653–663.

Some school districts have stopped participating in the National Spelling Bee out of concern for students' self-esteem.

In summary, having high self-esteem is a real benefit in some ways, such as in making us happier. In other regards, such as preventing delinquency or improving our academic performance, it isn't a particular benefit. Those mixed results don't mean we shouldn't care about the self-esteem of those around us. Rather, they suggest that the benefits of high self-esteem are largely limited to social and emotional areas and may not be as broad as people once thought.

Many people have suggested that self-esteem differs according to a person's sex and cultural background. Let's examine the extent to which that variation is true.

Culture, Sex, and Self-Esteem

Sex and culture are such powerful influences in our lives that it's easy to assume they affect almost everything about who we are and how we communicate. The effects are not always what we might guess, however.

CULTURE AND SELF-ESTEEM. Many people might assume that ethnic minorities in the United States would have lower self-esteem than non-Hispanic Caucasians—who form the majority ethnic group—because of the social stigmas that minorities often face.[51] In fact, the research tells a slightly different story. According to psychologists Jean Twenge and Jennifer Crocker, Hispanic Americans, Native Americans, and Asian Americans do tend to rate themselves lower than non-Hispanic Caucasians in self-esteem.[52] Beginning in the 1980s, however, African Americans have reported the highest self-esteem of all U.S. ethnic groups, including non-Hispanic Caucasians.[53] The differences among these groups aren't substantial, but they have been relatively consistent over the past few decades.

If ethnic minorities experience discrimination and social stigma, how do they maintain their self-esteem? Researchers believe that socially marginalized groups—a category that can also include sexual minorities and people with disabilities—use three general strategies. First, they value the things at which they excel. To the extent that one group excels academically, athletically, or artistically, for instance, that group will emphasize those activities more heavily than activities in which they perform less impressively. Second, they tend to attribute their problems to prejudices in society rather than to their own behaviors or decisions. Third, like most people, they compare themselves with others in their own group more than with people from other groups.[54]

Since the 1980s, African Americans have reported the highest self-esteem of all ethnic groups in the United States.

SEX AND SELF-ESTEEM. Unlike culture, sex does not by itself appear to affect self-esteem. Despite alarming reports that girls suffer from a shortage of self-esteem,[55] there is no scientific evidence, either among children or among adults, to support that belief. In fact, among ethnic minorities, self-esteem is higher for U.S. females than for U.S. males. There is no sex difference among non-Hispanic Caucasians, however.[56] Some experts have suggested that for ethnic minorities, experiences of racial discrimination are more damaging to the self-esteem of males than of females. That theory might explain why males have lower self-esteem than females among ethnic minorities but not among non-Hispanic Caucasians, at least in the United States.[57]

We've seen that self-esteem benefits us in some ways and not in others, and that it varies by culture and sex, but not always in the ways we might expect. In the following discussion, we'll tie self-esteem more directly to interpersonal communication by examining three fundamental interpersonal needs that appear to be facilitated by self-esteem.

The Self and Interpersonal Needs

In his *interpersonal needs theory,* social psychologist Will Schutz proposed that self-esteem interacts with three important interpersonal needs to affect our communication with others: the need for control, the need for inclusion, and the need for affection. As we'll see, each of these needs motivates us to interact with other people in particular ways.

NEED FOR CONTROL.   We all have a **need for control,** which is our motivation to maintain some degree of influence in our relationships. As infants, we relied almost completely on our caregivers to make decisions for us. As we grew up, however, we needed to play a more decisive role in determining the course of our relationships. In many relationships, people share control, so that each person has some say in what happens. We're often less satisfied in relationships when we feel we have no control.[58]

Research shows that the higher a person's self-esteem, the more that individual feels in control of the events in her or his life.[59] By the same token, many of us also have a need to relinquish control from time to time. Just as we're dissatisfied with having too little control, we can also feel overwhelmed by the responsibility of having too much control. Allowing others to exert influence over us is an important part of the interdependent nature of personal relationships. We're often most satisfied, therefore, with a moderate amount of control.

NEED FOR INCLUSION.   Our **need for inclusion** is our need to belong, to be included in the activities of others, and to have positive human contact. Some of us have a stronger need for inclusion than others, but even people whom we would describe as loners need some interaction with others. Studies have shown that people can experience mental and physical distress when their need for inclusion is not met.[60] For individuals with a high need for inclusion, then, the opportunities to form and maintain interpersonal relationships contribute to their self-esteem.

From a different perspective, people with higher self-esteem tend to be more outgoing and extroverted than people with lower self-esteem. For that reason they might be more motivated to seek out relationships that will meet their need for inclusion.[61] For example, they may be more likely to join social groups, religious organizations, or sports teams to meet others. Nevertheless, even people with a high need for inclusion also enjoy periods of solitude.

NEED FOR AFFECTION.   Finally, each of us also has a **need for affection.** We need to have people in our lives who love and appreciate us and who communicate their affection to us. We also need to give love and intimacy to others. Some researchers believe that people are born with the capacity for affection, and studies have shown that the more affection people give and receive, the healthier and happier they are.[62] People with higher self-esteem also tend to be more expressive of their affectionate feelings than people with lower self-esteem.[63]

need for control One's need to maintain a degree of influence in one's relationships.

need for inclusion One's need to belong to a social group and be included in the activities of others.

need for affection One's need to give and receive expressions of love and appreciation.

Affection is one of our most fundamental human needs.

AT A GLANCE

SCHUTZ'S INTERPERSONAL NEEDS

Need for Control	Our need to maintain some degree of control in a relationship
Need for Inclusion	Our need to belong to a social group and to have positive contact with others
Need for Affection	Our need to feel loved and appreciated by others

The "At a Glance" box summarizes Schutz's proposed three interpersonal needs. Schutz believed that all three needs are fundamental, meaning that everyone has them to some degree. Furthermore, the greater these needs are, he argued, the more motivated we are to seek and form relationships with people who can help us meet them. People with high self-esteem don't necessarily have stronger needs for inclusion, affection, and control than others do, but they appear to be more successful at meeting those needs through their communication with other people.

LEARN IT What social behaviors are enhanced by having high self-esteem? How does self-esteem differ between the sexes or among various ethnic groups? What three interpersonal needs did Schutz propose were fundamental?

APPLY IT This week, make a point of expressing affection—in whatever ways feel natural—to close family members, co-workers, and/or friends. Then, in a short report, briefly describe two or three instances of this expression of affection and explain how your efforts have supported both your own and others' need for affection.

REFLECT ON IT When do you feel better or worse about yourself? What factors, besides sex and culture, do you think influence self-esteem?

3 Presenting the Self: Image Management

As we've considered, your self-concept is related to *the way you see yourself.* When you communicate interpersonally, however, you are also concerned with *the way you want others to see you.* In some situations, you might want others to regard you as friendly, outgoing, and fun. In different situations, you might want people to look at you as reliable, competent, and serious. Perhaps there are circumstances when you'd like others to think of you as independent and open-minded.

image The way one wishes to be seen or perceived by others.

When you consider how you want others to perceive you, you're considering the kind of **image** you want to project. In this section, we'll see that managing your image is a collaborative, multidimensional, and complex process. We'll also consider the contributions of communication researcher Myra Goldschmidt, sociologist Erving Goffman, and other scholars whose work has helped us understand the process of image management.

Principles of Image Management

In its depiction of the development of Facebook, the film *The Social Network* (2010) visits the question of whether founder Mark Zuckerberg generated the idea for the networking site himself or pirated it from three classmates. When Zuckerberg's classmates sue him for intellectual property theft, he comes across in legal depositions as aggressive, impatient, and condescending. Partly as a result of the way Zuckerberg has presented himself, one of his lawyers indicates that they will be settling a second lawsuit out of court. The impression Zuckerberg would make in a trial, she believes, would lead to a highly unsympathetic jury.

The Social Network *portrays Mark Zuckerberg as having little concern for image management. In contrast, most people consider how they want others to perceive them.*

When your goal is to make a positive first impression, you've probably heard that it's best to "just be yourself." Indeed, many people try to project an image that accurately reflects their self-concept. Yet there are many times when the way you act reflects a specific image you wish to project, and you adjust your behavior accordingly. That projection might be "you just being yourself," or it might be an image that suits the occasion or the outcome you desire. This is the process of **image management.** Let's explore three fundamental principles of this process:

- Image management is collaborative.
- We manage multiple identities.
- Image management is complex.

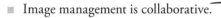

image management The process of projecting one's desired public image.

IMAGE MANAGEMENT IS COLLABORATIVE.
To some extent, managing your image is an individual process. After all, your image is yours. You also get a lot of help managing your image, however, from the people around you. As psychologist Dan McAdams has suggested, each of us develops a *life story,* or a way of presenting ourselves to others that is based on our self-concept but also influenced by other people.[64]

If others accept the image you portray, they'll tend to behave in ways that encourage that image. Let's say you see yourself as a confident person, and you project that image to others. If other people regard you as confident, they'll treat you as though you are—and their response to you will strengthen that part of your identity in your own mind. If others don't accept the image of yourself that you portray, however, they may see you as less credible or as untrustworthy. Trying to be someone you aren't, or portraying an image of yourself that isn't genuine, might mean that people don't take you seriously.

WE MANAGE MULTIPLE IDENTITIES.
Consider that all the people who interact with you know you only in a certain context. You have your circle of friends, who know you as a friend. You have your family members, who know you as a mother, a son, an aunt, a brother, a cousin, or a grandchild. Your boss and co-workers know you as an employee. Your doctor and your dentist know you as a patient, your professors know you as a student, and your landlord knows you as a tenant.

Significantly, each of these contexts carries its own distinctive role expectations, so you probably enact a somewhat different identity in each one. You likely communicate differently at work than at home, and your friends probably know you differently than your professors do. The point is that we all manage multiple identities; that is, we show different parts of ourselves to different people in our lives.

On occasion, people enact images of themselves that are inaccurate or dishonest. In the movie *Catch Me If You Can* (2002), actor Leonardo DiCaprio plays Frank Abagnale, a man who, in real life, fraudulently portrayed himself as a substitute teacher, a lawyer, a doctor, and an airline pilot before being captured and imprisoned by the U.S. government in the 1960s. Although their experiences are usually less dramatic than Abagnale's, many people present images of themselves that are not entirely accurate, such as a job applicant who exaggerates her work experience on her resume or a man who describes himself in a personal ad as younger than he is.

The challenge of managing multiple identities is especially pronounced for people with "invisible" medical conditions, which are illnesses or disorders that are not necessarily apparent to others. Conditions such as Down syndrome, stuttering, developmental disabilities, and confinement to a wheelchair are relatively "visible" because many people will notice those conditions after seeing or listening to someone who has them. In contrast, people can, to varying degrees, hide the fact that they have conditions such as cancer, diabetes, asthma, and depression if they don't want others to know. Most people can't identify a person with diabetes or asthma, for example, simply by looking at him or her.

For that reason, people with those and other invisible conditions have both the ability and the responsibility to determine how to incorporate their conditions into the image they project. For instance, many people must continually decide whom to tell about their conditions, when to make those disclosures, and how to do so. That decision can be particularly agonizing for individuals suffering from invisible conditions that are also socially stigmatized, such as mental health disorders and HIV-positive status, because of the fear of how others will react to their disclosures. The "Communication: Dark Side" box addresses that issue as it pertains to HIV-positive individuals.

Image management is similarly challenging for many sexual minorities. Like an invisible medical condition, a person's sexual orientation is not always evident in the way he or she looks, sounds, or communicates. That gives lesbian, gay, and bisexual people the ability to choose to whom to reveal their sexual orientation. Many find this to be a consequential decision, because sexual minorities are often discriminated against throughout the world, including much of the United States.[65] To avoid prejudice, sexual minorities may choose to "stay in the closet" and keep their sexual orientation a secret, even from their closest friends and relatives.

A person's decision to disclose his or her sexual orientation has some important health consequences. To begin with, long-term concealment of such a fundamental aspect of an individual's identity is stressful.[66] Over time, such stress can elevate the risks for cancer and infectious diseases,[67] rapid progression of HIV,[68] and suicide.[69] There is some evidence that those problems are magnified for lesbian, gay, and bisexual adolescents, who, in contrast to adults, may lack the social support and emotional maturity to manage the stress of concealing their sexual orientation.[70]

Although concealing one's sexual orientation can be problematic for health, so can disclosing it. For instance, a study of gay and bisexual men found that those who had disclosed their sexual orientation in their workplace experienced more daily stress and negative moods than did those who kept their orientation secret.[71] Other research has found that lesbians and gay men are at elevated risk for depression and stress even if they are open about their sexual orientation.[72]

communication dark side

RISKS OF DISCLOSING HIV-POSITIVE STATUS

It is traumatic for people to learn that they are infected with HIV. Being HIV-positive puts individuals at risk for developing AIDS, a terminal disease with no known cure. It also requires that people decide with whom they're going to share the news of their infection.

Many people with HIV may feel in a bind when deciding whether to disclose their condition to others. On the one hand, disclosing the illness may help them acquire both medical and emotional support, and it may encourage others to adopt healthier sexual or drug-use behaviors themselves. On the other hand, disclosure can be risky. Psychologists Valerian Derlega and Barbara Winstead explain that HIV-positive people may have several reasons for choosing not to disclose their illness:

- *Privacy:* It's no one else's business but their own.
- *Self-blame:* They feel guilty for being HIV-positive.
- *Communication difficulties:* They don't know how to tell others about it.
- *Fear of rejection:* They worry that others will reject or even hurt them.
- *Fear of discrimination:* They fear that employers, landlords, or others will discriminate against them.
- *Protection of others:* They don't want others to worry about them.
- *Superficial relationships:* They don't feel close enough to others to trust them with this information.

Despite these risks, Derlega and Winstead emphasize that disclosing HIV status can be useful in many ways. Not only can it help secure needed medical attention and emotional support, but it can also help to strengthen relationships, particularly with others who are also HIV-positive. It is also extremely important for the health and safety of a romantic or sexual partner. To protect potential partners, in fact, several U.S. states have enacted laws making it a felony to expose someone else knowingly to HIV without that person's consent, as would happen if an HIV-positive individual engaged in sexual behavior with a partner without informing that partner of his or her HIV status.

FROM ME TO YOU

Many of us are uncomfortable discussing HIV. In the United States, being HIV-positive is widely stigmatized because of its association with two marginalized groups: gay men and intravenous drug users. The stigma makes it easier to believe that if you don't belong to either of those groups, you can't or won't develop HIV. The truth, however, is that HIV infects people from all walks of life—homosexual and heterosexual, rich and poor, female and male, adult and child.

Source: Derlega, V. J., & Winstead, B. A. (2001). HIV-infected persons' attributions for the disclosure and nondisclosure of the seropositive diagnosis to significant others. In V. Manusov & J. H. Harvey (Eds.), *Attribution, communication behavior, and close relationships* (pp. 266–284). New York: Cambridge University Press.

IMAGE MANAGEMENT IS COMPLEX. If image management sounds complicated, that's because it often is. For instance, we may have competing goals in our interactions with others. Let's say you've been offered a prestigious internship at a start-up company in California's Silicon Valley, and you ask your older sister and her husband, who live close to that area, if you can move in with them for the semester. You probably want your sister to think of you as a mature, responsible adult rather than as the carefree teenager you were when she moved out of your parents' house. As a result, you will have to present your request in a way that preserves your image as a responsible person. At the same time, you want to persuade your sister and brother-in-law that you really need a place to stay and that you can't afford to rent one on your own because the internship pays poorly. This reality may cause you to project the image that you need help. Thus, you may find your image needs in conflict: You want to appear responsible but also in need of assistance. How to manage these competing image needs—while still persuading your sister to let you move in—can be complex.

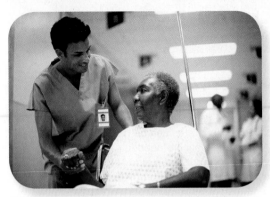

Helping others maintain their dignity, especially in situations that threaten it, is an important part of saving face.

Communication researcher Myra Goldschmidt found that when people ask others for favors, they often create narratives that help to maintain their images while still being persuasive.[73] To your sister, you might say things like "I need a place to stay for just a couple of months while I do this internship," and "I promise to help around the house." Such strategies can help preserve your image as a responsible individual even in a situation where that image might be threatened.

We've seen that image management is a collaborative process that often requires negotiating several identities in a complex way. How do we determine what our image needs are in the first place?

Managing Face Needs

Maybe you've heard the phrase "saving face." Helping someone save face means helping that person avoid embarrassment and maintain dignity in a situation that threatens it. The very reason we hate getting embarrassed is that it threatens the image of ourselves we're trying to project, and that threat is a function of our need to save face. Sometimes we associate face saving with collectivistic cultures such as Korea and Japan. In reality, saving face is important to people in many cultures.[74] Let's take a look at what happens when our desired public image is threatened.

FACE AND FACE NEEDS.   Each of us has a desired public image—a certain way that we want others to see and think of us—and we work to maintain that image. For instance, if you want others to see you as intelligent and competent, you will likely behave in ways that give that impression, and you will try to avoid situations that will make you look incompetent or uninformed. Sociologist Erving Goffman coined the term **face** to describe our desired public image and the term **facework** to describe the behaviors we use to project that image to others.[75] The "Got Skills?" box offers suggestions for improving your own facework abilities.

Researchers believe that our face is made up of three **face needs,** or important components of our desired public image.[76] You might find it easy to remember those face needs by noting that the first letters of their names—fellowship, autonomy, and competence—constitute the first three letters in the word *face.* **Fellowship face** refers to the need to have others like and accept us. That is the part of our identity that motivates us to make friends, join clubs or social groups, and behave pleasantly around others. **Autonomy face** refers to our need to avoid being imposed upon by others. It's our autonomy face that motivates us to be in control of our time and resources and to avoid having other people make decisions for us. Finally, **competence face** is our need to have others respect us and to acknowledge our abilities and intelligence. That need drives us to seek careers and hobbies that we're good at and to avoid situations in which we will embarrass ourselves. The "At a Glance" box summarizes the three face needs.

FACE THREATS.   Each of us has a different desired public image, and so our face needs vary. Fellowship, autonomy, and competence are largely independent face needs, so having a high level of one need does not necessarily affect a person's levels of the other two needs. For instance, some people have a very strong fellowship face need, meaning it is extremely important that others like them. Other people much prefer to be respected than liked. Similarly, one person may have a very high need for autonomy, whereas another person may not mind having decisions made for him or her. Those differences are part of what makes everyone's identity unique.

face A person's desired public image.

facework The behaviors one uses to project one's desired public image to others.

face needs Components of one's desired public image.

fellowship face The need to feel liked and accepted by others.

autonomy face The need to avoid being imposed upon by others.

competence face The need to be respected and viewed as competent and intelligent.

[FACEWORK]

Practice offering complaints in a nonthreatening manner.

WHAT?

Learn to protect the face needs of another person.

WHY?

Receiving complaints, such as grievances about poor service in a restaurant or car dealership, can threaten a person's competence face. When you are dissatisfied with something, you can express your complaints constructively—and, by so doing, perhaps even improve your chances of getting satisfactory resolution of the issue—if you know how to preserve the face needs of the individual to whom you are complaining.

HOW?

1. Imagine a specific situation in which you feel you must complain about poor service. List two or three ways in which your complaint might threaten the competence face of the person receiving it.

2. Write out sentences and phrases that would minimize those face threats. For instance, focus on describing the problem rather than assigning blame: "When I got my car back, I noticed that the 'check engine light' was on. Can you tell me why?"

TRY!

1. Role-play a conversation about poor service with another person. Try to minimize threats to your communication partner's competence face.

2. Ask the person for feedback on how well you communicated your complaint in a nonthreatening manner.

CONSIDER: *What skills did you learn? How will you apply them when you next need to express a complaint or problem?*

Although we all have our own face needs, we often become consciously aware of them only when they're threatened. Let's say you applied to join an honor society but were not accepted. The decision not to include you could threaten your fellowship face. It could also threaten your competence face by making you feel you weren't smart enough to get into the group. The rejection of your application, therefore, is a **face-threatening act** because it fails to fulfill one or more of your face needs.

Face-threatening acts often lead people to behave in ways that help restore their face. In the case of the honor society, you could say "I didn't really want to be in that society anyway."[77] Making such a statement doesn't mean you actually believe it. Indeed, you probably did want to be in the honor society, or you wouldn't have bothered applying. Rather, you would likely say this to manage your image with others by making it appear as though your face needs weren't threatened. This response is therefore a type of *defense mechanism* that helps minimize the effects of a face-threatening act.

Face threats are common experiences within many marginalized populations. For example, threats to autonomy face may arise among marginalized people who have to rely on others to meet their material needs or who feel they don't have a voice in

> **face-threatening act** Any behavior that threatens one or more face needs.

AT A GLANCE

THREE TYPES OF FACE

Fellowship Face	Our need to have others like and accept us
Autonomy Face	Our need not to be imposed upon by others
Competence Face	Our need to be respected for our intelligence and abilities

Having a visible disability can invite threats to fellowship, autonomy, and competence face.

decisions that affect them. Elderly people, for instance, frequently experience losses of autonomy as a result of various physical and cognitive limitations associated with aging.[78] Individuals with certain disabilities may also perceive threats to their autonomy if they are unable to do things that others can do, such as driving a car and going for a walk. Still other groups may feel their autonomy is threatened when they don't have the ability to make certain decisions for themselves, as in the case of lesbian and gay adults who (in most states) cannot legally marry their romantic partners.

Being marginalized also leads many people to feel disrespected and shamed. Such feelings can threaten both their fellowship face and their competence face. U.S. American society has stigmas associated with being homeless, poor, old, disabled, lesbian, gay, mentally ill, and (in some circles) even divorced, even though a person may have no choice about belonging to any such groups.[79] Stigmatized people might feel like outsiders who don't fit in with those around them, and those perceptions threaten their fellowship face by leading them to feel unaccepted. They may also perceive that others judge them not on the basis of their intelligence or abilities but simply because of their stigmatized condition—a perception that threatens their competence face by making them feel disrespected.

LEARN IT What does it mean to say that image management is collaborative? How are fellowship face, autonomy face, and competence face similar? How are they different?

APPLY IT Imagine you're asking someone in your family for a favor. Think about the types of images you would want to project to that person. With those images in mind, write out the words you would use to make your request.

REFLECT ON IT When do you notice that you have to manage multiple identities? What strategies do you use to do so? How do you usually react when your face needs are threatened?

4 Communicating the Self: Self-Disclosure

self-disclosure The act of giving others information about oneself that one believes they do not already have.

Now that we have explored how we form a self-concept and how we manage our image, let's complete our analysis by looking at how we communicate about ourselves, or *self-disclose*. **Self-disclosure** is the act of intentionally giving others information about ourselves that we believe to be true but that we think they don't already have.

From a highly intimate conversation with a romantic partner about our hopes and dreams to a mundane chat with a co-worker about where we dined last evening, self-disclosure involves sharing a part of ourselves with someone else.

In this section, we're going to look at several principles of self-disclosure and examine various benefits that self-disclosure can bring to us and to our relationships. Finally, we'll take stock of some of the risks of self-disclosing.

Principles of Self-Disclosure

Most of us engage in self-disclosure, in one form or another, on a fairly ongoing basis. Self-disclosure has several important attributes.

SELF-DISCLOSURE IS INTENTIONAL AND TRUTHFUL. For an act of communication to qualify as self-disclosure, it must meet two conditions: (1) We must deliberately share information about ourselves, and (2) we must believe that information is true. Let's say that, through a momentary lapse in attention, your friend Dean mentions his financial problems to you without meaning to. That wouldn't constitute an act of self-disclosure according to the definition just given, because Dean didn't share the information deliberately. Unintentionally telling another person something about yourself is an example of what is sometimes called *verbal leakage.*

Similarly, self-disclosing means sharing information that we believe is true. If you tell a co-worker that you've never traveled outside your home country, for instance, that qualifies as self-disclosure if you believe it to be true. It's your belief in the truth of the information that matters, not the absolute truth of the information. Perhaps you traveled outside the country when you were an infant and were too young to remember. If you believe the information you're providing is true, however, then it qualifies as self-disclosure. Intentionally giving people information about ourselves that we believe to be false is an act of deception, as we'll see in Chapter 12.

SELF-DISCLOSURE VARIES IN BREADTH AND DEPTH. **Social penetration theory,** developed by social psychologists Irwin Altman and Dalmas Taylor and depicted in Figure 3.3, illustrates how self-disclosure over time is like peeling away the layers of an onion: Each self-disclosure helps us learn more and more about a person we're getting to know.

According to social penetration theory, peeling away the layers to get to know someone requires sharing disclosures that have both breadth and depth. **Breadth** describes the range of topics you discuss with various people. With some people, you might disclose about only certain aspects of your life. For instance, you might tell your doctor all about your health but not about other aspects of your life. You might disclose only about your professional life with a co-worker, or only about your academic life with a professor. In those relationships, your self-disclosure has little breadth, because you disclose only about a limited range of topics. In contrast, with your relatives, close friends, and romantic partner you probably talk about several different aspects of your life, such as your work and school experiences, your financial concerns, your professional ambitions, your health, your spiritual or religious beliefs, your political opinions, and your desires for the future. Your disclosure in these relationships is characterized by greater breadth, because you disclose about a wider range of topics.

social penetration theory A theory that predicts that as relationships develop, communication increases in breadth and depth.

breadth The range of topics about which one person self-discloses to another.

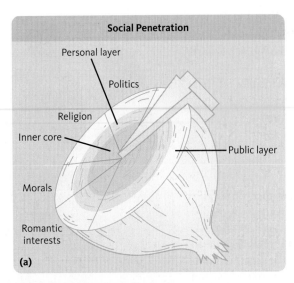

Social Penetration

Depth but no breadth

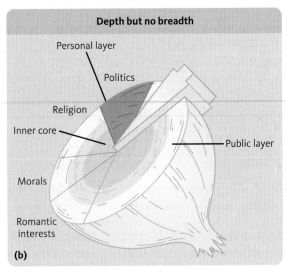

Breadth but no depth

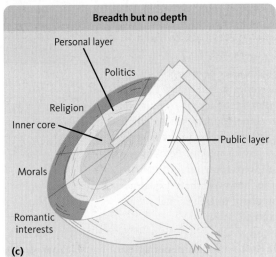

Breadth and depth

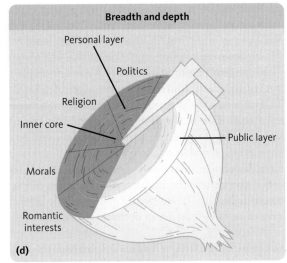

FIGURE 3.3 Social Penetration Theory Researchers use the image of a multilayered onion to represent the process of social penetration in a relationship. The outer layer of the onion represents breadth of self-disclosure. That layer is referred to as the "public layer" because it reflects details you would share with most people. The inner layers of the onion reflect depth of self-disclosure. We call those the "personal layers" because they represent details you would share only with people you know quite well. If you share personal details about your political ideas with someone, but nothing else, then your relationship has depth but not breadth. If you tell someone only superficial information about your political, religious, moral, and romantic experiences but do not provide more personal details on any of those topics, then your relationship has breadth but not depth. In our closest relationships, we usually disclose both superficial and private information about many issues, so those relationships have both breadth and depth.

depth The intimacy of the topics about which one person self-discloses to another.

The second dimension, **depth,** measures how personal or intimate your disclosures are. The depth of our self-disclosures is largely a function of how carefully we feel we must guard the information in the disclosures. Let's say Maya and her romantic partner are having problems. Maya might describe her problems in detail to her mother, not only because she values her opinion, but also because she trusts her mother to keep the information private. Because she doesn't feel the need to guard this information from her mother, Maya can engage in disclosure that has great depth. With her secretary, by contrast, Maya discloses that she is having difficulty, but she doesn't go into detail because she doesn't feel comfortable entrusting her secretary with the specifics. In this instance, Maya engages in self-disclosure of lesser depth.

SELF-DISCLOSURE VARIES AMONG RELATIONSHIPS. Not every relationship is characterized by the same breadth and depth of self-disclosure. Some relationships involve depth of disclosure but very little breadth. With your accountant, for instance, you might disclose in depth about financial matters but not about anything else. Likewise, you might tell your doctor intimate details about your health but very little about other issues in your life. In Figure 3.3b, this type of relationship is depicted by coloring one wedge of the circle from the outermost ring to the innermost but leaving the other circles untouched.

Other relationships are characterized by breadth of disclosure but very little depth. With casual friends at school or work, for example, you might disclose a little about several areas of your life—family, hobbies, political ideas, career ambitions—but not provide intimate details about any of them. As Figure 3.3c indicates, you would depict this type of relationship by coloring in several of the wedges on the circle, but only on the outermost ring, leaving the smaller internal rings untouched.

Still other relationships, such as romantic partnerships and close friendships, thrive only with high degrees of both breadth and depth. In such relationships, people typically share both public and private information about multiple aspects of their lives. Figure 3.3d, by coloring in several of the wedges around the circle—some of which extend all the way to the center—illustrates both the breadth and the depth of self-disclosure in those kinds of relationships.

SELF-DISCLOSURE IS A GRADUAL PROCESS. Even our closest relationships usually aren't close right away. Closeness develops over time as two people get to know each other and reveal more and more information about themselves. In new relationships, people often disclose slowly, sharing just a few details at first and offering more personal information only if they like and trust each other.[80]

When they started becoming friends, Deepak and Prasad shared mostly routine information, such as their hometowns, favorite sport teams, and occupations. As they got to know and trust each other more, they shared their opinions on politics, relationships, and religion. Only after they had known each other for quite a while did they feel comfortable talking about more personal things, such as Prasad's health problems and the challenges in Deepak's marriage. Although people in some relationships begin sharing intimate information quickly, self-disclosure usually moves in small increments.

ONLINE SELF-DISCLOSURE FOLLOWS A DIFFERENT PATTERN. One exception to the general pattern of gradual self-disclosure occurs in relationships formed online, such as through e-mail, chat rooms, or blogs.[81] You might predict that people would be less disclosive in computer-mediated contexts than in face-to-face settings, on the reasoning that they might not feel as engaged with online conversational partners or as comfortable sharing personal information. Just the opposite appears to be true, however. Research shows that the lack of face-to-face interaction in computer-mediated contexts encourages self-disclosure, so that people are often more disclosive at the start of an online relationship than in a face-to-face one.[82] For example, a study

FACT ? OR fiction

LET IT OUT: DISCLOSURE DOES A BODY GOOD

When you've gone through troubling times, have you ever noticed that you feel better after putting your feelings into words? Some people say they benefit from talking with supportive friends or counselors about their experiences. Others say that even writing about their feelings in a private journal makes them feel better, both mentally and physically. Is that idea fact or fiction?

A large body of research suggests that it's a fact. Multiple experiments by psychologist James Pennebaker and his colleagues have demonstrated that disclosing feelings in writing—particularly feelings related to experiences of trauma—produces measurable benefits in physical and mental health. In a typical study, participants write once a week for 20 minutes at a time over a three-week period about a traumatic event. People in a control group write on the same schedule about emotionally

neutral topics, such as what they did over the weekend. Pennebaker and his team have found that compared to the control group, participants who disclose about traumatic events experience significant improvements in their mental and physical health, some of which last several months after the experiment has ended. Pennebaker believes that suppressing emotions requires effort that can also impair a person's health. Expressing emotions in words—even in writing—may relieve people of the effort required to suppress their emotions and cause their health to improve as a result.

ASK YOURSELF

- How do you notice that you feel better, if at all, after disclosing your emotions?

- Are you generally more comfortable self-disclosing to members of one sex than to members of the other, or do you feel equally comfortable disclosing to both women and men?

Source: Lepore, S. J., & Smyth, J. M. (2002). *The writing cure: How expressive writing promotes health and emotional well-being*. Washington, DC: American Psychological Association.

we share personal information with others, they may feel more comfortable doing the same in return.

- *Emotional release:* Sometimes the best part of self-disclosing is the feeling of getting something "off your chest." Let's say that Caryn borrowed her sister Amy's car and accidentally put a small dent in the fender. Instead of telling Amy about the dent, Caryn hoped she wouldn't notice. Pretty soon, Caryn felt so guilty that she had trouble sleeping. When she finally disclosed the accident to Amy and apologized, she felt relief. Appropriate self-disclosures like Amy's can often provide emotional release.[95] Several studies have also shown that they can reduce the stress of holding on to a secret. That is an important benefit, because reducing stress can improve both mental and physical health.[96] You can read more about the connection between disclosure and health in "Fact or Fiction?"

- *Assistance to others:* You can self-disclose in ways that help other people, particularly when you're consoling people who are going through hard times. If your friend is having difficulty handling his parents' divorce, for instance, you might disclose how you managed traumatic situations in your own family. Your disclosure can provide comfort and signal to your friend that he's not alone. Many self-help programs, such as Alcoholics Anonymous, use this principle to help their members realize they are all going through a similar struggle.[97] Some disclosures even have the effect of protecting others against threats to their health—as in the situation where a person who is HIV-positive discloses that status to health care providers and potential sexual partners.[98]

Enhancement of relationships, reciprocity, emotional release, and assistance to others are not the only benefits provided by self-disclosure, but they're among the most important for interpersonal communication. Before we conclude that self-disclosure is always a positive behavior, however, let's take a look at some of its most notable risks.

Risks of Self-Disclosure

Communication scholar Malcolm Parks has argued that we spend so much time thinking about the benefits of disclosure that we tend to ignore the risks it entails for both the people who make the disclosures and those who receive them.[99] Here we'll look at four potential risks:

- *Rejection:* When we self-disclose, we allow others to know information about us that they didn't know before. Although such information sharing can lead to very good outcomes, such as emotional release and enhancing trust, it also involves some serious risks.[100] For instance, what if the people to whom we're disclosing don't like what we tell them? Let's say your brother confides in you that he's gay. His disclosure might bring you closer together, but if his sexuality is a problem for you, his disclosure could lead you to reject him. Often, the way a person reacts to a disclosure will determine whether its outcome is positive or negative.

- *Chance of obligating others:* The reciprocity of self-disclosure can be a very good thing if you are trying to get to know someone better. However, it can also lead the other person to feel obligated to disclose something back to you when he or she might not be comfortable doing so. Beyond the potential for creating awkward silences and feelings of discomfort, such feelings could encourage the person to avoid you.

- *Hurt to others:* Beyond making someone uncomfortable, it's possible to hurt others with disclosures that are too critical or too personal. Despite the maxim that "honesty is the best policy," uncensored honesty can lead to wounded feelings and even resentment. Imagine that your wife has asked you what you think of a childhood friend with whom she recently reunited over the Internet. You have never been a big fan of Sonya, but you find yourself torn between wanting to be honest and wanting to be nice, because their renewed friendship seems to be lifting your wife's spirits. Indeed, you may have been taught that if you can't say something nice, you shouldn't say anything at all. This rule for politeness is meant to reduce the chances that someone will be hurt by a self-disclosure that's too critical.

- *Violation of other people's privacy:* Inappropriate disclosures can even hurt people who aren't participating in the conversation. In September 2010, for instance, four U.S. teens—Tyler Clementi (18), Billy Lucas (15), Asher Brown (13), and Seth Walsh (13)—committed suicide after allegedly being taunted due to rumors about their homosexuality. Their deaths focused increased media attention on the problems that can ensue when people's privacy is violated through inappropriate disclosures.

People in many relationships, including families, friendships, and workplace relationships, share private information with one another that is not meant to be shared

gossip The sharing of an individual's personal information with a third party without the individual's consent.

with others. When we disclose that information to third parties without permission—a behavior we call **gossip**—we risk hurting people and damaging their trust in us.

Risks of Disclosing Online

Earlier in this chapter, we considered how disclosures made in online environments are often hyperpersonal, or of a more personal nature than they would be if they were shared face-to-face. The tendency to be hyperpersonal makes disclosing online particularly vulnerable to the risks discussed just above. As we will see in Chapter 11, researchers believe that communicating online has a "disinhibition effect," encouraging people to say or do things that they wouldn't if they were in face-to-face settings.[101] For instance, you might not feel comfortable talking about the intimate details of your health while sitting with a friend in a restaurant, but you might describe them in explicit detail to members of an online support group.

The disinhibition associated with computer-mediated communication can be liberating, because it helps us to feel free to express ourselves in ways we normally wouldn't. We have to be careful, however, that we don't disclose inappropriate information about ourselves or others. Because nearly all computer-mediated communication is written, recipients can save disclosures made online and even forward them to third parties. Consider the case of Lanny, who self-disclosed to an online chat room about his impatience with his boss's speech impediment. Another person in the chat room recognized Lanny's screen name and forwarded his postings to his boss, who found them personally offensive.

Many people have experienced regret or distress about information that they or others disclosed online, a phenomenon known as *postcyberdisclosure panic*.[102] Because disclosures are usually made online in the form of written text, and because people often feel uninhibited about disclosing online, it's wise to be especially careful about what you disclose in computer-mediated environments.

LEARN IT What is meant by breadth and depth of self-disclosure? In what ways can self-disclosure enhance relationships? What are the primary risks of self-disclosure? What aspects of online communication make a person particularly vulnerable to the risks of self-disclosure?

APPLY IT Choose one friend, one family member, and one school or work relationship. For each one, re-create the drawing in Figure 3.3, specifying both the depth and the breadth of disclosure that you typically share with that person. Notice the similarities and differences in breadth and depth across those three relationships.

REFLECT ON IT In what ways do you benefit from disclosing to other people? How do you feel when people share inappropriate disclosures with you?

MASTER the chapter

1 Understanding the Self: Self-Concept (p. 72)

- Your self-concept consists of your perceptions about who you are. Self-concept is multifaceted, partly subjective, and enduring but changeable.
- Personality, cultural and gender roles, reflected appraisal, and social comparison all influence the development of self-concept.
- Self-monitoring and the self-fulfilling prophecy are two pathways through which self-concept can shape communicative behavior.

2 Valuing the Self: Self-Esteem (p. 82)

- Your self-esteem is your subjective evaluation of your value and worth as a person. Having high self-esteem is a benefit in some ways and a liability in others.
- Ethnic groups appear to differ somewhat in their self-esteem. In the United States, women report higher self-esteem than men among ethnic minorities but not among non-Hispanic Caucasians.
- Humans have fundamental needs for control, inclusion, and affection; self-esteem is affected by the extent to which those needs are met.

3 Presenting the Self: Image Management (p. 88)

- Your image consists of the way you want others to perceive you. Most people manage multiple images in collaborative and complex ways.
- Humans have three kinds of face needs: fellowship face, autonomy face, and competence face. Behaviors that impinge on face needs are called face-threatening acts.

4 Communicating the Self: Self-Disclosure (p. 94)

- Self-disclosure is the deliberate act of giving others information about ourselves that we believe to be true and think they don't already have. It is intentional and involves true information, varies in breadth and depth, varies among relationships, usually follows a process, is usually reciprocal, serves many purposes, and is influenced by sex and culture.
- Benefits of self-disclosure include the enhancement of relationships and trust, the probability of reciprocity, emotional release, and the provision of assistance to others.
- Risks of self-disclosure include rejection, the chance of obligating others, the potential to hurt others, and the violation of another person's privacy.
- Some of the risks of self-disclosure are made more likely when self-disclosure takes place online.

KEY TERMS

DISCUSSION QUESTIONS

1. In what ways has your self-concept changed over the course of your adolescent and adult life? What parts of your self-concept have remained relatively constant?

2. When it comes to social comparison, what reference groups are particularly relevant to you?

3. What's good about gossip? In what ways can gossip produce positive relational outcomes?

4. What are some situations that threaten people's need for inclusion? Their need for affection? Their need for control? How do you generally react in those situations?

PRACTICE QUIZ

MULTIPLE CHOICE

1. **The motivation to maintain some degree of influence in our relationships is known as the need for**
   a. belonging
   b. control
   c. inclusion
   d. autonomy

2. **The name for the situation in which expectations cause people to act and communicate in ways that make the expectations come true is**
   a. self-fulfilling prophecy
   b. self-serving bias
   c. self-disclosure
   d. social comparison

3. **Craig hates being imposed upon by others. Craig has a high degree of**
   a. fellowship face
   b. competence face
   c. connectedness face
   d. autonomy face

4. **After Frances shares with James her intense fear of public speaking, James then feels compelled to share with Frances something personal about himself. That example illustrates that self-disclosure usually occurs incrementally and is guided by**
   a. the norm of reciprocity
   b. the rule of reciprocation
   c. disclosure rules
   d. the need for inclusion

5. **The aspects of self-disclosure that characterize social penetration theory are**
   a. breadth and depth
   b. honesty and intimacy
   c. quantity and quality
   d. good and bad

FILL IN THE BLANK

6. Your _____ consists of ways you tend to think and act across most situations.

7. Through _____ our self-concept is influenced by how we think other people see us.

8. The subjective evaluation of one's value and worth as a person is known as one's _____.

9. A behavior that threatens one's face need is known as a _____.

10. Disclosures made in an online environment would be described as _____ when they are more personal in nature than they would be face-to-face.

ANSWERS

Multiple Choice: 1 (b); 2 (a); 3 (d); 4 (a); 5 (a); **Fill in the Blank:** 6 (personality); 7 (reflected appraisal); 8 (self-esteem); 9 (face-threatening act); 10 (hyperpersonal)

RESEARCH LIBRARY

MOVIES

Catch Me If You Can (drama; 2002; PG-13)
This film portrays the life of Frank Abagnale, a former con man who fraudulently portrayed himself as a doctor, an attorney, a substitute teacher, and an airline pilot before being captured. It illustrates in a dramatic fashion the extent to which people can adopt and manage multiple identities.

Meet the Parents (comedy; 2000; PG-13)
In this popular movie, Greg Focker tries hard to make a good first impression on the parents of his fiancée. Despite his best efforts, however, he makes several poor impressions before finally being accepted by them. In a humorous way, this film illustrates many of the challenges of eliciting positive impressions from others.

BOOKS AND JOURNAL ARTICLES

Baumeister, R. F. (Ed.). (1993). *Self-esteem: The puzzle of low self-regard*. New York: Plenum.

Cupach, W. R., & Metts, S. (1994). *Facework*. Thousand Oaks, CA: Sage.

Goldschmidt, M. M. (2004). Good person stories: The favor narrative as a self-presentation strategy. *Qualitative Research Reports in Communication, 5,* 28–33.

Kelly, A. E., Klusas, J. A., von-Weiss, R. T., & Kenny, C. (2001). What is it about revealing secrets that is beneficial? *Personality and Social Psychology Bulletin, 27,* 651–665.

WEBSITES

www.utexas.edu/student/cmhc/booklets/selfesteem/selfest.html
This website, from the University of Texas Counseling and Mental Health Center, focuses on the benefits of self-esteem and offers suggestions for improving low self-esteem.

kevan.org/johari
This site allows you to create an interactive Johari window by selecting characteristics that you feel describe you and then by asking your friends and relatives to nominate their characteristics of you.

4 Interpersonal Perception

MAKING SENSE OF OUR SOCIAL WORLD

Moments into her speech accepting the 2009 MTV Video Music Award for best female video, country singer Taylor Swift—along with her audience—was stunned when rapper Kanye West suddenly appeared onstage, grabbed the microphone from her hands, and declared that a video from pop singer Beyoncé should have won the award instead. "Taylor, I'm really happy for you," West said. "I'll let you finish, but Beyoncé had one of the best videos of all time. One of the best videos of all time!" Visibly shaken, Swift walked offstage moments after West's outburst, leaving viewers to wonder why he had so rudely interrupted her acceptance speech.

W hen we encounter social behavior, especially behavior we find surprising, our nearly automatic reaction is to try to make sense of it. We need to understand what is happening if we are to know how to react to it properly. Therefore, getting along in our social world depends a great deal on our ability to make meaning out of other people's behaviors. When we talk about making meaning, we're talking about the process of perception. Our minds and senses help us understand the world, but they can also lead us to make mistakes, such as misinterpreting other people's behaviors. The more we learn about our perception-making abilities, the better we know ourselves, one another, and our world. We can all learn to perceive behavior more accurately, and this chapter focuses on how.

1 The Process of Perception

Despite being one of the most productive marketing managers at her publishing company, Gisele has a hard time earning favor from her supervisor Dale. Gisele enthusiastically presents new products and innovative marketing plans at her weekly meetings with Dale, but he seems interested only in the bottom line. Instead of sharing Gisele's excitement about fresh ideas, his concerns always center on how much a new product will cost and how much profit it will generate. Gisele has come to perceive Dale as an uninspired manager who is simply biding his time until retirement. Dale concedes that Gisele is energetic and smart, but he perceives her as naïve concerning the way business works.

Part of what makes Gisele and Dale's relationship so challenging is the differences in their interpersonal perceptions. In this section, we will examine the process of perception by defining interpersonal perception, identifying the stages of perception making, and probing factors that influence the accuracy of our perceptions of others.

Interpersonal Perception Defined

Gisele and Dale clearly have quite different perceptions of each other, but what does that mean, exactly? **Perception** is the process of making meaning from the things we experience in our environment, and when we apply this process to people and relationships, we engage in **interpersonal perception.**[1] We are involved in interpersonal perception constantly. Gisele experiences Dale's repeated references to costs and profits, for instance, and she makes meaning from them ("he has no enthusiasm for anything except the bottom line"). You notice what your friends, colleagues, relatives, and co-workers do and say, and their words and actions have meaning to you based on the way you interpret them.

> **perception** The process of making meaning from the things we experience in the environment.

> **interpersonal perception** The process of making meaning from the people in our environment and our relationships with them.

Three Stages of the Perception Process

Your mind usually selects, organizes, and interprets information so quickly and so subconsciously that you may think your perceptions are objective, factual reflections of the world. You might say you perceived that Kanye West was being rude to Taylor

Swift because he *was* being rude to her. In fact, you created that perception on the basis of the information you selected for attention (he interrupted her speech), the way you organized that information (interruption is an inconsiderate behavior), and the way you interpreted it ("he's being rude").[2]

Selection, organization, and interpretation are the three basic stages of the perception process. Let's examine each one.

SELECTION.   The process of perception begins when one or more of your senses are stimulated. You pass a construction site and hear two workers talking about the foundation they're pouring. You see one of your classmates smile at you. A co-worker bumps you on the shoulder as he walks past. If you notice these sensory experiences of hearing, seeing, and being bumped, then they can initiate your process of forming perceptions.

In truth, your senses are constantly stimulated by objects and events in your environment. It's simply impossible, though, to pay attention to everything you're seeing, hearing, smelling, tasting, and feeling at any given moment.[3] When you're walking past the construction site, for instance, you're probably no longer hearing the sounds of traffic going by.

Rather than paying attention to all the stimuli in your environment, you engage in **selection,** the process in which your mind and body help you choose certain stimuli to attend to. For example, you notice your classmate smiling at you without paying attention to what others in the classroom are saying or doing. You notice that your spouse failed to bring home dinner, but you ignore the fact that he got the car washed and picked up your dry cleaning. Clearly, the information you attend to influences the perceptions you form.

> **selection** The process of attending to a stimulus.

Importantly, we don't necessarily make conscious decisions about which stimuli to notice and which to ignore. Rather, as research indicates, three characteristics especially make a particular stimulus more likely to be selected for attention.

First, being unusual or unexpected makes a stimulus stand out.[4] For instance, you might not pay attention to people talking loudly while walking across campus, but hearing the same conversation in the library would probably spark your attention, because it would be unusual in that environment. Or perhaps you're walking back to your car after a night class and you don't take particular notice of other students walking along the same sidewalk, but you do notice an older, poorly dressed man pushing a shopping cart. His presence stands out to you because you aren't used to seeing people on campus who look like him.

Second, repetition, or how frequently you're exposed to a stimulus, makes it stand out.[5] For example, you're more likely to remember radio ads you've heard repeatedly than ones you've heard only once. Similarly, you tend to notice more characteristics about the people you see frequently than about those you see seldom, such as their physical appearance and behavior patterns.

Third, the intensity of a stimulus affects how much you take notice of it. You notice strong odors more than weak ones, for instance, and bright and flashy colors more than dull and muted ones.[6]

ORGANIZATION.   Once you've noticed a particular stimulus, the next step in the perception process is to classify it. This task, called **organization,** helps you make sense of the information by revealing how it is similar to, and different from, other things you know about. To classify a stimulus, your mind applies a *perceptual schema* to it, or a mental framework for organizing information.

> **organization** The process of categorizing information that has been selected for attention.

g@t connected

PEOPLE 2.0: PERCEPTIONS OF AVATARS

When interacting online, many people use avatars as representations of themselves. Although avatars are not "real" people, they signify real people, and so we become accustomed to perceiving them in many of the same ways we perceive the people around us. Including an avatar alongside an e-mail message or chat room posting can make our words seem more personal to others—but how is our avatar *really* being perceived? To find out, communication researchers Kristine Nowak and Christian Rauh had college students evaluate a series of avatars and report on their perceptions. The researchers learned that

- *Avatars should look as human as possible.* Some people create avatars that are based on images of animals or inanimate objects. Nowak and Rauh found, however, that human-looking avatars were perceived to be more credible and more attractive.

- *Avatars should have a defined gender.* Many avatars appear androgynous, meaning that it is difficult to tell whether the avatar is intended to be female or male. According to the research, people prefer interacting with avatars that they perceive as clearly male or female rather than androgynous.

- *Communicators prefer avatars that match themselves.* When asked to select the avatar they would most prefer to use as their own, the research participants showed a strong preference for human-looking avatars that matched their own gender.

If you create an avatar to use in computer-mediated communication, remember that others will perceive it as a representation of you. Consider the perceptions you want your avatar to create when you're communicating interpersonally, and notice the perceptions you form of others' avatars.

Source: Nowak, K. L., & Rauh, C. (2006). The influence of the avatar on online perceptions of anthropormorphism, androgyny, credibility, homophily, and attraction. *Journal of Computer-Mediated Communication, 11*, 153–178.

According to communication researcher Peter Andersen, we use four types of schema to classify information we notice about other people: physical constructs, role constructs, interaction constructs, and psychological constructs.[7]

- *Physical constructs* emphasize people's appearance, causing us to notice *objective* characteristics such as height, age, ethnicity, and body shape, as well as *subjective* characteristics such as physical attractiveness. As "Get Connected" illustrates, we use physical constructs to perceive not only people but also graphic representations of people, called *avatars*.

- *Role constructs* emphasize people's social or professional position, so we notice that a person is a teacher, an accountant, a father, a community leader, and so on.[8]

- *Interaction constructs* emphasize people's behavior, so we notice that a person is outgoing, aggressive, shy, sarcastic, or considerate.

- *Psychological constructs* emphasize people's thoughts and feelings, causing us to perceive that a person is angry, self-assured, insecure, envious, or worried.

Think about the first time you met your interpersonal communication instructor. What sensory information did you notice about him or her, and which schema did you apply to it? Perhaps you paid attention to your instructor's age, ethnicity, and clothing. If so, you probably organized those pieces of information as physical constructs, meaning you recognized that they all dealt with your instructor as a physical being. If you paid attention to how friendly or how demanding your instructor is, you probably organized those pieces of information as interaction constructs, recognizing that they all dealt with how your instructor behaves or communicates. If your focus was on how well your instructor taught, you were emphasizing role constructs by attending to your instructor's professional function in the classroom. Finally, if you took note of how happy or self-confident your instructor seemed, you focused on psychological constructs by paying attention to his or her disposition or mood.

Whichever schema we use to organize information about people—and we may use more than one at a time—the process of organization helps us determine the ways in which various pieces of information that we select for attention are related.[9] If, for example, you notice that your neighbor is a Little League softball coach and the father of three children, those two pieces of information go together because they both relate to the roles he plays. If you notice that he seems irritated and angry, those pieces of information go together as examples of his psychological state. In addition, you recognize them as being different from information about his roles, physical characteristics, or behaviors.

Perceptual schemas can also help us determine how other people are similar to and different from us. If your dentist is female, that's one way in which she is similar to (or different from) you. If she is friendly and outgoing, that's another similarity (or difference). Perceptual schemas help us organize sensory information in some meaningful way so that we can move forward with the process of perception.[10]

INTERPRETATION. After noticing and classifying a stimulus, you have to assign it an **interpretation** to figure out what it means for you. Let's say one of your co-workers has been acting especially friendly toward you for the last week. She smiles at you all the time, brings you little gifts, and offers to run errands for you during her lunch break. Her behavior is definitely noticeable, and you've probably classified it as a psychological construct because it relates to her thoughts and feelings about you. What does her behavior *mean,* though? How should you interpret it? Is she being nice because she's getting ready to ask you for a big favor? Does she want to look good in front of her boss? Or does she like you? If she does like you, does she like you as a friend—or as a potential romantic partner?

> **interpretation** The process of assigning meaning to information that has been selected for attention and organized.

To address those questions, you likely will pay attention to three factors to interpret her behavior: your personal *experience,* your *knowledge* of her, and the *closeness* of your relationship with her. Your personal experience helps you assign meaning to behavior. If co-workers have been nice to you in the past just to get favors from you later, then you might be suspicious of this co-worker's behavior.[11] Your knowledge of the person helps you interpret her actions. If you know she's friendly and nice to everyone, you might interpret her behavior differently than if you notice that she's being nice only to you.[12] Finally, the closeness of your relationship influences how you interpret a person's behavior. When your best friend does you an unexpected favor, you probably interpret it as a sincere sign of friendship. In contrast, when a co-worker does you a favor, you are more likely to wonder whether he or she has an ulterior motive.[13]

Experience, knowledge, and closeness can all affect how you interpret something that you perceive, but these factors don't necessarily suggest the same interpretation. Think back to the example of seeing a poorly dressed man pushing a shopping cart on campus at night. Perhaps you have had experiences dealing with panhandlers and

How would you describe Sarah Palin according to Andersen's four perceptual schemas?

homeless people in the city where you grew up, so you interpret his appearance and behavior as suggesting that he is a transient. Let's say you also know, however, that the drama department at your school is currently rehearsing a play about the challenges of homelessness. That knowledge leads you to interpret his appearance and behavior as suggesting that he is part of the dramatic production. In this example, your experience and knowledge lead you to quite different interpretations of the same situation. Because you don't know this man personally, the closeness of your relationship with him doesn't provide you with any additional clues to aid your interpretation.

We've seen that perception is a process, which means it happens in stages. That doesn't necessarily mean the process is always linear, however. The three stages of perception—selecting, organizing, and interpreting information—overlap.[14] How we interpret a behavior depends on what we notice about it, for example, but what we notice can also depend on the way we interpret it.

Let's assume, for example, that you're listening to a politician's speech. If you find her ideas and proposals favorable, then you might interpret her demeanor and speaking style as examples of her intelligence and confidence. In contrast, if you oppose her ideas, then you might interpret her demeanor and speaking style as examples of arrogance or incompetence. Either interpretation, in turn, might lead you to select for

---

AT A GLANCE

STAGES OF THE PERCEPTION PROCESS

Selection	We select certain sensory information for attention.
Organization	We categorize each piece of information to determine how it is similar to, and different from, other pieces of information.
Interpretation	We assign meaning to each piece of information.

attention only those behaviors or characteristics that support your interpretation and to ignore those that don't. Therefore, even though perception happens in stages, the stages don't always take place in the same order. The "At a Glance" box summarizes the three stages of perception.

We're constantly noticing, organizing, and interpreting things around us, including other people's behaviors. Like other skills, perception takes practice, and our perceptions are more accurate on some occasions than others.

Influences on Perceptual Accuracy

Because we constantly make perceptions, you might think we'd all be experts at it by now. In truth, perceptual mistakes are often easy to make. For example, perhaps your sister calls to check on you out of concern when you're feeling ill. Because your illness makes you short-tempered and grumpy, however, you perceive that she is calling only because she feels obligated. As another example, on your overseas trip you perceive that two adults you see in a restaurant are having a heated argument. In fact, as you later find out, they are engaging in behaviors that signify interest and involvement in that culture.

Why do we continue to make perceptual errors despite our accumulated experience? Three factors in particular influence the accuracy of our perceptions and can lead to errors: our physiology, our cultural and co-cultural backgrounds, and our social roles.

PHYSIOLOGICAL STATES AND TRAITS.   *Physiology* is the study of the mechanical and biochemical ways in which our bodies work. Many aspects of our physiology influence the way we perceive the world.[15] Here we focus specifically on physiological states and traits.

Physiological states are conditions that are temporary. We enter and leave various physiological states, meaning that their influence comes and goes over time. For instance, the physiological state of feeling tired alters our perception of time and can make us anxious. Therefore, the five minutes we're waiting in line at the grocery store might seem much longer.[16] Similarly, being hungry or sick seems to sap our energy and make us grumpy and impatient, reducing our ability to get along with others.[17] You can probably think of personal experiences that demonstrate how those or other aspects of your physiology have influenced your perceptual accuracy.

In contrast, our *physiological traits* are conditions that affect us on an ongoing basis. Compared with states, which are continually changing, traits are more enduring. For example, perception relies a great deal on our senses—our abilities to see, hear, touch, taste, and smell. A voice that sounds just right to a hearing-impaired person may seem too loud to others. A food you find too spicy might seem bland to someone else.[18] You might think a room is too hot, another person might think it's too cold, and a third person might think it's just right. Our senses help us perceive and understand the world. So, when our sensory abilities differ, our perceptions often do as well.

Another physiological trait is our biological rhythm, or the cycle of daily changes we go through in body temperature, alertness, and mood.[19] As levels of various hormones rise and fall throughout the day, our energy level and susceptibility to stress change as well. Consequently, there are times during the day when we interact positively with people, and other times when we feel cranky and are more easily annoyed.

Everyone's biological rhythm is a little different. You might be most refreshed and alert first thing in the morning, whereas your roommate might be a night owl who doesn't get going until late in the day. Most of the time, these differences aren't a huge

Your physiological traits influence how you react to various foods as well as how you perceive various behaviors.

problem. Research shows, however, that when romantic partners have very different biological rhythms, they report more conflict and less intimacy than partners whose rhythms are more closely matched.[20]

Consider the case of Aida and her partner Luca. Aida wakes up around 6 A.M. every day. Her biological rhythm gives her the most energy early in the morning, but by early evening she is drowsy and ready for bed. In contrast, Luca likes to sleep until 8 or 9 in the morning. He gets energized late at night and will often stay up until well past midnight. As a result of their different rhythms, Luca is grouchy whenever they both have to be up early, such as when they have to catch a morning flight. Similarly, Aida is unhappy whenever they both have to stay up late, such as when they babysit their nephews.

Because either Aida or Luca is always cranky during these times, they frequently get on each other's nerves. They also interpret each other's behavior in negative ways. For instance, when Luca forgets to put his clothes in the washing machine, Aida's short temper leads her to interpret his behavior as a deliberate attempt to annoy her instead of as an innocent oversight. Similarly, if Aida speaks impatiently to Luca, his own crankiness causes him to interpret her speaking tone as condescending rather than to consider that she may just be tired. Their tendency to interpret each other's behaviors negatively causes Aida and Luca to let even small annoyances turn into arguments. If their biological rhythms were more similar, however, they would feel energized and drowsy at the same times. Consequently, they would better understand each other and be less likely to feel out of sync with each other.

CULTURE AND CO-CULTURE. Another powerful influence on the accuracy of our perceptions is the culture and co-cultures with which we identify. Cultural values and norms have many different effects on the way we communicate interpersonally. In addition to affecting our behavior, culture influences our perceptions and interpretations of other people's behaviors.[21]

Let's say that Jason, an American, meets Rosella, an Italian, at their company's international sales meeting. Jason notices that Rosella stands very close to him and touches him frequently, and these behaviors make him uncomfortable. He might perceive that Rosella is being dominant and aggressive, because in the United States people usually maintain more personal space and touch new acquaintances less often than do Italians. Noticing Jason's discomfort, Rosella might perceive that he's shy or socially awkward, because Italians are used to closer interpersonal distances and more frequent touch.[22] In this situation, Rosella and Jason's cultural norms affect not only their own behavior but also their perceptions of each other's behaviors.

Co-cultural differences can also influence perceptions. Teenagers might perceive their parents' advice as outdated or irrelevant, for instance, whereas parents might perceive their teenagers' indifference to their advice as naïve.[23] Some middle-class people might perceive that wealthy people are constantly taking advantage of them, whereas wealthy people may see lower-class people as lazy or ungrateful.[24] Liberals and conservatives might each perceive the others' behaviors as rooted in ignorance.[25]

Each of us has multiple "lenses" through which we perceive the world. Some of those lenses are products of our cultural background. Many others are influenced by our age, social class, political orientation, education, religion, and hobbies, and by other elements of our co-cultures.

For people in many socially marginalized populations, the experience of feeling misunderstood by others is common. Consider Hasani, a high school teacher who has struggled with clinical depression for most of his adult life. Much of the time, Hasani controls his depression adequately with medication. Occasionally, however, he has a severe depressive episode during which he becomes physically and mentally immobilized. His illness causes him to miss work more frequently than normal and often requires his principal to find a substitute at the last minute.

Some of Hasani's colleagues and students perceive that he is taking advantage of a system that allows him to miss work without penalty. Because the disabling nature of depression isn't outwardly visible, it can be easy for others to perceive that Hasani is simply taking a day off whenever he is in a bad mood. This inaccurate perception is fueled by people's misunderstandings about depression.

SOCIAL ROLES.   A *social role* is a set of behaviors that are expected of someone in a particular social situation. Each of us plays several social roles, and those roles can also influence the accuracy of our perceptions. One example is gender roles. Gender and biological sex affect a range of communication behaviors, so it's not surprising that they influence the perceptions we form of others.[26]

After years of hard work and consistently high performance ratings, for example, Karin has finally been promoted to senior manager at the telecommunications company where she works. She now supervises a staff of 12 managers, 7 male and 5 female. Karin is experienced, highly motivated, and straightforward in her dealings with others. The women on her staff see her as powerful, assertive, and an excellent role model for female executives. To the men, however, she seems domineering, aggressive, and pushy, because they perceive her behavior as unfeminine. In this instance, women and men who otherwise have much in common (they are all managers under the same boss) perceive the same pattern of behaviors in completely different ways.

Our experience and occupational roles can also influence our perceptions of others' behaviors.[27] As a first-time mother, for instance, Charlotte was terrified when her infant son began jerking and convulsing while she was holding him one day. She was certain he was having a seizure, so she rushed him to the emergency room. Derek, an experienced pediatric nurse, recognized the problem immediately: The baby simply had the hiccups. He explained to Charlotte that newborns often don't make the "hiccup" sound, so it's easy to mistake the baby's jerking motion for something more serious. Because of the differences in their training and experience with babies, Derek and Charlotte perceived the same behavior quite differently.

LEARN IT   What does it mean to engage in interpersonal perception? How are selection, organization, and interpretation related to one another? How do physiological states or traits, culture, co-culture, and social roles affect our perception-making ability?

APPLY IT   Think of a perception you recently made of someone else's behavior. In writing, describe what the person did and what your perception was. Given what you now know about the effects of physiology, culture, and social roles on perception making, formulate at least two alternative perceptions that you might have made about the same behavior.

REFLECT ON IT   What sensory information are you attending to right now? How do your co-cultures influence the perceptions you make of others?

2 Fundamental Forces in Interpersonal Perception

Most of the time we believe we're seeing the world as it really is. For example, Karin's male managers saw her as aggressive and domineering, but did they perceive her in that way because she actually was—or, rather, because they disliked having a female boss? Even though we rely a great deal on our perceptions, research shows that those perceptions are vulnerable to a number of biases, many of which operate outside our conscious awareness. In this section, we examine seven fundamental forces that affect our perceptions.

Stereotyping Relies on Generalizations

stereotypes Generalizations about groups of people that are applied to individual members of those groups.

You're probably familiar with **stereotypes,** which are generalizations about a group or category of people that can have powerful influences on how we perceive those people.[28] Stereotyping is a three-part process:

- First, we identify a group we believe another person belongs to ("you are a blonde").
- Second, we recall some generalization others often make about the people in that group ("blondes have more fun").
- Finally, we apply that generalization to the person ("therefore, you must have more fun").

You can probably think of stereotypes for many groups.[29] What stereotypes come to mind when you think about elderly people, for instance? How about people with physical or mental disabilities? Wealthy people? Homeless people? Gays and lesbians? Science fiction fans? Immigrants? Athletes? What stereotypes come to mind when you think about yourself?

Stereotyping means classifying a person as part of a group, making a generalization about that group, and then applying the generalization to that person. What stereotypes come to your mind for this person?

Many people find stereotyping distasteful or unethical, particularly when stereotypes have to do with characteristics such as sex, race, and sexual orientation.[30] There's no question that stereotyping can lead to some inaccurate, even offensive, evaluations of other people. The reason is that stereotypes underestimate the differences among individuals in a group. It may be true, for instance, that elderly people are more conservative than other age groups, but that doesn't mean that every elderly person is conservative or that all elderly people are conservative to the same extent. Similarly, people of Asian descent are sometimes stereotyped as being more studious than those in other ethnic groups, but that doesn't mean every Asian person is a good student or that all Asians do equally well in school.[31]

Importantly, there is variation in almost every group. However, stereotypes focus our attention only on the generalizations. In fact, we have a tendency to engage in selective memory bias, remembering information that supports our stereotypes but forgetting information that doesn't.[32] During interpersonal conflicts, for instance, both women and men tend to remember only their partners' stereotypical behaviors.[33] Let's take a look at a conflict between Carmen and her boyfriend, Nick, regarding their division of household labor:

> **Carmen:** You were supposed to vacuum and put in a load of laundry when you got home; instead you're just sitting there watching TV. Why am I the one who has to do everything around here?
>
> **Nick:** Look, I'm sorry. I've had a long day, and all I want to do is sit here for a while and de-stress.
>
> **Carmen:** I understand that, Nick, but I've also had a long day; I'd like to just sit around doing nothing too, but this stuff has to get done, and it shouldn't be my responsibility to do it all.
>
> **Nick:** Whatever. Can't we talk about this later?

What do you think Carmen and Nick will remember most about this conflict after it's over? Nick may recall that Carmen nagged and criticized him, but he may forget that she also listened to what he was saying. Likewise, Carmen may report that Nick "tuned her out," but she may overlook that he also apologized. In other words, both may remember only the other person's behaviors that conformed to stereotypes for female and male behavior.

That is one reason why it's so important to check our perceptions before we act on them. After an argument like Nick and Carmen's, for instance, ask yourself what communication behaviors the other person engaged in that were not necessarily stereotypical. That may help you form a more accurate memory of the conflict; it may also help you to treat the other person as an individual and not simply as a representative of his or her sex.[34]

Note, however, that perceptions about an individual made on the basis of a stereotype are not always inaccurate.[35] Consider the stereotype that women love being around children. If you met a woman and assumed (on the basis of this stereotype) that she enjoyed being around children, you might be wrong— however, you also might be right. Not every woman enjoys spending time with children, but some do. By the same token, not every elderly person is conservative, but some are. Not every male florist is gay, but some are. The point is that just because your perception of someone is consistent with a stereotype, it isn't necessarily inaccurate. Just as we shouldn't assume a stereotypical judgment is true, we also shouldn't assume it is false.

At this point, you might be wondering whether you should abandon stereotyping altogether—but in fact doing so would be unrealistic. A more productive way of dealing with stereotypes involves two elements: awareness and communication. First, be aware of the stereotypical perceptions you make. What assumptions do you make, for instance, when you meet an elderly Asian woman, an African American teenage boy, or an adult in a wheelchair? It's natural to form perceptions of such individuals based on what you believe to be true about the groups to which they belong. Try to be aware of situations when you do so, however, and also try to remember that your perceptions may not be accurate. Second, instead of assuming that your perceptions of other people are correct, get to know them and let your perceptions be guided by what you learn about them as individuals. By communicating interpersonally, you can begin to discover how well other people fit or don't fit the stereotypical perceptions you formed of them.

To deal productively with stereotypes, we must first be aware of how they influence our perceptions and behavior. What stereotypes would you apply to this person?

The Primacy Effect Governs First Impressions

As the saying goes, you get only one chance to make a good first impression. There's no shortage of advice on how to accomplish this, from picking the right clothes to polishing your conversational skills. Have you ever noticed that no one talks about the importance of making a good *second* impression? What is so special about first impressions?

primacy effect The tendency to emphasize the first impression over later impressions when forming a perception.

According to a principle called the **primacy effect,** first impressions are critical because they set the tone for all future interactions.[36] Our first impressions of someone seem to stick in our mind more than our second, third, or fourth impressions do. In an early study of the primacy effect, psychologist Solomon Asch found that a person described as "intelligent, industrious, impulsive, critical, stubborn, and envious" was evaluated more favorably than one described as "envious, stubborn, critical, impulsive, industrious, and intelligent."[37] Notice that most of those adjectives are negative, but when the description begins with a positive one (intelligent), the effects of the more negative ones that follow it are diminished.

Asch's study illustrates that the first information we learn about someone tends to have a stronger effect on how we perceive that person than information we receive later on.[38] That's why we work so hard to make a good first impression in a job interview, on a date, or in other important social situations. When people evaluate us favorably at first, they're more likely to perceive us in a positive light from then on.[39]

Although first impressions are powerful, they aren't necessarily permanent.[40] For example, when Suzette first met her hairstylist Trey, she didn't like him at all. At the

Barney Stinson, a character on How I Met Your Mother, *is constantly looking for ways to impress women. For Halloween parties, Barney always brings a spare costume. That way, if he strikes out with the most desirable women, he has a second chance to make a first impression.*

time, he had just come from a contentious visit with the manager of his salon, and he was in a bad mood when Suzette sat down in his chair. As a result, he seemed distant and uninterested while he cut her hair. His behavior made a poor impression on Suzette, and she decided to switch to another stylist at the same salon after that. As she continued to see Trey on her subsequent visits, however, he would always greet her warmly and ask her about her family. Over time, Suzette began to realize that her initial negative impression of Trey was inaccurate and that he was actually a nice, caring person.

To reiterate, the primacy effect means that first impressions are powerful, not that they are unchangeable. When subsequent communication is more positive than initial interactions, as in the case of Trey and Suzette, negative first impressions can sometimes be overcome.

The Recency Effect Influences Impressions

recency effect The tendency to emphasize the most recent impression over earlier impressions when forming a perception.

We've considered the importance of making a good first impression. As standup comedians and most other entertainers know, it's equally important to make a good final impression, because that's what the audience will remember after leaving. The principle in play is the **recency effect,** which says that the most recent impression we have of someone is more powerful than our earlier impressions.[41]

As an example, let's say that Diego has been diagnosed with testicular cancer and has made appointments with two doctors, Dr. Tan and Dr. Meyer, to discuss his treatment options. The doctors make equally good first impressions by listening to Diego and asking him questions about his symptoms and his overall health. At the end of their visit, Dr. Tan explains the specifics of surgery, radiation therapy, and chemotherapy to Diego and asks him how he feels about each option before ultimately recommending surgery. Diego leaves the first appointment with a positive impression of Dr. Tan.

At Diego's other appointment, Dr. Meyer ends by telling him that he definitely needs surgery and that any doctor who says otherwise is wrong. To Diego, this approach makes Dr. Meyer seem pushy and unconcerned about Diego's feelings or his treatment preferences. Diego leaves the second appointment with a negative impression of Dr. Meyer. Significantly, Diego doesn't form this negative impression because their visit started poorly. On the contrary, he felt good about both doctors at the beginning of his appointments. Rather, the last impression Diego formed of Dr. Meyer before he left was negative, and that impression remains with him after the visit.

At first glance, it might seem as though the recency effect and the primacy effect contradict each other. Which is the more important impression—the first or the most recent? The answer is that *both* appear to be more important than any impressions that we form in between.[42] To grasp this point fully, consider the last movie you saw. You probably have a better recollection of how the movie started and how it ended than you do of everything in between.

The same observation applies to our perceptions of other people. Diego's impressions of Dr. Tan and Dr. Meyer aren't based on his perceptions of everything that happened during his appointments. What he remembers is how they started (positively for both doctors) and how they ended (positively for Dr. Tan, negatively for Dr. Meyer). Figure 4.1 illustrates the relationship between the primacy effect and the recency effect.

The recency effect says we are most influenced by our most recent impression of someone. Diego formed a positive impression of Dr. Tan in part because of how positively their interaction ended.

Our Perceptual Set Limits What We Perceive

"I'll believe it when I see it," people often say. Our perception of reality is influenced not only by what we see, however, but also by our biases, our expectations, and our desires. These elements can

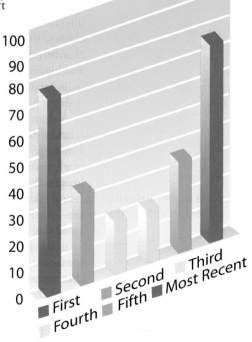

FIGURE 4.1 Our first impressions and our most recent impressions are more important than those that come in between.

assess your SKILLS

BEING ALTERCENTRIC

How much do you agree with each of the following statements? On the line before each, record your level of agreement on a 1–5 scale. Higher numbers mean you agree more; lower numbers mean you agree less.

In conversations with other people, I usually:

1. _____ Try to see things from their point of view.

2. _____ Don't assume they think the same way I do.

3. _____ Focus mostly on their ideas or opinions.

4. _____ Pay attention to their facial expressions and body language to figure out how they feel.

5. _____ Try to "put myself in their shoes."

6. _____ Attempt to avoid making assumptions about what they think or feel.

7. _____ Don't assume they're thinking whatever I'm thinking.

8. _____ Try to focus more on them than on myself.

Add up your scores and write the total on this line: _____. That total score represents the extent to which you try to be altercentric rather than egocentric when communicating with others.

- Between 8 and 18: Your conversation style is primarily egocentric.
- Between 19 and 29: You strike a balance between egocentrism and altercentrism.
- 30 or higher: You're fairly altercentric.

party for Marty. Paul is surprised, but not in a good way: The last thing he wanted was to spend his birthday at a loud, crowded party making conversation with people he hardly knew. So, he spends 30 minutes at the party and leaves. The next day, Marty is angry because Paul didn't appreciate the trouble he took to arrange the party. Paul is angry because he hates parties and that wasn't how he wanted to spend his birthday.

Paul and Marty are both being egocentric, because each is assuming that the other should react to the situation the way he would. Marty loves parties, so it doesn't even occur to him that Paul doesn't; he just thinks Paul is being ungrateful. Paul hates being in crowds, so he doesn't even consider that Marty was trying to do something nice for him.

The opposite of being egocentric is being *altercentric,* or focused on the perspective of another person instead of your own. To what extent do you communicate in altercentric ways? See the "Assess Your Skills" box to find out.

Positivity and Negativity Biases Affect Perception

Sometimes our perceptions are influenced more by positive or negative information than by neutral information. When we pay the most attention to positive information, we are exhibiting what researchers call a **positivity bias.**[51]

positivity bias The tendency to focus heavily on a person's positive attributes when forming a perception.

One form of the positivity bias is the tendency of people in love to look at each other "through rose-colored glasses," overestimating the partner's positive qualities while underestimating or ignoring his or her faults or shortcomings.[52] Perhaps you've been around people who have seen their love interests in that way. Research suggests that this is a normal stage of relationship development and that a certain amount of "idealizing" is healthy for new relationships.[53] Most relationships grow out of that stage, however. People who cling to an idealized view of their romantic partners may experience disappointment when they realize the person is not as perfect as they thought.

In the film *An Education* (2009), for instance, Carey Mulligan plays Jenny Mellor, a teenager who is about to start college when she falls in love with David Goldman (played by Peter Sarsgaard). Jenny eventually learns that David is a con man, but she is so enamored of him that she overlooks his shady behavior. When he proposes to her even though he is already married, Jenny confronts David and he disappears, leaving her in a state of despair fueled by the strong positivity bias she had for him. Later in this chapter, we'll further explore how looking through rose-colored glasses affects interpersonal behavior.

The opposite of the positivity bias is the **negativity bias,** or the tendency to weigh negative information more heavily than positive.[54] According to the negativity bias, even one piece of negative information can taint your perception of someone you would otherwise like. The negativity bias is particularly strong in competitive situations, such as job interviews and graduate school admissions.[55] When many people are competing for a limited number of opportunities, even seemingly minor pieces of negative information can ruin an otherwise positive impression.

negativity bias The tendency to focus heavily on a person's negative attributes when forming a perception.

Let's say you're calling references to check up on a person you have just interviewed for a key position on your work team. If the candidate is described as "innovative," you'll probably form a positive impression of her. If she's described as "rigid," your impression will probably be negative. What happens, however, if the candidate is described as both "innovative" and "rigid"? The answer is that you, like most people, will still form a negative impression. In other words, the negative information will override the positive.[56]

Positivity biases and negativity biases are particularly influential for communication and satisfaction in long-term relationships, such as marriages. People in almost any significant relationship will encounter positive events, such as the birth of a new child and a long-anticipated vacation. They will also encounter negative events, such as a prolonged conflict and an unexpected job loss. When they consider their relationship as a whole, however, satisfied couples tend to emphasize its positive characteristics; in other words, they are biased toward the positive. In contrast, dissatisfied couples tend to emphasize the negative characteristics.[57]

Stereotyping, primacy, recency, perceptual set, egocentrism, positivity, and negativity are all powerful influences, and simply knowing about them doesn't shield us from their effects. The more we know about perceptual errors, however, the better we can think critically and question our judgments to form more accurate perceptions of the people around us.

Carey Mulligan's character in An Education *discovers that her boyfriend is a con artist—but her positivity bias is so strong that she overlooks his behavior.*

LEARN IT What are the three stages of stereotyping? How are the primacy and recency effects related? How does a perceptual set influence interpersonal perception? What does it mean to be egocentric? What are the effects of the positivity biases and negativity biases?

APPLY IT Watch the movie *Crash* (2004), which highlights numerous cultural stereotypes. In a written report, identify as many stereotyped beliefs as you can from the movie, and briefly describe the ways in which each character's stereotyped beliefs influenced his or her behaviors toward other characters. Also, list examples of other perceptual influences, particularly egocentrism or negativity bias, that affected the characters' behaviors.

REFLECT ON IT What is one inaccurate stereotype that someone might have of you? When are you most likely to make egocentric perceptions of others?

3 Explaining What We Perceive

People have an almost constant need to make sense of the world. It's not enough just to notice someone's behavior, for instance—we are also driven to figure out *why* it happened. Why did Paul leave his party so soon? Why did Kanye interrupt Taylor's speech? We want to know.

Explaining Behavior Through Attributions

During a trip to Tokyo in November 2009, President Barack Obama made headlines when he greeted Japanese emperor Akihito with a nearly 90-degree bow. The president's behavior left many wondering, Why did he bow before a foreign leader?

> **attribution** An explanation for an observed behavior.

When we experience behavior we don't immediately understand, we usually try to make sense of it. We do so by formulating an attribution. An **attribution** is simply an explanation, the answer to a "why" question.[58] You notice your brother ignoring his girlfriend, for instance, and you wonder to what you should attribute his behavior. Your advisor asks you why you failed your history midterm, and you consider to what you should attribute that outcome. Attributions for behavior vary along three important dimensions—locus, stability, and controllability.[59]

Many observers wondered why President Obama would bow to a foreign head of state, as he did to Japanese emperor Akihito in November 2009.

LOCUS. Locus refers to where the cause of a behavior is "located," whether within ourselves or outside ourselves.[60] Some of our behaviors have internal causes, which means they're caused by a characteristic of ourselves. Other behaviors have external causes, meaning they're caused by something outside ourselves.

Let's say your boss is late to a lunch meeting, and you're trying to figure out why. Some internal attributions are that he has lost track of time, he's rarely punctual, and he's making you wait on purpose. Those attributions are all different, but they all identify some internal characteristic of your boss as the cause of his lateness. External attributions are that traffic is really heavy, that your boss has a long way to walk, and that his employees always have numerous questions for him in the morning. Again, those are all different attributions, but each one points to something in your boss's external environment—not within him personally—as the cause of his behavior.

STABILITY. A second dimension of attributions is whether the cause of a behavior is stable or unstable.[61] A stable cause is one that is permanent, semipermanent, or at least not easily changed. Why was your boss late for lunch? Rush-hour traffic would be a stable cause for lateness, because it's a permanent feature of many people's morning commutes. By contrast, a traffic accident would be an unstable cause for lateness, because accidents occur only from time to time in unpredictable places with unpredictable effects.

Notice that these are both external attributions. Internal causes for behavior also can be either stable or unstable, however. Imagine that you are trying to understand why your roommate snapped at you this morning. If you claim the reason is that she's a mean person, that would be a stable attribution, because most people's personalities don't change dramatically over the course of their lives. If you conclude that she snapped at you because she has the flu and is feeling tired, however, that's an unstable attribution, because having the flu is a temporary condition.

CONTROLLABILITY. Finally, causes for behavior also vary in how controllable they are.[62] If you make a controllable attribution for someone's behavior, then you believe that the cause of that behavior was under the person's control. In contrast, an uncontrollable attribution identifies a cause outside the person's control.

Let's say your brother is supposed to pick you up from the airport, but he isn't there when you arrive. You might assume he has failed to show because he has spent too much time hanging out with his friends beforehand and is running late. That is a controllable attribution, because the cause of his lateness (spending time with friends) is within his control. Alternatively, you might assume he got into a car accident. That is an uncontrollable attribution, because he couldn't help but be late if he wrecked his car.

Locus, stability, and controllability are all related to one another. However, different attributions can reflect different combinations of these dimensions. In fact, any combination of locus, stability, and controllability is possible.

For example, just because an attribution is internal doesn't necessarily mean it's also stable or uncontrollable. Referring back to an earlier example, one attribution for why your roommate snapped at you this morning is that she's not a "morning person." That is an internal attribution (she's not a morning person) that is stable (she's probably never been a morning person) and relatively uncontrollable (it probably has to do with her biological rhythms). A different attribution is that she was grumpy because she got only two hours of sleep, having been out partying most of the night before. That attribution is also internal (she's grumpy), but it is probably unstable (she isn't grumpy every morning) and controllable (she chose to stay up late the night before). Table 4.1 provides eight different attributions for a single behavior that represent all the possible combinations of locus, stability, and controllability.

Although most of us probably try to come up with accurate attributions for other people's behaviors, we are still vulnerable to making attribution mistakes.[63] Such errors can create problems for us because our response to other people's behaviors is often based on the attributions we make for those behaviors.

Eight Attributions for Rudeness

TABLE 4.1

We generally expect social interaction to be pleasant, so when someone is rude to us, we usually wonder why. Let's say Ricardo, the cashier at your grocery store, was especially rude today, and you're forming an attribution for his behavior. Below are eight attributions representing every possible combination of locus, stability, and controllability.

Internal, Stable, and Controllable	*He's a jerk.*	Personality traits (such as being a jerk) are internal and usually stable, but he should be able to control whether he acts like a jerk.
Internal, Stable, and Uncontrollable	*He's mentally challenged, and he doesn't always understand politeness.*	Although being mentally challenged is internal and stable, he can't help being mentally challenged.
Internal, Unstable, and Controllable	*He's hung over.*	Physical states such as being hung over are internal, but they aren't stable (because they will go away), and they are controllable (he didn't have to drink).
Internal, Unstable, and Uncontrollable	*He's got the flu.*	Illness is internal but unstable (because he'll get better). Presumably he didn't choose to get sick, so it's also uncontrollable.
External, Stable, and Controllable	*He's got a girlfriend who picks a fight with him every single morning; he needs to get out of that relationship.*	The source is external (a girlfriend); her influence is stable (they interact every day) but controllable (he can end the relationship if he wants).
External, Stable, and Uncontrollable	*The medication he takes to control his heart condition makes him impatient.*	Medication is an external source; it's stable (because it's for an ongoing condition) and uncontrollable (because he has to take it).
External, Unstable, and Controllable	*He's cranky because the air conditioning in his apartment isn't working; he should get it fixed.*	The air conditioning is an external cause; it's unstable (because it will eventually get fixed) and controllable (because he can get it fixed).
External, Unstable, and Uncontrollable	*Someone rear-ended his truck this morning, so he's upset.*	The source is external (another driver); it's unstable (it was a one-time incident) and uncontrollable (it was an accident).

Let's say that Adina and her 14-year-old son Craig get into an argument one night about whether Craig can go on a school-sponsored overseas trip. After their argument, they both go to bed angry. When Adina gets up the following morning, she finds that Craig hasn't done the dishes or taken out the trash, two chores he is responsible for doing every night before bed. It turns out that Craig was so flustered by the previous night's conflict that doing his chores slipped his mind. Adina makes a different attribution, however: She perceives that Craig didn't do the chores because he was deliberately disobeying her. On the basis of that attribution, she tells Craig he is grounded for a week and is not going on the school trip. Her actions only prolong and intensify the conflict between them.

If, instead, Adina attributed Craig's behavior to an honest oversight, she might have been able to overlook it instead of making it the basis for additional conflict. As we'll see in the next section, learning how to recognize common attribution errors will best equip us to avoid making mistakes that, as in the case of Adina and Craig, transform a bad situation into a worse one.

Recognizing Common Attribution Errors

We might think we always explain behavior in an objective, rational way, but the truth is that we're all prone to taking mental shortcuts when coming up with attributions. As a result, our attributions are often less accurate than they ideally should be. Three of the most common attribution errors are the self-serving bias, the fundamental attribution error, and overattribution.

SELF-SERVING BIAS. The **self-serving bias** refers to our tendency to attribute our successes to stable, internal causes while attributing our failures to unstable, external causes.[64] For example, if you got an *A* on your test, you did so because you're smart, but if you got an *F,* the reason is that the test was unfair or because you work so much to keep up with tuition payments that you didn't have time to study. Those attributions are called self-serving because they suggest that our successes are deserved but our failures are not our fault.

The self-serving bias deals primarily with attributions that we make for our own behaviors. However, research shows that we often extend that tendency to other important people in our lives.[65] In a happy marriage, for instance, people tend to attribute their spouse's positive behaviors to internal causes ("She remembered my birthday because she's thoughtful") and negative behaviors to external causes ("He forgot my birthday because he's been very distracted at work"). That tendency is especially pronounced among people who are currently in love and are seeing each other through rose-colored glasses, as the "Communication: Light Side" box explains. In distressed relationships, the reverse is often true: People attribute negative behavior to internal causes ("She forgot my birthday because she's completely self-absorbed") and positive behavior to external causes ("He remembered my birthday only because I reminded him five times").

The self-serving bias is a natural, self-protective tendency, although it is a form of self-delusion.[66] Virtually none of us is responsible for all our successes and none of our failures. If we're being honest, most of us would agree that our failures are sometimes our fault (you got an *F* because you didn't study). Similarly, most of us would admit that our successes sometimes result from factors outside our control (you got an *A* because of the curve, not because of your performance).

Those observations also apply to communication in relationships. We might like to think, for instance, that we are responsible for everything that is going well in our relationships but are not responsible for anything that is going poorly. Again, that attitude is unrealistic. As you've probably learned from your own experience, both people in an interpersonal relationship contribute to its positive and negative aspects. When you commit the self-serving bias and act as though you're responsible only for successes but not for failures, your actions are likely to cause resentment from others. For those reasons, it's important to be aware of our self-serving biases and to be honest about the attributions we make for our behavior and the behavior of others. Check out the "Got Skills?" box on p. 129 for hints on doing so.

FUNDAMENTAL ATTRIBUTION ERROR. Think about how you reacted the last time someone cut you off in traffic. Specifically, what attribution did you make for the driver's behavior? You might have said to yourself, "She must be late for something important" or "He must have a car full of noisy children," but you probably didn't. "What a jerk!" is likely to be closer to your reaction.

> **self-serving bias** The tendency to attribute one's successes to internal causes and one's failures to external causes.

I Like that

We often extend the self-serving bias to our relationships. Why did your partner remember your birthday? Was it because your partner is a thoughtful person or because you reminded him or her repeatedly?

SEEING THE WORLD DIFFERENTLY: LOVERS AND THEIR ROSE-COLORED GLASSES

Perhaps you've noticed that people in love perceive each other more positively than others do. Although they have little difficulty pointing out each other's good qualities, they seem unable even to notice each other's flaws and shortcomings. Indeed, it is as though being in love allows people to see past their partners' exteriors to appreciate the "real person" underneath. Colloquially, we call that ability "seeing through rose-colored glasses," to suggest that being in love makes one's partner—and perhaps everyone else as well—look rosier than usual.

Research has confirmed that people in love perceive and communicate with each other differently than people who are not in love. In a now-classic study, social psychologists Clyde and Susan Hendrick found that college students in love perceived greater commitment, satisfaction, and investment in their relational partners—and less interest in alternative partners—compared to those not currently in love. The love-stricken also reported engaging in less self-monitoring behavior (perhaps because they felt more unqualified acceptance from their romantic partners) and less thrill-seeking behavior (maybe because they found their romantic relationships more thrilling). The researchers suggest that seeing through rose-colored glasses is a normal, and even beneficial, phase for new lovers to experience, as it encourages them to ignore each other's faults while their feelings for each other deepen.

ASK YOURSELF

- Besides being in love with that person, what else might cause you to see someone through rose-colored glasses?

- Are there people you tend to see through rose-colored glasses? If so, how does that influence the attributions you make for their behavior?

Source: Hendrick, C., & Hendrick, S. S. (1988). Lovers wear rose colored glasses. *Journal of Social and Personal Relationships, 5,* 161–183.

---

fundamental attribution error The tendency to attribute others' behaviors to internal rather than external causes.

The reason for that response isn't crankiness. Rather, it's the tendency to commit what scientists call the **fundamental attribution error,** in which we attribute other people's behaviors to internal rather than external causes.[67] The high school student ran the pledge drive because she's a caring, giving person, not because she earned extra credit for doing so. The cashier gave you the wrong change because he doesn't know how to count, not because he was distracted by an announcement being made over the loudspeaker. That driver cut you off because he or she is a jerk, not because of noisy children or any other external factor that might have motivated that behavior.

The fundamental attribution error is so strong, in fact, that we commit it even when we know better. For instance, you can probably think of at least one actor you dislike simply because you don't like the characters he plays. Most of us understand that acting involves playing a role and pretending to be a character that someone else has created; an actor's words and behaviors clearly aren't his own. However, we often commit the fundamental attribution error by assuming (even subconsciously) that an actor's behavior reflects who he is as a person.

Just how strong is the fundamental attribution error? Consider that in one study people explained a person's behavior in terms of internal factors even after they were specifically told that it was caused by external factors.[68] In the study, college students talked with a young woman whose behavior was either friendly or unfriendly. Before their conversations, half the students were told the woman's behavior would be spontaneous, but the other half were told she had been instructed to act either friendly or unfriendly.

[SELF-SERVING BIAS]

Recognize the self-serving bias—and learn to avoid it.

WHAT?

Learn to avoid the self-serving bias when making attributions about your interpersonal behavior.

WHY?

To recognize and acknowledge that you share responsibility for both the positive and the negative aspects of your personal relationships.

HOW?

1. Choose a relationship that matters to you, and list its five most positive and five most negative characteristics.

2. Write out the ways in which (a) you contribute to the positive aspects of your relationship, and (b) the other person contributes to the negative aspects.

3. Next write out the ways in which (a) you contribute to the negative aspects of the relationship, and (b) the other person contributes to the positive aspects. If you find this task difficult, consider what the other person might say.

TRY!

1. The next time you encounter a problem in this relationship, stop yourself before you assign blame. Carefully consider the role that each of you played in creating that problem.

2. *Let your relationship partner hear you sharing the credit with him or her for the positive aspects of your relationship.*

3. Over the course of a week, in a short journal entry, document the times when you successfully avoid the self-serving bias. At the week's end, write a paragraph reflecting on what you have learned.

CONSIDER: *How does your interpersonal communication improve when you keep the self-serving bias in check?*

How did this information influence the students' attributions for the woman's behavior? The answer is that it had no effect at all. When the woman acted friendly, the students maintained it was because she is a friendly person, and when she acted unfriendly, they maintained it was because she is an unfriendly person. In both cases, students attributed the woman's behavior to her personality, even when they were specifically told that she was only behaving as instructed.

As interpersonal communicators, we should bear in mind that people's behaviors—including our own—are often responses to external forces. For instance, when the new doctor you're seeing spends only three minutes diagnosing your condition and prescribing a treatment before moving on to the next patient, you might conclude that she's not a very caring person. This would be an internal attribution for her behavior, which the fundamental attribution error increases your likelihood of making. If you think your doctor rushed through your consultation because she's uncaring, that attribution might lead you to give her a poor evaluation to your friends and co-workers or to switch to another doctor altogether.

Was your attribution correct, however? Ask yourself what external forces might have motivated the doctor's behavior. For example, she might have rushed through your consultation simply because another doctor's absence that day forced her to see twice as many patients as usual, not because she's an uncaring person. If that's the case, then you might have switched to another doctor for no reason, forgoing your opportunity to form a positive professional relationship with her. To the extent that we base our decisions on inaccurate attributions, we run the risk of needlessly damaging our relationships in the process.

overattribution The tendency to attribute a range of behaviors to a single characteristic of a person.

OVERATTRIBUTION. A third common attribution error is **overattribution,** in which we single out one or two obvious characteristics of a person and then attribute everything he or she does to those characteristics.[69] Let's use the example of Fatima, who is an only child. When you see her being impatient or acting selfishly, you might say to yourself, "That's typical of an only child." Maybe you notice that she pushes herself to make good grades, she is very conservative with her money, or she doesn't seem to enjoy the holidays. "Well, she is an only child!" you might say to yourself, as if that one characteristic *is* the underlying cause of everything she does.[70]

Overattribution is a form of mental laziness. Instead of trying to understand why Fatima might push herself so hard in school, we pick something obvious about her (she's an only child) and conclude that it must have something to do with that.

Although that example might seem inconsequential, overattribution can contribute to problematic behavior in some contexts. For instance, psychologists William Schweinle, William Ickes, and Ira Bernstein have studied overattribution in the context of marital aggression. On the basis of the principle of overattribution, the researchers predicted that when women communicate in a certain way, such as by being critical, men sometimes explain the behavior as being typical of women in general. In other words, they focus on one aspect of a person ("she's a woman") as the cause of her behavior ("because she's a woman, she's being critical").

Schweinle and his colleagues found that the more men engage in this form of overattribution with women in general, the more likely they are to be verbally abusive with their own wives.[71] The researchers noted that engaging in this form of overattribution causes men to perceive their wives as being critical even when they aren't, simply because they are women. As one result, men form defensive thoughts that provoke their verbal aggression.[72]

Overattribution is particularly easy to do with marginalized groups such as sexual minorities, homeless people, and people with disabilities.[73] Because members of these groups are marginalized, some people don't have much experience interacting with them. This lack of communication might make it easier to believe that the group a person belongs to is the primary cause of his or her behaviors. For that reason, it's important to remember that being homeless or gay might be one characteristic of a person, but it doesn't define the person completely, and it's not the cause of everything that person says or does.[74]

Humans are complex social beings. So, if we want to understand the reasons behind another person's behaviors, we need to look past his or her outward characteristics and consider what aspects of the individual's physical and/or social environment might be motivating his or her behavior.

Like other forms of perception, attributions are important but prone to error. That observation doesn't imply that we never make accurate attributions for other people's behavior. It simply acknowledges that the self-serving bias, the fundamental attribution error, and overattribution are easy mistakes to commit. The more we know about those processes, the better able we'll be to examine the attributions we make. The "At a Glance" box summarizes the three common attribution errors.

Overattribution can be easy to do with people in socially marginalized groups, such as individuals with an intellectual disability—especially when interaction with them is limited. Humans are complex social beings, though. We cannot understand people simply by characterizing their most obvious qualities.

LEARN IT What does it mean to say that attributions vary according to locus, stability, and controllability? How are the self-serving bias, the fundamental attribution error, and overattribution examples of attribution errors?

APPLY IT For one week, keep a list of all the attributions you give to someone else about something you have done. At the end of the week, go back through your list, and evaluate each attribution for accuracy. How many attributions fit the self-serving bias? How many were accurate? Were any of your attributions overly negative?

REFLECT ON IT When do you commit the fundamental attribution error? With which group(s) of people would you be most likely to make overattributions?

4 Improving Your Perceptual Abilities

We've examined how easy it is to make perceptual mistakes. We stereotype people. We assume they think the same ways we do. We attribute all their behaviors to one or two characteristics. Clearly, perception making is hard work. On the positive side, despite all those limitations, we can do a better job of it if we know how. Improving our perceptual ability starts with being mindful of what our perceptions are and what influences them. Next, it involves checking the accuracy of our perceptions. Before we examine those steps, though, imagine yourself in the following situation.

You have just started working at a store that sells and services swimming pools. You've noticed that the social atmosphere at the store seems playful and fun, but you sense tension between Dmitri, the store manager, and Min, one of the salespeople. Dmitri grew up in Greece, went to college in Canada, and has been living in the United States since he graduated. Min's parents emigrated from South Korea when she was an infant and raised Min and her older brother in the Pacific Northwest.

From what you've observed, Dmitri is friendly and informal with almost everyone, including his employees. Min is also friendly, but she communicates with others in a more formal, reserved manner than Dmitri. On a couple of occasions, you have seen Dmitri put his arm around Min and flirt with her. You have observed him doing the same with several other people as well; Dmitri is a very gregarious person. You've also heard from another employee, however, that Min has asked Dmitri not to behave that way toward her at work, although you are not certain whether that is true.

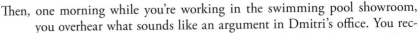

Then, one morning while you're working in the swimming pool showroom, you overhear what sounds like an argument in Dmitri's office. You recognize the voices as Dmitri's and Min's, and although you can't hear everything they're saying, you hear enough to figure out that Min is upset because Dmitri promoted another employee instead of her to the position of lead salesperson. Eventually you see Min walk out of Dmitri's office looking visibly upset. By that afternoon, you start hearing a rumor that Min has filed a harassment complaint against Dmitri.

We'll use this scenario throughout this section to illustrate how you can improve your perception-making abilities. As you imagine yourself in this scenario, consider what perceptions you would form. Has Dmitri harassed Min by denying her a promotion because she expressed discomfort at his flirtatious behavior?

Alternatively, is Min falsely accusing Dmitri of harassment because she is angry at not getting the promotion? Or are both parties at fault? Arriving at an accurate perception of the situation will be difficult given the limited information you have. Nevertheless, with effort, you can improve your perceptual ability.

Being Mindful of Your Perceptions

We form perceptions of people and situations constantly—so often, in fact, that we're sometimes unaware that we're doing it. We can improve our perceptual abilities, however, only when we're mindful of our perceptions. In other words, we must first be aware of what our perceptions are; then we must consider how they might be affected by our own characteristics, by the characteristics of the people we're perceiving, and by the context in which we're perceiving them.

KNOW YOURSELF.   How can several people observe the same event and form different—even contradictory—perceptions of it? As we've seen, the reason is that our individual characteristics often shape the way we perceive people and situations. One part of being mindful of your perceptions, therefore, is to ask yourself how they are influenced by your personal attributes.

For instance, how might your perception of Dmitri and Min's situation be affected by your sex? Perhaps you identify more with Min if you're female because you are projecting how you would feel in the same situation. Likewise, you might identify more with Dmitri if you're male. In the same vein, your cultural values and expectations might also influence your perception of the situation. If you grew up in a low-power-distance culture that values equality and workers' rights, you might be predisposed to perceive that Dmitri is abusing his power and victimizing Min. Conversely, if you were raised in a high-power-distance culture that values hierarchy and discourages the questioning of authority, you might be more likely to perceive that Min is overreacting and needlessly causing problems.

Remember that your physiological states and traits can also shape your perceptions. If you were tired or hungry when you overheard Dmitri and Min's exchange, for example, you might have felt short-tempered and been more likely than usual to rush to judgment one way or the other. That could have led you to select, organize, and interpret only those clues that supported your initial perception and to ignore any information that did not.

Your experiences with previous jobs could also bias your perceptions of Dmitri and Min by creating a perceptual set. Let's say that one of your closest friends at your last job was the victim of harassment. Noticing the pain and frustration she went through may have sensitized you to instances of harassment, leading you to "see" a situation as an example of harassment because that's what you expect to see.

Now let's take the opposite approach and imagine that your friend was wrongfully accused of harassment by a disgruntled employee. That experience might sensitize you to "see" even legitimate victims of harassment as simply vindictive and dishonest, because that's what you expect to see. In either case, your experiences would have created a perceptual set that shaped your perceptions.

We can't always change these influences on our perception-making ability. Try as we might, for example, we can't just choose to think like someone of a different gender or cultural background. But what we *can* do is ask ourselves how factors such as our experiences, sex, cultural background, and physiological states and traits might affect the perceptions we make. Acknowledging those influences is one of the first steps in improving our perceptual ability.

FOCUS ON OTHERS' CHARACTERISTICS: THE INFLUENCE OF GENDER AND CULTURE. Being mindful of our perceptions also means acknowledging how they are influenced by characteristics of the people we're perceiving. For instance, are you more inclined to believe Dmitri and Min's situation is an example of harassment because the supervisor is male and the employee is female? What if the situation involved a male employee accusing a female supervisor of harassment? Might that detail change your perception of the accusation's merit? You might think the sex of the people involved wouldn't matter—legally and ethically, it shouldn't—but several studies have shown that people are more likely to perceive harassment when the supervisor is male as opposed to female.[75]

Another characteristic of Min and Dmitri that may affect your perceptions of their situation is their cultural backgrounds. Culture has a strong influence on how we behave and communicate, so it should come as no surprise that it also influences the way we perceive behavior. When we observe interactions between people from our own culture, our shared knowledge about cultural norms enables us to perceive and interpret their behaviors with relative ease. However, when we observe interactions between people from other cultures, we are more likely to misinterpret their behaviors. One reason why this is true is that people's cultural backgrounds can activate stereotypes that can influence our perceptions.

For example, perhaps you stereotype Greek men as being naturally gregarious, so you see Dmitri's friendly behavior toward his employees merely as an expression of his nature, not as harassment. Or perhaps you stereotype Asian women (even those raised in the United States) as being accommodating and respectful of authority. If so, then you would likely perceive that Min wouldn't have argued with her supervisor unless she truly felt victimized. Neither of those stereotypes may actually be valid. Nevertheless, to the extent that you hold stereotyped beliefs that are relevant to Dmitri or Min, those beliefs can color the way you perceive the situation.

CONSIDER THE CONTEXT. The last step in being mindful of your perceptions is to consider how the context itself influenced them. In the example of Dmitri and Min, the context includes not only the argument you overheard but also the observations you made of Dmitri's and Min's communication behaviors before the argument. Let's say that when you started working at the store, your first impression of Dmitri was that he was inappropriately affectionate toward his employees. Because of the primacy effect, that first impression might encourage you to perceive his behavior toward Min as harassment. Conversely, let's say that you recently observed Min communicating in an unprofessional manner with two customers. Because of the recency effect, that recent negative impression might encourage you to perceive that she is accusing Dmitri unfairly.

Positivity biases and negativity biases can also shape your perceptions. If you really like Min and have always gotten along well with her, then you might be inclined to believe only positive things about her. That inclination could bias you toward believing her side of the story and concluding that Dmitri had in fact harassed her. However, if you and Min don't get along, then you might be inclined to believe the worst about her, and this inclination could bias you against believing her accusations.

Don't forget, too, that you heard only bits and pieces of Dmitri and Min's argument. It's possible, then, that your limited ability to hear the conversation caused you to miss parts of the argument that would have changed your perception of the situation. In other words, the context itself limited the information that you could select for attention. An important part of being mindful of your perceptions, therefore, is to ask whether there are pieces of information to which you didn't have access.

These three clues—knowing yourself, focusing on the characteristics of others, and considering the context—can all help you think critically about your perceptions by acknowledging the range of factors that can influence them.

Checking Your Perceptions

Being mindful of your perceptions is an important step toward improving your perceptual abilities, but it is only the first step. After you have considered which factors led you to form a particular perception, the next step is to check the accuracy of that perception. To do so, let's continue with the example of Dmitri and Min.

SEPARATE INTERPRETATIONS FROM FACTS. *Dragnet* was a radio and television police drama that debuted in the early 1950s. Its main character, Sgt. Joe Friday, was a detective best known for requesting "just the facts, ma'am." That phrase implies that objective facts are different from interpretations of those facts.

Let's say you saw Dmitri put his arm around a customer and kiss her on the cheek. If you were asked to describe the scene, you might say that "Dmitri was acting friendly with that woman" or "he was flirting with her" or even "he was coming on to her."

Which of those reports is factual? Technically, none of them is. Rather, they are all interpretations, because they all assign *meaning* to what you observed. You witnessed Dmitri's behavior and interpreted it as friendliness, as flirtation, or as a sign of sexual interest, so you described it in those ways. In fact, if you and two co-workers had witnessed the behavior, you could easily have interpreted it in three different ways.

Sgt. Joe Friday

If all three of your perceptions were subjective interpretations, then what are the facts here? The essential fact is that you saw Dmitri put his arm around the woman and kiss her on the cheek. That's what you objectively observed. Perhaps you also noticed other clues that helped you arrive at your interpretation, such as what occurred right before or how the customer reacted. The point is that *describing* what you actually saw or heard is not the same thing as *interpreting* it. If we are to check the accuracy of our perceptions, we must start by separating what we heard or saw from the interpretation we assigned it.

GENERATE ALTERNATIVE PERCEPTIONS. Once you have assigned meaning to an event, ask yourself what other meanings or interpretations you might have come up with. As we considered earlier, most people arrive at a perception and then pay attention only to information that supports their perception, ignoring any information that doesn't. A better approach is to look for alternative ways of perceiving the situation, even if they contradict your initial perception.

Your observations of Dmitri and Min, for example, might lead you to perceive that Min is accusing Dmitri of harassment only out of anger at not getting the promotion. What are alternative ways of perceiving the situation? One alternative we have already identified is that Dmitri has actually harassed Min. Are there others? Perhaps Dmitri feels threatened by Min and worries that he might put his own job in jeopardy by promoting her. Perhaps Min and Dmitri have had a contentious relationship for a long time. In that case, the conflict you witnessed wasn't about Min's promotion at all but instead reflected long-standing grudges on the part of both individuals.

The practice of generating alternative perceptions is important for two reasons. First, it requires you to look at information about the situation that doesn't match your original perception. For example, if you initially perceived that Min accused Dmitri of harassment only out of anger at not getting the promotion, then it would be easy for you to ignore your observations of Min's discomfort with Dmitri's overly friendly behavior because those observations don't support your perception. In contrast, to generate an alternative perception, you would have to take those observations into account.

Second, generating alternative perceptions encourages you to ask yourself what information you don't have that might be relevant. How much do you know about Dmitri and Min's history with each other, for instance? If you knew they used to be a romantic couple but had an emotional breakup just a few months before you started working at the store, that information might give you a more accurate context for interpreting their behaviors toward each other.

Keep in mind, however, that even if you are able to generate alternative perceptions, that doesn't necessarily mean your initial perception was inaccurate or should be discarded. In fact, looking at alternatives will sometimes make you even more convinced that your first perception was accurate. The purpose of considering alternative perceptions is to make certain you aren't ignoring or discounting clues from the situation simply because they are inconsistent with the perception you formed.

Once you have separated interpretations from facts and have considered alternative ways of perceiving the situation, you can engage in direct and indirect forms of perception checking.

ENGAGE IN PERCEPTION-CHECKING BEHAVIORS. Perception checking is the process of testing your perceptions for accuracy. This is an important step toward improving your perceptual abilities because when you act on the basis of inaccurate perceptions, you run the risk of turning a situation from bad to worse, as you saw Adina do with her son Craig earlier in this chapter. You can engage in either direct or indirect means of perception checking.

Direct perception checking involves simply asking other people if your perception of a situation is accurate. If you perceive that Min is angry at Dmitri, for instance, one way to find out if you're right is to ask her. Direct perception checking involves three elements:

1. Acknowledging the behavior you witnessed

2. Interpreting that behavior

3. Asking whether your interpretation was correct

Here's an example of how you might directly check your perception that Min is angry with Dmitri:

> "I heard you talking to Dmitri in his office [*acknowledging behavior*]. It sounded like you were pretty mad at Dmitri [*offering an interpretation*]. Is that true?" [*asking about your interpretation*]

[DIRECT PERCEPTION CHECKING]

Learn to check your perceptions directly.

WHAT?

Learn to use direct perception checking.

WHY?

To verify the accuracy of your interpersonal perceptions so that you can correct them when they are wrong.

HOW?

1. After formulating an interpretation of someone's behavior, describe the behavior to the person and then indicate how you interpreted it. For example, "You're shaking; you seem really nervous."

2. Ask the individual if your interpretation is correct. If it is, the other person will typically confirm it. If it isn't, the correct interpretation will usually follow ("No, I'm just cold right now").

TRY!

1. When you encounter an ambiguous behavior, formulate your interpretation but remember that it may be inaccurate.

2. If you feel it's appropriate, ask the other person whether your interpretation of his or her behavior is accurate.

3. Over a few weeks, take note of when your interpretations have been accurate and when they have not. Write a short journal entry reflecting on the differences between your successful and unsuccessful interpretations.

CONSIDER: *In cases when you interpreted the behavior incorrectly, what relevant information did you disregard when formulating your interpretation?*

got **SKILLS** ?

Depending on your relationship with Min, she may feel comfortable telling you how she feels: "Yeah, I'm furious with him!" Or she might downplay her feelings if she doesn't feel comfortable disclosing them to you: "I'm just a little upset about not getting the promotion, that's all." If your perception is wrong, she might tell you that: "No, I'm not mad at Dmitri at all; why would you think that?" She might even choose not to respond to your question: "I'd appreciate it if you could just leave me alone for a little while." Direct perception checking will be the most useful, therefore, when you approach people who are willing either to confirm your perceptions or to correct them. You can learn more about direct perception checking in the "Got Skills?" box.

In contrast, *indirect perception checking* involves listening and observing in order to seek additional information about the situation. Instead of asking Min if she is angry, for example, you might observe her facial expressions, listen to how she talks to others, and watch her body language when she's around Dmitri. If you notice that Min looks and sounds angry, that observation gives you additional confidence in the accuracy of your perception. If she seems to interact with Dmitri in a calm, pleasant manner, that observation might suggest that your perception was off base.

Neither direct nor indirect perception checking will provide foolproof results every time. As we saw, asking people if your perceptions are correct is useful only if they are willing to tell you. Indirect perception checking can fail, too, because your initial perception ("Min is angry") might lead you to pay attention only to clues that reinforce that perception. For instance, you might notice Min's distressed tone of voice without also noticing that her facial expression appears calm. Another danger of indirect perception checking is that you might pay attention to information that isn't relevant. To

FACT OR fiction ?

WHEN IT COMES TO PERCEPTION CHECKING, MORE INFORMATION IS ALWAYS BETTER

People sometimes criticize others for making snap judgments—that is, arriving at their perceptions on the basis of limited information. After listening to one speech, for example, you decide to vote for a political candidate without learning anything else about her. Or a customer comes into your store, and after taking one look at him, you perceive that he's trouble. It's easy to see how those on-the-spot judgments can be misleading and how your perceptions might have been more accurate if you'd had additional information.

In many cases, this observation is true: When forming perceptions of others, we should remember that first impressions can be misleading. That political candidate might *sound* good, but you may have a different perception of her when you learn that she has no experience. That customer might *look* suspicious, but you might think differently when you find out he's a youth minister just home from a long and tiring retreat. In many situations, the more information we can gather to check our perceptions, the more accurate our perceptions will be.

Research shows, however, that in certain cases our snap judgments are surprisingly accurate. Going further—gathering additional information about someone, such as through indirect perception checking—*can* make our perceptions more accurate, but it doesn't *always* make them more accurate.

You might think, for instance, that friends you have known for a long time would describe you more accurately than strangers would. An interesting experiment in 2002 proved otherwise, though. Participants in the study described themselves on personality inventories and then asked their close friends to describe them on the same inventories. Not surprisingly, the friends' reports matched the participants' self-reports fairly well. The researchers then asked complete strangers to walk through the participants' dorm rooms and then describe the participants' personalities. That is, the strangers filled out descriptions of the participants without even meeting them—just on the basis of the limited information they got from browsing around the participants' dorm rooms.

Interestingly—and perhaps surprisingly—the strangers were more accurate than the close friends in describing three of five dimensions of participants' personalities. This experiment illustrates that having more information about a person—as you would if you had known that person for years—does not necessarily make your perceptions of him or her more accurate. More information is sometimes better, but not always.

FROM ME TO YOU

The observation that more information is not always better might leave you feeling a little torn. On the one hand, it's useful to check your perceptions by gathering additional information; on the other hand, additional information can sometimes make your perceptions less rather than more accurate.

The trick to solving this paradox is to learn which pieces of information to pay attention to and which to ignore. That's a difficult skill to be taught, and in fact most of us learn it by our experience at forming and checking perceptions. Just knowing that more information isn't always better gives you an advantage. When you engage in indirect perception checking, you can ask yourself whether each new clue you gather about a situation is relevant to your perception. Over time, that practice should improve your perceptual accuracy.

Source: Gosling, S. D., Ko, S. J., Mannarelli, T., & Morris, M. E. (2002). A room with a cue: Personality judgments based on offices and bedrooms. *Journal of Personality and Social Psychology, 82,* 379–398.

determine whether Min is angry, for example, you might take careful note of the way she's sitting at her desk and how she's looking at others, even though those behaviors might not be affected by her emotion.

Although you might think that gathering more information will always lead you to make more accurate perceptions, there are instances when having more information makes your perceptions *less* accurate, as the "Fact or Fiction?" box details. For those reasons, it's often in your best interest to engage in both direct and indirect perception checking, so that each strategy can compensate for the shortcomings of the other.

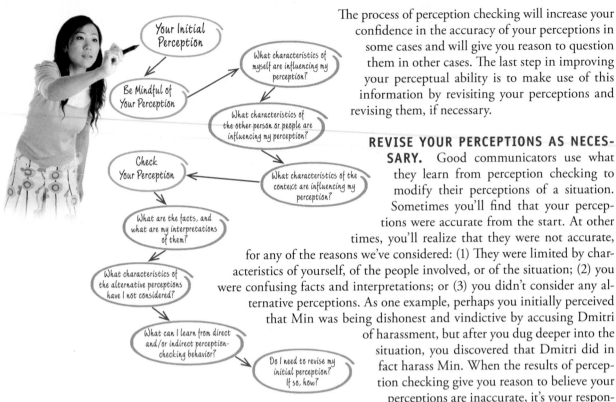

The process of perception checking will increase your confidence in the accuracy of your perceptions in some cases and will give you reason to question them in other cases. The last step in improving your perceptual ability is to make use of this information by revisiting your perceptions and revising them, if necessary.

REVISE YOUR PERCEPTIONS AS NECESSARY. Good communicators use what they learn from perception checking to modify their perceptions of a situation. Sometimes you'll find that your perceptions were accurate from the start. At other times, you'll realize that they were not accurate, for any of the reasons we've considered: (1) They were limited by characteristics of yourself, of the people involved, or of the situation; (2) you were confusing facts and interpretations; or (3) you didn't consider any alternative perceptions. As one example, perhaps you initially perceived that Min was being dishonest and vindictive by accusing Dmitri of harassment, but after you dug deeper into the situation, you discovered that Dmitri did in fact harass Min. When the results of perception checking give you reason to believe your perceptions are inaccurate, it's your responsibility as a communicator to revise them.

Improving your perceptual ability therefore involves two major strategies. First, you have to be mindful of the factors that influence what perception you form of a situation. Second, you have to check that

FIGURE 4.4 Improving Your Perceptual Ability. Improving your perceptual ability involves two stages. First you need to identify your initial perception by exploring characteristics about yourself, the other person, and the context of the situation that may be influencing your perception. Then you need to check your perception by considering what is factual and interpretive, and whether there may be alternative perceptions.

perception by separating facts from interpretations, considering alternative perceptions, engaging in direct and indirect perception checking, and revising your perception if necessary. With practice, these skills, which are represented in Figure 4.4, will help you improve your perceptions of people in interpersonal contexts.

LEARN IT What aspects of ourselves, the people we are perceiving, and the context can influence our perceptions? How do direct and indirect perception checking differ?

APPLY IT Distorted or inaccurate perceptions often provide the basis for comedy story lines. Spend a few days watching your favorite sitcoms, and pay attention to how the characters' perceptions are limited, how they might be affected by culture, and how they might confuse interpretation with fact. Document your findings in class or in a brief written report. Noticing these behaviors in others—even television characters—can help us to notice them in ourselves.

REFLECT ON IT How do you notice that your own perceptions are limited? When do you mistake interpretations for facts?

MASTER the chapter

1 The Process of Perception (p. 108)

- Interpersonal perception is the process of making meaning from the people and the relationships we encounter.

- The process of perception includes selecting stimuli for attention, organizing them into relevant categories, and interpreting their meaning.

- Physiological states and traits, cultures, co-cultures, and social roles all influence the accuracy of our perceptions.

2 Fundamental Forces in Interpersonal Perception (p. 116)

- Stereotyping is the process of applying generalizations about a group to a person we perceive to belong to that group.

- According to the primacy effect, our first impressions are more powerful than any of our later impressions.

- The recency effect maintains that the most recent impression we have formed will overshadow the impressions that came before it.

- Our perceptual set causes us to perceive only what we want or expect to perceive.

- When we are egocentric, we lack the ability to adopt another person's perspective.

- The positivity bias encourages us to focus on a person's positive aspects; the negativity bias encourages us to focus on his or her negative aspects.

3 Explaining What We Perceive (p. 124)

- Attributions, or explanations for behavior, vary according to their locus, stability, and controllability.

- The self-serving bias, the fundamental attribution error, and overattribution are common attribution mistakes.

4 Improving Your Perceptual Abilities (p. 131)

- Being mindful of your perceptions involves focusing on the aspects of yourself, others, and the context that are influencing what you perceive.

- Checking the accuracy of your perceptions involves separating interpretation from fact, generating alternative perceptions, engaging in direct and indirect perception checking, and revising your perceptions as necessary.

KEY TERMS

attribution (p. 124)
egocentric (p. 121)
fundamental attribution error (p. 128)
interpersonal perception (p. 108)
interpretation (p. 111)
negativity bias (p. 123)

organization (p. 109)
overattribution (p. 130)
perception (p. 108)
perceptual set (p. 120)
positivity bias (p. 122)
primacy effect (p. 118)

recency effect (p. 118)
selection (p. 109)
self-serving bias (p. 127)
stereotypes (p. 116)

DISCUSSION QUESTIONS

1. What inaccurate perceptions do people often have of you? Why are people prone to making those perceptual mistakes? What perceptual mistakes concerning other people do you find yourself making?

2. Why is the idea of stereotyping so distasteful to many people?

3. If we recognize that our perceptions are always limited, what can we do to improve our perception making? How can we make our perceptions *less* limited?

4. What is the difference between a fact and an interpretation? How can you tell the difference?

PRACTICE QUIZ

MULTIPLE CHOICE

1. A characteristic that does *not* make a particular stimulus more likely to be selected for attention is that
   a. it is unusual
   b. it is expected
   c. you are frequently exposed to it
   d. it is of high intensity

2. Lacking the ability to take another person's perspective is known as
   a. egocentrism
   b. id
   c. superego
   d. cultural relativism

3. Cherie sees her new partner as perfect, although her friends can see many flaws. Cherie is experiencing
   a. negativity bias
   b. positivity bias
   c. perceptual set
   d. egocentrism

4. Frankie believes that he got into graduate school at his top-choice university because he is a good student. Jolie believes that she was not accepted for admission to her first-pick university because she is an out-of-state student. Frankie and Jolie are engaging in
   a. overattribution
   b. attributional reasoning
   c. self-serving bias
   d. errors in judgment

5. The predisposition to perceive only what we want or expect to perceive is known as
   a. interpretation
   b. organization
   c. attribution
   d. perceptual set

FILL IN THE BLANK

6. The first of the three stages of perception is the _____ stage.

7. A _____ is a set of behaviors that is expected of someone in a particular social situation.

8. According to the _____, first impressions are crucial because they set the tone for future interactions.

9. The _____ posits that the most recent impression we have of someone is more powerful than our earlier impressions.

10. Singling out one or two obvious characteristics of a person and attributing everything he or she does to those characteristics is known as _____.

ANSWERS

Multiple Choice: 1 (b); 2 (a); 3 (b); 4 (c); 5 (d); **Fill in the Blank:** 6 (selection); 7 (social role); 8 (primacy effect); 9 (recency effect); 10 (overattribution)

RESEARCH LIBRARY

MOVIES

Crash (drama; 2004; R)

This movie illustrates tensions fueled by stereotypes among characters living in Los Angeles. The story portrays tense interactions involving an African American television director and his wife, a Mexican locksmith, a middle-aged Korean couple, a Caucasian district attorney and his wife, a Persian store owner, two carjackers, and others, each of whom acts on his or her stereotypes about ethnicity, age, and social class. The film is a powerful illustration of the ease with which we recall stereotypes and the extent to which they can affect our behavior.

Inception (drama; 2010; PG-13)

In this movie, Leonardo DiCaprio and Joseph Gordon-Levitt play corporate spies who steal information by entering the subconscious minds of their targets. When a wealthy client requests that they plant an idea in the mind of a competitor, the spies and their accomplices induce their target into a deep dream that blurs the line between perception and reality.

BOOKS AND JOURNAL ARTICLES

Goldstein, E. B. (2007). *Sensation and perception* (7th ed.). Pacific Grove, CA: Wadsworth.

Hughes, P. C., & Baldwin, J. R. (2002). Communication and stereotypical impressions. *Howard Journal of Communication, 13,* 113–128.

Kellerman, K. (1989). The negativity effect in interaction: It's all in your point of view. *Human Communication Research, 16,* 147–183.

Manusov, V., & Harvey, J. H. (Eds.). (2001). *Attribution, communication behavior, and close relationships.* Cambridge, England: Cambridge University Press.

WEBSITES

https://implicit.harvard.edu/implicit/demo/
This site describes the Implicit Association Test, an assessment of your prejudices toward others, and allows you to take the test for yourself.

http://changingminds.org/explanations/theories/stereotypes.htm
This website describes the process of stereotyping and provides additional detail not only on how people use stereotypes but also on how we can change our stereotypes.

5 Language

WORDS CAN HEAL OLD WOUNDS

Heartfelt words of apology can mend emotional wounds, restore relationships, and inspire change, even when those words come half a century after the fact. Such was the case when Elwin Wilson—a white southern man—apologized in 2009 for having attacked John Lewis—an African American—in the "whites only" waiting room of a Greyhound bus station in 1961. Lewis was a member of the U.S. House of Representatives in 2009, but at that earlier time he was a freedom rider in the racial equality movement of Martin Luther King Jr., while Wilson was a young man aggressively opposed to racial integration.

After the election of Barack Obama to the presidency in 2008, Wilson began a personal crusade to make amends to those he had wronged. When Wilson was reunited with Representative Lewis, the congressman said, "For you to come here today, it's amazing to me. It's unreal. It's unbelievable. Maybe, just maybe, others will come forward because there needs to be this healing. Good to see you, my friend."

Finding the right words can be challenging under the most ordinary circumstances, let alone extraordinary ones. We may not always know what to say to make someone feel comforted, informed, entertained, motivated, or persuaded. If we know how to use language effectively, however, we can employ it to accomplish those goals in our personal relationships—and many others.

1 The Nature of Language

Many species communicate in one form or another, but we humans are the only creatures on the planet who use language. Although most of us are born with verbal ability, we have to learn the specific languages we use; and, like most learned skills, our language abilities improve as we practice and learn about them.

In this chapter's opening story, Elwin Wilson communicated his sincere apologies to Representative John Lewis in words. Like Wilson, we use language as a way to represent or symbolize our thoughts and feelings.

> **language** A structured system of symbols used for communicating meaning.

We can understand **language** as a structured system of symbols used for communicating meaning. Many scientists believe that language evolved from early humans' use of gestures to communicate.[1] For instance, many of us hold out our hands when we ask for something. We share this gesture with other primates, such as chimpanzees. The human brain, however, appears to have a specific capacity for learning and using language that is not shared by other species. Researchers in the field of biolinguistics have proposed that our advanced cognitive capacity has allowed humans to develop the symbolic system we know as language.[2]

The human brain seems to have a specific capacity for learning and using language that is not shared by other species. This scan of the left half of the human brain contrasts the different areas used in aspects of language activity, including generating words, hearing words, seeing words, and speaking words.

Generating words

Hearing words

Seeing words

Speaking words

You can probably think of many behaviors and items that represent or symbolize some type of meaning. A smile often symbolizes happiness, for instance; a red traffic light symbolizes the need to stop. Many gestures also have symbolic meaning, in that they represent a particular concept or idea. For example, you probably wave to say "hello" or shrug your shoulders to say "I don't know." Significantly, although traffic lights, gestures, and facial expressions all symbolize meaning, none of those behaviors or items qualifies as a language. Instead, a language is characterized by the use of a specific type of symbol: words.

Words are the building blocks of verbal communication. As we'll see in this chapter, we use words to represent ideas, observations, feelings, and thoughts. Words have a profound influence on how we relate to others. One key point here is that the power of verbal communication isn't limited to the words we speak; it also includes the words we write. When we hear the term *verbal*, we sometimes think only of spoken language. In fact, written messages are also verbal, because they also use words. Keep that in mind as we take a look at some of the most important features of language.

Language Is Symbolic

Language is symbolic. That statement means that each word represents a particular object or idea, but it does not constitute the object or idea itself. For example, the word *barn* represents a structure often used for storing hay, grain, or livestock. The word itself is not the structure; rather, it merely symbolizes it. Similarly, the word *five* represents a specific quantity of something (one more than four and one fewer than six), but the word itself is not the quantity; it simply represents it.

One way to understand the symbolic nature of language is to remember that different languages have different words for the same thing. The English word *barn*, for instance, is *schuur* in Dutch, *celeiro* in Portuguese, 축사 in Korean, and σιταποθήκη in Greek. Those are completely different symbols, but they all represent the same object or idea. If you were to invent your own language, you could create any term you wanted to represent the concept of a barn.

As an illustration of the use of different symbols to represent the same idea, Figure 5.1 displays the word *speak* as represented in five different alphabets. These include (1) the Roman alphabet, with which you are already familiar; (2) Braille, an alphabet consisting of raised dots, used by people who are blind to read and write; (3) Morse code, a system of long and short sounds used to communicate by means of a telegraph machine; (4) American Sign Language, a system of gestures and body language used to communicate with people who have hearing impairments; and (5) Gregg shorthand, a symbolic alphabet used for rapid note taking. Notice how different those symbols look, even though they are all symbolizing the same idea.

We saw in Chapter 1 that the meaning of words—that is, what they symbolize—can change over time. For instance, *awful* used to mean "full of awe," and *neck* used to mean "a parcel of land" (as in "my neck of the woods"). Those terms now symbolize something different, and it is entirely possible that they will represent something different in the future. This example illustrates the important point that the symbolic nature of language is never static. Rather, it changes and evolves as words take on new meanings.

Language Is Arbitrary (Mostly)

Why do words symbolize the particular things they do? For the most part, words have only an arbitrary connection to their meanings.[3] Think of the word *car*. The actual word doesn't look like a car or sound like a car, so why does it make us think of one? The only reason is that speakers of English

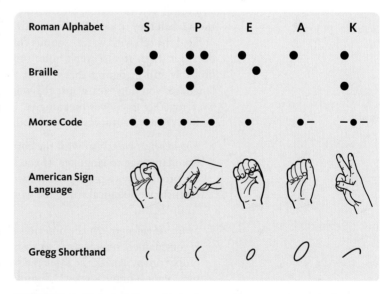

FIGURE 5.1 Alphabet Soup Many forms of language have their own alphabets. Here is the word SPEAK according to several different language systems.

have agreed to give the word *car* that particular meaning. We could just as easily call cars "whickles" or "geps" or "mumqualls." Those words don't mean anything, but they would if we assigned them a meaning. The point is that the meaning of almost all words is arbitrary: Words literally mean whatever we, as users of a language, choose for them to mean.

Language can be arbitrary precisely because it is symbolic. As we saw earlier, words only symbolize their meanings; they don't constitute their meanings themselves. For that reason, we can assign almost any word to symbolize a particular meaning, making the connection between language and meaning arbitrary.

onomatopoeia A word formed by imitating the sound associated with its meaning.

One major exception to that rule is **onomatopoeia,** a word formed by imitating the sound associated with its meaning. Words such as *buzz, meow, splash,* and *click* are all onomatopoetic words because their sounds reflect their meanings. For that reason, we can say that those types of words have an *iconic* connection to their meanings—that is, they serve as an icon or a representation of the meaning they symbolize—rather than an arbitrary one.

It's worth noting, however, that even onomatopoeia varies by language. To a U.S. American speaker of English, a dog goes "bowwow," but to an Indonesian, it says "gong gong." A sheep says "baa" to an English speaker, but "me'e'e" to the Navajo. The sound of a gunshot is "bang" in the United States but "pum" to the Spanish, "peng" to the Germans, and "pan" to the French.[4]

Language Is Governed by Rules

We have said that language is symbolic and that the meaning of most words is arbitrary. That assertion leads to an obvious question: How is it that we all understand one another? The answer is that every language is governed by rules.

Even if you can't state all the rules of your native language, you generally notice them when they're violated. To a native speaker of English, for instance, the statement "I filled the tub with water" sounds correct, but the phrase "I filled water into the tub" does not. Even if you aren't quite sure why the second sentence sounds wrong, you probably still recognize that it does. Along these same lines, when you learn a new language, you don't learn just the words; you also learn the rules for how the words work together to convey meaning.

Researchers distinguish among four types of language rules:

- *Phonological rules* deal with the correct pronunciation of a word, and they vary from language to language. If you speak French, for example, you know that the proper way to pronounce *travail* is "trah-VYE." In contrast, according to English phonological rules, the word looks as though it should be pronounced "trah-VALE."

- *Syntactic rules* govern the ordering of words within phrases. The question "What is your name?" makes sense to an English speaker because the words are in the proper order. To ask the same question in American Sign Language, we would sign "your – name – what?" Signing "what – your – name?" is incorrect.

- *Semantic rules* have to do with the meanings of individual words. These meanings may be arbitrary, as we have seen, but they are agreed upon by speakers of a language. When you hear the word *car,* for instance, you think of an automobile, not

RULES OF LANGUAGE

Phonological Rules	Deal with the correct pronunciation of words
Syntactic Rules	Dictate the proper order of words for the intended meaning
Semantic Rules	Govern the meanings of individual words
Pragmatic Rules	Deal with the implications or interpretations of statements

a washing machine, a rock concert, or an iPad. It is a semantic rule that connects *car* with "automobile" and not with one of the other meanings.

- *Pragmatic rules* deal with the implications or interpretations of statements. Think of the phrase "Nice to meet you," a common greeting among speakers of English. Depending on the context and the speaker's tone of voice, you might think the speaker really is happy to meet you, or you might infer that he or she is just saying so to be polite. If the speaker's tone is sarcastic, you might even infer that he or she is actually unhappy to meet you. In each instance, it is pragmatic rules that lead you to your conclusion.

The "At a Glance" box summarizes the four types of language rules.

As children acquire a language, they gain an almost intuitive sense of its phonological, syntactic, semantic, and pragmatic rules. That knowledge allows native speakers of a language to speak and write fluently. In contrast, people who are less familiar with the language are more prone to violate these rules.[5]

Language Has Layers of Meaning

Many words imply certain ideas that differ from their literal meanings. The literal meaning of a word—that is, its dictionary definition—is called its **denotative meaning.** Think of the word *home.* Its denotative meaning is "a shelter used as a residence." When you hear the word *home,* however, you probably also think of a concept such as "a place where I feel safe, accepted, and loved" or "a space where I am free to do whatever I want." Those are examples of the word's **connotative meaning,** the implications that a word suggests in addition to its literal meaning.

denotative meaning
A word's literal meaning or dictionary definition.

connotative meaning
A word's implied or secondary meaning, in addition to its literal meaning.

THE SEMANTIC TRIANGLE.   To illustrate the relationship between words and their denotative and connotative meanings, psychologist Charles Ogden and English professor Ivor Richards developed the *semantic triangle* (Figure 5.2).[6] In its three corners, the semantic triangle portrays three necessary elements for identifying the meaning in language. The first element is the *symbol,* which is the word being communicated. In the second corner is the *referent,* which is the word's denotative meaning. Finally, there's the *reference,* or the connotative meaning.

As the semantic triangle illustrates, if several listeners hear the same word, they might attribute the same denotative meaning to it but different connotative meanings. For instance, if I say "euthanasia," the word itself is the symbol, and its referent is a medically assisted death. To one listener, the word represents a merciful way to end a person's pain and suffering. To another person, it represents a form of homicide. To

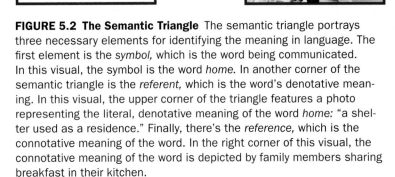

still other listeners, it represents an unfortunate—but sometimes justified—component of the death experience. These are all differences in the word's reference, or connotative meaning, rather than in its denotative meaning.

This example illustrates the essential point that the meanings of words are situated in the people who use them and not in the words themselves. Consequently, people may use a word such as *euthanasia* to connote a range of different meanings. As the transaction model of communication, discussed in Chapter 1, suggests, most words don't have meanings of their own but receive their meanings through the social interaction of the people who use them.

LOADED LANGUAGE.   In October 2008, the U.S. Congress passed the Economic Stimulus Act, which allowed the federal government to purchase up to $700 billion in troubled assets as a way to rouse the faltering economy. The law was highly controversial among members of Congress and other U.S. citizens, and the controversy was reflected in the language people used to describe it. For those who favored it, the Economic Stimulus Act was a "rescue plan," but for many who opposed it, it was a "bailout." Both of those terms are examples of **loaded language,** words with strongly positive or negative connotations. Notice that "rescue plan" sounds positive because it conjures images of a hero saving the innocent victims of a crisis. "Bailout," however, sounds negative because it connotes begrudgingly helping people deal with problems they themselves have created.

FIGURE 5.2 The Semantic Triangle The semantic triangle portrays three necessary elements for identifying the meaning in language. The first element is the *symbol,* which is the word being communicated. In this visual, the symbol is the word *home.* In another corner of the semantic triangle is the *referent,* which is the word's denotative meaning. In this visual, the upper corner of the triangle features a photo representing the literal, denotative meaning of the word *home*: "a shelter used as a residence." Finally, there's the *reference,* which is the connotative meaning of the word. In the right corner of this visual, the connotative meaning of the word is depicted by family members sharing breakfast in their kitchen.

loaded language Terms that carry strongly positive or strongly negative connotations.

Loaded language reflects the observation that denotations and connotations represent different layers of meaning. At a denotative level, for instance, the word *cancer* refers to a malignant growth or tumor in the body. For many people, however, the term connotes any evil condition that spreads destructively. For example, you might hear someone describe a condition such as poverty or bigotry as a "cancer on society." That example illustrates that people can use the word *cancer* as a loaded term when they wish to evoke feelings of fear, disgust, or anger on the part of listeners. People can also use loaded words to evoke positive emotions. Terms such as *peace, family,* and *freedom* have emotionally positive connotations, even though their denotative meanings are emotionally neutral.[7]

Language Varies in Clarity

Josh is driving his brother Jeremy to an appointment with a new physician, and Jeremy has the directions. As they approach an intersection, they have the following conversation:

Josh: I need to turn left at this next light, don't I?

Jeremy: Right.

Words such as mother *and* marriage *have emotionally positive connotations, even though their denotative meanings are neutral. A term such as* marriage *generates controversy among some groups of people when it is applied to same-sex couples.*

Which way should Josh turn? When Jeremy responded to Josh's question by answering "right," was he saying that Josh was correct in thinking he should turn left, or was he correcting Josh by instructing him to turn right? We don't really know, because Jeremy has used **ambiguous language** by making a statement that we can interpret to have more than one meaning. Jeremy's reply was ambiguous because the word *right* could mean either "correct" or "turn right" in this situation.

A certain amount of ambiguity is inherent in our language. In fact, according to the *Oxford English Dictionary* (*OED*), the 500 most frequently used words in the English language have an average of 23 meanings each. The word *set* has so many meanings—nearly 200, more than any other English word—that it takes the *OED* 60,000 words to define it![8]

One reason language varies in clarity is that some words are more concrete than others. A word that is *concrete* refers to a specific object in the physical world, such as a particular laptop computer, a specific restaurant, or an individual person. In contrast, a word that is *abstract* refers to a broader category or organizing concept of objects. According to English professor Samuel Hayakawa, words can be arrayed along a "ladder of abstraction" that shows their progression from more abstract to more concrete.[9]

An example of Hayakawa's ladder of abstraction appears in Figure 5.3. At the bottom of the ladder is a reference to all living beings, which is a broad, abstract category. Moving upward, the concepts become more and more concrete, referring to all animals, then all mammals, all primates, all *Homo sapiens,* and all males, before reaching the most concrete reference to a specific individual.

> **ambiguous language** Language having more than one possible meaning.

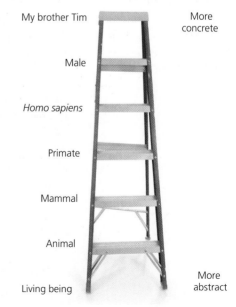

My brother Tim — More concrete

Male

Homo sapiens

Primate

Mammal

Animal

Living being — More abstract

FIGURE 5.3 Ladder of Abstraction According to English professor Samuel Hayakawa, words can be arrayed along a "ladder of abstraction" that shows their progression from more abstract to more concrete. In this figure, the bottom of the ladder refers to a living being, a broad, abstract category.

Language Is Bound by Context and Culture

Finally, the meaning in language is affected by the social and cultural context in which it is used. Societies and cultures differ in many ways, including their degree of individualism and their use of communication codes. Many of those differences are reflected in people's verbal messages. For instance, when you hear someone say, "I'm looking out for number one," you're hearing a very self-focused message that would be less common in a collectivistic than an individualistic society. In fact, a common Japanese adage is "It is the nail that sticks out that gets hammered down," which reflects the collectivistic culture of that nation.[10]

Studies have shown that for individuals who speak more than one language, the choice of language can affect their perceptions.[11] While completing a values test, for instance, students in Hong Kong expressed more traditional Chinese values while speaking Cantonese than while speaking English. Jewish and Arab students in Israel both described themselves as more distinct from outsiders when speaking their native languages than when speaking English. Just as each language is distinctive, the language we use leads us to see the world in a particular way.

In fact, the idea that language shapes our views of reality was proposed by anthropologist Edward Sapir and linguist Benjamin Whorf in what became known as the **Sapir-Whorf hypothesis.** Their notion was that language influences the ways that members of a culture see the world—and that the attitudes and behaviors of a culture's people are reflected in its language.[12]

The Sapir-Whorf hypothesis embodies two specific principles. The first, called *linguistic determinism,* suggests that the structure of language determines how we think. In other words, we can conceive of something only if we have a term for it in our vocabulary.[13] Imagine a language, for instance, that includes no word describing the emotion of envy. According to the principle of linguistic determinism, people who speak that language would not experience envy because their experiences of the world would be limited to what their language allowed them to communicate about.

The second principle, called *linguistic relativity,* suggests that because language determines our perceptions of reality, people who speak different languages will see the world differently. In his research, for instance, Whorf discovered that the language of the Hopi Indians makes no distinction between nouns and verbs. Whereas English uses nouns to refer to things and verbs to refer to actions, the Hopi language describes just about everything as an action or a process. Compared with English speakers, then, the Hopi tend to see the world as being constantly in motion.[14]

Sapir-Whorf hypothesis
The idea that language influences the ways that members of a culture see and think about the world.

LEARN IT What does it mean to say that language is symbolic? How is onomatopoeia an exception to the rule that language is arbitrary? How do syntactic rules differ from semantic rules? Describe the difference between a word's denotative meaning and its connotative meaning. When is a word or phrase ambiguous? What is the Sapir-Whorf hypothesis?

APPLY IT To observe how language evolves, invent a new word or expression. Write out a definition for it, and begin using it in everyday conversation with your friends. Take note of how well your word or expression catches on and whether your friends begin using it in their own conversations.

REFLECT ON IT In what ways is your language use affected by your culture? Where did you learn all the rules associated with your native language?

FACT OR fiction?

LANGUAGE DETERMINES WHAT WE CAN THINK ABOUT

The Sapir-Whorf hypothesis implies that if we don't have a word for a particular concept, we cannot experience that concept. It also implies that people who speak different languages will see the world differently because of the differences in their languages. Are these ideas fact or fiction?

It's hard to tell for certain, but the Sapir-Whorf hypothesis has been widely criticized by researchers. Three criticisms are common.

The first criticism centers on the cause-and-effect relationship between language and thought. The Sapir-Whorf hypothesis proposes that language shapes and constrains how we think. It is equally possible, though, that our thoughts shape and constrain our language. For instance, an experienced fashion designer might look at four jackets and label their colors "scarlet," "ruby," "crimson," and "vermilion." You might look at the same jackets and call them all "red." Does the designer think of the four colors as different because she has more terms for them than you do, or does she have more terms because she has more experience thinking about differences among colors? It's difficult to know for sure, but either idea is possible.

Second, even if people don't have a word for a particular experience, such as the stress of trying to speak a foreign language, that doesn't necessarily mean they don't have that experience. Perhaps you can recall feeling stress at learning another language, even if you didn't have a specific term for it.

Finally, as linguist Steven Pinker has pointed out, even people who don't acquire language, perhaps because of mental or cognitive deficiencies, are able to think, count, and interact with others. They wouldn't be able to do those things if language determined thought.

Those criticisms don't necessarily mean that the Sapir-Whorf hypothesis is entirely wrong. They suggest, however, that language doesn't shape and constrain our ways of thinking quite to the extent that Sapir and Whorf believed.

ASK YOURSELF

■ What did you think of the Sapir-Whorf hypothesis when you first read about it? Did it seem reasonable or unreasonable to you?

■ Do you think only in words? Do you ever think in numbers, colors, or sounds? If you didn't know any languages, would you lack the ability to think?

Source: Pinker, S. (1994). *The language instinct.* New York: HarperCollins.

The Sapir-Whorf hypothesis is provocative, but is it true? We'll examine some of the evidence in the "Fact or Fiction?" box.

2 Appreciating the Power of Words

English writer Rudyard Kipling, author of *The Jungle Book,* once called words "the most powerful drug used by mankind." To understand his point, think about how you feel when someone you love expresses affection to you, or when you listen to a speech by a politician you can't stand, or when you have to comfort a grieving friend. Words can literally change a person's day—or a person's life—in positive or negative ways.

Whole books have been written about the power of language. Here we'll focus on five important contexts in which words have special power: naming, persuasion, credibility and power, affection, and comfort.

Naming Defines and Differentiates Us

What's something that belongs to you yet is constantly used by others? The answer is *your name.*

A name is simply a linguistic device that identifies something or someone. Your name does more, however, than just differentiate you from others—it's also an important component of your sense of self. From the perspective of interpersonal communication, naming is one way we represent ourselves to others and one way we gain information about other people. Let's examine how names relate to identity and look at some common ways that names come about.

NAMING AND IDENTITY. As we considered in an earlier chapter, first impressions are often critical to the perception we form of someone. Although impressions are influenced by factors such as a person's appearance or behaviors, they can also be shaped by his or her name. A person's first name, for instance, frequently suggests information about the person's demographic characteristics. One such characteristic is the person's sex. In Western societies, for instance, we usually assign names such as Jacob, Michael, and Caleb only to males and names such as Emma, Savannah, and Nicole to females.

Names can also provide clues about a person's ethnicity. For example, you might infer that LaKeisha is African American, Huong is Asian, and Santiago is Latino. Some names even suggest a person's age group, so you might assume that Jennifer, Emily, and Hannah are younger than Edna, Mildred, and Bertha.

In addition to demographic information, names can suggest information about our disposition and sense of self. For instance, we might perceive an adult man who goes by the name William differently than one who goes by Billy, even though those are two forms of the same name. Indeed, research shows that we do make assumptions about people—accurately or not—on the basis of their names.[15]

In one study, for instance, people made more positive evaluations of men named David, Jon, Joshua, and Gregory than they did of men named Oswald, Myron, Reginald, and Edmund, even though they were given no information about the men other than their names.[16] Other studies have shown that people whose first names strongly suggest a non-white ethnicity sometimes experience discrimination based only on their names.[17]

NAMING PRACTICES. In the United States, the Social Security Administration keeps track of the most popular first names given to newborns throughout the country. Certain names have remained fashionable for quite some time. Beginning in 1880, for example, Mary and John were the most popular female and male first names nearly every year until 1926, when Robert took over the top spot for boys. Mary dominated the list for girls until 1947, when it was replaced with Linda. As times change, though, so do naming preferences. By 1985, Jessica and Michael were the most popular first names. Sophia and Aiden topped the list in 2010.[18] Table 5.1 lists the most popular first names since 1900.

TABLE 5.1

Popular Names over the Last Century

Year	Top Three Boys' Names	Top Three Girls' Names
2010	Aiden Jacob Jackson	Sophia Isabella Olivia
1975	Michael Jason Christopher	Jennifer Amy Heather
1950	James Robert John	Linda Mary Patricia
1925	Robert John William	Mary Dorothy Betty
1900	John William James	Mary Helen Anna

Practices of naming also vary according to culture and religion. In predominantly Catholic communities around the world, for instance, males are often given a feminine middle name, such as Marie or Maria. (In French Catholic families, men often have a compound first name, such as Paul-Marie, to accommodate the same tradition.) These naming practices appear to reflect cultural traditions rather than specific church doctrine. Among the Sikh of India, boys are given the surname Singh and girls the surname Kaur, although adults of both sexes often take these as middle names instead. The Sikh practice of giving common surnames to all boys and girls is meant to symbolize the abolition of class inequalities. Amish children receive their fathers' surname and are commonly given the first letter of their mother's maiden name as their middle name; thus, the son of Mary Jacobs would have the middle name J (with no period). This practice is intended to honor both the maternal and the paternal lineages.

Amish naming practices honor both maternal and paternal lineages.

In many parts of the world, it is also traditional for women to adopt their husband's last name when they marry, or at least to add his name to hers. So, when marrying George Rogers, Jean Levitt might become Jean Rogers, or Jean Levitt Rogers, or Jean Levitt-Rogers. Alternatively, she might choose to remain Jean Levitt. What factors influence that decision?

In a study by communication researchers Karen Foss and Belle Edson, married women who kept their birth names gave more importance to their personal concerns than to their relationships. In contrast, women who took their husband's names rated their relationships as more important than issues of self. Women who hyphenated their last names were in the middle, rating their relationships and personal concerns about equally.[19]

Other research has confirmed that women who retain their birth names at marriage score higher than other women on self-reports of masculinity and feminist attitudes.[20] However, name changers and name keepers don't appear to differ from each other in their self-esteem, autonomy, or reports about the balance of control in their marriages.[21]

To an extent, then, your name tells your story. Like your clothes or your hairstyle, it is a part of how you present yourself to others and how others relate to you.

We Use Words to Persuade

Persuasion is the process of moving people to think or act in a certain way. Every time we watch a TV commercial, read a billboard, or listen to a political speech, someone is trying to influence our beliefs or behavior. Much of our ability to persuade others comes from the language we use. Greek philosopher Aristotle (384–322 B.C.) described three forms of *rhetorical proof,* which are ways to support a persuasive argument. He explained that persuasive messages could be supported by appeals to ethos, pathos, and logos.

Let's say you're trying to persuade your neighbor to support a proposition that would raise his property taxes but increase the security of area schools. What are some ways of asking for his support that would encourage him to agree?

APPEALING TO ETHOS. Aristotle recognized that, to be persuaded, people needed to have positive regard for the person whose message they were considering. Consequently, a speaker who appears respectable and trustworthy is generally more persuasive than one who does not.[22] Aristotle used the term **ethos** to refer to a speaker's respectability, trustworthiness, and moral character.[23]

> **ethos** A speaker's respectability, trustworthiness, and moral character.

One strategy for persuading your neighbor, therefore, is to appeal to your level of knowledge and expertise with respect to the topic. Your neighbor may be inclined to defer to your opinion about the proposition if your opinion seems more trustworthy and better informed than his own. In contrast, if your description of the proposition comes across as ill informed, your neighbor may not respect it enough to find it persuasive.

Note that judgments about ethos always belong to the people with whom you're speaking. Listeners decide for themselves how much integrity, respectability, and trustworthiness a speaker has. Good persuasive speakers therefore establish and reinforce their ethos, knowing that it will enhance their persuasive abilities.[24]

APPEALING TO PATHOS. A second persuasive strategy is to appeal to people's emotions. When people are emotionally aroused, their receptivity to new ideas is enhanced. Aristotle used the term **pathos** to refer to listeners' emotions, and he understood that emotion can be a significant persuasive tool.

> **pathos** Listeners' emotions.

Although stirring virtually any emotion can be persuasive, people's interpersonal emotional appeals often focus on generating negative emotions—such as fear, guilt, disgust, anger, and sadness—particularly when a change in behavior is the desired outcome.[25] The reason is that we generally dislike experiencing such emotions, so we are motivated to respond to the persuasive appeal as a way of reducing those feelings. Some research has shown, however, that appealing to positive emotions—such as joy or gratitude—can be more effective when the goal is to change someone's opinions rather than his or her behaviors.

You might use an emotional appeal when asking your neighbor to support the school safety proposition. Since your goal is to affect his behavior (specifically, his voting behavior), you could employ a fear appeal by asking him to imagine how scared he would be if one if his own children were abducted from the school grounds. That fear might then motivate him to vote for the proposition increasing school security. Some additional examples of emotional appeals appear in Table 5.2.

APPEALING TO LOGOS. A third way to persuade people is to appeal to their sense of reason. If a particular belief, opinion, or

TABLE 5.2

Some Examples of Emotional Appeals

Suppose you were trying to persuade your aunt to stop smoking. Here are examples of appeals to pathos that you might use.

Type of Appeal	Example Statement
Appeal to fear	Thousands of people die from lung cancer every year; you could be next.
Appeal to guilt	Think about how many innocent children you're hurting every day with secondhand smoke.
Appeal to joy	Imagine how happy you'd be if you were free of your nicotine addiction.
Appeal to disgust	See this charred skin tissue? That's what your lungs look like right now.
Appeal to shame	You're an embarrassment to your family when you smoke.
Appeal to anger	Aren't you sick and tired of nicotine controlling every day of your life?
Appeal to sadness	Imagine saying goodbye to your kids because smoking claimed your life.

[APPEALING TO LOGOS]

Use logical arguments to persuade others.

WHAT?

Learn to persuade through the use of logic and reason.

WHY?

To encourage individuals to think or act in a particular way by appealing to their sense of reason, as when you are trying to get someone to end a dangerous practice (such as drinking and driving) or to persuade a person to contribute to a cause you support.

HOW?

1. Select someone you want to persuade and an issue on which you want to persuade the person. For example, suppose you want to persuade your father to pay for your study abroad next summer.

2. In a letter, lay out two specific reasons why the person should do as you suggest. Remember, your goal is to show why your suggested action makes sense. So, be sure to appeal to logic, not emotion.

3. For each reason, give evidence for your claims. For the study-abroad example, you might explain how study abroad helps students get better-paying jobs when they graduate. You might support that claim using information from your school's study-abroad office.

TRY!

1. Write your persuasive letter, but don't send it to the addressee. Rather, share it with a small group in your class or with your instructor, for feedback on ways to make the logic in your arguments more persuasive.

2. Once you have received feedback on your letter, you may either keep it or send it and see if it is persuasive.

CONSIDER: *In what instances is it more persuasive to appeal to reason than to emotion?*

got **SKILLS** ?

behavior makes good sense, then people will be inclined to adopt it if they have the capacity to do so. Logical appeals aren't always effective, particularly if some other force—such as an addiction—influences a person's behavior. When people are free to choose their beliefs, opinions, and behaviors, however, they are frequently persuaded by a solidly logical argument. Aristotle used the term **logos** to refer to listeners' ability to reason.

To **reason** means to make judgments about the world based on evidence rather than emotion or intuition. When we appeal to logos, we formulate logical arguments that support our position, and we provide specific information or evidence to bolster those arguments. To maximize our effectiveness, we attempt to select the arguments and evidence we believe will be most relevant to our listeners.

Perhaps you've heard your neighbor complain in the past about the high tax burden of living in your municipal area. That dissatisfaction suggests to you that he will not be excited about the prospect of a tax increase. To persuade him to support the school safety proposition, you might therefore explain to him how the increase in property taxes will be offset by a decrease in the city's emergency services fees, given that school security will be enhanced. To support your argument, you could show him the relevant figures from the county auditor's report, as published in your local newspaper. Rather than arousing his emotions or enhancing his personal respect for you, such a tactic appeals to your neighbor's sense of logic and reason. You can test your ability to appeal to reason by checking out the "Got Skills?" box.

> **logos** Listeners' ability to reason.

> **reason** To make judgments about the world based on evidence rather than emotion or intuition.

Credibility Empowers Us

credibility The extent to which others find someone's words and actions trustworthy.

Our **credibility** is the extent to which others perceive us to be competent and trustworthy. Some speakers have credibility on certain topics because of their training and expertise. You'll probably have more confidence in medical advice if you hear it from a doctor or a nurse, for instance, than if you hear it from the barista at your local coffee shop. If the advice is about making a great latte, however, you'll probably trust your barista more than your doctor or nurse. In either case, you are assigning credibility on the basis of the speaker's specific expertise.

It might seem as though training and expertise automatically give a person credibility. In fact, however, credibility is a perception that is influenced not only by a person's credentials but also by his or her actions and words. One journalist, for instance, might be perceived as highly credible because she always double-checks her facts and represents all opinions on an issue. Another journalist with the same training might be perceived as less credible if he has made factual errors in the past or if his writing seems slanted toward a particular view. Many people in the public eye, such as politicians, work hard to be perceived as credible, knowing they can lose public support if they aren't.

Language is intimately tied to issues of credibility. Irrespective of our training or credentials, our words can portray us as confident, trustworthy communicators, or they can make us appear unsure of ourselves. In either situation, our ability to get what we want out of our interpersonal interactions is affected by the credibility that our use of language gives us.

CLICHÉS.   Several forms of language have the potential either to enhance or to damage perceptions of a person's credibility. One language practice that can diminish credibility is the use of *clichés,* or phrases that were novel at one time but have lost their effect because of overuse. When politicians talk about "the promise of change" or businesspeople refer to "thinking outside the box," they may lose credibility with their audiences because those phrases are clichés that may make speakers sound uninformed or out-of-touch.

DIALECTS.   People can also affect perceptions of their credibility by using certain *dialects,* which are variations on a language that are shared by people of a certain region or social class. Many U.S. Americans, for example, can tell the difference between a speaker from the South and one from New England on the basis of the words these speakers use. The southern speaker might use words characteristic of a southern dialect, such as saying "y'all" to mean "you all," whereas the speech of the New Englander might reflect the dialect of that region, perhaps calling something "wicked good" rather than "very good."

According to *communication accommodation theory,* we may be able to enhance our credibility by speaking in a dialect that is familiar to our audience.[26] In contrast, when we use a dialect that is different from that of our listeners, we can cause them to see us as an outsider, and such a perception might lead them to question our credibility.

EQUIVOCATION.   Another form of language that sometimes influences a speaker's credibility is *equivocation,* or language that disguises the speaker's true intentions through strategic ambiguity. We often use equivocal language when we're in a dilemma, a situation in which none of our options is good.

Suppose, for example, that you're asked to provide a reference for your friend Dylan, who is applying for a job on the town police force. You are asked how well

g@t connected

EQUIVOCATION ONLINE: GENDER AND LANGUAGE IN BLOGS

Some research suggests that males use more direct, less equivocal language than females do, at least in face-to-face settings where such patterns reflect stereotypical gender roles. In online interaction—as in a blog—however, communicators may have more anonymity and therefore feel less need to behave in gender-typical ways.

To find out whether males and females differ in their language patterns in blogs, Georgetown University researchers David Huffaker and Sandra Calvert analyzed 184 randomly selected blogs that were maintained by adolescents. They found that

- *Young men used more direct language than did young women.* Just as in face-to-face communication, males' language on blogs was characterized by greater directness, certainty, and tenacity, and less equivocation and ambivalence, than females' language.

- *Young men used more active and aggressive language than did young women.* The language of male bloggers was more aggressive, less passive, and more focused on activity, motion, and accomplishment than was the language of female bloggers, a finding that is also consistent with gender stereotypes.

- *Young women and men disclosed relatively equally.* Contrary to the stereotype of women self-disclosing more than men, the researchers found no sex differences in self-disclosure about most topics. Females were more likely than males to disclose the URL to their personal web pages, although males were more likely than females to disclose their physical locations.

Although this is just one study and it focused only on blogs (as opposed to other forms of computer-mediated communication), its conclusions suggest that some sex differences in face-to-face language use are also reflected in the way people interact online.

Source: Huffaker, D. A., & Calvert, S. L. (2005). Gender, identity, and language use in teenage blogs. *Journal of Computer-Mediated Communication, 10*(2). http://jcmc.indiana.edu/vol10/issue2/huffaker.html

---

Dylan handles pressure. Though Dylan is your friend, you can immediately think of several occasions when he hasn't handled pressure well. Now you're in a bind. On the one hand, you want Dylan to get the job because he's your friend. On the other hand, you don't want to lie to the police lieutenant who's phoning you for the reference.

Several studies have shown that when we're faced with two unappealing choices such as those, we often use equivocal language to get ourselves out of the bind.[27] In response to the lieutenant's question about how well Dylan handles pressure, for instance, you might say: "Well, that depends; there are lots of different kinds of pressure." Note that such a statement doesn't give the lieutenant much information. Instead, it might imply that you don't know how well Dylan handles pressure but you don't want to admit that you don't know. It might also imply that you do know how well Dylan handles pressure but don't want to say. In either case, you are likely to come across as less credible than if you had answered the question directly.[28]

Researchers John Daly, Carol Diesel, and David Weber have suggested that those sorts of conversational dilemmas are common and that we frequently use equivocal language in such situations.[29] Other theorists, including the linguist Robin Lakoff, suggest that women use more equivocal language than men because equivocation reflects a lack of assertiveness that corresponds to feminine gender expectations.[30] Check out the "Get Connected" box to see whether such a difference in language use also appears online.

WEASEL WORDS.   A form of language related to equivocation is the use of *weasel words:* terms and phrases that are intended to mislead listeners by implying something that they don't actually say. Advertisers commonly use weasel words when making claims about their products. For instance, when you hear that "four out of five dentists prefer" a certain chewing gum, the implication is that 80 percent of all dentists prefer that brand. That would indeed be impressive—but that isn't what the statement actually said. For all we know, only five dentists were surveyed to begin with, making the support of "four out of five" appear much less impressive.

One way people use weasel words in interpersonal communication is by making broad, unsupported generalizations. To make herself sound intelligent and informed, for instance, Eva is fond of starting statements with "People say that . . ." or "It's widely known that . . ." These phrases are weasel words because they imply a broad level of agreement with whatever Eva is saying, but they provide no evidence of that agreement. That is, Eva never specifies which people say or know whatever she is claiming, or how many people say or know it, or why we should trust their beliefs or knowledge in the first place.

ALLNESS STATEMENTS.   One specific form of weasel words is an *allness statement,* or a declaration implying that a claim is true without exception. For instance, when you hear somebody claim that "experts agree that corporal punishment is emotionally damaging to children," the implication is that all experts agree. Note, however, that the speaker provides no evidence to back up that claim. Likewise, when someone says "There's no known cure for depression," the implication is that no cure exists. All the statement actually means, however, is that no cure is known to the speaker.

CHOOSING CREDIBLE LANGUAGE.   The various forms of speech we've examined can cause listeners to conclude that the speaker's words are imprecise, untrustworthy, and lacking in credibility. That perception can have negative effects on how other people respond to the speaker. Several studies have shown, for instance, that people perceive speakers who use such forms of language as less competent, less dynamic, and even less attractive than speakers whose language is free of those characteristics.[31] In fact, using even *one* of those forms is enough to taint someone else's perceptions of the speaker.[32]

More credible forms of speech avoid using weasel words and allness statements. Try this: Instead of claiming, for example, that what you're saying "is widely believed," simply state that *you* believe it, unless you do have evidence to support it. Instead of saying something like "experts agree" with what you're claiming, say that "some experts agree," and be prepared to give examples of those who do.

Language Expresses Affection and Intimacy

Language has a profound ability to communicate affection and create or enhance intimacy in our personal relationships. Affection and intimacy are closely related but not the same. *Affection* is an emotional experience that includes feelings of love and appreciation that one person has for another. In contrast, *intimacy* is a characteristic of close, supportive relationships. We humans use language both to convey our affectionate feelings for one another and to strengthen our intimate bonds with those who are most important to us.

Verbal statements can communicate affection or intimacy in many ways. Some statements express our feelings for another person, such as "I like you" and "I'm in love with you." Others reinforce the importance of our relationship with another person, such as "You're my best friend" and "I could never love anyone as much as I love you." Still others convey hopes or dreams for the future of the relationship, including "I can't wait to be married to you" and "I want us to be together forever." Finally, some statements express the value of a relationship by noting how we would feel without it, such as "I can't stand the thought of losing you" and "My life would be empty if I hadn't met you."

Statements like those are characteristic of our closest personal relationships. In fact, evidence suggests that communicating intimacy and affection is good both for relationships and for the people in them. For example, family studies researcher Ted Huston and his colleagues found that the more affection spouses communicated to each other during their first 2 years of marriage, the more likely they were still to be married 13 years later.[33] Other research has found that the more affection people receive from their parents during childhood, the lower their chances of developing depression, anxiety, and physical health problems later in life.[34]

We use language to convey affectionate feelings for others and to strengthen our intimate bonds.

Although verbal statements of affection and intimacy are probably more precise than nonverbal gestures (such as hugging), they can still be ambiguous. Consider, for instance, how many different meanings you can have when you say "I love you" to someone. Do you love that person romantically? As a platonic friend? As a family member? Research shows it's not uncommon for people to misinterpret verbal displays of affection—to think someone is expressing romantic love when he or she means to express platonic love, for instance.[35] That kind of situation can be very uncomfortable for both the sender and the receiver.

In many cases, nonverbal behaviors (such as tone of voice and facial expression) and contextual information help to clarify the meaning of an affectionate message. Nevertheless, there's still a risk of misinterpretation, especially when we use affectionate language with new friends or with people we don't know well.[36]

Words Provide Comfort and Healing

Finally, we use words to comfort people in distress. Exchanges of comfort can be mundane, as when a mother soothes a child with a stubbed toe. They can also occur in extraordinary circumstances, as when someone gives comfort and support to a young man who has lost his romantic partner to cancer.

Recall that verbal communication includes both written and spoken words. To convey support, we often use written messages. Consider that the greeting card industry is a $10 billion-a-year business. People send greeting cards not only to acknowledge birthdays and celebrate holidays but also to express verbal messages of comfort, such as through get-well and sympathy cards.[37] There are also cards that express gratitude and ones that convey hope. Bluemountain .com, a website from which people can send free electronic greeting cards, offers e-cards in several categories related to comfort and healing, including special cards for the families of deployed military personnel and for the remembrance of September 11 victims.[38]

USING LANGUAGE TO COMFORT OTHER PEOPLE. Perhaps you've tried to help someone who was grieving a significant loss but felt unsure about what to say. Professional counselors provide several specific tips for using language to comfort other people in times of loss:[39]

- *Acknowledge the loss:* "I'm so sorry to hear about your sister's accident. I know that everyone who knew her will miss her greatly."
- *Express sympathy:* "Words can't express how sorry I feel. Please know that my heartfelt sympathies are with you."
- *Offer a positive reflection:* "I will always remember your sister's wonderful sense of humor and her great compassion for others."
- *Offer assistance:* "Please remember I'm here for you, whatever you need. I'll give you a call this weekend to see if there's anything I can do for you."

In addition, many other situations call for words of comfort, such as a divorce, a job loss, or a serious illness. The words we use may be different in each case, but the underlying goals are the same: to acknowledge the person's feelings and to offer support.

USING LANGUAGE TO COMFORT OURSELVES. Just as we can use our words to comfort other people, we can also use them to comfort ourselves. Many people find that "journaling," or keeping a diary of their feelings, helps them find comfort and meaning even in traumatic events. In fact, some evidence indicates that writing about our thoughts and feelings can improve our health. Psychologist James Pennebaker has conducted many studies showing that when people write about a trauma they've gone through—such as physical abuse or the death of a loved one—they often experience reduced levels of stress hormones, strengthened immune systems, and a decrease in doctor visits.[40]

Pennebaker's theory is that holding in negative emotions requires effort that we might otherwise use to support our health. For that reason, expressing those emotions (even on paper) allows us to put that energy to better use. The healing effects of expressive writing can be so strong, in fact, that participants in Pennebaker's studies have seen improvements after only two or three writing sessions of 20 minutes each.

In a similar vein, communication scholars have shown that when people are in distress, writing about their positive feelings for a loved one can accelerate their recovery. In one experiment, for instance, participants were put through a series of stressful tasks, such as mentally solving complicated math problems under time constraints and watching video clips of married couples fighting.[41] Those tasks elevated their levels of the hormone cortisol, which the body produces under conditions of stress.

Research by psychologist James Pennebaker demonstrates the health benefits of expressing one's thoughts and feelings in a journal.

The participants were then assigned to one of three conditions. Participants in the first group were instructed to write a letter expressing their affection to someone they loved. The second group merely thought about a loved one but didn't put their feelings into words. Finally, the third group did nothing for 20 minutes. The researchers found that when people wrote about their affectionate feelings, their cortisol level returned to normal the most quickly. Putting their affectionate feelings into words accelerated their recovery from stress.

Just thinking about a loved one didn't provide any more benefit than doing nothing. Only those participants who translated their feelings into language recovered quickly from their elevated stress. As with Pennebaker's work, this study demonstrated the health benefits of using words to express one's feelings.

In summary, people use language to accomplish a number of important tasks. They assign people names and grant identities to others. They persuade others to adopt certain ideas or behaviors. They gain credibility and power. They convey affection and build intimacy with others. They provide comfort and support, both to others and to themselves. Many interpersonal situations require us to perform one or more of these tasks. Therefore, our understanding of how language serves those functions will help us communicate effectively in those contexts.

LEARN IT Which characteristics about a person are often implied by his or her name? How can you use an appeal to pathos to persuade someone? How is equivocation related to credibility? In what ways do we express affection to others verbally? What types of statements should messages of comfort contain?

APPLY IT When you're feeling stressed, try a version of Pennebaker's emotional writing activity. Sit quietly in a room with a pen and paper, and begin to write about your feelings. Why are you feeling stressed? What else are you feeling? Don't worry about punctuation and grammar; just write nonstop for at least 20 minutes. Even if you feel a little worse immediately afterward (because you've been thinking so hard about what's bothering you), notice how you feel later in the day. Does putting your feelings into words help your frame of mind?

REFLECT ON IT If you had to choose a different name for yourself, what would it be? Why? What makes one speaker more credible than another to you?

3 The Use and Abuse of Language

We've seen that language helps us achieve a wide variety of purposes. Now let's look at the ways in which language can vary in its form. Some forms, such as humor, are generally positive and can produce all sorts of good outcomes, such as entertaining others, strengthening relationships, and even contributing to healing. Others, such as hate speech, are known for the devastating hurt they can cause.

In this section, we explore several forms of language: humor, euphemism, slang, libel and slander, profanity, and hate speech. Many of these forms are neither entirely good nor entirely bad. Like many human inventions, language can be used well, and it can also be abused. We will look at examples of both.

Humor: What's So Funny?

A few years ago, psychologist Richard Wiseman designed a study with an ambitious goal: to discover the world's funniest joke. More than 2 million people from around the world visited his website and rated some 40,000 jokes for their level of humor. Here was the winning entry—the funniest joke in the world:

Two hunters are out in the woods when one of them collapses. He doesn't seem to be breathing, and his eyes are glazed. The other guy takes out his phone and calls the emergency services. He gasps: "My friend is dead! What can I do?" The operator says: "Calm down, I can help. First, let's make sure he's dead." There is a silence, then a gunshot is heard. Back on the phone, the guy says: "Okay, now what?"[42]

You may or may not find that joke funny, and you might even find it offensive. Nonetheless, you can probably recognize the humor in it. The joke contains what researchers believe to be the most important aspect of humor: a violation of our expectations. Most of us would interpret the operator's statement ("Let's make sure he's dead") as a suggestion to check the hunter's vital signs, not as a recommendation to shoot him. It's that twist on our expectations that makes the joke funny. In fact, researchers have discovered that specific parts of the brain process humor, and that without the violation of expectations—without the punch line—those neurological structures don't "light up" or provide the mental reward we associate with a good joke.[43]

Humor can enhance our interpersonal interactions in many ways. It can bring us closer to others and make social interaction more pleasant and enjoyable.[44] It can defuse stress, such as when people are in conflict with one another.[45] Within relationships, "inside jokes" can reinforce people's feelings of intimacy. Humor can provide so many personal and social benefits, in fact, that a good sense of humor is something both women and men strongly seek in a romantic partner.[46] Recent research shows that self-deprecating humor—jokes in which people poke fun at themselves—are seen as especially attractive in others.[47]

Not all effects of humor are positive, however. Humor can also be used to demean social or cultural groups, as in the case of racial jokes or jokes about elderly people or persons with disabilities. Moreover, even when they are made without the intention to offend, jokes told at another's expense can cause embarrassment or distress and might even qualify as harassment.[48] When using humor, it's therefore important to take stock of your audience to make certain that your jokes will amuse rather than offend.

Euphemisms: Soft Talk

euphemism A vague, mild expression that symbolizes something more blunt or harsh.

Some topics are difficult or impolite to talk about directly. In such cases, we might use a **euphemism,** a vague, mild expression that symbolizes something more blunt or harsh. Instead of saying that someone has died, for instance, we might say that he has "passed away." Rather than mentioning that she is pregnant, a woman might say she's "expecting." You can probably think of many euphemisms, such as "let go" (instead of "fired"), "sleep together" (instead of "have sex"), and "praying at the porcelain altar" (instead of "vomiting in the toilet").

In almost every case, the euphemistic term sounds less harsh or less explicit than the term it stands for, and that's the point. We use euphemisms when we want to talk about sensitive topics without making others feel embarrassed or offended.[49] Importantly, euphemisms require more than just a technical understanding of the language in which they're made; they also require an understanding of cultural idioms. The reason why such understanding is necessary is that euphemisms often have a literal meaning that differs from their euphemistic meaning. For example, at a literal level, the phrase "sleep together" means just that: to engage in sleep while together. If you didn't realize that the phrase is a cultural euphemism for "have sex," then you wouldn't understand the meaning when it is used in that way.

Many euphemisms change over time. What we today call "posttraumatic stress disorder" was called "shell shock" during World War I, "battle fatigue" during World War II, and "operational exhaustion" during the Korean War. Sometimes societies change euphemisms in order to treat the groups of people they refer to with greater dignity. The euphemism "differently abled," for instance, began as "lame," then became "crippled," then "handicapped," and then "disabled" before evolving into its present form. Those and other euphemisms may continue to evolve as our culture and cultural ideas develop over time.

Like humor, the use of euphemisms has good and bad points. As we've seen, euphemisms provide people a way to talk about sensitive topics—such as sexuality, disability, and death—without having to use uncomfortable language. That aspect is beneficial, particularly to the extent that people otherwise would avoid communicating about those important topics. Some researchers have warned, however, that the excessive use of euphemisms can desensitize people, causing them to accept situations they would otherwise find unacceptable.[50]

In line with that idea, communication researchers Matthew McGlone, Gary Beck, and Abigail Pfiester found that when a euphemism becomes conventional or commonplace, people may use it without thinking about what it really means.[51] Euphemisms that are common during times of war, for instance, include "friendly fire" (for firing on one's own troops) and "collateral damage" (for civilians killed inadvertently).[52] When euphemisms are used specifically to disguise or distort meaning, as those euphemisms exemplify, they are referred to as *doublespeak*.[53] Some language experts believe that using doublespeak for horrendous situations of military combat can lead people to feel emotionally detached from—or even accepting of—the horrors of war.[54] Using euphemisms competently therefore requires us to consider whether "softening" the topic of discussion will facilitate open communication—or encourage us to tolerate what we might otherwise find intolerable.[55]

Euphemisms are common during times of war. Do you think euphemistic language lessens our sensitivity to the harshness of combat?

Slang: The Language of Subcultures

Closely related to euphemism is **slang,** the use of informal and unconventional words that often are understood only by others in a particular group. If you grew up in Boston, for instance, you probably know that "rhodie" is a slang term for people from nearby Rhode Island. In Australia, "snag" is slang for "sausage." On the Internet, a "blog" is a web page featuring ongoing news or commentary, and a "hacker" is someone who creates or modifies computer software.

People have slang terms for all sorts of things. Many slang words are used in games, such as "quads" for four-of-a-kind in poker and "squash" for a one-sided match in professional wrestling. People in the medical community might refer to psychiatrists as the "Freud squad" or urologists as the "stream team." A "gym bunny" spends excessive amounts of time exercising at the gym; a "mall rat" spends excessive amounts of time hanging out at a shopping mall.

Slang can serve an important social function by helping people distinguish between those who do and don't belong to their particular social networks. Many social, cultural, and religious groups have their own terminology for certain ideas, and a person's ability to use a group's slang appropriately can "mark" him or her as belonging to that group. For instance, if you don't know that "bubbly-jock" means "turkey," you're probably not from Scotland, and if you don't know whether you're in "T Town" (Texarkana) or "Big T" (Tucson), chances are you're not a trucker.

A form of informal speech closely related to slang is *jargon*. As we saw in Chapter 2, jargon is the technical vocabulary of a certain occupation or profession. The purpose of jargon is to allow members of that occupation or profession to communicate with one another precisely and efficiently. For example, many law enforcement officers in North

slang Informal, unconventional words that are often understood only by others in a particular subculture.

Whether you're into gardening, political activism, or basketball, slang allows you to connect and identify with others who share your interests.

America talk to one another using "10-code," or number combinations that represent common phrases. In that jargon, "10-4" means you've received another person's message; "10-24" means your assignment is completed. Health care providers also use jargon specific to their profession. For instance, they refer to a heart attack as a "myocardial infarction," a headache as a "cephalalgia," and athlete's foot as "tinea pedis." Attorneys, engineers, dancers, airplane pilots, television producers, and military personnel are among many other occupations and professions that have their own jargon.

Like humor and euphemisms, slang and jargon are neither inherently good nor inherently bad. They can be used for positive purposes, such as to reaffirm one's membership within a particular social community. Whether you're into basketball, wine tasting, calligraphy, or restoring old cars, learning and using the slang appropriate to those interests serves as a type of membership badge, allowing you to connect with others like you. By the same token, however, the use of slang and jargon can also make people feel like outsiders. If you're a police officer, for instance, saying that you're "10-7" instead of "done for the day" might make those around you who are not in law enforcement feel excluded from the conversation. For that reason, you should consider how your use of slang and jargon might come across to those around you.

Defamation: Harmful Words

In January 2008, baseball pitcher Roger Clemens filed a lawsuit against former New York Yankees trainer Brian McNamee. In a report released a month earlier, McNamee had informed investigators that while working as Clemens's strength trainer, he had repeatedly injected the pitching ace with Winstrol, a performance-enhancing steroid, in violation of the law. In his lawsuit, Clemens claimed that McNamee's statements not only were untrue but had damaged Clemens's professional reputation.

Clemens's claim was that McNamee had engaged in **defamation,** language that harms a person's reputation or gives that person a negative image. Defamation comes in two forms. The first, **libel,** refers to defamatory statements made in print or some other fixed medium, such as a photograph or a motion picture. The second, **slander,** is a defamatory statement that is made aloud, within earshot of others.

For instance, let's say that Aliyah wants to open a day care center in a town where Toni also operates one. To discourage parents from using Aliyah's center, Toni circulates rumors that Aliyah has been charged with child molestation. That statement is defamatory because it would harm Aliyah's reputation and cause her financial damage in the form of lost business.

Does it matter whether Toni's accusation is true? Usually the answer is yes: Under most legal systems, a statement must be false to be considered libel or slander. There are situations, however, when even a true accusation can qualify as slander or libel. Such cases often involve public figures, like politicians and celebrities, and hinge on the importance of the information for the public. Disclosing in print that a senator has tested positive for HIV, for example, might qualify as libel even if it were true, if disclosing it serves no prevailing public interest.

Slander is more common than libel in interpersonal interaction. Although slander is a legal term, behaviors we would call gossiping or spreading rumors often amount to the same thing. If you've ever had someone spread rumors about you, you know

defamation Language that harms a person's reputation or image.

libel A defamatory statement made in print or in some other fixed medium.

slander A defamatory statement made aloud.

how painful that can be. Although gossip can serve some positive functions, such as reinforcing bonds of intimacy among people, the targets of gossip or rumors can experience profound distress.[56]

Profanity: Offensive Language

Profanity is a form of language that is considered vulgar, rude, or obscene in the context in which it is used. We sometimes call profane terms "swear words" or "curse words," and they come in many forms. Some profane terms are meant to put down certain groups of people, such as calling a woman a "bitch" or a homosexual man a "fag." (Many of those also qualify as hate speech, which we examine next.) Other profane terms are attacks on religious beliefs or figures considered sacred by followers of a particular religion. Others describe sexual acts or refer to people's sexual organs or bodily functions. Still others are general expressions of anger or disappointment, such as "Damn!"

Profanity is context-specific: What makes a word profane is that it is considered rude or obscene in the language and context in which it is used. For instance, calling a woman a "bitch" might be profane, but using the same term to describe a female dog is not. In the United States, "fag" is a derogatory term for gay men, but to the British, it refers to a cigarette.

Every language ever studied has included swear words. Some swear words translate among languages; for example, the expression "Damn!" in English is "Zut!" in French and "Verflucht!" in German and can be profane in all of them. Other expressions appear to be unique to certain languages; for instance, a Dutch speaker might say "Krijg de pest!" which translates to "Go get infected with the plague!"

Profanity has many different effects on social interaction. Often, it makes people feel uncomfortable or insulted. In recent years, some social groups have recognized that they can reduce the negative effects of certain profane terms themselves by making the terms more commonplace, thus lowering or eliminating their shock value. That practice is called *reclaiming the term.* For instance, when homosexuals call one another "queers," their intent is not to cause insult but rather to remove the power to insult from the word.

Not all effects of profanity are negative. In certain contexts, the use of profanity can act as a *social lubricant* by establishing and maintaining an informal social atmosphere. Profanity is a common element in comedy, for instance, partly because it creates an expectation that nothing is taboo in that context and that ideas can flow freely. In addition, using profanity within one's own social network can actually reinforce interpersonal bonds by sending the metamessage that "I feel comfortable enough with you to use profanity in your presence." Recent research has even shown that people have an increased tolerance for physical pain when they swear, perhaps because swearing activates the body's "fight-or-flight" system."[57]

> **profanity** A form of language considered vulgar, rude, or obscene in the context in which it is used.

"But it's not a four-letter word if I used *texting*!"

© Cartoonbank.com

Hate Speech: Profanity with a Hurtful Purpose

Hate speech is a specific form of profanity meant to degrade, intimidate, or dehumanize people on the basis of their gender, national origin, sexual orientation, religion, race, disability status, or political or moral views.[58] Calling people derogatory names,

> **hate speech** A form of profanity meant to degrade, intimidate, or dehumanize groups of people.

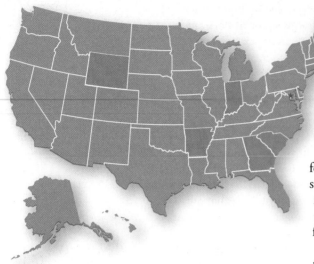

FIGURE 5.4 U.S. States with Hate Crime Laws At present, all U.S. states except Wyoming, Arkansas, Indiana, South Carolina, and Georgia have laws prohibiting hate crimes such as the use of hate speech.

intimidating them, and advocating violence against groups of individuals might all qualify as forms of hate speech. For instance, the terms "bitch" and "fag" can be used not only as profanity but also as hate speech if they're directed at women or homosexuals with the intent to degrade or intimidate them.

Several laws and regulations exist in North America to restrict hate speech or other acts of intimidation against minority groups and to punish people who engage in them (Figure 5.4). Many of those restrictions are found in campus speech codes, which dictate the types of statements that students, staff, and faculty can and cannot make on a college campus. There is little question that most, if not all, of the effects of hate speech are negative, a fact justifying laws and regulations to restrict it.

Still, hate laws and regulations are controversial. Supporters argue that the regulations are necessary to promote civility and to protect people—especially minority-group members—from the discrimination and even violence that hate speech can incite. Opponents counter that it is difficult to determine what qualifies as hate speech and what does not. They also maintain that restricting speech is a form of censorship and a violation of the First Amendment of the U.S. Constitution.[59] Given the complexities of defining hate speech and determining how best to respond to it, those points of contention are likely to be debated for some time.

Hate speech has recently received heightened societal attention given several widely publicized instances of suicide on the part of high school and college students after they were bullied for being gay (or being perceived to be gay). One response, highlighted in the "Communication: Light Side" box, has been an outpouring of supportive messages on the Internet that are directed at people who feel victimized by hateful speech and other bullying behavior because they are seen as different or abnormal for some reason.

As we've seen in this section, language comes in many forms, including humor, euphemism, slang, libel and slander, profanity, and hate speech. Some of those forms, such as humor, generally have positive effects but can also produce unwanted negative outcomes. Other forms, such as profanity, are generally negative even though they can have positive effects on the people using them. Understanding the positive and negative aspects of those diverse forms of language helps us to appreciate the power and complexity of verbal communication.

LEARN IT What makes a joke funny? What are the purposes of using euphemisms? In what ways does the use of slang reflect a person's subcultures? How is libel different from slander? What makes a word or a phrase profane? What is hate speech?

APPLY IT Many groups have their own slang. Talk to some people who have hobbies, interests, or jobs very different from yours, and learn some of the slang common to those groups. Document what you've learned in a short report.

REFLECT ON IT What euphemisms do you tend to use? Do you feel that prohibiting hate speech is a good idea or a bad one? Why?

REACHING OUT: PROVIDING WORDS OF COMFORT AND HOPE ONLINE

In 2010, a number of teenagers around the United States took their own lives in the wake of the relentless bullying they received for being different. Recognizing that many adolescents and young adults feel similarly picked on and degraded on a daily basis, columnist Dan Savage created the It Gets Better Project. This online video channel reaches out to young people who feel bullied by emphasizing the message that their lives will improve.

The site features short videos from adolescents and adults, many of whom experienced bullying themselves.

Some of the contributors are well known, such as singer Adam Lambert, designer Tim Gunn, Secretary of State Hillary Clinton, and Bishop Gene Robinson. Others are ordinary people who share words of comfort and

Suicides by teens such as Seth Walsh led to the It Gets Better Project.

hope. Videos are posted in many languages, including several in American Sign Language. Beyond casting widespread media attention on the problem of bullying, the project demonstrates how a simple message—such as "it gets better"—can offer hope to people at a time when their lives feel hopeless.

FROM ME TO YOU

Concerned that you might say or do something offensive, you might (if you are like many people) find yourself becoming rigid or hyper-polite around individuals from groups that are different from your own. However, that pattern of behavior in itself can serve to reinforce divisions among you and others. Think about it: It's hard for others to feel comfortable around you if you don't seem to feel comfortable around them.

People in many marginalized groups, for example, will tell you that they don't expect special treatment: What they often want the most is simply to be treated like anyone else. So relax! When you talk to people, try not to see them as members of a particular group but simply as people.

Source: www.itgetsbetter.org.

4 Improving Your Language Use

Using language is a skill that nearly all of us can improve on. In this section, we'll look at four pieces of advice that will help you become a better verbal communicator. Some tips may be more relevant to one situation than another, but each can assist you in refining your language use.

Consider the Effect You Wish to Create

When you speak—whether to one person or to several people—consider what you want your words to accomplish. Is your goal to make others feel comfortable around you? To persuade them? To inform them? To entertain them? You might even have multiple goals at once. Whatever your goals, you're more likely to achieve them if you consider how your use of language can help you.

One aspect of creating effective verbal messages is to make certain that what you're saying is appropriate to your audience. Considering your messages from your listeners' point of view will help you avoid three basic mistakes: shared knowledge errors, shared opinion errors, and monopolization errors.

SHARED KNOWLEDGE ERROR.   When you presume your listeners have information that they don't have, you are making the *shared knowledge error.* For example, when Devon is speaking to casual acquaintances, he refers to his friends and relatives by their names without explaining who they are. He also makes reference to events that occurred earlier in his life, before his acquaintances knew him.

We can communicate with close friends and family members that way because they usually know our personalities, our histories, and the other people in our social circles. We shouldn't presume, however, that strangers or casual acquaintances have this information. As competent communicators, we therefore must consider the perspectives of the people we're talking to and use language appropriate to what they do or do not know about us.

SHARED OPINION ERROR.   The mistake known as the *shared opinion error* occurs when you incorrectly assume that your listeners share your opinions. In diverse company, for example, it's often risky to express strong opinions on potentially controversial issues such as politics and religious beliefs, because by doing so you might offend people who don't share your positions. However, it's even riskier to speak as though you assume that everyone present agrees with you. When you communicate in that manner, other people may be more likely to confront you with their different points of view. In some situations, a healthy exchange of ideas can follow; but in others, the discussion can turn contentious, leading you to become defensive about your positions.

MONOPOLIZATION ERROR.   The *monopolization error* occurs when one speaker inappropriately dominates the conversation. No matter with whom she's speaking, for instance, Tara always does most of the talking by far. Such behavior may be appropriate, say, on the part of an instructor leading a classroom discussion. In interpersonal interaction, however, monopolizing a conversation can make other people feel as though the speaker isn't interested in what they have to say but only in presenting his or her own ideas. Remember that good interpersonal conversations involve a give-and-take of ideas, opinions, and comments—so don't forget to allow everyone to speak.

As those examples illustrate, the ways you use language influence those around you. Therefore, to communicate competently, it is essential that you consider what influence you want to have. That is particularly important for parents, teachers, supervisors, and others in positions of authority, because they often have a responsibility to set expectations for language use in their homes, classrooms, and work environments. If you don't want your children to use profanity, for instance, you can help set that expectation by not using it yourself—or at least by not using it in their presence. If you value supportive communication in your classroom or workplace, set an example by using appropriate humor and avoiding hate speech. In those ways, you will help ensure that your language use has positive effects on others.

Consider the influence you want your communication to have on others, especially if you are in a position of authority.

Separate Opinions from Factual Claims

Recall from Chapter 4 that factual claims ("she hit him") are different from interpretations ("she assaulted him"). Factual claims are also different from opinions. A factual claim makes a statement that we can verify with evidence and show to be true or false in an absolute sense ("I've taken piano lessons for 10 years"). An opinion expresses a personal judgment or preference that we could agree or disagree with but that is not true or false in an absolute sense ("I'm a terrific piano player"). Competent communicators know how to keep opinions and factual claims separate in verbal communication.

Distinguishing factual claims from opinions is often easier said than done, especially when we're dealing with strong opinions on emotionally heated issues. Let's say, for instance, that you and several friends are discussing an upcoming election in which you're choosing between two candidates. Half of you prefer Candidate C, the conservative, and the other half prefers Candidate L, the liberal. Consider the following statements you might make about the candidates, and indicate which are factual claims and which are opinions:

- *"Candidate C has more experience in government."* Because we can show this statement to be true or false by looking at the candidates' records, this is a factual claim.
- *"Candidate L is the better choice for our future."* This is an opinion, because it expresses a value judgment (this candidate is better), which we cannot objectively validate.
- *"Candidate C is immoral."* This is an opinion, because the truth of this claim depends on what morals you subscribe to. Morals are subjective; therefore, the statement can't be proved true or false in an absolute sense.
- *"Candidate L accepted illegal bribes."* This is a factual claim, because you can examine the evidence to discover whether it's true.

Opinions and factual claims require different types of responses. Suppose you tell me that "Candidate C has never held an elective office," and I reply by saying "I disagree." That isn't a competent response. You have made a factual claim, so by definition it is either true or false. Therefore, whether I agree with it is irrelevant. I can agree or disagree with an opinion, but a factual claim is either true or false no matter how I feel about it. Instead, if I had responded to your statement by saying "I think you're incorrect," that would be a competent reply because we would now be discussing the truth of your statement rather than my agreement with it.

As you develop the skill of distinguishing opinions from facts, keep two principles in mind. First, *opinions are opinions whether you agree with them or not.* If you believe abortion should be legal in the United States, for instance, you might be inclined to call that statement a fact. It isn't, though. It is a statement of opinion because it expresses an evaluation about what "should be." Second, *factual claims are factual claims whether they are true or not.* If you think it's untrue that religious people are happier than nonreligious people, for instance, you might be inclined to call that statement an opinion. It isn't, though. Even if the statement isn't true, it is still a factual claim because it expresses something that could be verified by evidence.

Separating opinions from factual claims takes practice, but it will help you respond competently to each type of verbal statement. Check out "Assess Your Skills" to see how well you can do right now. The "Apply It" exercise on p. 173 suggests some additional ways for you to practice that skill.

assess your SKILLS

HOW WELL CAN YOU DISTINGUISH OPINIONS FROM FACTUAL CLAIMS?

The ability to separate opinions from factual claims is an important skill for effective verbal communication. How well can you spot the difference? Read each of the following statements. Assuming nothing more than the statement tells you, indicate whether you think the statement is an opinion or a factual claim by placing a check mark in the appropriate column.

	Factual Claim	Opinion
1. Lady Gaga is the best singer in the world.	_____	_____
2. Television was invented in the 1920s.	_____	_____
3. Religious people are happier than nonreligious people.	_____	_____
4. The United States is better off with a Democrat as president.	_____	_____
5. Men talk as much as women do.	_____	_____
6. Same-sex couples should not be allowed to marry.	_____	_____
7. Children should be required to learn a foreign language.	_____	_____
8. Neil Armstrong was the first person to walk on the moon.	_____	_____
9. Dogs have a keener sense of smell than people do.	_____	_____
10. Abortion should be legal in the United States.	_____	_____

Statements 1, 4, 6, 7, and 10 are all opinions. Statements 2, 3, 5, 8, and 9 are all factual claims. How well did you do? If you missed some of the answers, don't worry—distinguishing opinions from factual claims can be harder than it seems.

As noted earlier, separating opinions from factual claims is especially challenging when we're dealing with emotionally charged issues such as religious values, ethics, and morality. The more strongly we feel about an issue, the more we tend to think of our beliefs as facts rather than opinions. In such cases we are less likely to consider the possibility that other people have opinions that differ from ours but are valid nonetheless.

Consider the heated debate over euthanasia, the practice of ending the life, in a minimally painful way, of a person or an animal that is terminally ill as a means of limiting suffering.[60] Supporters perceive euthanasia as an act of selfless mercy, whereas opponents consider it an act of selfish cruelty.[61] People on both sides of the issue feel their position is right. Some of them probably don't realize that both positions are opinions, not facts. Whether a behavior is merciful or cruel depends on individual beliefs, not on any objective standard.

Although it is probably more difficult to separate opinions from facts when you feel strongly about an issue, that's often when it is most important to do so. Instead of telling others that their positions on sensitive issues are right or wrong, tell them that you agree or disagree with their positions. That way, you express your own position but acknowledge that different—even contradictory—opinions may also exist.

Speak at an Appropriate Level

Efficacious linguistic devices must demonstrate isomorphism with the cerebral aptitude of the assemblage. If the meaning of that statement isn't exactly clear, the reason is that the language is inappropriately complex. What the statement simply means is that good messages must be understandable to listeners.

Part of being an effective verbal communicator is knowing how simple or how complex your language should be for your audience. A competent teacher, for instance, knows to use simpler language when teaching an introductory course than when teaching an advanced course, because students in each class will have different levels of understanding. When individuals use language that is too complex for their audience, they are "talking over people's heads." If you have experienced that situation, you know how hard it can be to understand what the speaker is trying to say.

When you talk over their heads, other people find it difficult to understand you.

The opposite problem is "talking down" to people, or using language that is inappropriately simple. Individuals often talk down by mistake. You might provide unnecessary detail when giving someone driving directions, for example, because you don't realize that she is familiar with the area. At other times, people use overly simple language on purpose. That behavior can make listeners feel patronized, disrespected, or even insulted.

Simple and complex language each has its appropriate place. To be a good communicator, you should practice your perspective-taking ability. Put yourself in your listeners' shoes, and then consider how simple or complex your words should be.

Own Your Thoughts and Feelings

People often use language that shifts responsibility for their thoughts and feelings onto others. Perhaps you always dread going to visit your Aunt Alice because whenever she doesn't understand you, she says, "You're not being clear," but when you don't understand her, she says, "You're not paying attention." By using that pattern of language, Alice blames you for misunderstandings but takes no responsibility for her own role in the communication process. Instead of a lack of clarity on your part, for example, the issue may be that Alice herself might not be paying attention. Instead of a lack of attention on your part, the problem may be that Alice might not be using clearly understandable language. Maybe you have encountered actual people who, like Alice, always seem to make others responsible for how they communicate.

Good communicators take responsibility for their thoughts and feelings by using I-statements rather than you-statements. An **I-statement** claims ownership of what a person is feeling or thinking, whereas a **you-statement** shifts that responsibility to the other person. Instead of saying, "You're not being clear," Alice might say, "I'm having a hard time understanding you." Rather than saying, "You make me mad," I might say, "I'm angry right now."

I-statements don't ignore the problem; they simply allow the speaker to claim ownership of his or her feelings. That ownership is important because it acknowledges that we control how we think and feel. Constructive I-statements include four parts that clearly express that ownership:

- "I feel _____" (expresses responsibility for your own feelings)
- "when you _____" (identifies the behavior that is prompting your feelings)

I-statement A statement that claims ownership of one's thoughts or feelings.

you-statement A statement that shifts responsibility for one's own thoughts or feelings to the listener.

[I-STATEMENTS]

Using I-statements helps you own your thoughts and feelings.

WHAT?

Learn to use I-statements.

WHY?

To acknowledge ownership and responsibility for your thoughts and feelings, as when you are dealing with an interpersonal issue such as a problem with something a friend or relative is doing—or not doing.

HOW?

1. Start by saying "I feel _____," which identifies your feelings.

2. Then say "when you _____," which identifies the behavior prompting your feelings.

3. Next say "because _____," which identifies what you find problematic about the behavior.

4. Finally, say "and I would appreciate it if you would _____," which suggests a solution to the problem.

TRY!

1. The next time you find someone's behavior problematic, don't say "You're making me angry" or "You're worrying me." Instead, express your message in the form of an I-statement.

2. Practice by imagining that your roommate has been leaving your house a mess, not paying you for groceries, and playing music while you're trying to sleep. In writing, craft two different I-statements you might use to address the situation with your roommate.

CONSIDER: *Why is it beneficial to acknowledge ownership of your thoughts and feelings?*

- "because _____" (points to the characteristic of the behavior that is prompting your feelings)
- "and I would appreciate it if you would _____" (offers an alternative to the behavior)

Let's say, for instance, that Colin is frustrated with Ji, his officemate, because she often leaves the door to their office open when neither of them is inside. Here's one way he might express those feelings:

> "You need to stop leaving our door open, because anyone can waltz in here and take whatever they want. You're really starting to make me mad."

This statement rightfully points out that the problematic behavior is Ji's; after all, she is the one who leaves the door open. What it doesn't do, however, is acknowledge that Colin's feelings of frustration belong to him. Now let's look at a more constructive way of communicating his feelings:

> "I get angry when you leave our office door open, because anyone could come in here and steal my briefcase or your purse. I would really appreciate it you would close the door whenever you step out of the office."

Notice how that statement doesn't ignore or downplay the problem. Rather, it allows Colin to take responsibility for his feelings of frustration and to identify clearly how he would like Ji to change her behavior.

The major benefit of using I-statements is that they are less likely than you-statements to cause a listener to become defensive.[62] By saying "You're really starting to make me mad," Colin sounds as though he is accusing Ji, a situation that would likely cause her to respond defensively. In contrast, by saying "I feel angry when you leave our office door open," Colin acknowledges that he is responsible for his own feelings, and he is only suggesting a change in Ji's behavior. Ji may still disagree with his assessment, but she will probably be less likely to feel that he is attacking or accusing her.

Learning to use I-statements can be challenging, because we might think that other people really are causing our thoughts and feelings; so it might feel right to say, "You're making me mad." Recall that other people can't control our thoughts and feelings unless we let them. Effective communicators speak in ways that acknowledge responsibility for and ownership of the ways they feel and think. To practice that ability, check out the "Got Skills?" box.

In summary, there are several ways to become a more effective verbal communicator. Consider the effect you want your language use to have on others around you and craft your verbal messages accordingly. Separate opinions from facts, particularly for highly sensitive or contentious issues. Use language that is appropriate for your audience. Take ownership of your thoughts and feelings, and let your language reflect it. The foregoing are among the most valuable ways of improving your verbal communication ability in interpersonal settings.

LEARN IT What is the shared knowledge error? How are opinions distinguished from facts? Why is it important to speak at an appropriate level? What are the four components of a constructive I-statement?

APPLY IT Separating facts and opinions can be difficult, not only when you're speaking but also when you're listening to others. Practice that skill by watching a television newscast or reading an Internet blog. Write down five statements you hear or read, and for each one, ask yourself if it is a fact, an opinion, or some other type of statement (such as an instruction). Remember that facts make claims that can be verified with evidence, whereas opinions express a person's judgments or evaluations about something. With practice, you'll sharpen your ability to distinguish opinions from facts.

REFLECT ON IT When someone "talks down to you," what does it make you think about that person? When do you tend to commit the monopolization error?

MASTER the chapter

1 The Nature of Language (p. 144)

- Language consists of words that represent, or symbolize, objects or concepts.
- The connection between most words and the objects or concepts they symbolize is arbitrary.
- Languages are governed by phonological, syntactic, semantic, and pragmatic rules.
- Words have both denotative and connotative meanings.

- Verbal statements vary in how ambiguous they are.
- The meaning of language is affected by the social and cultural contexts in which it is used.

2 Appreciating the Power of Words (p. 151)

- Naming is a fundamental way of giving identity to someone or something.
- Language can be used to persuade others to think or act in a particular way.

- Some forms of language are perceived as more credible than others.

- People use verbal behavior in personal relationships to convey affection and create intimacy.

- We can use words to provide comfort to others and also to ourselves.

- Libel is defamatory language that appears in print; slander is defamatory language that is spoken.

- Profanity is a form of language that is generally considered offensive.

- Hate speech is a form of profanity aimed at degrading or intimidating a specific group of people.

3 The Use and Abuse of Language (p. 161)

- Humor relies on a violation of expectations.

- Euphemisms allow us to discuss sensitive topics in a minimally discomforting way.

- Many subcultures have their own slang, which serves to mark membership in those groups.

4 Improving Your Language Use (p. 167)

- Avoid shared knowledge, shared opinion, and monopolization errors.

- Learn to separate opinions from statements of fact and to respond appropriately to each one.

- Speak at a level of understanding that is appropriate for your audience.

- Take ownership of your thoughts and feelings by using I-statements more than you-statements.

KEY TERMS

ambiguous language (p. 149)
connotative meaning (p. 147)
credibility (p. 156)
defamation (p. 164)
denotative meaning (p. 147)
ethos (p. 154)
euphemism (p. 162)

hate speech (p. 165)
I-statement (p. 171)
language (p. 144)
libel (p. 164)
loaded language (p. 148)
logos (p. 155)
onomatopoeia (p. 146)

pathos (p. 154)
profanity (p. 165)
reason (p. 155)
Sapir-Whorf hypothesis (p. 150)
slander (p. 164)
slang (p. 163)
you-statement (p. 171)

DISCUSSION QUESTIONS

1. With the Sapir-Whorf hypothesis in mind, what examples can you think of that illustrate how your language reflects your culture's behaviors and attitude?

2. The more you learn about persuasion, the greater your ability to persuade others. What are the ethical implications of having the ability to persuade?

3. Why do you think so many people laugh at jokes that put down other people? Can a joke be funny even if you find it distasteful? Explain.

4. There is much disagreement regarding hate speech laws: Supporters maintain they are necessary to promote civility; critics contend they amount to unconstitutional censorship. What do you think?

PRACTICE QUIZ

MULTIPLE CHOICE

1. The dictionary definition of a word is its _____ meaning, whereas the implication of that word is its _____ meaning.

a. denotative, connotative
b. connotative, denotative
c. denotative, relational
d. connotative, relational

2. **All of the following are elements in Ogden and Richard's semantic triangle** *except*
   a. symbol
   b. reference
   c. referent
   d. article

3. **A vague, mild expression that symbolizes something blunter or harsher is called a/an**
   a. eugenic
   b. equivocation
   c. euphemism
   d. emphasis

4. **Sophie wants a new bike, so she tries to make her dad feel sorry for her, saying she's the only student in her class who doesn't have a good bike. Sophie's persuasive strategy is to appeal to**
   a. pathos
   b. logos
   c. ethos
   d. equivocation

5. **Good communicators take responsibility for their own thoughts and feelings by using**
   a. I-statements
   b. you-statements
   c. we-statements
   d. they-statements

FILL IN THE BLANK

6. Because language is _____, each word represents a particular object or idea, but the word does not constitute the object or idea itself.

7. A word whose sound imitates its meaning is an example of _____.

8. _____ rules allow an individual to connect the word *laptop* with the concept "computer."

9. The idea that we can only conceive of something if we have a word for it is known as _____.

10. Terms and phrases that are intended to mislead listeners by implying something that they don't actually say are known as _____.

ANSWERS

Multiple Choice : 1 (a); 2 (d); 3 (c); 4 (a); 5 (a); **Fill in the Blank:** 6 (symbolic); 7 (onomatopoeia); 8 (semantic); 9 (linguistic determinism); 10 (weasel words)

RESEARCH LIBRARY

MOVIES

Babel (drama; 2006; R)
In *Babel,* a married couple from California is vacationing in Morocco when the wife is shot while riding a bus. The movie integrates their story with those of their nanny back home in San Diego; a Moroccan man and his teenage sons; and a hearing-impaired teenage girl in Japan. Underlying all four stories is the challenge of understanding—and being understood by—those whose languages are different from our own.

Windtalkers (drama; 2002; R)
This movie follows the story of U.S. Marines who are deployed to the Pacific during World War II to intercept and translate Japanese radio transmissions, which the U.S. military had discovered were being communicated using the ancient language of the Navajo. The translators, the "code-talkers," are heavily protected because of their value to the U.S. military mission. The story illustrates one direct application of the ability to understand and use language.

BOOKS AND JOURNAL ARTICLES

Huston, T. L., Caughlin, J. P., Houts, R. M., Smith, S. E., & George, L. J. (2001). The connubial crucible: Newlywed years as predictors of marital delight, distress, and divorce. *Journal of Personality and Social Psychology, 80,* 237–252.

Moore, C. J. (2004). *In other words: A language lover's guide to the most intriguing words around the world.* New York: Walker.

Pinker, S. (2007). *The stuff of thought: Language as a window into human nature.* New York: Viking.

WEBSITES

www.lsadc.org/
   This is the home page of the Linguistic Society of America, an organization founded in 1924 to advance the scientific study of language.
www.aclu.org/studentsrights/
   expression/12808pub19941231.html
   This web page, hosted by the American Civil Liberties Association, defines hate speech and presents an argument against prohibiting it through regulations or laws.

6 Nonverbal Communication

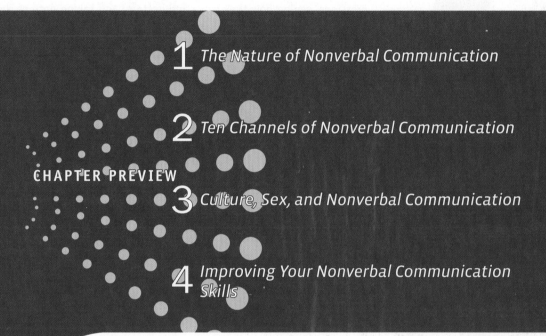

A TOUCHING MOMENT FOR THE FIRST LADY

In April 2009, during her first visit to England as First Lady of the United States, Michelle Obama created a public stir when she put her arm around Queen Elizabeth II as a gesture of friendship. Although such friendly physical contact is natural in U.S. culture, it was a breach of protocol in Great Britain, where visitors to the royal palace are sternly warned never to touch the queen unless reciprocating a handshake. The no-touch rule reflects a long historical tradition of considering kings and queens to possess divine powers, including the power to cure disease through touch. If a monarch's touch could heal, people believed, the ruler should conserve that power by not allowing others to touch him or her. Even though such beliefs are no longer widely held, official protocol still prohibits touching a king or queen in most instances. Many people in England were therefore shocked to see Michelle Obama with her arm around the queen. The queen's spokespeople insisted afterward, however, that she took no offense at the First Lady's affectionate gesture.

Marge Simpson uses her facial expressions, posture, and tone of voice to communicate her feelings about her husband and children.

Nonverbal communication is powerful. Sometimes the smallest gesture—a glance; a warm vocal tone; a brief, affectionate touch with a foreign head of state—can send unmistakable messages about ourselves to others. Moreover, so much of what we learn about other people's thoughts and feelings comes not through listening to their words but through observing their body language—watching their facial expressions, seeing how they move and gesture, and taking note of their eye contact. Those and other behaviors often convey enormous amounts of information about people in efficient and sometimes subtle ways.

1 The Nature of Nonverbal Communication

On the animated television show *The Simpsons,* Marge Simpson is seldom shy about expressing disapproval when her husband or her children misbehave. She frequently communicates her feelings through her facial expressions, posture, and the stressful grunting sound she makes when she's annoyed. Those and other nonverbal communication behaviors clearly convey Marge's state of mind to anyone who happens to be around her. What makes nonverbal behavior such an effective form of communication? We will find out in this section, first by differentiating nonverbal communication from verbal communication and then by examining five of its most important characteristics.

What Is Nonverbal Communication?

Nonverbal means just what it sounds like—not verbal. Nonverbal communication requires neither words nor language. How, exactly, do we communicate with others, if not with words and language?

The answer is, in many ways. We can tell a great deal about people by watching their facial expressions and listening to their tone of voice. When you listen to your doctor tell you the results of your recent blood tests, for instance, you might hear the tension in her voice and determine that something is wrong, or you might see the pleasant look on her face and conclude that everything is fine. We also interpret people's gestures and notice the way they carry themselves. Perhaps you see two people punching each other but you determine from their behaviors that they are playing rather than genuinely fighting.

In addition, we frequently make judgments about people on the basis of their appearance. While scanning personal ads online, for example, you might be more drawn to some people than to others based on their photographs. Sometimes we even perceive others according to the way they use their time and the space around them. Perhaps you tried talking to your boss about your recent evaluation, but you felt ignored because he kept looking at his new iPhone. People routinely communicate more information through their appearance and nonverbal behaviors than they do through language. When it comes to interpersonal communication, looks and actions often do speak louder than words.

We can define **nonverbal communication,** then, as behaviors and characteristics that convey meaning without the use of words. Nonverbal communication behaviors frequently accompany verbal messages to clarify or reinforce them. For instance, if someone asks you for directions to the bookstore and you point and say "It's that way," your nonverbal behavior (pointing) clarifies the meaning of your verbal message. In contrast, if you just say "It's that way" without pointing, then your verbal message is ambiguous—and not very helpful. At other times, however, nonverbal communication behaviors convey meaning on their own. For example, if you ask me where the bookstore is and I shrug my shoulders, you will probably infer from my behavior that I don't know the answer to your question, even though I never actually said so.

Nonverbal behavior is a powerful way of communicating, and it comes naturally to many of us. Yet there's a lot more to interpreting nonverbal behavior than you might think. The more you learn about nonverbal communication, the better you will be able to understand it.

nonverbal communication Behaviors and characteristics that convey meaning without the use of words.

Five Characteristics of Nonverbal Communication

It's difficult to imagine life without nonverbal communication. Communicating nonverbally is particularly critical for people who lack language skills, such as infants, who can only vocalize without words, and for individuals with certain types of neurological problems, such as a stroke, that limit their language use. But even people with language ability depend immensely on nonverbal communication. For example, because she had only a limited knowledge of Spanish, Bergitta depended on nonverbal behaviors while traveling through Bolivia, Uruguay, and Argentina. She was frequently amazed at how well she could understand others simply by observing their gestures and facial expressions. Her communication was more challenging than it would have been if she had known the language, but she was still able to understand—and be understood by—others through nonverbal behaviors. Let's look at five key characteristics of such nonverbal communication.

NONVERBAL COMMUNICATION IS PRESENT IN MOST INTERPERSONAL CONVERSATIONS. Whether you talk to people one-on-one or in a group, you have access not only to the words they speak but also to several dimensions of nonverbal communication. In many situations, you can watch people's facial expressions for signs of how they're feeling. For instance, you might tell from his facial expression that your supervisor is bored at his business lunch and eager to leave. Voice also conveys data about a person's state of mind. At a party, you can determine from the tone of her voice when your host is being serious and when she's kidding. Even the way people dress and smell can send you information. Glancing around the room at a large business event, you might be able to guess which people are managers and which are staff members by the formality of their clothing. We are flooded with nonverbal signals in many kinds of social situations.

In other communication contexts, such as talking on the telephone and sending e-mail, we don't have access to as many nonverbal cues as we do in face-to-face conversation. We still make use of what's available, however. Even if we haven't met those to whom we're speaking on the telephone, for instance, we can make judgments about their voices—noticing, for example, how fast they're talking, how loudly, with what tone, and with what type of accent. In electronically mediated communication—such as e-mail, instant messaging, and text messaging—we can introduce nonverbal cues

Communication in computer-mediated formats, such as e-mail, instant messaging, and text messaging, relies heavily on language. Even in these environments, however, people can still introduce nonverbal facial expressions through the use of emoticons (a word that means *emotional icons*). Here are some of the most common emoticons:

Smiles	:)	🙂
Laughs	:D	😃
Frowns	:(	🙁
Winks	;)	😉
Kisses	:X	😚
Confusion	:/	😕
Sticking out tongue	:P	😛

FIGURE 6.1 Emoticons: Nonverbal Communication in Cyberspace Emoticons help readers decipher the sender's emotions. Interestingly, there are sex differences in emoticon use that mirror sex differences in facial expressions during face-to-face communication. For instance, women use emoticons more often than men, particularly when communicating with other women. In cross-sex communication, though, men tend to match women's use of emotions, but women do not tend to match men's use of them. The sexes also differ in *why* they use emoticons: Women tend to use them primarily to express joy or humor, whereas men are more likely to use them to communicate sarcasm. Sources: Microsoft, Inc. (2006). The first smiley :-). Retrieved January 19, 2006, from http://research.microsoft.com/~mbj/Smiley/Smiley.html; Walther, J. B., & D'Addario, K. (2001). The impacts of emoticons on message interpretation in computer-mediated communication. *Social Science Computer Review, 19,* 324–347; Witmer, D., & Kaztman, S. (1997). On-line smiles: Does gender make a difference in the use of graphic accents? *Journal of Computer-Mediated Communication, 2*(4). Retrieved May 23, 2000, from http://www.ascusc.org/jcmc/vol2/issue4/witmer1.html; Wolf, A. (2000). Emotional expression online: Gender differences in emoticon use. *Cyber Psychology & Behavior, 3,* 827–833.

emoticons Textual representations of facial expressions.

through the use of **emoticons,** the familiar textual representations of facial expressions (Figure 6.1). There are also other cues to help us make judgments in electronic media, such as pauses and the use of all capital letters.

Most of our interpersonal communication includes at least some form of nonverbal communication. Going further, when we only have a few nonverbal signals to go on, we pay them extra attention. For example, vocal characteristics such as pitch and tone are important nonverbal cues in face-to-face conversation, but they are even more important on the telephone because so many other nonverbal signals, such as facial expressions and gestures, are unavailable to us. By the same token, when people lose the ability to use one of their senses to communicate, they typically compensate by relying more heavily on their remaining senses. Deaf people, for example, pay extra attention to visual cues when communicating with others because they are unable to interpret vocal characteristics. Similarly, blind people often rely more heavily on hearing and touch to help them communicate, because they are unable to see gestures or facial expressions.

NONVERBAL COMMUNICATION OFTEN CONVEYS MORE INFORMATION THAN VERBAL COMMUNICATION.

Go to the self-help section of almost any bookstore, and open up titles such as *How to Read a Person Like a Book*[1] and *What You Do Is More Important Than What You Say.*[2] You'll probably get the impression that nearly all the information people get by communicating with others comes through nonverbal behavior. In fact, some unreliable but frequently cited studies have estimated that as much as 93 percent of meaning is transmitted nonverbally.[3] Nonverbal communication isn't quite that powerful, however. More realistic estimates from nonverbal communication scholar Judee Burgoon

Nonverbal communication often involves multiple channels at once. During a face-to-face conversation, speakers can attend to facial expressions, eye behaviors, tone of voice, gestures, posture, and touch as sources of information.

suggest that 65 to 70 percent of meaning comes from nonverbal clues.[4] Importantly, even Burgoon's more conservative statistics suggest that people communicate more through nonverbal behaviors than words.

The most likely reason why nonverbal communication adds up to such a significant percentage is that it makes use of many **nonverbal channels,** which are the various behavioral forms that nonverbal communication takes. Some of those channels rely on our sense of vision, such as facial expressions, gestures, and personal appearance. Vocal characteristics, such as loudness, pitch, and tone of voice, engage our sense of hearing. We also use our senses of touch and smell to communicate. We often express different messages with a handshake and a hug, and we convey subtle messages about attraction to others through our use of smell.

nonverbal channels The various behavioral forms that nonverbal communication takes.

We sometimes rely on clues from nonverbal channels to make sense of a situation when talking to others isn't a good option. As the son of an alcoholic, for instance, Rick has learned that his mother Claudia has very unpredictable mood swings. When Rick visits his mother, he's never really sure how she'll be feeling. Some days, she's outgoing and upbeat; other days, she's withdrawn and negative. Occasionally, she'll start yelling at the slightest provocation. Over time, Rick has noticed that he can tell which mood Claudia is in—cheerful, depressed, or angry—simply by looking at her posture and facial expression.

NONVERBAL COMMUNICATION IS USUALLY BELIEVED OVER VERBAL COMMUNICATION.

It's not uncommon to get conflicting messages between what a person says and does. Most of the time, we believe the nonverbal clues.[5]

Let's say you're waiting for your friend Dante at your favorite bookstore café. When he walks in, Dante slumps down on the seat next to you, rolls his eyes, and sighs heavily. You ask him how he's doing, and he says, "It's been a *great* day." Dante's verbal behavior is sending you one message ("I'm having a great day"), but his nonverbal behavior is suggesting something quite different ("I'm having a lousy day"). Which of those contradictory messages do you believe? Most of us would put more stock in what Dante is *doing* than in what he is *saying.* In other words, as multiple studies have shown, we would believe his nonverbal message.

we do so to avoid misunderstanding and to provide listeners with greater clarity about our meaning. Several *nonverbal* behaviors also help us to achieve the goal of communicating clearly.

Suppose, for example, that you're sitting at the dinner table with your sister and she leans over to you, lowers her voice to a whisper, and cups her mouth with her hand, as though she's about to tell you a secret. That combination of nonverbal behaviors sends you the message "What I'm about to say is meant for only you to hear." In other words, her nonverbal behavior metacommunicates her intentions to you.

We often use nonverbal behaviors such as facial expressions and gestures to indicate how someone else should interpret our messages. For instance, we might smile and wink to indicate that we're being sarcastic or raise our eyebrows to signal that what we're saying is very serious. All those are examples of how we can use nonverbal cues to metacommunicate with others.

Nonverbal behaviors can be metacommunicative. When a friend or relative whispers and covers her mouth with her hand, those behaviors convey that what she's telling you is meant to be a secret.

Functions of Nonverbal Communication

Later we will see that nonverbal behaviors come in a number of forms, or channels. People use those channels for many reasons. Here, let's look at six common functions of nonverbal communication in personal relationships.

MANAGING CONVERSATIONS.   Even though conversations involve the exchange of verbal communication, we use several nonverbal behaviors to help our conversations with others go smoothly. In particular, nonverbal cues assist us in inviting, maintaining, and ending conversations.

- *Inviting conversations:* Three nonverbal cues are especially relevant for inviting conversations: personal space, physical appearance, and eye contact. First, you're most likely to initiate conversations with people who are physically closest to you rather than with people who are farther away.[12] Therefore, whom you happen to be standing by partly determines whom you'll talk to. Second, you'll be more inclined to initiate conversations with people you find physically attractive.[13] Because attractive people are often sought out as conversational partners, you may not always succeed in striking up conversations with them. Their physical attractiveness, though, will often motivate you to try. Finally, you'll be more likely to talk with people who make eye contact with you.[14] Conversely, when people avoid making eye contact with you, they're often signaling that they're unavailable for conversation.

- *Maintaining conversations:* During a conversation, you'll probably use gestures, eye contact, and tone of voice as **turn-taking signals**—nonverbal signs that indicate when each person's speaking turns begin and end. For example, you might raise a finger, a gesture that indicates you have something to say or that signals that you're not yet finished with your speaking turn. Eye contact can serve similar turn-taking functions. Research shows that most of us maintain more eye contact with a conversational partner when we're listening than when we're speaking.[15] You can therefore withhold eye contact while you're speaking as a way of signaling that you're not yet done with your turn.

turn-taking signal Nonverbal behavior that indicates when a person's speaking turn begins and ends.

- *Ending conversations:* Changes in eye behavior and posture are particularly common strategies for ending a conversation. When communication scholar Mark Knapp and his colleagues induced experimental participants to try to end conversations, the most frequent nonverbal leave-taking behavior was breaking eye contact.[16] Because we tend to look at people when we're listening to them, one way we can signal that we're ready for a conversation to end is to break eye contact with the other person. A second strategy is to angle our posture away from the person and toward the direction in which we wish to go. That behavior, called *left-positioning,* signals that we are preparing to leave the site of the conversation.[17]

EXPRESSING EMOTIONS. The fact that many nonverbal human behaviors communicate information about emotional state means that interpreting another person's emotions can give us important clues about how best to interact with that person. The two most expressive nonverbal channels for emotion are facial expressions and vocal behaviors.

- *Facial expressions of emotion:* Many of us "wear" our emotions on our face.[18] Facial expression is such a central part of our experience as social beings that we begin signaling our emotions through facial displays very early in life. For instance, studies have shown that infants begin smiling in response to external stimuli, such as a pleasant voice and a gentle touch, around the end of the first month of life.[19] By 10 months of age, most infants smile more in the presence of a parent than a stranger, suggesting they are happier when the parent is present.[20]

- *Vocal expressions of emotion:* The voice is also remarkably emotionally expressive.[21] We sometimes can tell how a person is feeling not by what he or she says but by the way his or her voice sounds. Experimental research on vocal displays of emotion has shown that many emotions affect the pitch of the voice. Specifically, the emotions of anger, surprise, happiness, fear, and affection tend to cause a higher-than-normal vocal pitch, whereas disgust, boredom, and extreme grief are conveyed by a lower vocal pitch.[22] Sadness, unless it is extreme, typically does not cause the pitch of the voice to change.[23]

MAINTAINING RELATIONSHIPS. Communication plays a central role in how most of us maintain our close relationships, and nonverbal behaviors are especially important for several key features of those relationships. Those behaviors include attraction and affiliation, power and dominance, and arousal and relaxation.

- *Attraction and affiliation:* Many nonverbal behaviors send messages

immediacy behavior Nonverbal behavior that conveys attraction or affiliation.

of attraction or affiliation. Researchers call those **immediacy behaviors.** When two people flirt, for example, they use their eye contact to signal attraction; they stand or sit close to each other; they touch each other playfully; and they use expressive tones of voice to convey the message that they are interested in each other.[24] People in many cultures use the same types of behaviors in initial interactions to signal that they are attracted to each other and wish to explore the possibility of future interaction.[25]

In more established relationships, nonverbal behavior is a common means of expressing affection and love. We hug, kiss, and hold hands with the people we love, and we speak to them in softer and higher-pitched tones of voice. Those kinds of behaviors help to reinforce feelings of affiliation, intimacy, and love, whether with our romantic partners, our family members, or our friends.[26] As the "Get Connected" box details, we can even use immediacy behaviors when interacting with others online.

- *Power and dominance: Power* is the potential to affect another person's behavior, and *dominance* is the actual exercise of that potential. Adults often convey messages about their power and status nonverbally. For example, supervisors touch subordinates more than subordinates touch superiors, and a powerful person is more likely to keep a less-powerful person waiting than vice versa.[27]

    Many of us also use *artifacts*—objects or visual features of an environment, to be examined further below—as status symbols. For instance, we might hang college diplomas on our office walls to signal our level of education or leave our expensive cars parked conspicuously in the driveway to signal our wealth. People also use nonverbal behaviors to assert dominance and control over others. Teachers do that, for example, when they use a certain look to convey disapproval about a child's behavior. Police officers control drivers' behaviors when they hold up a hand to signal "stop." Finally, some of us use silence to stop others from continuing to speak when we're in an uncomfortable conversation.

- *Arousal and relaxation: Arousal* refers to an increase in energy. We experience arousal in two fundamentally different ways depending on whether it is accompanied by positive or negative emotions. When it is accompanied by positive emotions, we experience arousal as excitement. Most of us express excitement through nonverbal cues such as an increase in eye contact with others, more laughter, faster rate of speech, higher vocal pitch and volume, and closer proximity to others.[28] When arousal is accompanied by negative emotions, however, we experience it as anxiety. Feeling anxious tends to cause fidgeting and random movement, nervous smiling or laughter, the use of more gestures and self-adaptors, higher vocal pitch and rate of speech, and the use of more filler words.[29]

    The opposite of arousal is *relaxation,* which we feel in situations of decreased energy. As with arousal, we experience relaxation in two different ways depending on the emotion involved. When relaxation is accompanied by positive emotion, we experience it as contentment. Feeling content leads most of us to smile more than usual, have a more relaxed posture, and increase our eye contact with and proximity to those around us.[30]

    In contrast, when relaxation is accompanied by negative emotion, we experience it as depression. Some people suffer from clinical depression, a psychiatric disorder thought to be caused by problems with chemicals called neurotransmitters, which relay signals between neurons and other cells in the brain.[31] Others just feel down from time to time, experiencing some of the symptoms of depression without the underlying psychiatric problems. In either case, feeling depressed

IMMEDIACY IN THE ONLINE CLASSROOM

Because immediacy reduces emotional and psychological distance between people, it's easy to understand why immediacy behaviors are valuable in a classroom. Isn't it the case that when you find your instructors more personable and approachable, you often find it easier to learn from them? Do you lose that advantage in online courses, by not having face-to-face communication with your instructors?

Not necessarily, researchers say. Online instructors can promote immediacy in several ways, such as by using photos and emoticons in their written messages, responding quickly to students' comments, and making themselves available for interaction with students in a virtual world such as Second Life. They can also encourage social interaction among the students themselves, a strategy that increases everyone's sense of inclusion and belonging.

To determine what benefits those types of immediacy behaviors have, a study looked at 145 students in online classes and found that

- *Instructor immediacy predicts how much students learn.* Just as in face-to-face classes, students learned and understood more of the content of the course when their online instructors used high-immediacy behaviors as compared to low-immediacy behaviors. Perhaps students felt more comfortable discussing course material and asking questions with high-immediacy teachers.

- *Instructor immediacy predicts how students feel about the course.* Students in online courses with high-immediacy instructors rated those courses more positively than did students who had low-immediacy instructors. Students in the former group were also more likely to recommend the course to their friends.

Immediacy behaviors certainly have to take different forms online than in face-to-face communication, but it is by no means impossible to be highly immediate in computer-mediated interaction. Good instructors—and good communicators—find ways to make technology fit their interpersonal communication needs.

Source: Baker, J. D. (2004). An investigation of relationships among instructor immediacy and affective and cognitive learning in the online classroom. *Internet and Higher Education, 7,* 1–13.

often leads people to smile less, make less frequent eye contact, and use fewer gestures and more self-adaptors.[32]

FORMING IMPRESSIONS. Many of us enjoy people watching while, say, sitting in a coffee shop or waiting at the airport. We pay attention to what individuals look and sound like and how they behave, and we use that information to form impressions about them. Those impressions are also strongly affected by people's nonverbal behaviors. In particular, nonverbal cues influence two general types of impressions: those related to a person's demographic characteristics and those related to a person's sociocultural characteristics.

- *Demographic impressions:* A person's *demographic characteristics* include his or her age, ethnic background, and sex. Research indicates that on the basis of visual cues, most of us can accurately classify a person into broad categories for age—such as infant, teenager, or elderly adult—and ethnicity—such as Asian, Hispanic, or non-Hispanic white.[33] Making a finer distinction, such as whether a woman is 50 or 60 years old or whether a man is Cambodian or Vietnamese, is more challenging. Similarly, most people can correctly identify an individual's biological sex by attending to visual cues such as the shape of the face and the body, hairstyle, clothing, jewelry, and cosmetics.[34]

  The voice is another nonverbal channel that helps us form demographic impressions of others. Vocal behaviors tend to be particularly good clues as to a person's age, sex, and sexual orientation. As people age, for instance, their vocal pitch and rate of speech typically decrease.[35] Consequently, many of us can determine a person's age with relative accuracy by listening to the sound of his or her voice.[36] By the same token, women and men's voices differ from each other in average pitch and vocal quality.[37] As a result, listeners can distinguish between male and female adult voices with nearly perfect accuracy.[38]

- *Sociocultural impressions:* People's *sociocultural characteristics* include their socioeconomic status, which is an index of how much money and education a person has and how prestigious his or her career is. They also include the cultural and co-cultural groups with which people identify.

  Personal appearance is usually the most informative nonverbal channel for forming sociocultural impressions. When you see a woman in an expensive, tailored business suit, for instance, you're likely to infer that she is of higher socioeconomic status than a woman wearing torn jeans and a sweatshirt.[39] You may not be accurate in your impression of those particular women, but the quality of a person's clothing is a relatively reliable visual cue to his or her socioeconomic status.[40]

  Many organized co-cultural groups, such as those associated with particular sports interests or music preferences, adopt fashions that identify their members. You might infer, therefore, that a young man in a football jersey and tennis shoes is a sports fan, whereas a young woman in black pants and a black shirt featuring a skull and crossbones is into alternative rock.

INFLUENCING OTHERS.   You probably find yourself in many social situations in which you wish to influence others' behaviors. Perhaps you're trying to persuade your friends to sponsor you in a marathon for cancer research—or you might be trying to get a good tip from the diners you've been serving. In those and many other contexts, you can use nonverbal behaviors to influence others. Nonverbal communication can be persuasive when it is applied as part of several strategies, including creating credibility and promoting affiliation.

- *Creating credibility:* One of the most effective strategies for influencing other people's behaviors is to project an image of credibility. We often do that by adopting a personal appearance that conveys expertise and authority. Consider uniforms. A judge's black robes, a doctor's white lab coat, and a police officer's badge and uniform all symbolize particular forms of experience and authority.[41] Other nonverbal cues are also influential. Speaking loudly, quickly, and expressively, with a good deal of pitch variation, makes a person sound more credible.[42] The use of eye contact and gestures that clarify the verbal message also enhances a person's credibility.[43] In particular, maintaining eye contact with someone while one is speaking powerfully influences persuasiveness.[44]

- *Promoting affiliation:* We are more persuaded by people we like than by people we don't.[45] Nonverbal behaviors that promote a sense of affiliation, closeness, and liking can therefore enhance our persuasive ability.

One behavior that often contributes to a sense of affiliation is touch.[46] Because we share more touch within close relationships than casual ones, being touched in appropriate, familiar ways can make us feel close to others. Several experiments have demonstrated that casual touches—such as a brief touch to the hand, forearm, or shoulder—make people more likely to comply with our requests.[47]

Affiliation is also enhanced by *interactional synchrony,* which is the convergence of two people's behaviors. When you mirror another person's posture, gestures, facial expressions, or vocal behaviors, you may cause that person subconsciously to perceive you as similar to him or her.[48] That perception is consequential for persuasion, because people like people who are similar to themselves.[49]

Your personal appearance, clothing, and demeanor can give you the credibility to influence others.

CONCEALING INFORMATION. A final function of nonverbal communication is to help people conceal information. Despite the cultural adage that "honesty is the best policy," people frequently decide not to be entirely truthful in their conversations with others. As we'll see in Chapter 12, individuals have many reasons for choosing to conceal information. Sometimes people lie to benefit themselves, such as faking an illness to get out of work. Sometimes they lie to avoid hurting themselves, such as concealing marital infidelity. Often, however, people choose to be deceptive to avoid hurting others—for example, by saying they're happy to receive a gift that they actually dislike.

One of the most commonly studied facial behaviors that can indicate deception is smiling. Most research studies have found that people don't differ in how much they smile when they're being honest as opposed to being deceptive. Rather, they differ in *how* they smile.[50]

When we're telling the truth, we're more likely to use a genuine smile that reflects actual positive emotion. That is the kind of smile we display when we hear good news or smell a delicious dinner cooking. When we're being dishonest, we're more likely to use a false smile, one that makes it appear as though we're happy even though we aren't. That is the smile we display when we run into a co-worker we don't like and are trying to appear glad to see him. Both types of smile draw the edges of the mouth upward, but a genuine smile also causes the skin around the eyes to wrinkle, whereas a false smile does not.

Attempting to conceal information can also influence certain vocal behaviors, particularly the pitch of the voice. Several studies have demonstrated that people speak with a higher pitch when they are deceiving than when they're telling the truth.[51] In one study, for instance, student nurses were asked to watch either a pleasant nature film or a grotesque film depicting amputations and burns. After viewing each film, the student nurses were told to convince an interviewer that the film they had just watched was pleasant and enjoyable. In one condition, therefore, the students were to be truthful, and in the other they were to be deceptive. By recording the participants' voices and analyzing them later, the researchers determined that the students' vocal pitch was significantly higher when they were attempting to deceive the interviewer than when they were telling the truth.[52]

Managing conversations, expressing emotions, maintaining relationships, forming impressions, influencing others, and concealing information are not the only functions of nonverbal behavior, but they are among the most valuable. In its own way, each of these functions helps us to communicate with others in efficient, productive ways.

LEARN IT What determines whether a form of communication is verbal or non-verbal? Why are we more likely to believe nonverbal behaviors than words when the two conflict? In what ways can nonverbal behavior help manage conversations or improve persuasion?

APPLY IT Consider how the tone of one's voice can influence meaning. Take a simple phrase such as "She made me do that." Say it first as though you're angry, then surprised, and, finally, sarcastic. Describe in a journal entry how your voice changes each time, even though the words are the same.

REFLECT ON IT How accurate do you think you are at interpreting other people's nonverbal behaviors? Why do you suppose that some people are better at "reading" nonverbal behavior than others?

2 Ten Channels of Nonverbal Communication

Nonverbal communication engages nearly all our senses, so it's probably no surprise that we experience it in so many different forms, or channels. In this section, we consider ten channels: facial displays, eye behaviors, movement and gestures, touch behaviors, vocal behaviors, the use of smell, the use of space, physical appearance, the use of time, and the use of artifacts.

Facial Displays

facial display The use of facial expression for communication.

It's hard to overstate the importance of **facial displays,** or facial expressions, in non-verbal communication. Indeed, according to the *principle of facial primacy,* the face communicates more information than any other channel of nonverbal behavior.[53] That principle is especially true for three important functions of facial displays: identity, attractiveness, and emotion.

IDENTITY. The face is the most important visual clue that humans use to identify one another.[54] You usually don't hang pictures of people's hands or feet on the wall; rather, you hang pictures of their faces, because the appearance of the face is the most reliable clue to identity. It's your face that appears on your driver's license and in your passport to help authorities identify you. Likewise, it's your face that appears in your high school yearbook to help your classmates remember you.

ATTRACTIVENESS.   The face also plays a major role in attractiveness. Even though we like to think that "beauty is in the eye of the beholder," there is remarkable consistency in what people find attractive in faces, both within and across cultures. Two properties that appear to be especially important in assessing attractiveness are symmetry and proportionality.

Symmetry refers to the similarity between the left and right sides of the face. For most of us, the two sides of our face look similar, but they aren't exactly alike. For both women and men, however, attractive faces have greater symmetry than unattractive faces.[55] Look at the photos in Figure 6.2 for an example of symmetric and asymmetric faces.

Proportionality refers to the relative size of one's facial features. Is your nose too big for your face? Are your ears too small? On a proportional face, all the features are of the proper size, not in an absolute sense but relative to one another.

Just as with symmetry, attractive faces have greater proportionality than unattractive ones. Unlike symmetry, which can be measured objectively, proportionality is a subjective judgment we make about a person's face. It makes a difference for the attractiveness of a face, however. Our tendency to find proportional faces attractive is a major reason why *rhinoplasty*, a surgical procedure to alter the size and shape of the nose, is one of the most commonly performed cosmetic surgeries in the United States.[56]

> **symmetry** The similarity between the left and right sides of the face or body.

> **proportionality** The size of facial features relative to one another.

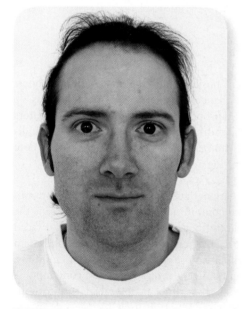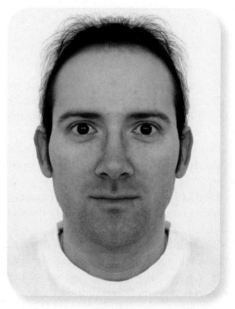

FIGURE 6.2 Facial Symmetry All else being equal, symmetrical faces are more attractive than asymmetrical faces. Researchers often study facial symmetry by taking a photograph of a face and modifying it with computer software to make it appear more symmetrical. For instance, the image on the left is an original, unretouched photo of an adult man's face, and the image on the right is a modified version of the same face that increases its symmetry. Research indicates that most people would find the face on the right more attractive. Which face do you find more attractive? Why?

FACT ? OR fiction

IN THE EYE OF WHICH BEHOLDER?
CULTURES VARY WIDELY IN PERCEPTIONS OF BEAUTY

Most of us have heard the cliché that "beauty is in the eye of the beholder," meaning that what one person finds attractive may not be appealing to another. This idea dates back at least to the third century B.C., a fact indicating that humans have long considered beauty to be subjective. If that were the case, we would expect to find little agreement from person to person, and from culture to culture, about what is physically attractive. How true is it that beauty is a matter of individual taste?

Not very true, according to research. In fact, a host of studies has shown just the opposite: People are remarkably consistent when it comes to judging attractiveness. In 2000, developmental psychologist Judith Langlois and her colleagues reviewed 130 of these studies and found that within cultures, people showed 90 percent agreement with one another when judging how attractive someone is. Moreover, people from different cultures agreed in their judgments of attractiveness 94 percent of the time. Thus, although we sometimes think of beauty as being culturally specific, Langlois and her team found that there was more agreement *across* cultures than within cultures in assessing attractiveness.

The researchers' findings indicate that people are much more similar than different when it comes to judging looks. Therefore, people who are considered attractive by one social group are much more likely than not to be considered attractive by other groups.

ASK YOURSELF

- Why does the idea that "beauty is in the eye of the beholder" persist?
- What do you find most physically attractive in members of the other sex? In members of your own sex?

Sources: Rubenstein, A. J., Langlois, J. H., & Roggman, L. A. (2002). What makes a face attractive and why: The role of averageness in defining facial beauty. In G. Rhodes & L. A. Zebrowitz (Eds.), *Facial attractiveness: Evolutionary, cognitive, and social perspectives* (pp. 1–33). Westport, CT: Ablex; Langlois, J. H., Kalakanis, L. E., Rubenstein, A. J., Larson, A. D., Hallam, M. J., & Smoot, M. T. (2000). Maxims or myths of beauty: A meta-analytic and theoretical review. *Psychological Bulletin, 126,* 380–423.

Because the nose occupies such a prominent position, making its size more proportional to that of other facial features often enhances a person's facial attractiveness.

It may seem odd to identify symmetry and proportionality as primary contributors to facial attractiveness, because we so often think of attractiveness as a highly individual assessment. As the "Fact or Fiction?" box explores, however, we're much more similar than dissimilar when it comes to judging a person's attractiveness.

EMOTION.   Recall from our earlier discussion that nonverbal behaviors communicate emotions more effectively than verbal communication. Because the face is the major channel of nonverbal behavior, we should not be surprised to learn that facial behavior is our primary means of communicating emotion. Our face enables us to make hundreds of different expressions, which we use to convey a host of emotions, from happiness, surprise, and determination to anger, fear, sadness, and contempt.

How accurately we decode those emotions from other people's facial expressions depends on several factors. The first factor is the emotion itself. As we saw in the earlier discussion of facial expressions, certain emotions are easier to decode than others. Happiness seems to be the easiest to decode. In one study, for instance, people accurately interpreted facial expressions of happiness more often than expressions of sadness or surprise.[57]

Another factor that affects our ability to decode messages is sex. In general, women tend to be better than men at decoding facial displays of emotion.[58] That observation

FIGURE 6.3 Facial Expressions in American Sign Language Facial expression plays a vital role in communicating ideas in American Sign Language (ASL). In some instances, the same hand sign is associated with different meanings if it is accompanied by different facial expressions. Both photographs feature the hand sign for "you," for example, but they involve different facial displays. The photo on the left would be interpreted as a question, such as "Are you?" or "Did you?" The photo on the right, however, would be interpreted as an exclamation, such as "It's you!" Although the hand sign is the same in the two photographs, the meaning differs because of the accompanying facial expression.

is true across different cultures. It might reflect the fact that in many societies, women are taught to be more friendly, supportive, and nurturing than men, so they learn better decoding skills as result.[59] Finally, people who are very outgoing and extroverted tend to be better at interpreting facial emotion displays than people who are shy or introverted.[60]

As a way to convey meaning, facial expressions are also extremely important to people who communicate through sign language. In sign language, facial expressions are sometimes called *nonmanual signals* because they work alongside hand signs to help express a particular meaning. For instance, when someone asks a yes-or-no question using sign language, his or her eyes are wide open, the eyebrows are raised, and the head and shoulders are pushed forward. Sometimes a person can change the entire meaning of a sign just by changing the facial expression that goes with it (Figure 6.3).[61]

Eye Behaviors

Because the eyes are part of the face, it may strike you as odd that researchers study eye behavior separately from facial behavior. However, just as facial behavior communicates more than any other nonverbal channel, the eyes communicate more than any other part of the face—thus, specialists treat **oculesics,** the study of eye behavior, as a separate nonverbal channel.

When people think about eye behavior, eye contact first comes to mind, for good reason. Eye contact plays a role in several important types of relational interaction. We use eye contact to signal attraction to someone and to infer that someone is attracted to us. We use it to gain credibility and to come across as sincere or trustworthy. We use it to persuade others and to signal that we are paying attention and understanding what others are saying. We can even use eye contact when we want to intimidate

oculesics The study of eye behavior.

someone or take a dominant or authoritative position in a conversation or a group discussion. Indeed, there are few times when we feel as connected to other people—in either positive or negative ways—as when we are looking each other in the eyes. As we'll see later in the chapter, however, those functions of eye contact often vary by culture.

Another eye behavior that has communicative value is pupil size. The pupil is the dark spot right in the center of each eye, which you can see in a mirror. Your pupils control how much light enters your eyes; as a result, they continually change in size. In darker environments, they dilate, or open wider, to take in all available light. In brighter environments, they contract, or become smaller, to avoid taking in too much light at once. What communication researchers find interesting, however, is that your pupils also dilate when you look at someone you find physically attractive and when you feel any kind of arousal, whether it is a positive response, such as excitement or sexual arousal, or a negative response, such as anxiety or fear. Watching how a person's pupils react to different social situations or conversational partners can therefore tell us something about his or her interest and arousal.

Movement and Gestures

Think about the different ways you can walk. When you're feeling confident, you hold your head high and walk with smooth, consistent strides. When you're nervous, you probably walk more timidly, stealing frequent glances at the people around you. Your *gait,* or the way you walk, is one example of how your body movement can communicate a particular message about you to others, such as "I feel proud" or "I feel scared." The study of movement is called **kinesics.**

kinesics The study of movement.

Now consider how you use your arms and hands to communicate. Perhaps it's to wave at your neighbor when you see her at the grocery store. Maybe it's to hold up two fingers to signal that you want two hot dogs at the football game concession stand. The use of arm and hand movements to communicate is called **gesticulation.** Research indicates that most people—even people who are born blind—use gestures even before they begin speaking.[62] Communication scholars divide gestures into several forms:

gesticulation The use of arm and hand movements to communicate.

■ **Emblems** are any gestures that have a direct verbal translation. Whenever you see an emblematic gesture, you should be able to translate it into words. Examples include the wave for "hello" or "goodbye" and the upright extended palm for "stop."

emblem A gesture with a direct verbal translation.

■ **Illustrators** are gestures that go along with a verbal message to clarify it. If you hold up your hands a certain distance apart when you say that fish you caught was "this big," your gesture serves as an illustrator to clarify what you mean by "this big."

illustrator A gesture that enhances or clarifies a verbal message.

■ **Affect displays** are gestures that communicate emotion, or *affect.* Some people wring their hands when they're nervous, and some cover their mouth with their hands when they're surprised. Those are both affect displays because they coincide with particular emotions.

affect display A gesture that communicates emotion.

■ **Regulators** are gestures that control the flow of conversation. One regulator with which you're probably very familiar is raising your hand when you're in a group and wish to speak. Gestures such as that help regulate who is speaking, and when, so that communication can flow smoothly.

regulator A gesture that controls the flow of conversation.

■ **Adaptors** are gestures that are used to satisfy some personal need, such as scratching an itch or picking lint off one's shirt. When we do those behaviors to our-

adaptor A gesture used to satisfy a personal need.

Gestures comprise body movements that have communicative meaning, and we begin to use them when we are young children. How would you interpret the gestures used by each of these people?

selves, we call them *self-adaptors*. When adaptors are directed at others (say, picking lint off someone else's shirt), they're called *other-adaptors*.

Touch Behaviors

Touch is the first of our five senses to develop. Even before an infant can see, hear, taste, or smell, his or her skin can respond to stimuli in the environment. Touch is the only sense without which we cannot survive. No matter how much we may cherish our other senses, it's entirely possible to survive without being able to see, hear, taste, or smell. Without our sense of touch, however, we would constantly be susceptible to burn, frostbite, and other potentially life-threatening injuries.

Haptics is the study of how we use touch to communicate. In terms of human communication, there are five major areas in which touch plays a critical role in conveying meaning: affection, caregiving, power and control, aggression, and ritual.

> **haptics** The study of how people use touch to communicate.

AFFECTIONATE TOUCH.   Sharing affection is one of the most important functions of touch. Behaviors such as hugging, kissing, and handholding communicate love, intimacy, commitment, and safety; they are commonplace in many romantic relationships, parent–child relationships, and friendships.[63] One reason affectionate touch is so important is that it contributes to our physical and mental well-being. Infants who are regularly cuddled experience faster physical development than those who are not, and people who are touched during stressful events experience less stress than those who are not.[64]

In recent years, concerns over sexual abuse of children have caused many public school districts to adopt strict "no touch" policies that prevent teachers, counselors, and other school staff from touching students in any way unless it is a medical emergency. As educator Tony Del Prete explains, "In an effort to keep one step ahead of sexual offenders, more and more schools are sending the message to adults—hands off! Touching children in schools has become virtually taboo."[65]

No matter how much we cherish our other senses, touch is the only sense we cannot survive without.

Although such zero-tolerance policies are designed to protect children, many experts have wondered whether preventing children from being touched actually does more harm than good. For example, researcher Tiffany Field, an internationally recognized expert on touch, believes that no-touch policies are "not a good idea, because children need touch for survival. Their growth and development thrive on touch. And how will they learn about love and affection if not through touch?"[66]

CAREGIVING TOUCH.   You're often touched by others while receiving some form of care or service. When you get your hair cut, have your teeth cleaned, receive a massage, or work with a personal trainer, you're touched in ways that correspond to those activities. Babysitters touch young children while cleaning or dressing them, and nursing home employees touch elderly residents while changing a bandage or helping them take a medication. Each of those actions is an example of caregiving touch because it is done in the course of providing a specific type of care or service.

Caregiving touch is distinguished from affectionate touch because it doesn't necessarily reflect any affection or positive emotion for the person being touched. When a physician touches you as part of a physical exam, for example, you don't infer from her touch that she has personal feelings for you. Rather, you interpret her touch as task-oriented. Your general expectation is that caregiving touch should be limited to caregiving contexts. Although you allow a dentist to touch your teeth and gums as part of a dental exam, for example, you probably wouldn't be comfortable allowing the same kind of touch if you ran into him at an art fair.

The fact that caregiving touch is task-oriented doesn't mean it isn't beneficial. Indeed, several forms of caregiving touch have important health benefits. For instance, adolescents and adults who receive therapeutic massage show improvement in a host of medical conditions, ranging from depression and stress to asthma, diabetes, cancer, multiple sclerosis, and HIV.[67] Caregiving touch can also induce calm and relieve stress for nursing home residents, as well as patients in a hospital or clinic.[68]

POWER AND CONTROL TOUCH.   Touch is sometimes used to exert power over other people's behavior. We occasionally touch people merely to suggest a certain course of behavior, as when the host of a party puts his hand on a guest's back to lead her in a certain direction. In other instances, we touch people to protect them by restricting their movement, such as when a nursing aide holds the arm of an elderly patient to help him walk without falling.

Although those behaviors involve some degree of control, they are intended to be friendly and helpful. In other cases, however, we touch people to control their behavior against their wishes. That type of touch can constitute a legitimate exercise of power, such as when police officers hold a suspect on the ground while applying handcuffs. It can also embody an illegitimate or unlawful exercise of power, such as when bullies hold an adolescent immobile to steal from him.

The use of control touch became controversial in the United States in 2010 when the Transportation Security Administration (TSA) adopted new airport passenger screening procedures requiring agents to pat down travelers in very invasive ways while searching for weapons. Some believed the searches violated passengers' privacy rights, whereas others considered them to be justified in the service of national security.

AGGRESSIVE TOUCH.   Behaviors done to inflict physical harm—such as punching, pushing, kicking, slapping, and stabbing—are forms of aggressive touch. Using touch behaviors to inflict physical harm on others almost always constitutes a criminal act. In fact, in some U.S. states, even acting as though you are going to touch

Pat downs by the Transportation Security Administration have stirred controversy. In what ways do the pat downs represent power and control touch?

someone to inflict harm, such as raising your hand as if you're about to strike, is a crime whether you actually touch the person or not. In those states, threatening to hit somebody is called "assault," and hitting the person is called "battery."

Despite such laws, incidents of violence and abuse using aggressive touch are still common, both in North America and in many societies around the world. Research indicates that although men are more likely than women to be the victims of violence at the hands of a stranger, women are more likely than men to be victimized by a close relational partner, such as a spouse.[69]

RITUALISTIC TOUCH. Some touches are ritualistic, meaning that we do them as part of a custom or a tradition. In North America, shaking hands is one such example: When we shake hands with people as part of a greeting ritual, we understand that the handshake does not convey any particular meaning about the relationship (the way that, say, holding hands would). By contrast, the greeting ritual in many cultures involves kissing on the lips or on the cheeks; people in those cultures would also understand those touches to be part of a ritual, not necessarily expressions of love or affection. Other ritualistic touches take place in the context of athletics. For example, basketball, wrestling, soccer, water polo, and many other sports involve body-to-body contact between players.[70]

Vocal Behaviors

Perhaps you have a high, breathy voice or a deep, booming voice. Maybe you usually talk very fast or quite loudly. Perhaps you have an accent that indicates where you grew up. And there may be times when you speak with a particular tone of voice to suggest that you are irritated, amused, or bored. We refer to those and other characteristics of the voice collectively as **vocalics.** We also refer to them as **paralanguage** (meaning "beside language") to indicate that they go along with the words we speak to convey meaning.

Some people are surprised to learn that the voice is a channel of nonverbal communication. After all, we speak with our voices, and spoken communication is verbal, right? That's true, but the only aspect of spoken communication that is verbal is *what we say*—the words themselves. Everything else about our voices, including the following characteristics, is nonverbal.

- *Pitch:* The pitch of the voice is an index of how high or deep it sounds. Every person's voice has an average *fundamental frequency,* which is the pitch one's voice hits the most often. On average, women's voices have a higher pitch than men's voices, and adults have deeper voices than children.

- *Inflection:* The inflection in the voice refers to the variation in its pitch. Voices that have a great deal of inflection are usually described as very expressive; those with little inflection are said to be monotone.[71]

- *Volume:* Volume is an index of how loud or quiet one's voice is. Most of us alter our vocal volume as the social context demands, such as by speaking quietly in a library and more loudly at a crowded reception. Everyone's voice also has an *average volume,* meaning that some people generally speak more loudly than others.

- *Rate:* The average adult speaks at a rate of approximately 150 words per minute,[72] but an individual might speak faster when excited or slower when unsure of himself or herself.

- *Filler words:* Filler words are non-word sounds such as "umm" or "er" that many people use to fill the silence during pauses while they're speaking. If we have to pause while speaking—say, to remember the word we want to use or the fact we want to describe—we can use filler words during the pause to indicate that we intend to continue speaking.

- *Pronunciation:* Pronunciation reflects how correctly a person combines vowel and consonant sounds to say a word. For example, how would you pronounce the word *victuals*? Although it looks as though it should be pronounced VIK-TULES, its correct pronunciation is VITTLES.

- *Articulation:.* Articulation, or *enunciation,* refers to how clearly one speaks. People who mumble or who speak with their mouth full demonstrate poor articulation. In contrast, people whose words are clear and easily understandable are good articulators.

- *Accent:* An accent is a pattern of pronouncing vowel and consonant sounds that is representative of a particular language or geographic area. Everyone speaks with an accent—even you—although individuals typically notice only those accents that are different from theirs.

- *Silence:* Silence is the absence of sound. We frequently use silence to convey meaning in conversations.[73] For instance, we often become silent when we are unsure how to respond to a question or when we have said as much as we wish to about a topic. We might also give someone the "silent treatment," ignoring him or her to convey defiance or disdain.[74] Finally, we can use silence to indicate that we do not wish to answer a question, perhaps to avoid embarrassment or offense.[75]

The Use of Smell

Of all the channels of nonverbal behavior, you might have the hardest time figuring out what smell has to do with human communication. It turns out that your sense of smell, called **olfactics,** operates subtly but powerfully to influence your reactions to others. In fact, two phenomena that are central to the human experience and to communication—memory and sexual attraction—are profoundly affected and regulated by smell.

olfactics The study of the sense of smell.

MEMORIES. Smells can affect our communication behavior by influencing our memories and moods. Have you ever smelled a particular scent—maybe a certain food or cologne—and instantly remembered a specific person, event, or place? Maybe the aroma of banana bread makes you think of your grandmother's kitchen, or the odor of motor oil reminds you of your uncle who used to work on cars. Those connections are examples of *olfactic association,* the tendency of odors to bring to mind specific memories. Why do olfactic associations matter for communication? It happens that memories often come with specific emotions, so when a smell reminds us of a particular person or place, it has the potential to affect our mood and behavior.

SEXUAL ATTRACTION. Smell also affects our communication by playing a role in determining to whom we are sexually attracted. Although you may think of sexual attraction as being driven mostly by visual cues—whether you think an individual *looks* attractive—in fact, your judgments about a person's sexual attractiveness are strongly affected by the way he or she smells to you. More specifically, research tells us that when we are looking for opposite-sex romantic partners, we are drawn to people whose natural body scent is the most different from our own. Why?

If two people have very similar scents, scientists have determined that their genes are also very similar, and that similarity can increase the probability of their producing genetically abnormal children. People produce much healthier children when they mate with partners who are genetically dissimilar to them. It happens that a person's natural body scent sends a signal to your brain that tells you how similar his or her genes are to yours. The more dissimilar a person's body odor is to yours, therefore, the more sexually attractive you will instinctively judge that individual to be.

Of course, not all instances of sexual attraction coincide with the desire to reproduce. Nonetheless, nature has connected smell to sexual attraction to help motivate healthy mate choices when procreation is our goal. We don't sniff out a person's scent profile consciously, however.

The Use of Space

When we interact socially, we constantly negotiate our use of space. That behavior becomes particularly apparent when our personal space is limited. Think of being in a crowded elevator or on a full airplane. Why do so many of us find such situations to be uncomfortable? The scientific study of spatial use, known as **proxemics,** explains that we each have a preferred amount of personal space that we carry like an invisible bubble around us. How much personal space each of us prefers depends on our temperament, the type of situation we're in, and how well we know the people around us.

proxemics The study of spatial use.

Anthropologist Edward T. Hall discovered that in Western cultures, people use four *spatial zones,* or levels of personal distance, when interacting with one another.[76]

intimate distance The distance most people in Western cultures maintain with intimate partners; ranges from 0 to 1½ feet.

personal distance The distance most people in Western cultures maintain with friends and relatives; ranges from 1½ to 4 feet.

social distance The distance most people in Western cultures maintain with casual acquaintances; ranges from 4 to 12 feet.

public distance The distance most people in Western cultures maintain with public figures during a performance; ranges from 12 to 25 feet or more.

In Western cultures, violating the norms for personal space can cause psychological discomfort.

Intimate distance, which ranges from 0 to approximately 1½ feet, is the zone we willingly occupy with only our closest and most intimate friends, family members, and romantic partners. With other friends and relatives, we typically maintain a **personal distance,** which Hall defined as extending from 1½ to about 4 feet. With customers, casual acquaintances, and others whom we don't know very well, we occupy a **social distance.** That ranges from about 4 to 12 feet and conveys more formal, impersonal interaction. Finally, **public distance** typically applies when someone is giving a speech or performing in front of a large audience. Public distances are usually 12 to 25 feet or greater, depending on the circumstance.

In interpersonal interaction, one factor that influences physical proximity is a person's disability status. Many people who do not have physical disabilities stand or sit farther away from individuals with physical disabilities than they do from others. In fact, communication scholars Dawn and Charles Braithwaite have suggested that people often shy away from interacting with persons with disabilities in the same way they tend to avoid people from other cultures.[77] Some researchers think that happens because people are inherently cautious around anyone they think of as different from themselves.[78]

Physical Appearance

Whether we intend to or not, we make all sorts of judgments about people on the basis of how they look. In particular, we have a strong predisposition to attribute positive qualities to physically attractive people, a tendency researchers refer to as the **halo effect.** In other words, when a person *looks* good, most of us subconsciously assume that he or she *is* good. Indeed, research has shown that we think attractive people are friendlier, more competent, and more socially skilled than less attractive people.[79]

Those perceptions translate into some real advantages for attractiveness. For instance, attractive people have higher self-esteem and date more frequently than less attractive people.[80] We are also nicer and more cooperative toward attractive people and more lenient toward attractive criminal defendants.[81] So if it seems at times that good-looking people get all the breaks, research tells us that is often the case. Much as we may like to claim otherwise, most of us are strongly influenced by physical appearance when making assessments about other people.

That preference for beauty has a dark side, however. Because physical attractiveness is so highly valued, some people go to dangerous extremes to achieve it. As you'll see in the "Communication: Dark Side" box, one of the unfortunate effects of the quest for beauty is the prevalence of eating disorders.

halo effect The tendency to attribute positive qualities to physically attractive people.

EATING DISORDERS AND THE PRESSURE TO BE ATTRACTIVE

There's little question that being physically attractive is an advantage. Because of the halo effect, we think attractive people are nicer, smarter, friendlier, more honest, and more competent than unattractive people, and we treat them accordingly. From childhood, most of us are taught to prize physical attractiveness. Unfortunately, this emphasis on physical looks can create enormous social and psychological pressures for people to make themselves as attractive as possible.

Because of the pressure to be attractive, and because being attractive often means being thin, an alarming number of people suffer from eating disorders.

The U.S. National Institute of Mental Health identifies two major types of eating disorders: anorexia nervosa and bulimia nervosa. *Anorexia nervosa* derives from the desire to be as thin as possible. People with anorexia pursue thinness relentlessly, through excessive dieting and exercise, self-induced vomiting, and the abuse of laxatives or diuretics. Anorexia is associated with major health risks, including low blood pressure, cardiac arrest, clinical depression, and suicide.

Bulimia nervosa is characterized by bingeing on large quantities of food and then compensating for overeating by vomiting, abusing laxatives or diuretics, and/or fasting. Whereas people with anorexia are often excessively thin, people with bulimia are often of normal weight for their age and height. Bulimia elevates the risk of several

health problems, including gastrointestinal disorders, clinical depression, and tooth decay (stemming from frequent purging).

Even people without eating disorders can take extreme measures to achieve thinness. Some undergo a procedure called *vertical banded gastroplasty*—better known as stomach stapling—that surgically alters the stomach to restrict food intake so that they will lose weight. A different procedure called *abdominoplasty*—or a tummy tuck—surgically removes excess skin and fat from the abdomen to make a person appear thinner.

FROM ME TO YOU

If you've never had an eating disorder, it might be easy to dismiss anorexia and bulimia as merely a symptom of *narcissism,* an unhealthy obsession with the self. Similarly, if you have never experienced clinical depression, you may wonder why depressed patients can't just "snap out of it." Eating disorders and depression are illnesses, however. People suffering from those disorders need not only medical treatment but also compassion and support from their relatives and friends.

Sources: National Institute of Mental Health: http://www.nimh.nih.gov/health/publications/eating-disorders/what-are-eating-disorders.shtml; National Eating Disorders Association: www.nationaleatingdisorders.org.

The Use of Time

Chronemics is the way people use time. You might not immediately think of time usage as nonverbal behavior, but the way we give (or refuse to give) our time to others can send them important messages about the way we feel about them. Because most of us spend our time on the people and activities that matter to us, for instance, the way we use time communicates messages about what we value. When we give our time to others, we imply that we value those people.

chronemics The use of time.

Our use of time also sends messages about power. When you go to see someone who is in a position of power over you, such as your supervisor, it is not uncommon to be kept waiting. However, you would probably consider it bad form to make a more powerful person wait for you. Indeed, the rule seems to be that the time of powerful people is more valuable than the time of less powerful people.

The Use of Artifacts

artifact An object or a visual feature of an environment with communicative value.

Each of us has certain physical environments that we inhabit and control, such as a house or an apartment, a residence-hall room, and an office. **Artifacts** are the objects and visual features within an environment that reflect who we are and what we like. One office you routinely visit, for instance, may be plush and opulent, with an oak desk, leather furniture, soft lighting, and expensive paintings on the walls. Another office may be plain and basic, featuring metal desks and chairs, fluorescent lighting, and bare walls. What messages might those different artifacts convey about the occupants of those two offices?

The way we place artifacts such as furniture within an environment can facilitate or inhibit interpersonal interaction. For example, teachers at Phillips Exeter Academy, a private preparatory school in New Hampshire, practice the "Harkness method" of teaching, which involves arranging up to 12 students and a teacher around an oval table. That arrangement is meant to diminish the separation between students and teachers, encouraging everyone to interact in an open, engaging way. In contrast, people who wish to discourage conversation in their offices or work environments might place their desks so that their back is to others.

The color of our environments can also influence nonverbal behavior by affecting our mood and disposition.[82] Specifically, "warm" colors such as red, orange, and yellow tend to be arousing, whereas "cool" colors such as blues and greens have calming effects.[83] Some researchers have suggested that those associations may have been formed early in human history, when individuals associated blues and greens with nature and nighttime—and therefore with being passive—and bright colors with sunshine and daytime—and therefore with being active.[84]

Artifacts reflect who we are and what we like. What messages would you infer about the owner of this chair?

Because the ten channels by which we communicate with others nonverbally encompass almost all our senses, nonverbal communication is a truly engaging experience. The "At a Glance" box summarizes those nonverbal channels. However, not everyone enacts nonverbal behavior in the same ways. As we'll see in the next section, culture and sex are both powerful influences on nonverbal communication styles.

LEARN IT What are three primary communicative functions of the face? How is eye behavior affected by culture? When is a gesture an emblem? Why is touch the most important sense for survival? Which aspects of the voice are verbal and which are nonverbal? How does smell affect memory and sexual attraction? What are Hall's four spatial zones? What is the halo effect? How does the use of time communicate messages about value? What is an artifact?

APPLY IT Dress in conservative business attire, and visit a restaurant, a department store, a bank, or some other business. Take note of how quickly you are helped by the employees and how friendly and eager they are to serve you. Now repeat the experiment in casual or shabby clothing. What differences do you notice in other people's behaviors toward you? What differences do you notice in your own behavior?

REFLECT ON IT What olfactic associations do you have? Why do you think the halo effect is so powerful?

3 Culture, Sex, and Nonverbal Communication

Suppose you've won an Olympic gold medal. As you stand atop the podium listening to your national anthem, with your friends and family beaming with pride from the stands, imagine the immense joy you would feel. In which nonverbal behaviors would you likely be engaged? How would you stand? What expression would be on your face? What gestures might you make?

It's easy to imagine that everyone would behave the same way you would in that situation. Research tells us, however, that our ways of communicating nonverbally are affected not only by our individual emotions and the demands of the situation but also by two major influences on nonverbal communication: culture and sex.

Culture Influences Nonverbal Communication

Many Americans who tune in to the Olympic Games on TV are surprised by certain of the nonverbal behaviors of athletes from different cultures. With regard to greeting behaviors, for example, foreign athletes may stand closer to—or farther from—one another other than is typical in U.S. culture. The reason is that those and many other nonverbal behaviors are shaped by the cultural practices with which people are raised.

Consider these many ways in which culture influences nonverbal communication:

- *Emblems:* The specific messages that an emblem symbolizes often vary by culture. The "come here" gesture commonly used in the United States means "goodbye" in China, Italy, and Colombia.[85] Gestures such as A-OK, thumbs up, and crossed fingers have sexual or obscene meanings in many parts of the world.[86]

4 Improving Your Nonverbal Communication Skills (p. 207)

- The ability to interpret nonverbal messages is a function of being sensitive to those messages and deciphering their meanings.

- The ability to express nonverbal messages can be enhanced by spending time with expressive people and taking part in activities that exercise your expressiveness.

KEY TERMS

adaptor (p. 194)
affect display (p. 194)
artifact (p. 202)
chronemics (p. 201)
emblem (p. 194)
emoticons (p. 180)
facial display (p. 190)
gesticulation (p. 194)
halo effect (p. 200)
haptics (p. 195)

high-contact culture (p. 204)
illustrator (p. 194)
immediacy behavior (p. 186)
intimate distance (p. 200)
kinesics (p. 194)
low-contact culture (p. 204)
nonverbal channels (p. 181)
nonverbal communication (p. 179)
oculesics (p. 193)
olfactics (p. 199)

paralanguage (p. 198)
personal distance (p. 200)
proportionality (p. 191)
proxemics (p. 199)
public distance (p. 200)
regulator (p. 194)
social distance (p. 200)
symmetry (p. 191)
turn-taking signal (p. 184)
vocalics (p. 198)

DISCUSSION QUESTIONS

1. In what ways would you alter your personal appearance if you were trying to look friendlier? Smarter? More liberal? Wealthier? What aspects of personal appearance convey such messages?

2. How do you feel when someone keeps you waiting? What messages do you get from the ways other people use time?

3. Touch is a form of nonverbal communication that is highly affected by social and cultural rules. What are some of the rules of touch that you perceive?

4. Why do you suppose we tend to believe nonverbal cues, even when they contradict a person's words? Give an example of a situation in which you would believe a person's verbal message instead of his or her nonverbal message.

PRACTICE QUIZ

MULTIPLE CHOICE

1. All of the following are characteristic of nonverbal communication *except*
   a. nonverbal communication is present in most interpersonal conversations
   b. nonverbal communication usually conveys more information than verbal communication
   c. nonverbal communication is the secondary means of communicating emotion
   d. nonverbal communication is metacommunicative

2. When Jorge proposed to Janie, she put her hand on her heart to signal her love for him. Which type of gesture did Janie enact?
   a. regulator
   b. adaptor
   c. affect display
   d. emblem

3. When a manicurist touches Suzi's hands while giving her a manicure, the type of touch Suzi receives is
a. affectionate
b. caregiving
c. ritual
d. power and control

4. Which of the following vocal behaviors is an index of how high or low a voice sounds?
a. inflection
b. volume
c. pitch
d. rate

5. Three behaviors that systematically change when people attempt to deceive are
a. smiling, eye blinking, pupil dilation
b. eye blinking, fidgeting, wincing
c. pupil dilation, wincing, smiling
d. none of the above

FILL IN THE BLANK

6. _____ is the first of the five senses to develop in humans.

7. People in _____ cultures stand close together and touch one another often.

8. Non-word sounds such as "umm" and "uh" are called _____ words.

9. Turning your posture away from the person you're speaking to, as a signal that you want to end the conversation, is called _____.

10. _____ is the convergence of two people's nonverbal behaviors.

ANSWERS

Multiple Choice: 1 (c); 2 (c); 3 (b); 4 (c); 5 (a); **Fill in the Blank:** 6 (touch); 7 (high-contact); 8 (filler); 9 (left-positioning); 10 (interactional synchrony)

RESEARCH LIBRARY

MOVIES

Nell (drama; 1994; PG-13)
This film tells the story of Nell, a young woman brought up in social isolation in the backwoods of North Carolina. Other than her deceased mother and twin sister, Nell has never met anyone until she is discovered by Jerome, a local doctor, and Paula, a psychologist who wants to study Nell in her laboratory. Because Nell speaks her own language, which is incomprehensible to outsiders, the movie provides many opportunities to witness communication via nonverbal signals.

Two Can Play That Game (comedy; 2001; R)
In this romantic comedy, Shanté discovers that her boyfriend Keith has been keeping company with other women. She decides to lure Keith back to her using various tricks and games, only to discover later that Keith is playing games with her. In several scenes, the characters use nonverbal behaviors (particularly affectionate behaviors) to convey messages to each other.

BOOKS AND JOURNAL ARTICLES

Andersen, P. A. (2007). *Nonverbal communication: Forms and functions* (2nd ed.). Long Grove, IL: Waveland.

Guerrero, L. K., & Floyd, K. (2006). *Nonverbal communication in close relationships.* Mahwah, NJ: Lawrence Erlbaum Associates.

Herz, R. S., & Inzlicht, M. (2002). Sex differences in response to physical and social factors involved in human mate selection: The importance of smell for women. *Evolution and Human Behavior, 23,* 359–364.

Manusov, V., & Patterson, M. L. (Eds.). (2006). *The Sage handbook of nonverbal communication.* Thousand Oaks, CA: Sage.

WEBSITES

www6.miami.edu/touch-research/
This site, from the Touch Research Institute in Miami, describes research demonstrating the many benefits of touch and touch therapy.

www.scienceofsmell.com
This website is the home page of the Smell and Taste Treatment and Research Foundation, a research institute in Chicago focusing on the importance of olfactics and taste in perception, relational communication, and health.

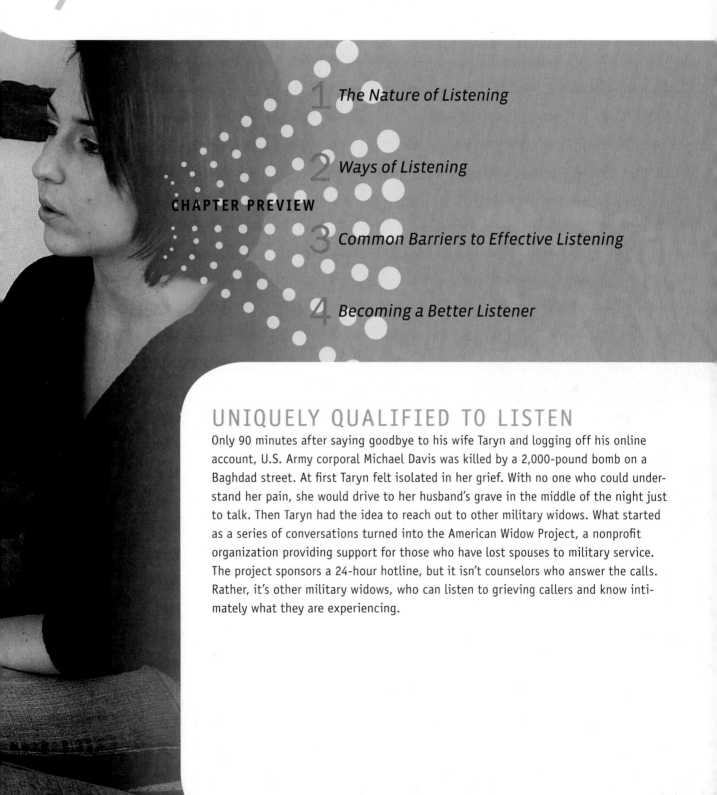

7 Listening

UNIQUELY QUALIFIED TO LISTEN

Only 90 minutes after saying goodbye to his wife Taryn and logging off his online account, U.S. Army corporal Michael Davis was killed by a 2,000-pound bomb on a Baghdad street. At first Taryn felt isolated in her grief. With no one who could understand her pain, she would drive to her husband's grave in the middle of the night just to talk. Then Taryn had the idea to reach out to other military widows. What started as a series of conversations turned into the American Widow Project, a nonprofit organization providing support for those who have lost spouses to military service. The project sponsors a 24-hour hotline, but it isn't counselors who answer the calls. Rather, it's other military widows, who can listen to grieving callers and know intimately what they are experiencing.

Y ou've probably had the experience of feeling as though someone was hearing you but not really listening. If so, you most likely felt frustrated. As you might imagine, problems with listening are fairly common in interpersonal relationships.[1]

Those problems arise because listening effectively is more difficult than you might think. Like other aspects of communication, listening is a skill you have to learn and practice. When you listen properly, the activity adds a great deal to the quality of your relationships. When you don't, your communication and relationships both suffer.

1 The Nature of Listening

The National Day of Listening acknowledges the importance of effective listening behaviors.

In 2008 the nonprofit group StoryCorps instituted the National Day of Listening to encourage Americans to listen to one another. The idea is that on the day after Thanksgiving, those who are interested spend one hour recording an interview with a loved one. Among the questions StoryCorps suggests posing are "What are some of the most important lessons you have learned in life?" and "How would you like to be remembered?" Participants are encouraged to archive the recordings of their interviews and to share them with relatives and friends so that everyone can experience the joy of listening.

If you're like most people, you probably don't give much thought to how well you listen. You can take classes to become a better speaker or better writer, but few schools offer courses to improve your listening skills. Yet most people spend much more time listening than speaking, writing, or engaging in other communicative behaviors. That's one reason why listening effectively is such a valuable skill.

What Is Listening?

Many people find effective listening hard to define. When someone complains "You never listen!" what exactly does that mean?

listening The active process of making meaning out of another person's spoken message.

We can define **listening** as the active process of making meaning out of another person's spoken message.[2] Two details about that definition are important to note. First, listening is an active process. That means it isn't automatic; rather, you have to *make* yourself listen to someone. Second, listening isn't just about hearing, or receiving input, but also about creating *meaning* from what you hear. Even if you and someone else are hearing the same message, you may construct different meanings for it, an indicator that the two of you are listening differently.

To understand that point, imagine you are listening to your brother's description of his new officemate, and you conclude that he finds her very competent and likable. After listening to the same description, however, your mother concludes that your brother feels threatened by his officemate's intelligence and self-confidence. The two of you heard the same description, but you listened to it differently. Each of us listens with a particular style, and that style influences what we hear and what meaning we make of it. What's your listening style? Check out the "Assess Your Skills" box to find out.

assess your SKILLS

PEOPLE, ACTION, CONTENT, TIME: WHAT'S YOUR *LISTENING STYLE?*

People listen for various reasons—sometimes to learn, sometimes to evaluate, and sometimes to provide empathy. Researchers have identified four distinct styles, each consisting of a different set of attitudes and beliefs about listening. Research suggests that most of us have one primary style that we use the most often. Which of the following styles best describes you?

- *People-oriented style:* This style emphasizes concern for other people's emotions and interests. As the name suggests, someone with a people-oriented style tries to find common interests with others. For instance, when Palik listens to his middle school students, he tries to understand what they are thinking and feeling so that he can relate to them effectively.

- *Action-oriented style:* This style emphasizes organization and precision. An action-oriented listener likes neat, concise, error-free presentations. For example, Monica approves when her interns fill her in on the week's activities in a clear, straightforward way, and gets frustrated when she can't understand them.

- *Content-oriented style:* This style emphasizes intellectual challenges. Someone with a content-oriented style likes to attend to details and think things through. Emma really enjoys listening to political commentators, for instance, because they make her think about her own social and political views.

- *Time-oriented style:* This style emphasizes efficiency. Someone with a time-oriented style prefers conversations that are quick and to-the-point. As an emergency room physician, for example, Ben relies on short and fast reports of a patient's condition from paramedics and nurses, and he gets impatient when they take more of his time than is necessary.

Each style has its distinctive strengths and weaknesses, so none is inherently better than the others. If you're primarily a people-oriented listener, for example, you're likely to get to know other people well, but you might not be able to work as efficiently as a time-oriented listener. Action-oriented listeners might do best in majors that emphasize clarity and precision, such as engineering and computer science, whereas content-oriented listeners might prefer majors that involve greater ambiguity and room for debate, such as art and political science.

Regardless of your primary listening style, research demonstrates that we adopt different styles for different situations. For instance, you might prefer a time-oriented style when you're in a rush but a people-oriented style when you're visiting loved ones. Similarly, you might adopt a content-oriented style when listening to your professor give a lecture but an action-oriented style when listening to the evening news.

Sources: Imhof, M. (2004). Who are we as we listen? Individual listening profiles in varying contexts. *International Journal of Listening, 18,* 36–45; Watson, K. W., Barker, L. L., & Weaver, J. B. (1995). The listening styles profile (LSP-16): Development and validation of an instrument to assess four listening styles. *International Journal of Listening, 9,* 1–13.

Listening to someone doesn't necessarily mean you're listening *effectively*. Effective listening involves listening with the conscious and explicit goal of understanding what the speaker is attempting to communicate. You might never know for certain whether you have understood a speaker's meaning exactly as he or she intended. However, if you're listening with the goal of understanding the speaker's meaning as best you can, you're listening effectively.

There are several barriers that make effective listening difficult, and different situations call for different types of listening. Understanding those dimensions of listening can help you improve your ability to listen effectively. That's a worthwhile goal, as we'll consider next.

The Importance of Listening Effectively

One of the reasons it's important to understand listening is that we do it so much of the time. How much of your day do you think you spend listening? In one study, researchers Kathryn Dindia and Bonnie Kennedy found that college students spent more time listening than engaging in any other communication activity. As shown in Figure 7.1, participants spent 50 percent of their waking hours listening.[3] In comparison, they spent only 20 percent of the time speaking, 13 percent reading, and 12 percent writing. Overall, then, they spent as much time listening as they did performing all other communication behaviors combined. Other studies have found similar results, at least with college students, suggesting that most of us spend a similar percentage of our communication time listening.[4]

The ability to listen effectively is important to our success in a variety of contexts. For example, good listening skills are vital in the workplace. Suppose, for instance, that your employees don't listen when you tell them the alarm they will soon be hearing will signal a fire drill, not a real fire. Some of them might panic, and others might injure themselves as they rush frantically from their work spaces. As another example, imagine that your manager at work doesn't listen when her employees warn her about problems with the company's equipment. As a result, a critical production line breaks down, stalling operations for a week.

Those examples illustrate how consequential effective listening can be in the workplace. In a survey of 1,000 human resource professionals, participants ranked listening as the single most important quality of effective managers.[5] The top 10 qualities appear in Table 7.1. In other research, listening topped the list of the most important communication skills in families and in personal relationships.[6] Indeed, being a good listener is vital to just about every social and personal bond we have.[7]

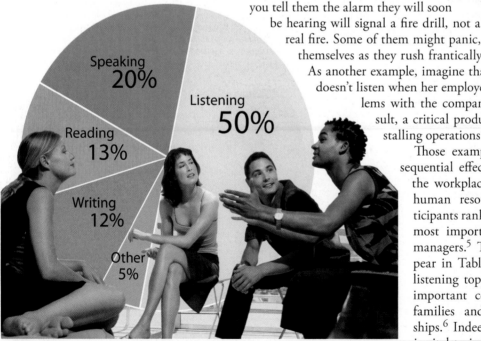

FIGURE 7.1 Percentages of Various Communication Activities

Speaking 20%

Reading 13%

Writing 12%

Other 5%

Listening 50%

TABLE 7.1

Most Important Attributes of Effective Managers, According to 1,000 Human Resource Professionals Surveyed

1. Ability to listen effectively and counsel
2. Ability to work well with others one-on-one
3. Ability to work well in small groups
4. Ability to gather accurate information from others to make a decision
5. Ability to write effective business reports
6. Ability to give feedback
7. Knowledge of job
8. Ability to present a good public image for the company
9. Ability to use computers
10. Knowledge of finance

Source: Windsor, J. L., Curtis, D. B., & Stephens, R. D. (1997). National preferences in business and communication education: A survey update. *Journal of the Association for Communication Administration, 3,* 170–179. Material is adapted from Table 4, p. 176.

Listening well doesn't affect just our relationships; it also has implications for our physical health. When a pharmacist gives us instructions about how to take a medication, for instance, we need to listen carefully, to avoid taking the medication improperly. When a doctor tells us what foods to avoid and when a nurse instructs us about caring for a wound, we need to be sure we've understood.

If listening skills are so valuable, why don't we work harder to improve them? One reason is that many of us overestimate our listening abilities. In one study, 94 percent of corporate managers rated themselves as good or very good at listening, whereas not a single one rated himself or herself as poor or very poor. Several of their employees told quite a different story, however: They rated their managers' listening skills as weak.[8] Studies like those indicate that there is little association between how good we think we are at listening and how good other people think we are.[9]

Listening skills are particularly important in the workplace. However, one study found that many employees rated their employers' listening skills as weak.

Some Misconceptions About Listening

Are you surprised to learn that people often overestimate their listening abilities? Here are some other misunderstandings about the listening process.

MYTH: HEARING IS THE SAME AS LISTENING. Some people use the terms *hearing* and *listening* interchangeably, but they aren't the same activity. Hearing is merely the perception of sound. Most people hear sounds almost continuously—you hear the neighbor's dogs barking, the television playing in the background, the car alarm that wakes you in the middle of the night. Hearing is a passive process that occurs when sound waves cause the bones in your inner ear to vibrate and send signals to your brain.

Just because we're hearing something doesn't mean we're listening to it. Unlike hearing, listening is an active process of paying attention to a sound, assigning meaning to it, and responding to it. Hearing is a part of that process, but listening requires much more than just perceiving the sounds around you.

By the same token, we sometimes listen without hearing, and our understanding can be impaired as a result. That point is illustrated humorously in a series of television ads aired a few years ago by the Cingular/AT&T telephone company. Each ad depicted a cell phone call between two people in which they unknowingly lost their cellular connection halfway through the conversation. In every case, one speaker interpreted the other's silence as meaningful, when in fact it was simply the result of the dropped call. For instance, just after telling her husband that she was expecting a baby, one woman's call was dropped without her knowledge. Although her husband exclaimed his excitement about the pregnancy, all she heard was silence, which she incorrectly interpreted as indifference or fear on his part. Even though she was trying to listen, then, she wasn't hearing.

MYTH: LISTENING IS NATURAL AND EFFORTLESS. It's easy to think of listening as a completely natural, mindless process, much like breathing. However, listening is a learned skill, not an innate ability like hearing. We have to acquire our listening abilities. Just as we are taught to speak, we have to be taught to listen—and to listen effectively.[10] Many of us are taught by our experiences. Perhaps you can recall instances when you didn't listen effectively to a supervisor's instructions about how to accomplish a work project, and you made poor decisions as a result. Maybe you have been in situations with a romantic partner when you didn't listen as effectively as you could have, and an unnecessary argument followed. Good communicators learn from their mistakes, so such experiences have probably taught you the importance of effective listening.

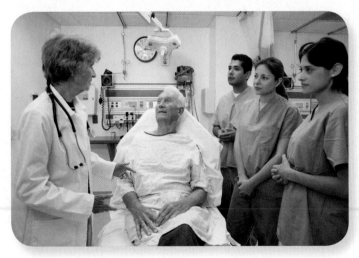

Recognizing the importance of good listening skills in the health care field, several medical schools in the United States have added coursework to teach young doctors how to listen effectively to their patients.

We also learn through instruction, such as the instruction you are receiving in your interpersonal communication course. The more you learn about what makes listening effective and what barriers to watch out for, the better equipped you'll be to listen effectively to other people.

The fact that listening is a skill also means that people vary in their listening abilities. Just as some people are better athletes, singers, or writers than others, some people are better listeners than others. Finally, as with most skills, you can improve your listening ability through education and training.[11] Counselors and social workers are trained to listen effectively to clients, a skill that improves the quality of services they provide. In recent years, medical schools around the United States have added coursework and role-play activities on effective listening and other interpersonal skills to their curricula for training physicians. People in many professions—from education and the ministry to customer service and politics—can benefit from training in effective listening.

MYTH: ALL LISTENERS HEAR THE SAME MESSAGE. We might assume that when several people are listening to the same message, they are all hearing and understanding the message in the same way. As we learned in Chapter 4, however, our perceptions of what we see and hear are always limited. Our experiences, our biases, and even our gender and culture all influence how we create meaning from the information we take in.

The safer assumption is that all listeners are hearing something slightly different, because each of us is filtering the message through our own unique experiences and biases. As communication scholar Ben Broome points out, even the most skilled listener can't "step outside" himself or herself entirely.[12] Broome is not implying that no one can ever understand another person's meaning. Rather, he is encouraging us to learn to be aware of how different people might interpret and understand the same message differently.

Culture and Sex Affect Listening Behavior

Cultural messages shape many communication behaviors, and listening is no exception. In particular, listening behavior appears to be affected by how people in a given culture think about the importance of time. In individualistic cultures, people often look upon time as a resource. For example, Americans commonly say that "time is money," and they view time as a commodity that can be saved, spent, and wasted. People in such cultures typically place a premium on efficiency and expect others to do the same. They value direct, straightforward communication, and listeners become impatient with speakers who don't "get to the point."[13] In contrast, collectivistic cultures such as Korea emphasize social harmony over efficiency. As part of their listening behavior, people in those cultures often pay close attention to nonverbal behaviors and contextual cues to determine the meaning of a speaker's message.[14]

Fewer studies have focused on sex, but research has identified some differences between women and men in listening behavior. For one, men are more likely than women to interrupt someone they are listening to.[15] Women have been shown to maintain eye contact while listening to their conversational partners more than men do.[16] Some commentators have even gone so far as to suggest that women and men have completely different styles of listening—but is that true? Check out "Fact or Fiction?" to find out.

LEARN IT How is listening different from hearing? Approximately how much of a person's communication time is spent listening? Why isn't listening a natural, effortless process? How do people in individualistic and collectivistic cultures listen differently?

APPLY IT The next time you have a conversation with someone, focus your attention on what she or he is saying rather than on how you're going to respond. With practice, you can learn to listen more intently to others.

REFLECT ON IT In what situations do you find you have difficulty listening effectively? How do you think your own cultural values and experiences influence the way you listen?

SEX MATTERS: MEN AND WOMEN LISTEN DIFFERENTLY

In this book we examine several stereotypes about how women and men communicate. Some are outright false, others are true, and still others are true but highly exaggerated. One stereotype that relates to listening is that women and men have different listening styles. Specifically, the idea is that women are more interested in people, whereas men are more interested in facts. Is the stereotype fact or fiction?

Recent research suggests that it is a fact. In a study of adults' listening styles, researchers Stephanie Sargent and James Weaver found that women scored themselves higher on people-oriented listening than men did. Those results suggest that women use their listening skills to learn about people and make connections with others. By contrast, men scored themselves higher on content-oriented listening than women did, suggesting that men use their listening skills to take in content and solve intellectual challenges.

Research shows that women and men have different styles of listening. Women are more likely than men to say they use their listening skills to learn about people and make personal connections. Men are more likely to say they use their listening skills to solve intellectual challenges.

The study's findings don't mean that women don't engage in content-oriented listening and that men don't engage in people-oriented listening—they do. Rather, it shows that women and men—overall—have different approaches to listening, as the stereotype suggests.

You might recall that people often overestimate their listening abilities. How, then, can we have confidence in the results of a study that relies on self-reports? Because virtually every study of listening styles uses a self-report method for collecting data, that's a critical question. The answer is that self-reporting on *how* one listens is different from self-reporting on *how well* one listens. Research indicates that although many of us exaggerate how well we listen, we are much more accurate at reporting what our styles of listening are.

How can we use the information about sex differences in listening styles to improve our communication abilities? When we're communicating with members of the other sex, we can consider their listening tendencies and formulate our messages accordingly. Let's say you're describing a recent conflict you had with your romantic partner to different groups of friends. Because you know that men tend to focus on the content of what they're

hearing, you might tailor your description to highlight what the conflict was about and what each person's position was. Because you know that women tend to focus on the interpersonal aspects of what they're hearing, you might adapt your description to focus on what the conflict taught you about your relational partner and yourself. It's important to remember that the sex differences in listening preferences are just tendencies. Nevertheless, they can provide clues to how best to communicate with members of each sex.

ASK YOURSELF

■ How do these general sex differences compare with the behaviors of the women and men you know?

■ Is one style of listening better than another? How might the particular context or situation affect whether women's style or men's style of listening is appropriate?

Source: Sargent, S. L., & Weaver, J. B. (2003). Listening styles: Sex differences in perceptions of self and others. *International Journal of Listening, 17,* 5–18.

2 Ways of Listening

Until now, we've been viewing listening as though it were a single, unified activity. In truth, listening effectively consists of several stages, all of which are equally important.

Stages of Effective Listening

Judi Brownell, a professor of organizational communication, is an expert on listening who developed the **HURIER model** to describe the six stages of effective listening: hearing, understanding, remembering, interpreting, evaluating, and responding.[17] ("HURIER" is an acronym for those stages.) We don't necessarily have to enact the stages in order; sometimes listening effectively requires us to go back and forth among them. When we listen effectively, however, those are the behaviors we adopt. Let's take a closer look at each one.

HEARING. Recall that hearing is the physical process of perceiving sound. That is where the listening process begins. As we've considered, we can hear someone without listening to what he or she is saying. We tend to do so when we're tired, uninterested in what the person is saying, or hearing multiple voices at once as in a crowded restaurant. Although we sometimes hear without listening, however, we can't really listen to people unless we can hear them, or at least have access to their words. In computer-mediated communication, we can also pay close attention to another person's words even if they are written rather than spoken. In face-to-face interaction, though, hearing is the first step in effective listening. People with hearing impairments find ways to overcome that challenge, such as reading lips and using sign language.

Although hearing another person's words is the first step in effective listening, it can also violate the person's privacy if he or she doesn't wish to be heard. Advances in communication technology unfortunately make privacy violations common. Check out the "Communication: Dark Side" box to learn what to do if you think you're a victim.

UNDERSTANDING. It's not enough simply to hear what someone is saying—you also have to understand it. To understand means to comprehend the meanings of the words and phrases you're hearing.[18] If someone is speaking in a language you don't understand, you might be able to hear that person, but you won't be able to listen effectively. The same is true when you hear technical language or jargon that is unfamiliar to you: Even if the speaker is speaking your language, you can't effectively listen if you don't understand the words. If you're uncertain whether you understand what a speaker is saying, the most effective course of action is usually to ask the person questions to check your understanding.

REMEMBERING. The third stage of the HURIER model is remembering, or being able to store something in your memory and retrieve it when needed.[19] Remembering what you hear is important for interpersonal communication because it can help you to avoid awkward situations. For instance, you might have had the embarrassing experience of running into someone whose name you couldn't remember, even though you had met the person on several prior occasions. In such interpersonal encounters, remembering what you heard previously can help you communicate with others more effectively.

HURIER model A model of effective listening that involves hearing, understanding, remembering, interpreting, evaluating, and responding.

UNINVITED LISTENING: CELL PHONE SNOOPING

As important as listening is, we don't *always* want others to listen to us. As communication technology advances, however, so does the capacity for electronic eavesdropping, such as listening to other people's cell phone calls without their knowledge or consent. Inexpensive and widely available software makes cell phone snooping possible. Once installed on your phone—a process that takes only a few minutes—the software permits a stalker to listen to your calls, read your text messages, and even eavesdrop on your face-to-face conversations by activating your speakerphone feature.

A 2009 Department of Justice report indicates that those invasions of privacy are often part of a larger pattern of stalking by jealous current or former romantic partners. If someone has installed eavesdropping software on your cell phone, changing your phone number won't solve the problem. Experts suggest that you either have your cellular service provider reinstall the operating software or simply purchase a new phone.

FROM ME TO YOU

None of us likes to think our own privacy might be invaded. To reduce the chances of unauthorized listening, keep your phone in your direct possession as much as possible and restrict access to it—such as by locking it in a desk drawer—when you cannot carry it.

Source: See Baum, K., Catalano, S., Rand, M., & Rose, K. (2009, January). *Stalking victimization in the United States*. Washington, DC: U.S. Department of Justice, Bureau of Justice Statistics.

Research shows that most people can recall only 25 percent of what they hear—and of that portion, they remember only about 20 percent of it accurately.[20] The average person is therefore not especially good at remembering.

Fortunately, remembering is a skill you can practice and improve. *Mnemonic devices* are tricks that can improve short- and long-term memory. Such devices come in several forms. If you've ever studied music, for instance, perhaps you learned to recall the lines of the treble staff—EGBDF—by treating the letters as an initialism for a phrase, such as "every good boy does fine." You might also develop rhymes to help you remember certain rules, such as when spelling in English "*i* before *e*, except after *c*." Another mnemonic device is the *acronym,* a word formed from the first letters or parts of a compound term. If you remember the elements of Brownell's effective listening model by learning the word *HURIER,* you are employing that type of mnemonic device. Research suggests that using mnemonic devices can significantly enhance memory.[21]

The process of interpreting involves paying attention to a speaker's verbal and nonverbal behaviors so you can assign meaning to what she has said.

INTERPRETING. Besides hearing, understanding, and remembering, an effective listener must interpret the information he or she receives. The process of interpreting has two parts. The first part is paying attention to all the speaker's verbal and nonverbal behaviors so that you can assign meaning to what the person has said. Suppose your friend Maya says, "It's a beautiful day outside." On the basis of her facial expressions and tone of voice, you might interpret this message either as sincere—meaning that Maya thinks today's weather is beautiful—or as sarcastic—meaning she thinks the weather is awful. Those are very different interpretations of Maya's message, even though her words are the same.

The second part of interpreting is signaling your interpretation of the message to the speaker. If you interpret Maya's statement as sincere, you might smile and say you're looking forward to getting outside to enjoy the great weather. However, if you interpret her statement as sarcastic, you might laugh or respond with a sarcastic remark of your own. Signaling not only lets the speaker know you're following along with what he or she is saying but also allows you to confirm your interpretations. Suppose that Maya intended her comment about the weather to be sarcastic but you interpreted it as sincere. If you smiled and said you were looking forward to getting outside, that response would probably signal to Maya that you have misinterpreted the intent of her statement. She might then say, "I was just kidding" to correct your interpretation.

EVALUATING.   Several events happen at the evaluation stage. For one, you're judging whether the speaker's statements are accurate and true. You're also separating facts from opinions and trying to determine why the speaker is saying what he or she is saying. Finally, you're considering the speaker's words in the context of other information you have received from that speaker or other sources. All those activities help you to be an active, engaged listener rather than a passive recipient of information.

RESPONDING.   The last stage of effective listening is responding, or indicating to a speaker that you're listening. We sometimes call that process *giving feedback,* and we do it both verbally and nonverbally using a variety of strategies.[22] Below are seven types of listening responses, arranged in order from the most passive to the most active strategies:

- *Stonewalling:* Responding with silence and a lack of facial expression. Stonewalling often signals a lack of interest in what the speaker is saying.
- *Backchanneling:* Nodding your head or using facial expressions, vocalizations such as "uh-huh," and verbal statements such as "I understand" and "That's very interesting" to let the speaker know you're paying attention.
- *Paraphrasing:* Restating in your own words what the speaker has said, to show that you understand. Check out the "Got Skills?" box for tips on practicing that useful skill.
- *Empathizing:* Conveying to the speaker that you understand and share his or her feelings on the topic.
- *Supporting:* Expressing your agreement with the speaker's opinion or point of view.
- *Analyzing:* Providing your own perspective on what the speaker has said.
- *Advising:* Communicating advice to the speaker about what he or she should think, feel, or do.

Depending on the situation, some of those responses may be more useful or appropriate than others. For instance, if you're listening to a friend who has just lost her favorite uncle

In the HBO series The Sopranos, *Tony Soprano (played by James Gandolfini) was a powerful, dangerous man with a large ego and many dark secrets. Dr. Jennifer Melfi (played by Lorraine Bracco) had the daunting task of counseling him. During therapy sessions, Dr. Melfi used backchanneling, paraphrasing, and analyzing as effective ways of responding. Because of Tony Soprano's involvement in crime, she was often unable to empathize or support and was reluctant to advise.*

[PARAPHRASING]

Paraphrasing is handy listening skill.

WHAT?

Learn to restate a speaker's message in your own words.

WHY?

To indicate that you understand the message and to give the speaker a chance to correct your interpretation if necessary, as when someone is giving you driving directions or providing advice.

HOW?

1. When you encounter a statement whose meaning is potentially ambiguous, determine what you *think* the statement means.

2. Formulate a way of making the same statement using different words.

3. Respond to the speaker: "So what you're saying is . . . " and then make the statement in your own words.

TRY!

1. Role-play a conversation about politics with a classmate. When you're unclear about the meaning of one of your partner's statements, paraphrase it.

2. Your partner will likely either confirm your interpretation of the statement or correct it. Either way, your understanding of his or her meaning will be enhanced.

CONSIDER: *Why is it useful to check your understanding of a speaker's statements when you're listening?*

---

to heart disease, empathizing and supporting are probably the most helpful responses. Stonewalling, backchanneling, or paraphrasing might make it seem as though you don't care about your friend, and analyzing or advising may seem insensitive. In comparison, if you're an accountant listening to a client who is wondering how she can make the most of her stock portfolio, then analysis and advice are probably called for.

In addition to the specific situation, our cultural expectations influence our ideas concerning appropriate listening responses, particularly with respect to appropriate nonverbal behavior. As we considered in Chapter 6, for instance, most Americans expect listeners to maintain eye contact with them while they're speaking. For that reason, they often assume that listeners who look down or away aren't listening. In many Native American cultures, however, looking down or away while listening is a sign of respect.[23]

The "At a Glance" box recaps the HURIER model. According to Brownell, the model's six stages characterize effective listening no matter why we happen to be listening. Let's shift gears a bit and take a look at a closely related topic: the most common types of listening.

Types of Listening

When we talk about different types of listening, we're referring to the varying goals we have when we listen to other people. Sometimes we listen to learn. At other times, our goal is to evaluate. On still other occasions, our goal is to empathize. Those goals aren't necessarily distinct; sometimes we listen with more than one of them in mind. When we distinguish among types of listening, we therefore are considering what our primary listening goal is at a given time.

INFORMATIONAL LISTENING. Much of the listening you engage in during class or at work is **informational listening,** or listening to learn. Whenever you watch the news or listen to driving directions or pay attention to a professor's lecture, you're engaged in informational listening.

informational listening
Listening to learn something.

HURIER MODEL OF EFFECTIVE LISTENING

Hearing	Physically perceiving sound
Understanding	Comprehending the words we have heard
Remembering	Storing ideas in memory
Interpreting	Assigning meaning to what we've heard
Evaluating	Judging the speaker's credibility and intention
Responding	Indicating that we are listening

Informational listening is both very common and extremely helpful. Indeed, it is one of the most important ways we learn. It is also the most passive type of listening. When we're engaged in informational listening, we are simply taking in information. Even though we may be listening effectively and even taking notes, we are listening primarily to learn something new rather than to analyze or support the speaker's information.

CRITICAL LISTENING. When your goal is to evaluate or analyze what you're hearing, you are engaged in **critical listening.** You listen carefully to a commercial to determine whether you want to buy the product it's advertising. You listen to a political speech and evaluate the merits of what you're hearing. You listen critically to your mother's description of her recent medical appointment to determine how worried she is about the results of her blood test.

A key point is that "critical" listening doesn't necessarily mean disapproving of or finding fault with what you're hearing. Instead, it means analyzing and evaluating the merits of what a speaker is saying. Compared with informational listening, therefore, critical listening is a more active, engaging process. It requires you not only to take in information but also to assess and judge it. As we will see at the end of this chapter, practicing critical listening is one of the best ways of becoming a better listener.

critical listening Listening with the goal of evaluating or analyzing what one hears.

EMPATHIC LISTENING. Perhaps the most challenging form of listening is **empathic listening,** which occurs when you are trying to identify with the speaker by understanding and experiencing what he or she is thinking or feeling.[24] When you are talking to a friend who has just his job or listening to a family member describe the stress of her divorce, you can use empathic listening to give comfort and support.

Effective empathic listening requires two skills. The first, *perspective taking,* is the ability to understand a situation from another individual's point of view.[25] The second skill, *empathic concern,* is the ability to identify how someone else is feeling and then experience those feelings yourself.[26] When you're listening to a co-worker describing his recent diagnosis of a particular disease, for instance, you can practice perspective taking by trying to think

empathic listening Listening in order to experience what another person is thinking or feeling.

about the situation as he is thinking about it. You can practice empathic concern by imagining how he must feel and then sharing in those emotions.

Empathic listening is different from *sympathetic listening,* which means feeling sorry for another person. If your neighbors lost their grandson to leukemia, for instance, you might be able to sympathize with them even if you can't truly understand their feelings. In contrast, the goal of empathic listening is to understand a situation from the speaker's perspective and to feel what he or she is feeling. For example, you might be listening to a friend who didn't get into her first-choice graduate school and trying to convey that you share her disappointment. Listening empathically is a challenge, because your perceptions can cause you to focus on how *you* would be feeling in the same situation rather than how *the speaker* is feeling.

OTHER TYPES OF LISTENING.   Informational, critical, and empathic listening aren't the only types of listening in which we engage. For example, we sometimes engage in *inspirational listening,* which is listening in order to be inspired. That type of listening is common when we're listening to a sermon or motivational speech. At other times, we engage in *appreciative listening,* which is listening for pure enjoyment. We listen appreciatively when someone tells a funny story or sings one of our favorite songs. Appreciative listening also comes into play when we watch a TV show or film we enjoy, or attend a performance featuring talent we admire. When it comes to interpersonal interaction, however, informational, critical, and empathic listening are often the most common and most important types.

LEARN IT   What are the differences between interpreting a message and responding to it? How are the goals of informational, critical, and empathic listening different?

APPLY IT   Develop a mnemonic device to help you remember the seven types of listening responses in order from most passive to most active (stonewalling, backchanneling, paraphrasing, empathizing, supporting, analyzing, advising). Record the device in a journal and then practice it, particularly as you review for quizzes or exams.

REFLECT ON IT   When do you have a hard time understanding a speaker? Which type of listening are you the best at?

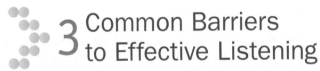

3 Common Barriers to Effective Listening

In the movie *The Break-Up* (2006), Brooke Meyers (played by Jennifer Aniston) asks her boyfriend Gary Grobowski (played by Vince Vaughn) to bring home a dozen lemons for a dinner party she is throwing for their families. Gary doesn't listen, and he brings home only three lemons. Brooke is distressed, because their company is arriving shortly. She expresses her concern to Gary, who continues to watch television while talking to her:

Brooke: You got three lemons.

Gary: What my baby wants, my baby gets; you know that.

Brooke: I know, but I wanted 12, baby wanted 12.

Gary: Why would you want 12 lemons?

Brooke: Because I'm making a 12-lemon centerpiece.

Gary: So no one's actually even eating them, they're just show lemons?

Brooke: Yeah, they're just show lemons. To go in the center of the table. I'm glad you find that amusing, but I cannot fill a vase with only three lemons.

Brooke isn't upset just because she doesn't have the right number of lemons. She's also upset because Gary didn't listen to her when she asked him to bring home a dozen lemons, and she gets increasingly frustrated because he continues watching television during their conversation instead of paying attention to her.

This scene raises the question, Why are so few of us good listeners? One answer is that several problems get in our way, acting as barriers to our ability to listen well. In this section, we examine several obstacles to effective listening.

Noise

How many stimuli are competing for your attention right now? How many different stimuli demand your attention at work when your boss, customers, and co-workers all try to talk to you at once? In the context of listening, *noise* refers to anything that distracts you from listening to what you wish to listen to.

Most of us find it more difficult to listen to a conversational partner when there are other sounds in the environment, such as a TV or loud music.[27] It isn't just sound that can distract us, though. If we're hungry, tired, or in an environment that is especially cold or hot, those influences can also qualify as noise because they interfere with our ability to listen effectively.[28]

When you're faced with such distractions, try to focus your attention on your conversational partner and listen intently to what he or she is saying. To do so, you must be conscious of noise in your environment and identify those factors that are drawing your attention away from your conversation. Eliminating or ignoring those noise sources—for example, by turning off your car radio or ignoring your ringing cell phone—will help you focus on your partner. If you're being distracted by noise that you can't ignore or reduce at the time, you might reschedule your conversation for a time when fewer stimuli are competing for your attention.

Pseudolistening and Selective Attention

At one time or another, you've probably pretended to be paying attention to someone when you weren't really listening. That behavior is called **pseudolistening.** When you pseudolisten, you use feedback behaviors that make it seem as though you're paying attention, even though your mind is elsewhere.

A variation of pseudolistening is **selective attention,** which means listening only to what you want to hear and ignoring the rest.[29] When you engage in selective attention, you are listening to some parts of a person's message and pseudolistening to other parts. In her job as an insurance adjuster, for instance, Sue-Ann receives an evaluation from her supervisor every January. Usually, most of her supervisor's comments are positive, but some of them suggest ways in which Sue-Ann could improve her performance. The problem is, Sue-Ann doesn't listen to those suggestions. Instead, she listens selectively, paying close attention to her supervisor's praise and only pretending to listen to her critiques.

pseudolistening Using feedback behaviors to give the false impression that one is listening.

selective attention Listening only to what one wants to hear.

Engaging in pseudolistening and selective attention occurs for many reasons. Maybe you're bored with what the speaker is saying, but you don't want to seem rude. Maybe you don't understand what you're hearing, but you're too embarrassed to admit it. Maybe you're paying attention to something else while someone is talking to you, or maybe you simply don't like what the other person is saying. Whatever the reason, pseudolistening and selective attention not only are barriers to effective listening but also can be a source of frustration for the speakers you're pretending to listen to. This frustration arises because people are often aware when others aren't listening to what they're saying. How do you feel when you know someone is only pretending to listen to you or is paying only partial attention to what you're saying?

Information Overload

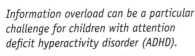
information overload The state of being overwhelmed by the amount of information one takes in.

A third barrier to effective listening is **information overload,** the state of being overwhelmed by the huge amount of information one is required to take in every day. We talk to people, watch television, listen to the radio, search the Internet, and thumb through all sorts of printed matter. At times, the sheer volume of information we have to attend to can seem overwhelming. When it does, we find it harder to listen effectively to new information.

SOURCES AND EFFECTS OF INFORMATION OVERLOAD.

As just one example of information overload, consider how many advertising messages you see or hear on a daily basis. These might include ads on television, in magazines and newspapers, on billboards, on people's clothing, in junk mail, and during movie previews. You might receive ads by fax, hear them on the radio, and find them in product inserts. You perhaps see them at gas pumps, at automated teller machines, on banners flying behind airplanes, and on the stickers you peel off fruit. You might also receive ads in the form of e-mail spam and pop-up announcements on the Internet. Researchers have estimated that the average U.S. American is exposed to between 600 and 625 advertising messages each day.[30]

You might conclude that information overload is a product of the digital age, which has made overwhelming amounts of information easily available. In fact, the term *information overload* was coined in 1970 by sociologist Alvin Toffler in a book titled *Future Shock,* which discussed the downside of rapid technological change.[31]

Clearly, then, people were experiencing the distracting effects of information overload even before computer-mediated communication was widely used. The problem is simply amplified in the digital age, as the "Get Connected" box describes.

Information overload can be a particular challenge for children with attention deficit hyperactivity disorder (ADHD).

One of the biggest problems arising from information overload is that it can interrupt people's attention. If you're e-mailing with an important client, for instance, your ability to pay attention to her messages can be compromised repeatedly by each new radio advertisement you hear, each new faxed announcement you receive, and each new pop-up ad you see. Those interruptions may seem small and inconsequential, but when you consider their effects on the entire population over time, they become a significant distraction. In fact, a 2007 analysis by a New York–based management research firm estimated the annual cost to U.S. companies of unnecessary interruptions from information overload to be a staggering $650 billion.[32]

Information overload can be particularly troubling for people with *attention deficit hyperactivity disorder,* or ADHD. People with ADHD are often easily distracted and have trouble focusing their attention for very long. They

g@t connected

MANAGING INFORMATION OVERLOAD ONLINE

Between Facebook, Twitter, e-mail, and your cell phone, keeping up with the people in your life can seem like a full-time job. Texting alone can overwhelm: The average American adult sends and receives almost 1,200 text messages every month. You've learned in this chapter that information overload hampers your ability to listen effectively in face-to-face conversations. Scientists have discovered that the same effect occurs in electronically mediated communication.

When you're swamped with texts, posts, voice mails, and tweets, you experience what researchers call *conversational overload,* which reduces your ability to attend to those messages adequately. To understand how conversational overload affects communication online, a group of researchers examined 2.6 million newsgroup postings and found that

- *People are more likely to attend to—and respond to—simple messages than complex ones.* Paying attention to a message requires cognitive energy, and each person has only so much to spend. When their attention is already stretched thin, people attend to messages that are simple and direct.

- *When people feel overloaded, they end or reduce their communication.* People experience overload when the energy required to attend to their communication tasks exceeds what they are willing or able to invest. In those situations, a very common strategy is to reduce the number of incoming messages, such as by withdrawing from a newsgroup or closing a Facebook account.

Good listening skills are as important in electronically mediated communication as they are in face-to-face interactions. The better you can prevent barriers to effective listening—including information overload and conversational overload—the more effective an interpersonal communicator you'll be.

Sources: Lenhart, A. (2010, September). *Cell phones and American adults.* Washington, DC: Pew Research Center; Jones, Q., Ravid, G., & Rafaeli, S. (2004). Information overload and the message dynamics of online interaction spaces: A theoretical model and empirical exploration. *Information Systems Research, 15,* 194–210.

are often also overly active and restless.[33] ADHD is a developmental disorder whose symptoms usually appear during childhood. A majority of children diagnosed with ADHD will continue to suffer from it during adulthood.[34] Because of their impaired ability to focus and their tendency to become easily distracted, people with ADHD may have an especially difficult time coping with the volume of information most of us encounter every day.

AVOIDING OVERLOAD FROM COMPUTER-MEDIATED AND OTHER SOURCES.
There are several strategies to reduce the distracting effects of information overload. During meetings and important conversations, for instance, turn off the ringer on your cell phone or PDA so you won't be distracted by incoming calls, text messages, or e-mails. Set filters on your e-mail system to reduce spam, and use a pop-up blocker to eliminate pop-up ads when you're online. Contact the Direct Marketing Association to have your address removed from junk-mail lists. Use your digital video recorder (DVR) to record your favorite TV shows so you can watch them at your convenience and skip the commercials. Using such strategies will help reduce the distractions of information overload and allow you to focus your attention on more important things, including your conversational partners.

Glazing Over

A fourth reason why effective listening is challenging is that our minds think so much faster than most people talk. Most of us are capable of understanding up to 600 words per minute, but the average person speaks fewer than 150 words per minute.[35] That leaves quite a bit of spare time for the mind to wander. We frequently use that time to engage in what researchers call **glazing over,** or daydreaming during the time we aren't actually listening.

For instance, Rochelle picks up her 6-year-old daughter and her 9-year-old son every afternoon, and they describe what they did in school during the drive home. Although she listens to what they say, Rochelle frequently allows her mind to wander during this time. She thinks about the novel she's reading, daydreams about taking a Caribbean vacation, and ponders next week's grocery list. Because her children speak more slowly than she can listen, and because their reports of their school activities are similar every day, Rochelle often glazes over when she's listening to them.

Glazing over is different from pseudolistening, or only pretending to listen. When you're glazing over, you actually *are* listening to what the speaker is saying—you're just allowing your mind to wander while doing so. Glazing over can lead to at least three problems. First, it can cause you to miss important details in what you're hearing. If you're glazing over while listening to a lecture in your communication theory course, for instance, you might fail to hear a critical piece of information about the term paper assignment. Second, glazing over might lead you to listen less critically than you normally would. For example, if your mind is wandering while you're listening to a salesperson describe the terms of a car loan, you might not realize that the deal isn't as good as it sounds. Finally, glazing over can make it appear to a speaker that you aren't listening to what he or she is saying, even though you are. Consequently, you can come across as inattentive or dismissive. An effective listener will work to keep his or her focus on what the speaker is saying instead of daydreaming or thinking about other topics.

Rebuttal Tendency

Regan has recently started work as a customer service representative for an electronics retailer, but his first two weeks on the job have not gone well. He knows he should listen nonjudgmentally to customers as they describe their frustrations with the products they bought, and then offer them his assistance and advice. Instead, Regan begins arguing with customers in his mind, even while they're still speaking. Rather than listening carefully to their concerns, Regan jumps to conclusions about what the customers have done wrong, and he formulates his response even before the customers have stopped talking.

Regan is enacting a **rebuttal tendency,** which is the propensity to debate a speaker's point and formulate one's reply while the person is still speaking.[36] According to research by business professor Steven Golen, thinking only of how one is going to respond to a speaker, arguing with the speaker in one's mind, and jumping to conclusions before the speaker has finished talking are all barriers to effective listening, for two basic reasons.[37] First, the rebuttal tendency uses mental energy that should be spent paying attention to the speaker. That is, it's difficult to listen effectively when all one is thinking about is how to respond. Second, by not paying close attention to the speaker, a listener can easily miss some of the details that might change how the listener responds in the first place.

To understand that second point, consider Regan's experience during his second shift. A customer returned a wireless Internet router she was having trouble installing.

glazing over Daydreaming during the time not spent listening.

rebuttal tendency The tendency to debate a speaker's point and formulate a reply while the person is still speaking.

As usual, Regan was quick to conclude that she hadn't followed the instructions, and he was crafting his response as she continued talking. Consequently, he didn't hear her explain that she'd already had a technician guide her through the installation procedure and inform her that the router was defective. If he had heard that important detail, Regan could have exchanged the product quickly and sent the customer on her way. Instead, he spent 10 minutes telling her to do what she had already done, leaving her frustrated and dissatisfied.

Closed-Mindedness

Another barrier to effective listening is **closed-mindedness,** the tendency not to listen to anything with which one disagrees.[38] Closed-minded individuals refuse to consider the merits of a speaker's point if it conflicts with their own beliefs. They also tend to overreact to certain forms of language, such as slang and profanity, and to stop listening to speakers who use them.[39]

closed-mindedness The tendency not to listen to anything with which one disagrees.

Many people are closed-minded only about particular issues, not about everything. As an educator, for instance, Bella prides herself in being open to diverse opinions on a range of topics. When it comes to her religious beliefs, however, she is so thoroughly convinced of the merits of her position that she refuses even to listen to any religious ideas that she doesn't already accept. For all practical purposes, she closes her mind to the possibility that any religious ideas besides her own could have any value whatsoever. Many of her fellow teachers find Bella's closed-mindedness offputting. In addition, it prevents Bella not only from learning more about others' religious traditions but also from teaching others about her faith, because she won't talk about religion with anyone who doesn't already share her beliefs.

Bella should remember that we can listen effectively to people even if we disagree with them. As the Greek philosopher Aristotle (384–322 B.C.) once wrote, "It is the mark of an educated mind to be able to entertain a thought without accepting it." When we refuse even to listen to ideas we disagree with, we limit our ability to learn from other people and their experiences. If you find yourself feeling closed-minded toward particular ideas, remind yourself that listening to an idea does not necessarily mean accepting it.

Competitive Interrupting

Normal conversation is a series of speaking "turns." You speak for a while, then you allow another person to have a turn, and the conversation goes back and forth. Occasionally, though, people talk when it isn't their turn. People interrupt for many reasons. Sometimes, the reason is to express support or enthusiasm for what the other person is saying ("Yeah, I agree!"); sometimes it's to stop the speaker to ask for clarification ("Wait, I'm not sure what you mean"); and sometimes it's even to warn the speaker of some impending danger ("Stop! You're spilling your coffee!").

For some people, however, interrupting is a way to dominate a conversation. Researchers use the term **competitive interrupting** to describe the practice of interjecting oneself when other people are speaking in order to take control of the conversation. For those who engage in competitive interrupting, the goal is to ensure that they get to speak more than the other person does and that their ideas and perspectives take priority. You can probably think of people who engage in such behavior—individuals with whom you feel you "can't get a word in edgewise."

competitive interrupting Using interruptions to take control of a conversation.

Research shows that most interruptions aren't competitive. However, talking with a competitive interrupter can be frustrating.[40] Some people respond to constant interruptions by becoming competitive themselves, thereby turning the conversation into a battle of wits. Other people withdraw from the interaction.

The "At a Glance" box summarizes the barriers to effective listening. Each of those barriers can be overcome. With training and practice, most of us can improve our abilities to listen well.

LEARN IT What constitutes noise? What do people do when they pseudolisten? How does information overload affect listening ability? What does it mean to glaze over? When people have a rebuttal tendency, what do they tend to do while they're listening? What does it mean to be closed-minded? When are interruptions competitive?

APPLY IT For one week, keep a diary of times when you feel that other people haven't listened to you effectively. For each instance, try to identify the barriers to effective listening. After the week is over, read back through your notes and reflect on times when the same barriers have affected your own listening ability. Assess how you might avoid those barriers to effective listening in the future.

REFLECT ON IT In what ways do you notice information overload in your own life? What topics do you tend to be closed-minded about, if any?

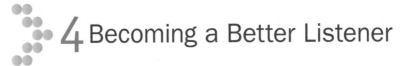

4 Becoming a Better Listener

We've looked at several examples of ineffective listening in this chapter. In the movie *The Break-Up,* Gary didn't listen to Brooke when she said she needed a dozen lemons. Regan doesn't listen effectively to his customers' complaints, and Rochelle glazes over when listening to her children describe their school day. Clearly, listening effectively can be a challenge. Fortunately, effective listening is a skill that can be developed through education and practice. Author Mary Lou Casey once wrote that "what people really need is a good listening to," and her sentiment suggests that we can do much good in our interpersonal relationships if we sharpen our listening abilities. In this section, we'll look at strategies you can use to improve your skills in informational, critical, and empathic listening.

Becoming a Better Informational Listener

When you engage in informational listening, your goal is to understand and learn from the speaker's message. For instance, you might be attending a presentation about saving for retirement, or you might be listening to your CEO talk about a merger your firm has just completed. How can you make the most of such opportunities?

SEPARATE WHAT IS AND ISN'T SAID.   One key strategy for improving your informational listening skills is to beware of the tendency to "hear" words or statements that aren't actually said. Think about the last time you saw a television commercial for a pain reliever, for instance. A common tactic for advertisers is to claim that "nothing is more effective" than their product. What do you learn from hearing that statement? In other words, how would you paraphrase it?

The advertisers are hoping you learn that their particular pain reliever is the strongest one available . . . but that's not really what they said, is it? All they said is that nothing is *more* effective, which means there may be several other products that are *just as* effective as theirs. It may also mean that all the products are equally ineffective! If you listened to this ad and concluded that this product is the most effective one available, you arrived at that conclusion on your own (although it was definitely the conclusion the advertiser wanted you to form). When you are engaged in informational listening, be careful to distinguish between what is actually being said and what you are simply inferring.

Perhaps the most effective way to determine whether you have understood a speaker's message is to paraphrase it—to restate the speaker's message in your own words to clarify the meaning of the message. If you paraphrase a statement in a way that accurately reflects its meaning, speakers tend to reply by confirming your understanding.

Let's suppose that while leaving a theater after watching a movie, your roommate Chad and you have the following exchange:

Chad: I think we should swing by that new barbecue place on the way home.

You: You want to pick up some dinner?

Chad: Yeah, I'm starving.

You think Chad is trying to imply that he's hungry and wants to get some food, but that isn't actually what he said. To check your understanding, you therefore paraphrase his statement by putting it into your own words. Because you understood Chad's statement correctly, he replied by confirming your interpretation.

Conversely, if you paraphrase a statement in a way that changes its meaning, a speaker generally will correct your misunderstanding. Let's say the exchange with Chad goes like this:

Chad: I think we should swing by that new barbecue place on the way home.

You: You want to pick up some dinner?

Chad: No, I want to see if my friend Blake is working tonight.

In this second instance, your interpretation of Chad's statement was inaccurate. By paraphrasing his statement, you invited him to correct your understanding—and he did. Paraphrasing is one of the most efficient ways to determine whether you have correctly distinguished between what a speaker has and has not said.

AVOID THE CONFIRMATION BIAS.   The **confirmation bias** is the tendency to pay attention only to information that supports one's values and beliefs while discounting or ignoring information that doesn't.[41] It becomes a problem for listening when it causes us to make up our minds about an issue without paying attention to all sides.

Let's say your close friend Tim is having a conflict with his girlfriend, Molly. Tim confides in you about the negative things Molly has been saying and doing, and because he's your friend, you're biased toward believing him. When Molly comes to talk to you about the situation, you therefore tune her out because you've already made up your mind that she's at fault.

In this case, you're falling victim to the confirmation bias. Because you've made up your mind that Tim is behaving fairly, you will pay attention only to information that confirms your belief and will tune out information that doesn't. Good informational listeners are aware that their beliefs are not necessarily accurate. Therefore, a strategy for improving your informational listening skills is to ask yourself whether you have listened to all sides of an issue before you form a conclusion, or whether you are simply avoiding information that would lead you to question your beliefs.

LISTEN FOR SUBSTANCE MORE THAN FOR STYLE.   The psychological principle called the **vividness effect** refers to the tendency for dramatic, shocking events to distort one's perceptions of reality.[42] We watch news coverage of a deadly plane crash, for instance, and we become nervous about getting on a plane, even though the probability of dying in a plane crash is only about 1 in 8 million.[43] Two days after the 1999 massacre at Columbine High School, 63 percent of Americans surveyed thought a shooting at their own child's school was likely, even though only 10 percent of all schools report even one experience of violent crime in a year.[44]

The same effect can occur within interpersonal situations. If your parents went through a traumatic divorce when you were a child, for instance, that experience may have convinced you that a marriage is more likely to fail than is actually the case. Dramatic events are more vivid and memorable than everyday events, so we pay more attention to them. You can experience much the same problem during informational listening if you focus only on what's most vivid. In class, for instance, you might be more entertained by a lecture with dramatic stories and flashy PowerPoint slides than by one that's dry. That doesn't mean that the flashy presentation contains better information than the dry one or that you'll learn more from it. Similarly, you might love being in classes with engaging, humorous teachers. That doesn't necessarily mean, however, that you'll learn more from them than from teachers who are disengaged and serious.

confirmation bias The tendency to pay attention only to information that supports one's values and beliefs while discounting or ignoring information that doesn't.

vividness effect The tendency for dramatic, shocking events to distort one's perception of reality.

Good informational listeners look past what is dramatic and vivid and focus on the substance of what they're hearing.

Being a good informational listener, then, means being able to look past what is dramatic and vivid to focus on the substance of what you're hearing. That process begins with being aware of the vividness effect and remembering that vivid experiences can distort your perceptions. The next time you go through a dramatic event or listen to a particularly entertaining speaker, ask yourself whether you are listening and paying attention to accurate information or are being swayed by the drama of the event or the charisma of the speaker.

Becoming a Better Critical Listener

Many interpersonal situations require you to assess the credibility of what you're hearing. Here are three ways to get better at it.

BE A SKEPTIC.   Being a good critical listener starts with being skeptical of what you hear. Despite its reputation, **skepticism** isn't about being cynical or finding fault; rather, it's about evaluating the evidence for a claim. Recall from our discussion of the confirmation bias that people often pay attention only to evidence that supports their existing beliefs. Being skeptical means setting aside your biases and being willing to be persuaded by the merits of the argument and the quality of the evidence. A good critical listener doesn't accept claims blindly. Instead, he or she questions them to determine whether they're valid.[45]

skepticism The practice of evaluating the evidence for a claim.

Consider the following example. Your co-worker Fahid has come up with a business opportunity. He tells you about his plan and asks you to invest in it. If you're a poor critical listener, you may base your decision on how you feel about Fahid or how excited you are at the prospect of making money. In contrast, if you're a good critical listener, you'll set aside your feelings and focus on the merits of Fahid's idea. Does he have a sound business plan? Is there a market for his product? Has he budgeted sufficient funds for advertising? Did he explain in detail how he would use your investment? Being a critical listener doesn't mean that you automatically criticize his plans; it does mean that you carefully evaluate them to determine whether they make sense.

EVALUATE A SPEAKER'S CREDIBILITY.
Besides analyzing the merits of an argument, a good critical listener pays attention to the speaker's credibility. Credibility is a measure of how reliable and trustworthy someone is. All other things being equal, you can generally presume that information you hear from a credible source is more believable than information you get from a noncredible source.

Several qualities make a speaker more or less credible. One is expertise. It makes more sense for us to trust a physician's medical advice than a professional athlete's, for instance, because the doctor is a medical expert and the athlete is not. At the same time, it doesn't make sense to trust a physician for legal or financial advice, because he or she isn't an expert on law or finance.

It's easy to confuse having *expertise* with having *experience*. Having experience with

Good critical listeners practice skepticism by evaluating the merits and the evidence for an argument.

something may give a person credibility on that topic or area, but it doesn't necessarily make the individual an expert. After raising six children, for instance, Hannah is a very experienced parent and thus has credibility insofar as she can draw on her many experiences to give advice to other moms. However, Hannah isn't an expert on parenting, because her only source of credibility is her individual experience. For instance, she doesn't have a degree in child development, nor is she a recognized authority on parenting issues.

Yet individuals can be experts on topics with which they have no personal experience. As a board-certified obstetrician and gynecologist, Tyrell is an expert on pregnancy and women's health, even though, as a man, he has no direct experience with either. Similarly, Young Li is an outstanding marital therapist who has helped countless couples even though she has never been married herself. How can a man be a good obstetrician, and a single person be a good marital therapist? The answer is that they are drawing on their training and expertise to help others, not on their individual experiences.

Another characteristic that affects a speaker's credibility is bias. If the speaker has a special interest in making you believe some idea or claim, that fact tends to reduce his or her credibility. If a tobacco company executive claimed publicly that there were health benefits to smoking, for instance, a good critical listener would be highly skeptical, because the executive is a biased source.

Sometimes you have to dig below the surface to investigate the source behind a particular idea so that you can meaningfully evaluate the idea's credibility. For example, you might be intrigued to hear about a research report claiming that using your cell phone while driving does not increase your risk of being in a collision. The study, you assume, may have been conducted by a reputable research team at a major university, a fact that would enhance its credibility. After you investigate, however, perhaps you discover that the study was funded by a group that lobbies on behalf of the telecommunications industry. Given its purpose, such a group would have a vested interest in the study's producing results that are favorable to cell phone use. The fact that a study is funded by a group with a vested interest in its results doesn't necessarily mean the study's conclusions are wrong. However, it does mean that you should be skeptical when you are exposed to them.

UNDERSTAND PROBABILITY. Evaluating the merits of a claim means speculating about the likelihood that the claim is true. That process can be tricky, because we sometimes confuse what's possible with what's probable, and what's probable with what's certain. An event or a fact is *possible* if there's even the slightest chance, however small, that it might be true. To be *probable,* a statement has to have greater than a 50 percent chance of being true. A statement is *certain* only if its likelihood of being true is 100 percent, nothing less. An illustration of the relationship among possibility, probability, and certainty appears in Figure 7.2.

Take a claim such as "I can survive without water for a month." There's a possibility that claim could be true, but the likelihood is very small. The claim certainly isn't probable, and a good critical listener wouldn't treat it as though it were. In contrast, the statement "I will get married someday" is not only possible, it's also probable, because a very large majority of people marry at least once. Does that fact mean that the claim is certain, therefore? The answer is no, because there's a chance, however small, that it may not happen. For a claim to be certain, there can be absolutely no chance that it isn't true.

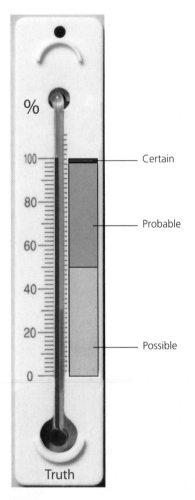

FIGURE 7.2 Possibility, Probability, and Certainty A statement is *possible* if its likelihood of being true is between 1 percent and 50 percent. It is *probable* if its likelihood of being true is between 51 percent and 99 percent. It is *certain* only if its likelihood of being true is 100 percent.

A claim such as "I will die someday" is certain, because every living creature eventually dies. People who are good at critical listening understand the differences among possibility, probability, and certainty. They bear in mind that just because a claim is possible, that doesn't mean it's worth believing.

Determining the probability of claims you hear isn't always easy. Suppose that Manuel visits his uncle Alfredo, who has been a vegetarian for most of his adult life. "If you eat red meat, you'll eventually die of heart disease," Alfredo constantly warns his nieces and nephews.

How should Manuel evaluate the probability of his uncle's claim? He should start by determining whether the claim is possible. In this case, it is, because there is a possibility that people who eat red meat will die of heart disease. He should then ask himself whether the claim is certain. In this case, it isn't, because many people who eat red meat do not die of heart disease. Manuel therefore knows that the chances that Alfredo's claim is true are between 1 percent and 99 percent. Thus, although he cannot accept the claim as a certainty, neither can he reject it as an impossibility. What he should do is to consider the probability that the claim is true. To determine probability, he needs to research the link between heart disease and the consumption of red meat. With that information, he can assess whether Alfredo's claim is probable—that is, true more often than it is false—or improbable—that is, false more often than it is true.

Becoming a Better Empathic Listener

Within our relationships, a common goal for listening is to provide empathy and support. Being a good empathic listener can be difficult at times, but it's not impossible.

LISTEN NONJUDGMENTALLY. When we listen to learn, and especially when we listen to evaluate, we often make judgments about the information we're taking in. Good empathic listening, however, is about being open-minded and nonjudgmental.

Two strategies are particularly helpful. The first is to listen without interrupting. Being supportive and empathic means letting the other person say what he or she needs to say without breaking in. Fight the urge to jump into the conversation, and simply listen. Second, don't offer advice unless asked. When you're hearing other people tell you their problems, your tendency is likely to be to respond with advice on how to solve those problems.[46] A good empathic listener will remember that people aren't always looking for advice—often, they just want someone to listen to them.

ACKNOWLEDGE FEELINGS. Empathizing involves understanding how someone else is feeling and trying to relate to those feelings. It's not the same thing as sympathizing, which means feeling sorry for the other person. An important strategy for good empathic listening, therefore, is to acknowledge a speaker's feelings and allow him or her to continue expressing them.

We do so by responding to speakers with *continuer statements,* phrases that identify the emotions a person is experiencing and allow him or her to communicate them further. By contrast, it is important to avoid *terminator statements,* phrases that fail to acknowledge a speaker's emotions and thereby shut down the person's opportunity to express them. After listening to a patient describe her concerns about the progress

[LISTENING EMPATHICALLY DURING GRIEF]

Offer an empathic ear when someone needs it.

WHAT?

Learn to listen empathically when another person is experiencing grief.

WHY?

To provide support to individuals at difficult times in their life, as when they lose a parent or other close relative, a dear friend, or a cherished pet.

HOW?

1. Tell the person that you are willing to listen and help however you can.

2. Let the person express his or her feelings without judgment. There is no right or wrong way to grieve.

3. Avoid telling the person "I know how you feel" unless you have experienced the same type of loss yourself.

4. Encourage the person to take care of his or her physical and other needs.

5. Listen patiently, and don't diminish the person's grief with a statement such as "You have to be strong," which can make the person feel ashamed of his or her feelings.

TRY!

1. When someone you know experiences a significant loss, tell the person you are available to listen if he or she wants to talk. Allow the person to decide when it is time to talk.

2. Find a quiet, comfortable place to listen, and minimize distractions. Do not answer text messages or cell phone calls. Give the person 100 percent of your attention.

3. If you're unsure of what to say, remember that you needn't say much at all. Your job is to allow the other person to speak.

CONSIDER: *During times of grief, why does it help to be listened to?*

---

of her illness, for instance, empathic physicians can use a continuer statement such as "That must make you feel very uncertain" or "I can imagine how scary this must be" to reassure the patient that they understand and appreciate her feelings. Physicians with less empathic ability are more likely to use terminator statements such as "We're doing everything we can" and "You just need to give this some time." Those types of responses imply to the patient that her feelings are unimportant.

In a recent study, researchers examined conversations between advanced cancer patients and their oncologists.[47] With permission, the researchers recorded nearly 400 conversations between patients and oncologists and listened for times when patients expressed negative emotions such as sadness, fear, and anxiety. When those moments arose, the researchers found that oncologists replied with continuer statements only 22 percent of the time. Younger physicians were more likely than older ones to use continuers, and female physicians were more likely than male physicians to do so. Those findings don't mean that oncologists lack empathy. Rather, the data suggest that they may have trouble communicating their empathy through emotionally supportive listening responses. Such responses are particularly important for individuals who are struggling with terminal illnesses.

There are times when it may be difficult to empathize with other people. If you have never lost a parent, for instance, it would be very difficult for you to understand that experience. When you find yourself in such a situation, resist the urge to tell the speaker "I know how you feel." Unless you really do understand the speaker's experience, he or she might find your statement disrespectful or insincere, even if you mean it as a show of support. Instead, use your listening skills to try to understand how the person is feeling. See the "Got Skills?" box to learn more about that skill.

COMMUNICATE SUPPORT NONVERBALLY.   One of the most important aspects of being a good empathic listener is to communicate your support nonverbally. When you're listening rather than speaking, your nonverbal behaviors convey your interest, understanding, and empathy to the speaker.

Perhaps the most important nonverbal behavior in this situation is eye contact. Speakers often watch your eye behaviors to see whether you're paying attention to what they're saying. If you allow yourself to be distracted by your environment, you can convey the message that you aren't really listening. Other important behaviors are your use of facial expressions and touch. A reassuring smile and a warm touch can make people feel as though you understand, support, and empathize.[48]

LEARN IT What is the vividness effect? When should you question another person's credibility? Why is it important to listen nonjudgmentally?

APPLY IT Television commercials offer ample opportunity to sharpen your critical listening skills. Spend some time watching advertisements and thinking about the claims they're making. How credible are the sources? How probable are the claims? Do the commercials encourage you to make inferences that aren't supported by evidence? If so, how do they do this? Write up your findings in a brief report.

REFLECT ON IT In what situations do you find it difficult to engage in informational listening? Whom do you know who is a particularly good empathic listener?

MASTER the chapter

1 The Nature of Listening (p. 216)

- Listening is the active process of making meaning out of another person's spoken message.
- The ability to listen effectively is important to success in a variety of communicative contexts.
- Listening is a learned skill that includes more than merely hearing.
- Cultural differences in the directness of verbal communication affect expectations for listening.

2 Ways of Listening (p. 223)

- Effective listening has six stages: hearing, understanding, remembering, interpreting, evaluating, and responding.

- People engage in informational listening, critical listening, and empathic listening in interpersonal contexts.

3 Common Barriers to Effective Listening (p. 228)

- Noise is anything that distracts you from listening to what you wish to listen to.
- Pseudolistening uses feedback behaviors that make it seem as if you're paying attention even when you aren't; selective attention means listening only to what you want to hear.
- Information overload refers to the state of being overwhelmed by the large amount of information each of us takes in daily.

- Glazing over is daydreaming during the time you aren't spending on listening.
- The rebuttal tendency is the tendency to debate a speaker's point and formulate your reply while the person is still speaking.
- Being closed-minded means failing to listen to anything with which you disagree.
- Some people engage in competitive interrupting, or interrupting to take control of a conversation.

4 Becoming a Better Listener (p. 234)

- Becoming a better informational listener means separating what is and isn't said, avoiding the confirmation bias, and listening for substance.
- Becoming a better critical listener means being skeptical, evaluating a speaker's credibility, and understanding probability.
- Becoming a better empathic listener means listening nonjudgmentally, acknowledging feelings, and communicating support nonverbally.

KEY TERMS

closed-mindedness (p. 233)
competitive interrupting (p. 233)
confirmation bias (p. 236)
critical listening (p. 227)
empathic listening (p. 227)

glazing over (p. 232)
HURIER model (p. 223)
informational listening (p. 226)
information overload (p. 230)
listening (p. 216)

pseudolistening (p. 229)
rebuttal tendency (p. 232)
selective attention (p. 229)
skepticism (p. 237)
vividness effect (p. 236)

DISCUSSION QUESTIONS

1. What does it mean to listen? How is listening different from hearing? In what instances do you hear someone without listening?

2. Which type of listening—informational, critical, empathic—do you engage in the most often? Which type do you enjoy the most? Why?

3. When do you notice yourself falling victim to the confirmation bias? What can you do to prevent it?

4. What does it mean to be skeptical? How does being skeptical help you to be a better listener?

PRACTICE QUIZ

MULTIPLE CHOICE

1. **Which of the following is *not* a part of the definition of listening?**
   a. It is an active process.
   b. It involves the creation of meaning.
   c. It deals with only spoken messages.
   d. It occurs automatically.

2. **Using facial expressions and a verbal statement such as "I understand" to let the speaker know you are paying attention is an example of the type of listening responses called**
   a. analyzing
   b. empathizing
   c. paraphrasing
   d. backchanneling

3. **Assigning meaning to what we hear illustrates the HURIER model's stage of**
   a. hearing
   b. remembering
   c. interpreting
   d. responding

4. **The type of listening that involves trying to understand a situation from the speaker's perspective is**
   a. empathic listening
   b. informative listening
   c. critical listening
   d. persuasive listening

5. **In class, Charyn cannot keep her mind off her problems at work. However, she pretends to listen to the professor's lecture. Charyn is experiencing the barrier to effective listening known as**
   a. information overload
   b. noise
   c. pseudolistening
   d. glazing over

FILL IN THE BLANK

6. Regarding the relationship between hearing and listening, _____ is a passive process, whereas _____ is an active process.

7. _____ occurs when someone listens only to the part of the message that she or he wants to hear and ignores the rest.

8. The _____ occurs when shocking and dramatic events distort an individual's perception of reality.

9. The first stage of effective listening, according to the HURIER model, is _____.

10. _____ is the tendency not to listen to anything with which you disagree.

ANSWERS

Multiple Choice: 1 (d); 2 (d); 3 (c); 4 (a); 5 (c); **Fill in the Blank:** 6 (hearing; listening); 7 (selective attention); 8 (vividness effect); 9 (hearing); 10 (closed-mindedness)

RESEARCH LIBRARY

MOVIES

Dead Man Walking (drama; 1995; R)
This drama depicts the true story of Sister Helen Prejean, a Roman Catholic nun who befriends convicted murderer Matthew Poncelet in the weeks leading up to his execution. By listening empathically, Sister Helen provides comfort to Poncelet before his death and helps his victim's family come to terms with their loss.

The Interpreter (drama; 2005; PG-13)
In this gripping thriller, Nicole Kidman portrays Silvia Broome, a foreign-language interpreter at the headquarters of the United Nations in New York. Her job is to listen carefully to what speakers are saying and to interpret their speech into another language simultaneously. While in the building after hours one night, she overhears a threat against a foreign leader made in an obscure African language in which she happens to be fluent. Attempts to verify and protect against the threat rely heavily on the credibility of Broome's skills as a listener.

BOOKS AND JOURNAL ARTICLES

Burley-Allen, M. (1995). *Listening: The forgotten skill: A self-teaching guide.* New York: Wiley.

Carrell, L. J., & Willmington, S. C. (1996). A comparison of self-report and performance data in assessing speaking and listening competence. *Communication Reports, 9,* 185–191.

Harris, R. M. (2006). *The listening leader: Powerful new strategies for becoming an influential communicator.* Westport, CT: Greenwood.

Wolvin, A., & Coakley, C. (1996). *Listening.* Dubuque, IA: Brown & Benchmark.

WEBSITES

www.listen.org
    This website is the home page of the International Listening Association, a professional organization promoting research and teaching about the importance of effective listening.

www.cnr.berkeley.edu/ucce50/ag-labor/7article/article40.htm
    This site, sponsored by the University of California at Berkeley, focuses on listening skills and offers a free one-hour workshop in effective empathic listening for download.

8 Emotion

AWASH IN EMOTION

In an episode of the Fox television show *Glee,* Kurt Hummel (played by Chris Colfer) sat at the bedside of his father Burt (played by Mike O'Malley), who had recently suffered a heart attack and was in a coma. Kurt was overwhelmed with a wide range of emotions. He felt guilty about an argument they'd had the last time they spoke. He was fearful of losing his father and saddened at the thought of life without him. He felt grateful for the support of his friends and ashamed that he had neglected them earlier. And when his dad began to squeeze his hand, Kurt felt surprised, happy, and profoundly hopeful that Burt might recover. The intensity of Kurt's many emotions helped him to realize how important his father was to him.

more attentive to what they were feeling and therefore more likely to express it. In comparison, cold weather inhibits the sensitivity of nerves, causing people to be less attentive to various sensations and therefore less expressive of what they feel.

CO-CULTURES.   Co-cultures can also affect how we deal with emotions. Some co-cultures encourage people to examine their emotions directly and express them freely. For example, an artistic co-culture, such as a theater group or a community of sculptors, might encourage the ability to express and respond to emotions for its value in the creation and appreciation of those art forms.

Other co-cultures, however, discourage people from dealing openly with their emotions. As one example, many military personnel returning from active combat duty avoid seeking treatment for post-traumatic stress disorder (PTSD) because they perceive that the military co-culture stigmatizes such treatment. PTSD is an anxiety disorder that some people develop after experiencing a severely troubling event, such as combat or a natural disaster. In a study of soldiers returning to the United States from combat in Iraq and Afghanistan, medical researchers found that as many as 77 percent of individuals with signs of PTSD refused treatment, citing their fear of being stigmatized by the military as a primary concern.[90] Those results are significant because when PTSD is untreated, it frequently leads to other problems, including drug and alcohol abuse.

Display Rules

display rules Unwritten codes that govern the ways people manage and express emotions.

Another factor influencing the expression of emotion is what psychologists Paul Ekman and Wallace Friesen call display rules.[91] **Display rules** comprise five unwritten codes that govern the ways people manage and express their emotions, and they vary according to the individual's social situation. Display rules include:

- *Intensification:* Exaggerating your emotion to appear as though you are experiencing it more intensely than you are. For example, you may pretend to be overjoyed about seeing an old acquaintance at an event, when in fact you find it only mildly pleasant. In that case, you intensify your emotion to make your acquaintance feel good.

- *De-intensification:* The opposite of intensification—that is, downplaying an emotion to appear as though you are experiencing it less intensely than you are. You may be extremely angry with a co-worker for missing a deadline, but in the presence of your supervisor you decide it's best to seem only mildly annoyed. In that situation, you de-intensify your emotion to be polite or to avoid damaging your colleague's reputation.

- *Simulation:* Acting as though you're feeling an emotion that you actually aren't experiencing. You may not really care about your neighbor's good news, but you act happy anyway when you hear about it because you want to appear supportive.

- *Inhibition:* The opposite of simulation—that is, acting as though you're indifferent or emotionless when you're actually experiencing an emotion. For example, it may make you jealous to see your romantic partner flirting with someone else, but you choose to act as though it doesn't bother you because you don't want to appear vulnerable in front of the other person.

EMOTION DISPLAY RULES	
Intensification	Acting as though you're terrified when you're only mildly worried
De-intensification	Acting as though you're mildly worried when you're actually terrified
Simulation	Acting as though you're terrified when you are really indifferent
Inhibition	Acting as though you're indifferent when you are actually terrified
Masking	Acting as though you're terrified when you're actually sad

- *Masking:* Expressing one emotion when you are actually experiencing a completely different one. You may be sad and nervous when your son or daughter leaves home for college, but you behave as though you're happy so that you don't spoil his or her excitement.

Additional examples of Ekman and Friesen's five display rules appear in the "At a Glance" box.

Technology

Many people use a technological device—such as an iPad or a Black-Berry—so often that they may not realize how the technology affects the way they experience and express emotions. In fact, technology in-fluences emotional behaviors in at least three ways.

First, as we saw in Chapter 6, text-based communication technologies, such as e-mail and text messaging, don't allow us to see or hear the nonverbal signals of emotion from our communication partner. That is, we can't use the person's facial expressions or tone of voice to figure out what he or she is feeling. However, there are other means of representing emotions within the text. They include using emoticons, which are text-based representations of facial expressions, such as :) for a happy face and :/ for a confused face. They also include embed-ding statements about one's own emotion into the text. Sometimes we do so in abbreviated form, such as writing "j/k," which stands for "just kidding," to convey that we are joking or being sarcastic. In such ways, we compensate for the limitations of channel-lean forms of communication on the expression of emotion.

Communication technology impacts how we experience and express emotion.

A second way technology affects our experience and expression of emotion is by increasing our opportunities for sharing emotions. Social networking websites, such as Facebook and MySpace, allow us to stay in contact with current friends or to re-establish contact with old ones. In that way, technology provides us with ongoing op-portunities to share positive and negative experiences in our lives with others.

In addition, when we go through emotionally challenging experiences, the Internet provides multiple opportunities to discuss those experiences with people who have also gone through them. We can find online chat rooms and support groups for a wide range of emotional experiences, including losing a loved one, dealing with a signifi-cant job loss or a serious illness, and having to provide care for an elderly relative. In

9 Interpersonal Communication in Friendships and Professional Relationships

FRIENDSHIPS FORGED

Centuries ago, the Greek philosopher Aristotle observed that when people "share salt"—which means enduring a difficult experience together—they forge bonds of friendship that are not easily broken. Such was the case for 33 men who were trapped together for 69 days in the fall of 2010 after a cave-in at the San José mine near Copiapó, Chile. The miners, who ranged in age from 19 to 63, survived their ordeal by staying busy, holding one another accountable for assigned tasks, and maintaining support and optimism throughout the group. According to experts who have studied the effects of shared trauma—such as being lost at sea or fighting in battle together—the experience of enduring and surviving such a horrific event together will join these men to one another emotionally for the rest of their lives.

I magine what life would be like without friends. Families and romantic relationships are important to us, but friends and acquaintances contribute significantly to our well-being, too. Sometimes we look to friends for social and emotional support. At other times, we seek out our friends when we just want to hang out and relax or when we need help making a decision or dealing with a problem. Friends lift our spirits and remind us we're not alone in the world. And, occasionally, they help us through traumatic experiences, as the Chilean miners did for one another.

This chapter illustrates the importance of social relationships—such as those between friends, close acquaintances, and co-workers—and focuses on how we use interpersonal communication to manage those relationships. All relationships are social to some extent. Because romantic and familial relationships often meet different social needs than do friendships, acquaintanceships, and workplace relationships, we will reserve those relationships for the next chapter.

1 Why Social Relationships Matter

Ann Atwater and C. P. Ellis were never destined to become friends. In the 1970s, Atwater—a poor African American welfare mother—was a civil rights activist in Durham, North Carolina, where Ellis was a leader in the Ku Klux Klan, a violent white supremacist organization. During 10 days of community talks about school desegregation, Ellis came to believe that both whites and minorities would benefit from desegregation, and he and Atwater became partners in the civil rights movement. They also became close personal friends. Together, they struggled against oppression and social stereotypes, and they leaned on each other heavily for support. When Ellis died of Alzheimer's disease in 2005, Atwater, having lost a dear—and most unlikely—friend, gave the eulogy at his funeral.

Having strong social ties with friends, neighbors, co-workers, and others improves the quality of our life in multiple ways. In this section, we'll see that we form social

relationships because we have a strong need to belong. We'll also examine some benefits of our social relationships, as well as certain costs we incur by maintaining them.

We Form Relationships Because We Need to Belong

In his book *Personal Relationships and Personal Networks* (2007), communication scholar Mac Parks wrote: "We humans are social animals down to our very cells. Nature did not make us noble loners."[1] He's right. One reason social relationships matter is that it's in our nature to form them. In fact, evolutionary psychologists argue that our motivation toward social relationships is innate rather than learned.[2] That fundamental human inclination to bond with others is the idea behind psychologist Roy Baumeister's theory called the **need to belong.**[3] Need-to-belong theory posits that each of us is born with a drive to seek, form, maintain, and protect strong social relationships. To fulfill that drive, we use interpersonal communication to form social bonds with others at work, at school, in our neighborhoods, in community and religious organizations, on sports teams, in online communities, and in other social contexts. According to Baumeister's theory, each of those relationships helps us feel as though we aren't alone because we belong to a social community.

The need-to-belong theory also suggests that for us to satisfy our drive for relationships, we need social bonds that are both interactive and emotionally close. For example, most of us wouldn't be satisfied if we had emotionally close relationships with people with whom we never got to communicate. Being cut off from social interaction can be physically and psychologically devastating. That's one of the reasons why solitary confinement is considered such a harsh punishment.[4] Women and men who are deployed for military service,[5] and many elderly individuals who live alone,[6] also experience loneliness when they don't see their families or friends for extended periods.

By the same token, interacting only with people who have no real feelings for us would be largely unrewarding as well. Imagine that you moved to a large city where you didn't know anyone. Even though you'd have plenty of interactions with people—taxi drivers, grocery store clerks, an eye doctor—you wouldn't encounter anyone you

It is in our nature to develop social relationships.

need to belong A hypothesis that says each of us is born with a fundamental drive to seek, form, maintain, and protect strong social relationships.

Deployed military personnel and elderly individuals who live alone often experience intense loneliness when they don't see their relatives or friends for extended periods of time.

Some standards of beauty—such as the preferred body type—vary from culture to culture.

particularly healthy genes, children produced with attractive people are likely to be healthy, because they will inherit those genes.[21]

A popular cultural saying is that "beauty is only skin deep." That maxim suggests that physical beauty or attractiveness is superficial, meaning that it reflects only people's outer appearance but offers no indication of who they are or how they behave. Indeed, perhaps you've heard someone assert that an individual is physically handsome or beautiful but that "it's what's on the inside that really counts." Despite the popularity of that belief, however, decades of research demonstrate that in reality we pay an enormous amount of attention to physical appearance when we're forming social and personal relationships.[22]

What makes one person more physically attractive than another is a combination of social and genetic characteristics. Some notions of beauty vary widely from culture to culture. Consider weight, for example. In North America and Western Europe, a thin, physically fit body type is generally considered the most attractive. In many African and Australian tribal cultures, however, an overweight body is considered the most attractive, at least for women.[23]

Cultures also vary in the ways in which they manipulate or mutilate the body to achieve physical attractiveness. One example is the practice of wearing lip plates. Girls in the Mursai of southern Ethiopia and the Mebêngôkre Indians of Brazil have their lips pierced at a young age and a large wooden or clay plate inserted into the hole. As the girls grow older, their lip plates are increased in size, and those with the largest plates are considered the most desirable as mates.[24] Similarly, women in the Padaung tribe of Myanmar often wear metal rings around their necks to make their necks appear longer than they are. Women with the longest necks are considered the most attractive and most desirable as mates.[25]

Other aspects of physical attractiveness are cross-cultural. For instance, people around the world prefer bodies and faces that are symmetrical—similar on the left and right sides—and that have features that are proportional in size to one another. Across cultures, men are also attracted to women who appear healthy and young, because those characteristics signal their ability to produce healthy offspring.[26] Similarly, women across cultures are attracted to men who look powerful and appear to have resources, because those characteristics signal their ability to provide for a family.[27]

USING SOCIAL COMMENTS IN AN ONLINE COURSE

If you've ever taken an online class, perhaps you've experienced the challenge of having to work collaboratively with people you don't know. Scientists have discovered that in such situations, people use *social comments*—words that build or reinforce relationships—to minimize feelings of emotional and geographic distance.

In one study, researcher Deana Molinari spent a semester analyzing comments made by undergraduate nursing students in an online course. She focused her attention on how the students communicated about group problem-solving tasks that were relevant to the course material. After analyzing nearly 500 individual messages produced over the span of the semester, Molinari found that students used social comments for four specific purposes:

- *To reveal themselves:* Students communicated about their experiences and personal interests as a way of self-disclosing to others in the class.

- *To forge ties with others:* Students asked others personal questions, expressed approval or validation of others' ideas, and conveyed interest in one another's lives to build virtual relationships.

- *To contribute to task solutions:* Once students felt comfortable with one another, they communicated more about the correct processes for solving problems they had been assigned to solve.

- *To find personal meaning:* Many students sought to find meaning in the learning experience by tying the content to their personal experiences.

Although many online courses do not offer the same opportunities for building social and personal relationships as do traditional face-to-face courses, competent communicators adapt by making the best use of those communication channels that are available to create a sense of social connection.

Source: Molinari, D. L. (2004). The role of social comments in problem-solving groups in an online class. *The American Journal of Distance Education, 18,* 89–101.

WE ARE ATTRACTED BY PROXIMITY. Another important predictor of attraction is *proximity,* which refers to how closely together people live or work and how often they interact. We're more likely to form and maintain social relationships with people we see often than with people we don't.[28] We tend to know our next-door neighbors better than the neighbors down the road, and we're more likely to become friends and maintain friendships with our classmates and co-workers than with people we rarely see.

Some researchers have suggested that the Internet has reduced the influence of physical proximity on attraction. With chat rooms, instant messaging, and other forms of online interaction, we're free to develop friendships with virtually anyone, no matter how geographically distant they are. Indeed, research has shown that a vast majority of Internet users have formed social relationships with people they met online.[29]

As the "Get Connected" box explores, offering socially oriented comments allows people in online college courses—who often haven't met in real life—to get to know one another and to develop a sense of community. Websites such as Facebook and MySpace allow us to make friends and communicate with them regularly, even if they live in different cities or different countries. Although our choices of online friends may still be influenced by physical appearance and our perceived similarity, they need not be bound by physical proximity.

WE ARE ATTRACTED BY SIMILARITY. You've probably had the experience of getting to know someone and marveling at how much you have in common. When we meet people with backgrounds, experiences, beliefs, and interests similar to our

In the movie I Love You, Man *(2009), Peter and Sydney find their similarities—and their differences—attractive.*

own, we find them to be comfortable and familiar; sometimes it's almost as if we already know them. It turns out that we find similarity to be very attractive. Research shows we're more likely to form social relationships with people who are similar to, rather than different from, ourselves.[30]

We find similarity to be attractive for at least two reasons. One reason is that we often find social validation in people who are similar to us. Liking people who are similar to us is, in a way, like liking ourselves. You might be especially drawn to people who share your hobbies, your sense of humor, or your way of seeing the world, for instance, because those people make you feel better about who you are.[31] We don't necessarily think about that at a conscious level, but it may nonetheless be one of the reasons we find similarity attractive.

A second reason we find similarity attractive is that it is in our genetic interests to do so.[32] For our primitive ancestors, similarity—particularly in physical appearance and behavior—was one of the most reliable ways to distinguish relatives from nonrelatives. That was important, because two people who look and behave similarly are more likely to share genetic material with each other than are two people who look and behave differently. And humans, like many other species, are motivated to help those with whom they share genetic material. That is why, for instance, we love our own children more than we love other people's children and why we give more of our resources to family members than to strangers.[33] When we help our genetic relatives, we help our own genes survive into future generations. Again, we don't so consciously. Rather, researchers believe that over millennia, humans have developed the motivation to help their genetic relatives because it ensures the survival of their own genes.[34]

WE ARE ATTRACTED BY COMPLEMENTARITY. Of course, no one is *exactly* like you—we all differ from one another in various ways. We may believe that opposites attract, but in reality similarity is often more attractive than difference. Even though we're attracted to similarity, however, we can also be attracted to people who are different from ourselves if we see their differences as *complementary*—that is, as beneficial to ourselves because they provide a quality we lack. Someone who's shy might be drawn to a more outgoing person because that friend can help him become more sociable. A person who prefers to plan activities ahead of time might be attracted to a friend who's more spontaneous.

The key to attraction based on complementarity is that the people involved have to see their differences as positive. We may not be drawn to people with religious beliefs or political orientations that are radically different from our own, for instance. If we are convinced our beliefs and orientations are correct, we may see such differences as negative. Because religious beliefs and political orientations often reflect our fundamental ways of viewing the world, we may look upon opposing viewpoints as threatening to our own, and that perspective may decrease our attraction to someone else. If we enjoy engaging in other ways of thinking, however, then we may see differences in beliefs and orientations as complementary, and we thus might view a person with dissimilar beliefs as attractive—and as a potential friend.[35]

Uncertainty Reduction Theory

A second major theory of why we form relationships focuses not on interpersonal attraction but on the uncertainty we feel when we don't know others very well. Let's say you meet someone and want to get to know the person better. What does it mean to get to know someone? According to communication scholars Charles Berger and Richard Calabrese, it means reducing our level of uncertainty about the person.[36]

When you first meet a new co-worker, for instance, you don't know much about her, so your uncertainty about her is high. Berger and Calabrese's **uncertainty reduction theory** suggests that you will find uncertainty to be unpleasant, so you'll be motivated to reduce your uncertainty by using communication behaviors to get to know her. At first, you'll probably talk about basic information, such as where she lives or what she likes to do in her spare time. As you get to know her better, she will probably disclose more personal information about herself. You may also learn about her by paying attention to nonverbal cues, such as her personal appearance, voice, and gestures. According to uncertainty reduction theory, each new piece of information you gain reduces your uncertainty more.

Importantly, uncertainty reduction theory also suggests that the less uncertain you are, the more you will like the person. Because we dislike being uncertain about people, we will like people more as our uncertainty about them is decreased. The relationship between liking and uncertainty, as reflected in uncertainty reduction theory, is illustrated in Figure 9.1.

Predicted Outcome Value Theory

You have just read that as your uncertainty about your new co-worker is reduced, you probably will like her more. What happens, however, if you don't like the information you learn about her? Will you still like her more or want to get to know her better? Communication professor Michael Sunnafrank offered a slightly different way to think about how we form relationships. In his **predicted outcome value theory,** he suggested that when we first communicate with others, we try to determine whether continued communication with them will be worth our effort.[37]

If we like what we learn about someone during our initial conversations, we predict positive outcomes for future communication with that person, meaning we will want

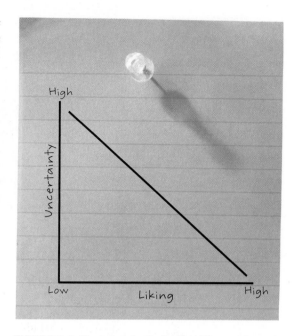

FIGURE 9.1 Uncertainty Reduction Theory According to uncertainty reduction theory, as uncertainty about a person goes down, liking for that person goes up.

uncertainty reduction theory A theory suggesting that people are motivated to reduce their uncertainty about others.

predicted outcome value theory A theory predicting that we form relationships when we think the effort will be worth it.

Sometimes we like people less the more we learn about them. Predicted outcome value theory suggests we'll use avoidance behaviors to signal our lack of interest in such people.

First Interaction

Did you like what you learned?	Yes	No
Predicted outcome value	Positive	Negative
Predicted behavior pattern	Approach	Avoidance

FIGURE 9.2 Predicted Outcome Value Theory Predicted outcome value theory says we project how positive our interactions with people will be in the future, and we behave toward them accordingly.

approach behaviors Communication behaviors that signal one's interest in getting to know someone.

to get to know the person better. In contrast, if we don't like what we learn about someone during our initial conversations, we predict negative outcomes for future communication, and we won't be motivated to continue to get to know him or her.[38]

There are many reasons why we might predict positive outcomes when we first communicate with a particular individual. We might find that we have many things in common with her or that she has a great sense of humor and is fun to be around. We might also find that she is very knowledgeable about something we're interested in, such as kayaking or designing web pages, so we can learn more about those hobbies by being around her. If we value those qualities, then Sunnafrank's theory predicts that we will engage in communication behaviors aimed at getting to know her better, such as increasing verbal communication and nonverbal immediacy around her.[39]

In other cases, we might predict negative outcomes when we first get to know someone. After spending time with a new acquaintance, for instance, we might discover that she's always criticizing people, she's boring, or she's very defensive. If we dislike those qualities, predicted outcome value theory proposes that we will reduce our verbal and nonverbal communication with her or avoid her altogether. Figure 9.2 illustrates the process of predicted outcome value theory.

Understanding Relationship Formation

Attraction theory, uncertainty reduction theory, and predicted outcome value theory all help us to understand how, and with whom, we form social relationships. According to attraction theory, we want to get to know people when we feel some measure of physical, social, or task attraction to them. Any of those forms of attraction will motivate us to engage in **approach behaviors,** which are communication behaviors that signal interest in another person. Approach behaviors include verbal statements, such as introducing yourself to someone and asking about him or her. They also include nonverbal actions, such as smiling and maintaining eye contact with the person. We use such communication behaviors to express our desire to get to know others, and attraction theory predicts that they are the result of physical, social, and/or task attraction.

According to uncertainty reduction theory, the primary purpose of engaging in approach behaviors is to collect information about the other person to reduce our uncertainty about him or her. The more our uncertainty is reduced, the more we will like the person. As we have seen, that assumption might be true if most of what we learn about the person is positive. What if we find out, however, that he or she is bigoted, obnoxious, or dull? According to uncertainty reduction theory, we may still like the person more because our uncertainty has been reduced.

According to predicted outcome value theory, however, we should like the person less, because the outcomes we'd predict from knowing him or her would seem less positive. As a result, we should no longer be motivated to engage in approach behaviors with the person. Rather, we would likely engage in **avoidance behaviors,** which are communication behaviors that signal a lack of interest in someone else. As with approach behaviors, avoidance behaviors include both verbal actions, such as saying "please leave me alone," and nonverbal behaviors, such as avoiding eye contact with the person and not spending time with him or her. According to predicted outcome value theory, therefore, we're motivated to form relationships with people only when the initial information we learn about them is positive.

Yet merely *forming* a social relationship doesn't necessarily mean we'll want to *maintain* it. Some friendships start strong but fade over time, whereas others grow and flourish. Two theoretical traditions in particular—cost/benefit theories and the concept of relational maintenance behaviors—help us understand why and how we maintain social relationships.

avoidance behaviors Communication behaviors that signal one's lack of interest in getting to know someone.

Theories About Costs and Benefits

Suppose you've been drawn to someone, you've gotten to know her, and the two of you have become friends. At that point, you've completed the process of forming a social relationship. How will you decide whether you want to stay in the relationship or let it die out? One way is by examining the give-and-take of relational costs and benefits.

Recall that relationships carry costs as well as rewards. You invest certain resources in a friendship, such as your time, attention, and money. In return, you receive certain benefits from it, such as emotional support, entertainment, and help. Two specific theories—social exchange theory and equity theory— help us understand how those costs and benefits influence which relationships we are most likely to maintain.

SOCIAL EXCHANGE THEORY AND RELATIONSHIP FORMATION. The guiding principle of **social exchange theory** is that people seek to maintain relationships in which their benefits outweigh their costs.[40] Think of your relationship with a neighbor. There are costs involved in being neighborly. You have to be willing to help when needed, and you may experience a loss of privacy if your neighbor is aware of your comings and goings. There are also benefits to a neighborly relationship, such as knowing someone can watch your home when you're away and having someone close by whose company you enjoy. The question, according to social exchange theory, is whether you think the benefits outweigh the costs. If you do, then you're likely to maintain that relationship; if not, then you're less inclined to maintain it.

social exchange theory A theory predicting that people seek to form and maintain relationships in which the benefits outweigh the costs.

An important concept in social exchange theory is your **comparison level,** your realistic expectation of what you want and think you deserve from a relationship. Your expectations are based on both your experiences with social relationships and the prevailing cultural norms for such relationships. Perhaps you think neighbors should be friendly and should help you out when you need it but otherwise should mind their own business. Those ideas would form part of your comparison level for your own neighborly relationships. Similarly, you might believe that friends should care about your well-being, always keep your secrets, and support you even when they disagree with your decisions. Those desires and expectations would be part of your comparison level for your own friendships.

comparison level A person's realistic expectation of what the person wants and thinks he or she deserves from a relationship.

Equally important is your **comparison level for alternatives.** That concept refers to your beliefs concerning how good or bad your current relationship is compared with your perceived options. Are you satisfied with your neighborly relationships, or do you think you could find better neighbors if you moved? Likewise, are you happy

comparison level for alternatives A person's assessment of how good his or her current relationship is, compared with other options.

WHAT?	WHY?	HOW?	TRY!
Learn to provide verbal relational assurances.	To help maintain important social relationships, such as those with friends and co-workers.	**1.** Through either verbal or nonverbal behaviors, stress your commitment to your relationship. **2.** As you have the opportunity, assure your friend or relational partner that you value him or her and intend to stay in that relationship for the foreseeable future.	**1.** Tell a good friend how much you care about him or her and how glad you are that you're friends. **2.** Discuss something that would be fun to do with this friend in the future, such as going on a road trip together. **CONSIDER:** *In what other ways can you assure your friend of his or her value to you?*

frequently, express their affection and appreciation for others, and don't complain. In other words, they're pleasant and fun to be around. As you might guess, those types of behaviors tend to make people well liked.[44] In contrast, behaviors such as complaining, being critical of others, and pouting when things don't go one's way reflect low positivity.

OPENNESS.   *Openness* describes a person's willingness to talk with his or her friend or relational partner about their relationship. People who use that relational maintenance strategy are likely to disclose their thoughts and feelings, ask how their friend feels about the relationship, and confide in their friend. Although it's possible to have too much openness in a relationship, an optimal amount will help maintain the relationship and keep it strong.[45] When people refuse to share their thoughts and feelings with others or don't reciprocate others' disclosures, they are displaying low amounts of openness.

ASSURANCES.   Stafford and Canary define *assurances* as verbal and nonverbal behaviors that people use to illustrate their faithfulness and commitment to others. A statement such as "Of course I'll help you; you're my best friend" sends the message that the communicator is committed to the relationship, and it reassures the friend or partner that the relationship has a future.[46] In contrast, when individuals don't acknowledge the importance of their friendships, they convey the message that they aren't very committed to them. Practice your ability to give assurances by checking out the "Got Skills?" box.

SOCIAL NETWORKS.   The term *social networks* refers to all the friendships and family relationships one has. An important relational maintenance behavior is to share one's social networks with another person. Two close friends, for instance, are likely to know each other's families, co-workers, and other friends. When that happens, we say that the friends' social networks have converged. Research shows that convergence is an important way to keep relationships stable and strong.[47] Individuals undermine

THE FIVE PRIMARY RELATIONAL MAINTENANCE BEHAVIORS

Positivity	Acting friendly, being courteous, refraining from criticism
Openness	Being willing to discuss your relationship
Assurances	Expressing and stressing your faithfulness and commitment
Social Networks	Introducing one person to your other friends, family members, and co-workers
Sharing Tasks	Performing your fair share of the work in your relationship

that convergence when they speak poorly of the friends and relatives of their friends or actively avoid spending time with them.

SHARING TASKS.   As the term suggests, *sharing tasks* means performing one's fair share of the work in a friendship. If your friend gives you a ride to the airport whenever you need it, for example, then it's only fair that you help her paint her apartment when she asks. If your roommate cooks you dinner, it would be fair for you to do the dishes afterward. As we've seen, being in a social relationship requires investments of energy and effort. One way of maintaining a relationship, then, is to make certain the two parties are contributing equally.[48] When you expect your friends to do favors for you without reciprocating, you are not sharing tasks equally.

Understanding Relationship Maintenance

To understand social relationships, we need to examine both why people maintain such relationships and how they maintain them. Social exchange theory and equity theory both explain why people maintain their relationships by focusing on the rewards and costs of those relationships. As we've considered, your social relationships bring you certain rewards, such as pleasure, safety, and material help, and they also invoke certain costs, such as your time, attention, and financial resources. Are the rewards you get from a particular relationship worth the costs of that relationship? Social exchange theory and equity theory both help you answer that question, although they do it in slightly different ways.

SOCIAL EXCHANGE THEORY AND RELATIONSHIP MAINTENANCE.   Social exchange theory leads us to compare the costs and rewards of our current relationships with those of our alternatives. Suppose you are deciding whether to maintain a relationship with your friend Betsy. One alternative would be simply to end that friendship. Another option would be to replace her with a different friend. According to social exchange theory, whether you stick with Betsy or adopt one of those alternatives depends on your perception of the costs and rewards associated with each option. From the perspective of this theory, you ultimately will choose the option that benefits you most.

EQUITY THEORY AND RELATIONSHIP MAINTENANCE.   In contrast to social exchange theory, equity theory leads us to compare how much the current relationship costs and rewards ourselves with how much it costs and rewards our partner. If you're debating whether to stay friends with Betsy, you would therefore consider how your ratio of costs and rewards compares with hers. What you're striving for, according to

Sally Field's character in Mrs. Doubtfire *used to see her husband's free spirit and sense of humor as benefits. Over time, however, she came to regard those traits as costs.*

equity theory, is a balance between your own cost/benefit ratio and Betsy's. From the perspective of this theory, we prefer relationships in which we receive benefits equal to—not greater than or less than—those of our partners.

SHIFTS IN COSTS AND BENEFITS. Importantly, some of the characteristics we think of as benefits can turn into costs. In the movie *Mrs. Doubtfire,* Miranda Hillard (played by Sally Field) separates from her husband, Daniel (played by Robin Williams). She then hires a housekeeper named Mrs. Doubtfire who, unbeknownst to her, is actually her husband in disguise. In a conversation with Mrs. Doubtfire, Miranda describes Daniel as having a wonderful sense of humor and the ability to make her laugh. Early in their marriage, she regarded that trait as a benefit. Over time, however, Daniel's inability to take himself or his parental responsibilities seriously took its toll on her patience. In other words, his humorous nature, which Miranda had previously considered a benefit, had become a cost.

Of course, the opposite is also true: Costs can turn into benefits. For example, you may regard a friend's political views to be a cost if they are radically different from yours, because you feel irritated and defensive when he expresses them. Over time, you may come to realize that his ideas have expanded your way of thinking and helped you to understand certain political issues. What you first regarded as a cost to your friendship may now seem like a benefit.

In summary, once we form relationships, we maintain them through our communication behaviors. Some of the most important types of relationship maintenance behaviors are behaving positively, being open, giving our partner assurances, involving our partner in our social networks, and sharing tasks. Additional ways of maintaining one's social relationships include doing favors for a friend and always asking the friend about his or her day. Many friends also maintain their relationships by participating together in their shared interests, such as watching sporting events, going to movies, and trying out new recipes.[49] In various ways, each of those behaviors conveys one's appreciation and value of a friend, as well as enjoyment of the person's company. Because friendships are largely voluntary, feeling appreciated and valued can motivate individuals to stay in them.

LEARN IT What is the difference between physical, social, and task attraction? According to uncertainty reduction theory, how is uncertainty related to liking? According to predicted outcome value theory, when we predict positive relational outcomes, what are we motivated to do? What is a comparison level for alternatives? What does it mean to be under-benefited and to be over-benefited? What behaviors do people enact to maintain their relationships?

APPLY IT Choose one of your friendships, and make a point of practicing the five relational maintenance behaviors—positivity, openness, assurances, social networks, and sharing tasks—with that friend over the next several weeks. In a journal entry, describe the ways in which you enacted each of those communicative behaviors and the responses they elicited from your friend.

REFLECT ON IT Do you feel over-benefited in any of your relationships? Which relational maintenance behaviors are most important in your social relationships?

3 Characteristics of Friendships

Your various friendships are likely as different and individual as your friends themselves. Some of those friendships are probably long-term and seem almost like family ties. Others may be specific to certain contexts, such as work, school, and the place where you volunteer. Yet even though each is unique in some ways, nearly all friendships have certain qualities in common. In this section, we take a look at five common characteristics of friendships.

Friendships Are Voluntary

One of the defining characteristics of friendship is that it is *voluntary*.[50] We choose our friends and they choose us, and we don't have to be friends with anyone we don't want to be. That's part of what makes a friendship so special: Both friends are in the relationship by choice.

Friendship is voluntary, but that doesn't mean we choose our friends arbitrarily. As we learned in the previous theoretical discussions about relationship formation and maintenance, attraction and the balance of costs and rewards all affect whom we pursue and maintain as friends.

The fact that friendships are voluntary also doesn't mean that they flourish on their own. On the contrary, they require communication behaviors on our part and on the part of our friends. Not only do we have to interact with others to form friendships in the first place, we also have to use relationship maintenance behaviors such as positivity, openness, assurances, network convergence, and sharing tasks to maintain them.

Five common characteristics of friendships—such as the friendship between these two women—are that they are voluntary, usually develop between peers, are governed by rules, differ by sex, and have a life span.

communication light side

FACEBOOK FRIENDS: 302 IS THE MAGIC NUMBER

As valuable as friends are to us, research suggests it's possible to have *too many* friends—at least on Facebook.

That idea may seem counterintuitive to you. In *real life,* after all, having many friends signals that you are popular, admired, and well liked by others, all of which cast you in a positive light. It might therefore seem that having several hundred (or even several thousand) Facebook friends would make you appear especially impressive.

Communication researchers at Michigan State University discovered otherwise, however, when they asked students to rate the likability of a person depicted in a Facebook page with either 102, 302, 502, 702, or 902 friends. As you might expect, the person shown on the Facebook page was rated as least likable when only 102 friends were advertised. However, likability scores peaked at 302 friends and dropped continually after that. In other words, the experimental subject was seen as more likable with 302 friends than with 502, 702, or even 902 friends.

The researchers suggested that people who have several hundred Facebook friends or more might be perceived as shallow because it would be so difficult to maintain high-quality friendships with that many people. Their study indicates that to appear likable but not shallow, the optimal number of Facebook friends to have is approximately 300.

Source: Tong, S. T., Van Der Heide, B., Langwell, L., & Walther, J. B. (2008). Too much of a good thing? The relationship between number of friends and interpersonal impressions on Facebook. *Journal of Computer-Mediated Communication, 13,* 531–549.

Since friendship is voluntary, does that mean we should strive to have as many friends as possible? Friends certainly bring us many benefits, but in some contexts—such as on a Facebook page—it might be possible to have *too many* friends, as the "Communication: Light Side" box explains.

Friendships Are Usually Between Peers

peer Someone of similar power or status.

A second important characteristic of friendship is that it is usually a relationship between equals. A **peer** is someone similar in power or status to oneself. Your instructors, boss, and parents aren't your peers because those people all exercise some measure of control over you, at least temporarily. Most of us conceive of friendship as a relationship with peers—that is, people who are our equals, no more or less powerful than we are.

Does that mean we can't become friends with our instructors, boss, and parents? Not at all—in fact, many of us consider those people to be very good friends. We can have satisfying friendships with individuals who have some type of power over us. Those relationships can also be complicated, however. When a friend exercises power over you, it can cause conflicts between the voluntary nature of your friendship and the involuntary nature of your parent–child, teacher–student, or employer–employee relationship. For instance, a professor who is also your friend may vacillate between giving you a good grade and giving you the poorer grade you might have earned. In such a situation, he may feel that the expectations of your friendship and the expectations of your professional relationship are in conflict.

Friendships Are Governed by Rules

In some ways, a friendship is like a social contract to which both parties agree. By being someone's friend, you acknowledge—at least implicitly—that you expect certain things from that person and that he or she can expect certain things from you. Those expectations are possible because friendships have rules. Even if the rules aren't explicitly stated, most people within a given society usually know and understand them.[51]

As you'll see in the "At a Glance" box, researchers have identified and studied many of the underlying rules of friendship. Some of these rules relate to specific behaviors (such as standing up for your friends and not publicly criticizing them), whereas others relate to the way you should think or feel about your friends (trusting them and not being jealous of their other friendships). Perhaps you've been in a friendship in which one or more of those implicit rules was broken. For example, maybe a friend has been criticizing you behind your back or has consistently failed to show up when you made plans together. Just as with communication rules in general—discussed in Chapter 1—friendship rules often become explicit only when someone violates them. As research tells us, most people agree there are right and wrong ways to treat friends.[52]

Friendships Differ by Sex

You've probably noticed some differences between the friendships you have with women and the ones you have with men. In fact, researchers have written volumes about sex differences and similarities in friendships and friendship behaviors. In this section, we examine those differences and similarities separately for same-sex and opposite-sex friendships.

AT A GLANCE

FRIENDSHIP RULES

Researchers Michael Argyle and Monika Henderson have confirmed that people have certain rules for friendships. When the parties to the relationship observe those rules, the friendships tend to be stronger. Here are some of the most important friendship rules Argyle and Henderson found. What rules would you add to this list?

- Stand up for your friend in his or her absence.

- Trust each other.

- Offer help when your friend needs it.

- Don't criticize your friend in public.

- Keep your friend's secrets.

- Provide emotional support when needed.

- Respect your friend's privacy.

- Don't be jealous of his or her other friends.

Source: Argyle, M., & Henderson, M. (1984). The rules of friendship. *Journal of Social and Personal Relationships, 1,* 211–237.

SAME-SEX FRIENDS.   One of the most consistent findings concerning same-sex friendships is that women and men value different aspects of their respective friendships. Essentially, friendships among women tend to place greater emphasis on conversational and emotional expressiveness, whereas men's friendships focus on shared activities and interests.[53]

Best friends Juanita and Lindsay, for instance, frequently get together just to talk and catch up. Their visits often include sharing their feelings about what's going on in their lives. During those talks, Juanita and Lindsay listen to each other and express their support and affection for each other. Sometimes, they engage in an activity while they talk, such as attending Lindsay's daughter's basketball game or driving to the bus station to pick up Juanita's sister; sometimes, they simply talk. Juanita and Lindsay agree that their ability to share, disclose, and express feelings with each other is what makes their friendship satisfying.

In contrast, when Alex thinks about his closest male friends, he thinks of Jake, his golfing buddy, and Davin, his patrol partner on the police force. The time he spends with those friends almost always revolves around some type of activity. With Jake, it's usually playing a round of golf and then having nachos and beer at a sports bar. With Davin, it's working together during the many hours they spend on patrol. Alex feels close to each friend because he enjoys their company when they are engaged in these activities.

Significantly, Alex's time with Davin and Jake allows them to talk about what's happening in their lives. During a long patrol shift, for instance, Alex and Davin frequently talk about their children's activities and their plans for the future. Similarly, during a recent round of golf, Jake told Alex how much he missed his recently deceased father. Most often, though, Alex and his friends simply enjoy the time they spend together doing activities, even if their time together doesn't involve much conversation. For Alex, it's the *doing,* not the *talking,* that makes a friendship close.

Although research has confirmed that those sex differences exist, it has also identified two important qualifications about these differences. First, as with nearly all sex differences in behavior, those differences in same-sex friendships are just averages. They don't characterize all friendships. Some women's friendships focus more on shared activities than on conversation, and some men routinely share personal conversations with their male friends even if they aren't engaged in an activity together.

Second, the fact that women's and men's relationships differ does not mean that friendships are more important to one sex than to the other. Some people believe that

Studies show that men's friendships often focus on shared activity, whereas women's friendships often privilege shared conversation. Men and women often value opposite-sex friendships as opportunities to communicate in ways that are important to the other sex.

because women self-disclose more to one another than men do, women's friendships are closer and more satisfying than men's are. In fact, however, research has demonstrated that women and men report equal levels of closeness in their same-sex friendships.[54] What differs between the sexes is simply the characteristics that make those friendships close. For women, the key characteristic is shared conversation; for men, it's shared activity.

OPPOSITE-SEX FRIENDS. What do we know about opposite-sex friendships? Research suggests that both men and women value those relationships as a chance to see things from each other's perspective.[55] Opposite-sex friendships can provide opportunities for men to be emotionally expressive and for women to enjoy shared activities that their same-sex friendships do not.[56]

In addition, many opposite-sex friends feel some degree of physical or romantic attraction toward each other,[57] and they often communicate in ways that resemble romantic relationships, such as by flirting with each other[58] and sharing sexual humor.[59] In fact, a study of more than 300 American college students conducted by communication scientists Walid Afifi and Sandra Faulkner found that half of the students reported having engaged in sexual activity with a nonromantic opposite-sex friend.[60] Although some research has suggested that sexual activity changes the fundamental nature of an opposite-sex friendship from platonic to romantic,[61] more than half of the students in Afifi and Faulkner's study who had engaged in sexual activity with an opposite-sex friend reported no such change in the nature of their relationship.

Whether they are attracted to each other or not, many opposite-sex friends have specific reasons for not wanting their friendship to evolve into a romantic relationship. In surveys of more than 600 American college students, communication scholars Susan Messman, Dan Canary, and Kimberly Hause discovered that people keep their opposite-sex friendships nonromantic for six primary reasons:[62]

- They aren't physically attracted to their friend.
- Their relatives and other friends wouldn't approve of a romantic relationship with the friend.
- They aren't ready to be in a romantic relationship.
- They want to protect their existing friendship.
- They fear being disappointed or hurt.
- They are concerned about a third party, such as a sibling, who is romantically interested in the friend.

Studies show that overall, both women and men consider their same-sex friends to be more loyal and helpful than their opposite-sex counterparts.[63] At the same time, however, opposite-sex friendships allow women and men to enjoy those aspects of friendship most valued by the other sex. Thus, it appears that same-sex and opposite-sex friendships offer unique rewards.

Friendships Have a Life Span

As important as friendships are to us, most are not permanent. Rather, as with most relationships, friendships have a life span: They are initiated, they are maintained, and eventually many of them end. Communication scholar and friendship expert William Rawlins has proposed that most friendships move through a life span consisting of six stages.[64]

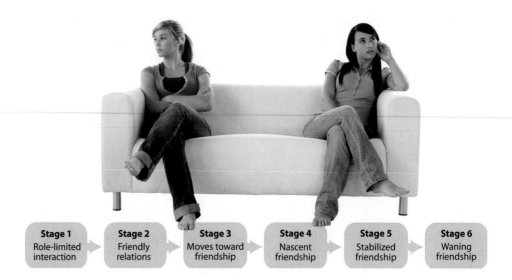

| Stage 1 Role-limited interaction | Stage 2 Friendly relations | Stage 3 Moves toward friendship | Stage 4 Nascent friendship | Stage 5 Stabilized friendship | Stage 6 Waning friendship |

Suppose two strangers, Naya and Emily, have been called for jury duty on the same day, and they meet in the jurors' waiting lounge. Let's see how their relationship might progress through Rawlins's six stages.

- *Role-limited interaction:* At the *role-limited interaction* stage, Naya and Emily meet and interact for the first time. Because they are strangers at this stage, their communication follows social and cultural norms for interaction between strangers. They are civil and polite but share little personal information.

- *Friendly relations:* After chatting for a while, Naya and Emily may enter the *friendly relations* stage. At that point, their conversation becomes friendlier. For example, they may share personal stories or anecdotes. Naya and Emily may intend for their friendly interaction simply to make their wait in the jurors' lounge more enjoyable. However, it can also be an invitation for friendship.

- *Moves toward friendship:* Suppose Emily e-mails Naya the following week to ask if she'd like to go to an art gallery opening. Emily's invitation can signal progression to the *moves toward friendship* stage. At this stage, Naya and Emily's communication becomes more social and less bound by norms and rules.

- *Nascent friendship:* If Naya and Emily continue getting together and enjoying their interactions, they may enter the *nascent friendship* stage. At that point, they begin to think of themselves as friends. Their communication continues to become more personal and less prescribed.

- *Stabilized friendship:* Over time, Naya and Emily's relationship may progress to the *stabilized friendship* stage. At that point, they consider their friendship to be fully established. They trust each other strongly and may even adjust their attitudes and opinions to be more in line with each other's.

- *Waning friendship:* After many years of close friendship, Naya and Emily may enter the *waning friendship* stage. That stage marks the decline of their friendship. Their friendship may simply become more distant and casual, or it may end altogether.

There are many reasons why a friendship comes to an end.[65] Research suggests that we can divide those reasons into two general categories: events that cause friends to dislike each other, and changes in life circumstances that decrease opportunities for communication and attention. Let's look at each situation.

FRIENDS CAN GROW TO DISLIKE EACH OTHER. Some friendships end because the friends no longer like each other. Although two people initially may have become friends because of their perceived similarity or their social attraction to each other, they can develop negative feelings toward each other that cause them to end their friendship. Studies have demonstrated that negative feelings are most likely to arise when one friend:

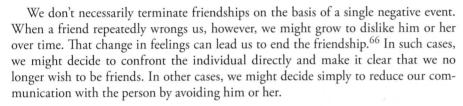

- Constantly nags or criticizes the other
- Betrays the other's confidence or trust
- Behaves in a hostile or physically violent way around the other
- Begins abusing alcohol or other drugs
- Fails to provide help or support when the other friend needs it
- Becomes intolerant of the other friend's romantic partner or other friends
- Feels he or she no longer has anything in common with the other friend

We don't necessarily terminate friendships on the basis of a single negative event. When a friend repeatedly wrongs us, however, we might grow to dislike him or her over time. That change in feelings can lead us to end the friendship.[66] In such cases, we might decide to confront the individual directly and make it clear that we no longer wish to be friends. In other cases, we might decide simply to reduce our communication with the person by avoiding him or her.

FRIENDS' LIFE CIRCUMSTANCES CAN CHANGE. Although friendships sometimes end because of negative feelings, many friends simply "drift apart." As our lives change and evolve, we may have less opportunity to interact with particular friends. That doesn't necessarily mean we develop any negative feelings for them. It does mean, however, that some friendships end simply from lack of attention.

According to research, one of the most common life changes that can end a friendship is physical separation.[67] Recall that physical proximity is one of the main reasons we're attracted to potential friends. Friendships are relatively easy to maintain with people you see all the time. If one friend moves away, however, keeping up the friendship becomes much more of a challenge.[68] Friends may keep in touch for a while after being separated, but their communication often declines over time, causing them to lose track of each other.

Other changes in life circumstances can also cause friendships to fade. When one friend gets married or has a baby, for instance, his or her attention is understandably diverted toward the new spouse or child. As a result, he or she has less time and opportunity to interact with friends. The demands of work or school can also make it difficult to spend time with friends. Experiencing a chronic illness can likewise limit opportunities to see friends. That may be particularly true with illnesses that impair social abilities, such as depression and chronic anxiety.

It is important to note that in those situations we don't necessarily *want* the friendship to end. Rather, we may simply no longer have the necessary time, energy, and attention to maintain it. If the friend is particularly important to us, however, we can use our communication and relational maintenance behaviors to keep the friendship going. It may take only an occasional phone call or e-mail message to maintain contact and let a friend know we still care about him or her. We can even use the Internet to help us restore communication with friends with whom we've lost touch.

LEARN IT What does it mean to say that friendship is voluntary? What is a peer? Which rules are common for friendships in North America? Do people report feeling greater loyalty to same-sex or opposite-sex friends? Why do friendships come to an end?

APPLY IT Working alone or in a small group, generate a list of what you consider to be the five most important rules for friendships, and rank-order them in terms of their importance. For each rule, identify one or two interpersonal communication behaviors that help you follow that rule in your own friendships.

REFLECT ON IT Do you have any friendships that you feel are involuntary? What do you value differently about your same-sex and opposite-sex friendships?

4 Social Relationships in the Workplace

Nearly all of us will be employed at some point in our lives, and our jobs will require us to interact with other people. It's therefore realistic to assume that most of us will have to relate to and communicate with people we know from work, whether they are co-workers, superiors, subordinates, or customers. In fact, many public agencies and private corporations expect their employees to communicate with one another in well-defined ways. Those expectations might include communicating honestly, treating people with dignity, listening to others, and being open to other people's opinions. All such communication behaviors contribute to a civil and respectful work environment. They can also make it easier for employees to form workplace friendships.[69]

As you may know from experience, friendships at work can be a double-edged sword. On the one hand, having friends at work is great, because friends can make the workday pleasant and help and support you when you need it. On the other hand, friendship roles and work roles often conflict. For instance, your workplace friends might wish to chat with you, but if you have tasks to complete by a tight deadline, you might not have time for them.

Workplace friendships can also be more challenging to control than regular friendships. As a part of our job, we are usually required to see and interact with our supervisors, co-workers, and customers whether we want to or not. Interaction with regular friends, in contrast, is usually voluntary and easier to control. If you have an argument with a regular friend, for example, you can choose to avoid him or her for a period of time while you both cool down. Because of your work responsibilities, however, you may not have that option with workplace friends.

To deal successfully with the challenges of workplace friendships, it's important to understand their dynamics. Let's examine those dynamics in three specific workplace relationships: between co-workers, between superiors and subordinates, and with clients.

Social Relationships with Co-Workers

You are probably most likely to form workplace friendships with your immediate co-workers. One reason that is true is that co-workers are usually peers rather than superiors or subordinates, so their levels of power and responsibility are similar to yours.[70] Another reason is that immediate co-workers share with you common experiences, such as working for the same company, the same department, and the same supervisor. In addition, you probably spend a great deal of time with your co-workers, perhaps even more than you spend with your friends outside work. Those characteristics can form a ready-made basis for friendship.[71]

Research has shown that the quality of people's friendships with their co-workers affects their job satisfaction.[72] All other things being equal, the closer you are to your co-workers, the happier you are at work.

As beneficial as friendships with co-workers are, however, they are also very challenging. The reason that is true is that the relationship has both a *social dimension* and a *task dimension,* and those different aspects of the friendship frequently come into conflict. The social dimension is your personal relationship with the co-worker; the task dimension is your professional relationship. Let's say, for

Research indicates that having high-quality workplace friendships is important to overall job satisfaction. As beneficial as they are, however, workplace friendships can be challenging to maintain.

example, that you're friends with your co-worker Kellie, who's up for a promotion. As her friend, you want her to have the promotion, but as her co-worker, you don't believe she has really earned it. It's easy to see how those mixed feelings could be troublesome for your friendship.

Clearly, then, to maintain friendships with your co-workers, you need to balance the personal and professional sides of the relationships at all times. For instance, you might decide it's important to tell Kellie you support her, to voice enthusiasm if she receives the promotion, and to express disappointment if she doesn't, because she's your friend. Even though you don't feel she has earned the promotion, your friendship with Kellie may motivate you to be supportive of her anyway.

Alternatively, you might remind Kellie that the promotion is very competitive, that she is competing with employees who have more experience and seniority than she does, and that she shouldn't be surprised if she doesn't get it. You might even say "I'm telling you this as your co-worker" to make it clear that you are speaking from the perspective of your professional relationship rather than your personal one. Which approach you choose will probably depend on how close your friendship is and on what your experiences with similar situations have been.

Social Relationships Between Superiors and Subordinates

As challenging as friendships among co-workers can be, friendships between superiors and subordinates are considerably more complicated, because they include a power difference that co-worker friendships generally do not have.[73] Recall that one of the defining characteristics of friendship is that it's a relationship between equals. So, when two friends are a supervisor and an employee, the power difference between them introduces a task dimension that friendships between co-workers usually don't have.

Genuine friendships between superiors and subordinates certainly aren't impossible to form or maintain. Indeed, research shows that being friends with your boss usually adds to your job satisfaction.[74] That makes sense: If you like your supervisor, you'll probably enjoy working for him or her.

The challenge arises because what's best for the superior–subordinate relationship isn't always what's best for the friendship. If you're the employee, you might dislike or disagree with your boss's decisions concerning the company's policies or future direction, particularly when those decisions affect you. Conversely, if you're the supervisor, you may agonize about such decisions because you realize that what's best for the company is not always what's best for each individual employee.

To understand those stresses, imagine that your supervisor announces that the company will reduce the clerical staff on whom you depend to get your work done. Now imagine that to accommodate a new business strategy, your boss cancels a promotional campaign you've been developing, including a photo shoot you were looking forward to. In such cases, it can be hard not to take your boss's actions personally, and that kind of response can strain your friendship.[75] In a study of superior–subordinate friendships, communication scholar Theodore Zorn found that superiors commonly experienced those types of tensions between their work responsibilities and their friendships with subordinates.[76]

Given all those strains, you may be wondering whether friendships between superiors and subordinates are ultimately doomed. In fact, despite the challenges, such friendships are possible to maintain. That is especially true if both parties acknowledge that their friendship and their work relationship might conflict and agree to keep those relationships separate as best they can.

It's often best if people in power-imbalanced friendships acknowledge the potential conflicts their friendships can entail and discuss them directly, particularly if they started their relationship as peers, and one of them was later promoted. By acknowledging the potential for conflicts and establishing their expectations for how to address them before they occur, a supervisor and employee can lay the groundwork for a successful friendship. That doesn't mean they won't experience the tensions that often accompany that type of relationship. Rather, it means they can agree ahead of time on how to handle those tensions so that the strains don't damage either their professional relationship or their friendship. Refer to the "Got Skills?" box for tips on how to do so.

One situation that's extremely problematic for superior–subordinate relationships is the case in which the subordinate feels he or she has been sexually harassed. In the United States, the Equal Employment Opportunity Commission (EEOC) defines *sexual harassment* as unsolicited, unwelcome behavior of a sexual nature. You might intend to be friendly or supportive by putting your arm around a subordinate, for instance, but if the subordinate feels uncomfortable by your behavior, it may constitute harassment.

According to the EEOC, sexual harassment can occur in two forms. The first, known as *quid pro quo* (Latin for "this for that"), happens when a supervisor offers an employee rewards in exchange for sexual favors. A statement such as "I'll give you tomorrow off if you have a drink with me tonight" can qualify as quid pro quo harassment if it is directed at a subordinate. The second form, known as *hostile work environment,* occurs when work conditions are sexually offensive or intimidating. Telling sexually suggestive jokes when both men and women are present or making derogatory comments about a person's sexual orientation can qualify as hostile work environment harassment.

Sexual harassment is a serious and pervasive problem in many organizations, and its victims often suffer long-term emotional and psychological harm. Competent communicators must consider how other people might interpret their verbal and nonverbal behaviors in the organizational context. How well could you identify sexual harassment if you saw or heard about it? Go to the "Assess Your Skills" box to find out.

[SEPARATING SOCIAL AND TASK DIMENSIONS IN SUPERIOR–SUBORDINATE RELATIONSHIPS]

Keep the social and task dimensions of work relationships separate.

WHAT?

Discuss the boundary between the social and the task dimensions of a superior–subordinate relationship.

WHY?

To equip the relationship to handle future conflicts between its social and task dimensions.

HOW?

1. If you begin to develop a friendship with a superior or subordinate, recognize early in the friendship that your priorities as friends may conflict with your priorities as co-workers.

2. Find time to address the situation openly and candidly with your superior or subordinate *before* such a conflict arises. Try to agree on ground rules for managing such conflicts when you experience them.

TRY!

1. Role-play a conversation with a classmate pretending to be your subordinate.

2. Say "There will probably be occasions when we have to put our friendship aside and focus on what's best for the company. Sometimes that will mean I'll have to make decisions that you don't like. When that happens, please don't take it personally; remember that I'm just doing my job."

3. Talk through how each of you might react in the event of such conflict, and practice negotiating ground rules to preserve both the social and the task dimensions of your relationship.

CONSIDER: *What strategies for managing social/task conflict seem most promising to you?*

got **SKILLS** ?

Social Relationships with Clients

In most professions, you'll interact with customers. For instance, you may sell your company's products to the same retail stores or medical offices each month and get to know the buyers there. Likewise, you may work for a financial or technology firm that offers ongoing consulting services to long-term business clients. Depending on the nature of your job, you may have clients you see or talk to regularly, so it's reasonable to expect that you may form social relationships with some of them.[77] Those relationships can be highly rewarding personally, and they can also benefit your organization because they can be a major reason why your customers continue to buy from you or your company.[78] After all, most of us prefer dealing with a salesperson or a service provider with whom we have developed a comfortable and trusting relationship.

At the same time, friendships with customers invoke some of the same task–social tensions that friendships with co-workers, employers, and employees do. Your customers may be your friends, but they still expect you to furnish a high-quality product or service, and you still expect them to provide full and prompt payment. If either party doesn't uphold its end of the bargain, then the customer–provider relationship can be disrupted, and the friendship can suffer.

MASTER the chapter

1 Why Social Relationships Matter (p. 278)

- Each of us has a need to belong that motivates us to seek, form, maintain, and protect strong social relationships.
- Social relationships bring us emotional, material, and health rewards.
- Social relationships incur costs in our time, our energy, and other resources.

2 Forming and Maintaining Social Bonds (p. 283)

- We value attraction in the form of physical appearance, proximity, similarity, and complementarity.
- Uncertainty reduction theory says we are driven to reduce uncertainty about others by getting to know them.
- According to predicted outcome value theory, we form relationships when we think there is value in doing so.
- Social exchange theory predicts that we form relationships in which the benefits outweigh (or are at least equal to) the costs.
- According to equity theory, a good relationship is one in which our ratio of costs and rewards is the same as our partner's.

- People use several relational maintenance behaviors, including positivity, openness, assurances, social networks, and shared tasks.

3 Characteristics of Friendships (p. 295)

- We generally expect friendships to be voluntary.
- Most friendships are between peers, or people of equal status.
- Friendships are governed by rules, many of which are implicit.
- Some characteristics of friendship differ according to the sexes of the friends involved.
- Friendships have a life span; they develop over time and we don't necessarily expect them to be permanent.

4 Social Relationships in the Workplace (p. 302)

- Having positive social relationships with co-workers increases job satisfaction.
- Social relationships between superiors and subordinates can be very positive but are also complicated by the inherent power difference within them.
- Positive social relationships with customers can be highly rewarding, both personally and professionally.

KEY TERMS

approach behaviors (p. 288)

avoidance behaviors (p. 289)

comparison level (p. 289)

comparison level for alternatives (p. 289)

equity theory (p. 291)

interpersonal attraction (p. 283)

need to belong (p. 279)

over-benefited (p. 291)

peer (p. 296)

physical attraction (p. 283)

predicted outcome value theory (p. 287)

relational maintenance behaviors (p. 291)

social attraction (p. 283)

social exchange theory (p. 289)

task attraction (p. 283)

uncertainty reduction theory (p. 287)

under-benefited (p. 291)

DISCUSSION QUESTIONS

1. How strong is your own need to belong? In what ways do you see your need for social relationships influencing the decisions you make (such as where to live and how to spend your free time)?

2. What are some of the biggest costs associated with maintaining your friendships? Which of your friendships have ended because the costs exceeded the rewards?

3. What would social exchange theory and equity theory have to say about being over-benefited in a friendship?

4. Give examples of the social and task dimensions of a relationship with a co-worker.

MULTIPLE CHOICE

1. **Attraction to someone's personality is known as**
   a. task attraction
   b. physical attraction
   c. semantic attraction
   d. social attraction

2. **Uncertainty reduction theory posits that**
   a. uncertainty about someone creates mystery and facilitates attraction toward him or her
   b. we like uncertainty because what we do not know cannot hurt us
   c. uncertainty is unpleasant, and we seek to reduce it through communication
   d. none of the above

3. **According to equity theory, a good relationship is one in which**
   a. the rewards outweigh the costs
   b. the costs outweigh the rewards
   c. the ratio of costs to rewards is equal for both people
   d. none of the above

4. **Behaviors people use to express their faithfulness and commitment to others constitute the relationship maintenance behavior known as**
   a. positivity
   b. openness
   c. sharing tasks
   d. assurances

5. **Sexual harassment that happens when a supervisor offers an employee rewards in exchange for sexual favors is known as**
   a. quid pro quo
   b. hostile work environment
   c. sexual scheming
   d. unlawful demands

FILL IN THE BLANK

6. The theory that says that each of us is born with a desire to seek, form, and maintain social relationships is _____.

7. We can be attracted to others who are different from ourselves if their differences are perceived as _____, or beneficial to ourselves.

8. The behaviors that signal our lack of interest in another person are _____.

9. Because friendships are _____, we choose our friends and they choose us.

10. Relationships between superiors and subordinates can be complicated because they include a _____ difference that co-worker relationships generally do not.

ANSWERS

Multiple Choice: 1 (d); 2 (c); 3 (c); 4 (d); 5 (a); **Fill in the Blank:** 6 (need-to-belong theory); 7 (complementary); 8 (avoidance behaviors); 9 (voluntary); 10 (power)

RESEARCH LIBRARY

MOVIES

I Love You, Man (comedy; 2009; R)
Paul Rudd stars in this comedy as Peter Klaven, a real estate agent who gets engaged to be married and discovers he has no male friends to include in his wedding party. His brother and fiancée intervene by setting him up on "man-dates" so that he can develop some male friendships. He ends up being socially attracted to a most unlikely friend, played by Jason Segel.

In Good Company (comedy; 2005; PG-13)
In this comedy, Dan Foreman (played by Dennis Quaid) is a senior advertising salesman whose new supervisor, Carter Duryea (played by Topher Grace), is half his age. The film depicts the challenges of negotiating a superior-subordinate relationship with a younger, inexperienced supervisor. When Carter begins dating Dan's daughter, the tension between Carter and Dan's social and professional relationships is amplified.

BOOKS AND JOURNAL ARTICLES

Baumeister, R. F., & Leary, M. R. (1995). The need to belong: Desire for interpersonal attachments as a fundamental human motivation. *Psychological Bulletin, 117,* 497–529.

Bukowski, W. M., & Newcomb, A. F. (Eds.). (1998). *The company they keep: Friendship in childhood and adolescence.* New York: Cambridge University Press.

Parks, M. R. (2007). *Personal relationships and personal networks.* Mahwah, NJ: Lawrence Erlbaum Associates.

Parks, M. R., & Floyd, K. (1996). Meanings for closeness and intimacy in friendship. *Journal of Social and Personal Relationships, 15,* 517–537.

Winstead, B. A., Derlega, V. J., Montgomery, M. J., & Pilkington, C. (1995). The quality of friendships at work and job satisfaction. *Journal of Social and Personal Relationships, 12,* 199–215.

WEBSITES

www.policylink.org/CHB/SocialRelationships/default.html
This site comments on the associations between social relationships and health, particularly mental health. The site is sponsored by Policy Link, a research and advocacy group promoting economic and social equity.

www.apa.org/monitor/apr07/social.html
This website, sponsored by the American Psychological Association, discusses research showing how having social relationships at work contributes to job satisfaction.

10 Interpersonal Communication in Romantic and Family Relationships

IN SICKNESS AND IN HEALTH

The movie *Love and Other Drugs* (2010) features Anne Hathaway as Maggie Murdock, a young woman who has Parkinson's disease. Maggie is befriended by Jamie Randall (played by Jake Gyllenhaal), a pharmaceutical sales representative known to be charming but emotionally shallow. After a brief affair, Jamie realizes, to his surprise, that he has developed genuine feelings for Maggie. His feelings lead to conflict for Maggie, who wants to be loved but is afraid of being a burden on anyone because of her medical condition. The film concludes with both Jamie and Maggie realizing that true intimacy requires a commitment to support one's partner and a willingness to accept that support.

Although traditions vary around the world, forming romantic relationships is a practically universal human activity: 95 percent of us will get married.

monogamy Being in only one romantic relationship at a time and avoiding romantic or sexual involvement with others outside the relationship.

infidelity Having romantic or sexual interaction with someone outside of one's romantic relationship.

polygamy A practice in which one person is married to two or more spouses at once.

In this scene from the TV show The Good Wife, *Julianna Margulies's character talks with her incarcerated husband, who has been unfaithful to her in their marriage.*

they are unemployed and lack the social support and financial resources employment provides.[11]

People in every known society form romantic unions. Although many romantic relationships share certain characteristics, there is also diversity among them. Let's look at variations in the extent to which romantic relationships are exclusive, voluntary, based on love, composed of opposite-sex partners, and permanent.

ROMANTIC RELATIONSHIPS AND EXCLUSIVITY. One common expectation for romantic relationships is that they are exclusive. Usually, exclusivity takes the form of **monogamy,** which means being in only one romantic relationship at a time and avoiding romantic or sexual involvement with people outside the relationship. Exclusivity is an expression of commitment and faithfulness that romantic partners share and trust each other to uphold. As a result, relational **infidelity,** which means having romantic or sexual interaction with someone outside of one's romantic relationship, is often an emotionally traumatic experience for the partner who is wronged.

Not all romantic partners expect their relationship to be exclusive, however. Instead, some couples choose to have "open" relationship in which romantic and/or sexual involvement with people outside the relationship is accepted.[12] Although it's difficult to know exactly how common that type of relationship is, research indicates that open relationships are observed between heterosexuals,[13] bisexuals,[14] gay men,[15] and lesbians alike.[16]

Not only are some romantic relationships not exclusive, but exclusivity isn't always an expectation for marriage. In fact, many countries—primarily in Africa and southern Asia—allow the practice of **polygamy,** in which one person is married to two or more spouses at the same time. Some people in open or polygamous relationships report that they appreciate the closeness and intimacy they share with multiple partners. Others indicate that feelings of jealousy and resentment can lead to increased conflict in such relationships.[17]

ROMANTIC RELATIONSHIPS AND VOLUNTARINESS. Another common expectation for romantic relationships is that they are voluntary, meaning that people choose for themselves whether to become romantically involved—and if they decide to, they, and not others, select their romantic partner. That expectation presumes that a relationship is strong and satisfying only if both partners have freely chosen to participate in it. One indicator of that expectation in the United States is the abundance of online and in-person dating services, which allow customers to browse the profiles of prospective partners and choose those with whom they want to make contact. In fact, one such service—Match.com—claims more than 20 million registered clients.[18]

Even if people enter into romantic relationships voluntarily, they do not always stay in them voluntarily. Indeed, research shows that many people are unhappy in their relationships but stay in them anyway.[19] According to relationship scholars Denise Previti and Paul Amato, the most common reasons people stay in relationships involuntarily are

- They want to provide stability for their children.
- Their religious beliefs disallow separation or divorce.
- They are concerned about the financial implications of separating.
- They see no positive alternatives to their current relationship.[20]

In much of the world, however, it is common for other people—usually parents—to select a person's romantic partner. According to the practice of *arranged marriage* (which is most common in the Middle East and other parts of Asia and Africa), people are expected to marry the partner their parents select for them. Sometimes, children can reject their parents' selection of a spouse, in which case the parents look for someone else. In other cases, children may be pressured to marry the person their parents have chosen for them. In either situation, an arranged marriage is not entirely voluntary.

The fact that arranged marriages aren't voluntary doesn't necessarily mean that people whose marriages are arranged are dissatisfied with the relationship. Indeed, people who expect their marriages to be arranged might prefer this practice to the task of choosing a spouse on their own. For people who expect to choose their own romantic partner, however, the practice of arranged marriage would likely decrease their satisfaction with their relationships.

ROMANTIC RELATIONSHIPS AND LOVE. In much of the Western world, people think of marriage and other romantic relationships as being based on love. In individualist societies such as the United States and Canada, that is, people tend to believe not only that they should get to choose their romantic partner but that their choice should be based on love and attraction.[21] Indeed, the typical American wedding ceremony (whether religious or civil) emphasizes the importance of love in the marital relationship, whereas the lack of love is frequently cited as a reason why relationships fail.[22]

Whether or not they love each other, however, some people enter into romantic relationships for other reasons. Some form relationships for financial stability.[23] Others establish relationships to gain, consolidate, or protect power,[24] such as when members of royal or politically powerful families intermarry.

Would you marry someone you didn't love? Many people in collectivistic societies would say yes. In countries such as China and India, for instance, the choice of a spouse has more to do with the wishes and preferences of family and social groups than it does with love, even if the marriage isn't arranged. One study found that only half of the participants in India and Pakistan felt that love was necessary for marriage, whereas 96 percent of the U.S. American participants did.[25] Sociologist Frances Hsu explained that when considering marriage, "an American asks, 'How does my heart feel?' A Chinese [person] asks, 'What will other people say?'"[26]

someone on an airplane and strike up a conversation. "What's your name?" and "Where are you from?" are common questions people ask at this initial stage.

EXPERIMENTING.   When you meet someone in whom you're initially interested, you might move to the **experimenting stage,** during which you have conversations to learn more about that person. Individuals at the experimenting stage might ask questions such as "What movies do you like?" and "What do you do for fun?" to gain basic information about a potential partner. This stage helps individuals decide if they have enough in common to move the relationship forward.

INTENSIFYING.   During the **intensifying stage,** people move from being acquaintances to being close friends. They spend more time together and might begin to meet each other's friends. They start to share intimate information with each other, such as their fears, future goals, and secrets about the past. They also increase their commitment to the relationship and may express that commitment verbally through statements such as "You're really important to me."

INTEGRATING.   The **integrating stage** occurs when a deep commitment has formed, and the partners share a strong sense that the relationship has its own identity. At that stage, the partners' lives become integrated with each other, and they also begin to think of themselves as a pair—not just "you" and "I" but "we." Others start expecting to see the two individuals together and begin referring to the pair as a couple.

BONDING.   The final stage in Knapp's model of relationship development is the **bonding stage,** in which the partners make a public announcement of their commitment to each other. That might involve moving in together, getting engaged, or having a commitment ceremony. Beyond serving as a public expression of a couple's commitment, bonding also allows individuals to gain the support and approval of people in their social networks.

A brief summary of the five stages of relationship development appears in the "At a Glance" box.

INDIVIDUAL AND CULTURAL VARIATIONS IN RELATIONSHIP FORMATION.
Not every couple goes through the stages of relationship development in the same way. Some may stay at the experimenting stage for a long time before moving into the intensifying stage. Others may progress through the stages very quickly. Still others may go as far as the integrating stage but put off the bonding stage. Researchers have found that same-sex romantic relationships develop according to the same kinds of steps.[38]

experimenting stage The stage of relationship development when individuals have conversations to learn more about each other.

intensifying stage The stage of relationship development when individuals move from being acquaintances to being close friends.

integrating stage The stage of relationship development when a deep commitment has formed, and there is a strong sense that the relationship has its own identity.

bonding stage The stage of relationship development when the partners publicly announce their commitment.

AT A GLANCE

KNAPP'S STAGES OF RELATIONSHIP DEVELOPMENT

Initiating	Meeting and interacting with each other for the first time
Experimenting	Having conversations to learn more about each other
Intensifying	Moving from being acquaintances to being close friends
Integrating	Forming a deep commitment and developing a relationship with its own identity
Bonding	Making a public announcement of commitment to each other

Polygamy is common in many countries.

Relationship formation is not necessarily the same in all cultures. In countries that practice arranged marriage, for instance, the process of forming a marital relationship would look much different. It would include negotiation and decision making by the parents and less input (if any) from the children. In countries where polygamy is common, the integration and bonding stages would also look different, because one person may be joining multiple spouses at once. As noted earlier in the chapter, cultures vary in their expectations about romantic relationships—and as their expectations differ, so do their ways of forming relationships.

Differing Relational Types Among Romantic Couples

Even if people follow the same basic path toward developing their romantic relationships, they won't necessarily end up with the same type of relationship. Rather, research on marital relationships indicates that romantic couples embody distinct relational types. Communication researcher Mary Anne Fitzpatrick has spent many years studying patterns of marital communication. Her work suggests that people form and maintain marriages by relying on *marital schemata,* which represent their cognitive models for what marriage is and should be.[39] Fitzpatrick's research has found that three types of marriages are especially common: traditional, separate, and independent.[40]

- *Traditional couples* take a culturally conventional approach to marriage. They believe in gender-typical divisions of labor in which wives are in charge of housework and childrearing, and husbands are responsible for home repair and auto maintenance. When conflict arises, spouses in traditional couples engage in it rather than avoid it.

- *Separate couples* are similar to couples in traditional marriages except that the spouses are autonomous rather than interdependent. They often have their own interests and social networks, and they think of themselves as separate

- Families come in multiple forms, including natural families, blended families, single-parent families, and extended families.
- Family roles, rituals, stories, and secrets are important aspects of how families communicate.

4 Creating a Positive Communication Climate (p. 330)

- Sending confirming messages is an important way of emphasizing positivity.
- Several specific types of communication messages help a communicator to avoid generating defensiveness in other people.
- Whether it is evaluative or non-evaluative, feedback should always be constructive.

KEY TERMS

avoiding stage (p. 331)

bonding stage (p. 324)

circumscribing stage (p. 331)

commitment (p. 314)

communication climate (p. 338)

communication privacy management (CPM) theory (p. 328)

confirming messages (p. 338)

defensiveness (p. 340)

dialectical tensions (p. 317)

differentiating stage (p. 331)

disconfirming messages (p. 339)

divorce (p. 331)

evaluative feedback (p. 343)

experimenting stage (p. 324)

family of origin (p. 335)

family of procreation (p. 335)

infidelity (p. 320)

initiating stage (p. 323)

integrating stage (p. 324)

intensifying stage (p. 324)

interdependence (p. 315)

intimacy (p. 314)

investment (p. 315)

monogamy (p. 320)

non-evaluative feedback (p. 342)

polygamy (p. 320)

rituals (p. 336)

stagnating stage (p. 331)

supportiveness (p. 340)

terminating stage (p. 331)

DISCUSSION QUESTIONS

1. What are some of the ways you invest in your intimate relationships? In what ways do investments in romantic relationships differ from those in familial relationships?

2. When do you notice autonomy–connection, openness–closedness, and predictability–novelty tensions in your relationships? How do those tensions reveal themselves in your communication behaviors?

3. How do you differentiate people in your family from people who are not in your family? How important are genetic ties, legal bonds, and role behaviors?

4. Why do you think positivity is so important for stable, satisfying relationships?

PRACTICE QUIZ

MULTIPLE CHOICE

1. The idea that our actions influence other people's lives as much as they influence our own is known as
   a. independence
   b. dependence
   c. interdependence
   d. autonomy

2. Johann and his partner Cris go out to dinner and see a movie every Friday night. This routine is beginning to bore Johann but provides stability that Cris values. The dialectical tension Johann and Cris are experiencing is
   a. openness–closedness
   b. autonomy–connection
   c. presence–absence
   d. predictability–novelty

3. Questions such as "What movies do you like?" are common at this stage of Knapp's relational model
   a. initiating
   b. intensifying
   c. differentiating
   d. experimenting

4. **According to Fitzpatrick, the type of couple most likely to avoid conflict is**
   a. traditionals
   b. separates
   c. independents
   d. interdependents

5. **In Gottman's research, the type of couple characterized by engaging in frequent conflict episodes that include personal attacks and criticism is referred to as**
   a. validating
   b. volatile
   c. conflict-avoiding
   d. hostile

FILL IN THE BLANK

6. Repetitive behaviors that have special meaning for a family are known as _____ .

7. According to Gottman, couples who talk openly about disagreements and stay calm throughout conflict episodes are called _____ couples.

8. According to _____ theory, in a romantic relationship, partners jointly own information about their problems.

9. _____ is a feeling of excessive concern with guarding ourselves against the threat of criticism or attacks to our ego.

10. A romantic relationship is _____ when the partners are "going through the motions" of a relationship that is no longer satisfying.

ANSWERS

Multiple Choice: 1 (c); 2 (d); 3 (d); 4 (b); 5 (d); **Fill in the Blank:** 6 (rituals); 7 (validating); 8 (communication privacy management); 9 (defensiveness); 10 (stagnating)

RESEARCH LIBRARY

MOVIES

It's Complicated (comedy; 2009; R)
In this movie, Jane (played by Meryl Streep) and Jake (played by Alec Baldwin) are divorced spouses with three grown children. Jake is remarried to a much younger woman, while Jane is being courted by Adam (played by Steve Martin). During that time, Jake and Jane secretly begin seeing each other again. Their children are unhappy about their affair because they are still recovering from their divorce. Jane and Jake decide to end their affair. The movie portrays in a comedic way many of the tensions inherent in forming and ending romantic relationships.

Rachel Getting Married (drama; 2008; R)
This story focuses on Kym (played by Anne Hathaway), who is released from drug rehabilitation for a few days to attend the wedding of her sister Rachel. Kym's troubled past and present draw attention away from her sister's nuptials, prompting resentment from Rachel and conflict with her mother. The plot follows the family's attempts to manage their conflicts and reconcile their relationships.

BOOKS AND JOURNAL ARTICLES

Amato, P. R. (2000). The consequences of divorce for adults and children. *Journal of Marriage and the Family, 62,* 1269–1287.

Fitzpatrick, M. A. (1988). *Between husbands and wives: Communication in marriage.* Newbury Park, CA: Sage.

Floyd, K., & Morman, M. T. (Eds.). (2006). *Widening the family circle:* New research on family communication. Thousand Oaks, CA: Sage.

Vangelisti, A. L. (Ed.). (2003). *The handbook of family communication.* New York: Routledge.

WEBSITES

www.gottman.com
   This is the website of the Gottman Institute, where psychologist and marital therapist John Gottman uses his research to help romantic couples and families improve their communication.
www.families.com
   This site hosts blogs and forums on multiple issues related to families. It is not an academic site, but it provides one example of how people communicate about family issues and how they publicly portray their family relationships.

11 Interpersonal Conflict

MANAGING CONFLICT? THERE'S AN APP FOR THAT

People in romantic relationships routinely cite conflict as one of the biggest relational challenges they face. Although it is largely inevitable in close relationships, conflict can lead to hurt feelings, damaged trust, and even relational dissolution. In the digital age, however, help is never more than a few mouse clicks away. An iPod app called Marriage Advice gives users guidance for managing conflict in their romantic relationships. The app explains why conflict can become problematic for a relationship, how to find a conflict counselor, and when to consider leaving the relationship. Every relationship is different, of course, but an app like Marriage Advice aims to offer practical suggestions that most couples can follow to improve their communication.

Almost every relationship experiences conflict from time to time. Managing conflict can be productive, but it is also very challenging. As you'll see in this chapter, though, conflict management is a normal part of our interactions with others. You can learn to deal with conflict constructively if you have the appropriate skills. Several features of this chapter will help you develop those skills.

1 The Nature of Interpersonal Conflict

What exactly is conflict, and what is it like to experience conflict in relationships? In this section, we will define interpersonal conflict and identify the characteristics all conflicts have in common. Then we will take a look at some of the many ways people think about conflict in their relationships.

Defining Interpersonal Conflict

interpersonal conflict An expressed struggle between interdependent parties who perceive incompatible goals, scarce resources, and interference from one another.

You may recall from Chapter 10 that communication scholars William Wilmot and Joyce Hocker define **interpersonal conflict** as "an expressed struggle between at least two interdependent parties who perceive incompatible goals, scarce resources, and interference from the other party in achieving their goals."[1] According to Wilmot and Hocker, an interaction must have all those elements to qualify as interpersonal conflict. Let's focus in on the key elements in their definition.

CONFLICT IS AN EXPRESSED STRUGGLE. Having a conflict means more than just disagreeing. You may disagree with President Obama's foreign policies or your children's taste in music, but you don't really have a conflict until you've made the

Conflict is often communicated verbally, but it can also be conveyed with nonverbal behaviors that express anger, concern, or disappointment.

other person aware of your feelings. Conflict, therefore, is a *behavior*. Sometimes we express our disagreements verbally, but we can also express them through a nonverbal behavior such as a mean look or a harsh tone of voice.

CONFLICT OCCURS BETWEEN INTERDEPENDENT PARTIES. Although all conflicts involve disagreements, a disagreement becomes a conflict only if the parties depend on each other in some way—that is, if the actions of each party affect the well-being of the other. You may have noticed that conflict is particularly common in relationships with high degrees of interdependence, such as those you have with your parents, children, instructors, bosses, and close friends. If two parties are completely independent of each other, then even though they may disagree, their disagreement isn't considered to be an interpersonal conflict.

It's possible to have conflicts within yourself as well. For example, you might occasionally feel conflicted about how you spend your time. Perhaps part of you thinks you should spend more time with your friends and family, but another part of you thinks you should devote more time to your schoolwork. This is conflict, but it isn't *interpersonal* conflict. Rather, it's *intrapersonal*, because it is occurring within yourself. Therefore, it operates outside the realm of interpersonal conflict.

CONFLICT IS ABOUT GOALS THE PARTIES SEE AS INCOMPATIBLE. Conflict stems from perceiving that our goals are incompatible with another person's goals. Labeling goals as "incompatible" doesn't simply mean that they are different. Rather, two goals are incompatible when it's impossible to satisfy both of them. You want to change lanes on the freeway, but the driver next to you won't let you in. You want to spend your tax refund on a new flat-screen television, but your spouse wants to spend it on a family vacation.

Note that the first sentence in the previous paragraph explicitly refers to our *perceptions* that our goals are incompatible. In reality, it may be possible to resolve the conflict in a manner that allows both parties to achieve their goals. (See the discussion of conflict strategies later in the chapter.) The point here is that parties in a conflict perceive that their goals are mutually exclusive, even if that perception is not objectively true.

CONFLICT ARISES OVER PERCEIVED SCARCE RESOURCES. There's little sense in fighting over something one has in abundance. Rather, people tend to have conflict over resources they perceive to be limited. Many relational partners have conflict over money, for instance. When individuals feel they don't have enough money for everything they need and want, they can easily have conflict over how to spend the money they do have.

Time is another resource that people often perceive to be scarce. Therefore, people frequently engage in conflicts over how they should spend their time. Perhaps your romantic partner wants you to split your vacation time between hiking and being with his or her family. If you perceive that you don't have adequate time for both activities, then you can experience conflict over how you will spend your time.

CONFLICT INCLUDES INTERFERENCE. Two parties might have opposing goals with respect to some issue, but they won't have genuine conflict until they act in ways that prevent each other from achieving their goals. You might disapprove of your roommate's smoking habit, for instance, but you won't have true conflict until you behave in ways that interfere with his habit. Complaining about his smoking, for instance, might diminish the enjoyment he derives from it. Hiding his cigarettes or throwing them out would make it more difficult for him to smoke. In either case, you are interfering with your roommate's ability to achieve his goal.

Thinking About Interpersonal Conflict

When you think about your own experiences with interpersonal conflict, what words or images come to mind? It turns out that people often think about conflict using figurative language, such as metaphors.[2] Researchers have identified a number of metaphors people use to describe conflict. Reflect on how well each of the following common metaphors about conflict reflects the way you view your own conflict experiences:

- *Conflict is a war.* Conflict is a series of battles, with winners and losers.
- *Conflict is an explosion.* Conflict is like hearing a time bomb ticking and then watching something blow up.
- *Conflict is a trial.* Each side presents its arguments and evidence, and whoever argues best wins the conflict.
- *Conflict is a struggle.* Conflict is a difficult and ongoing part of life.
- *Conflict is an act of nature.* Conflict simply happens to people; it cannot be prevented or controlled.
- *Conflict is an animal behavior.* Only the strong survive; conflict is a natural part of all creatures' lives.
- *Conflict is a mess.* Conflict is messy, and it contaminates other aspects of life.
- *Conflict is miscommunication.* Conflict stems from misunderstandings and breakdowns in communication.
- *Conflict is a game.* Conflict is a fun competition in which participants test their skills against each other.
- *Conflict is a heroic adventure.* Conflict is about taking risks and conquering new territory.
- *Conflict is a balancing act.* Engaging in conflict is like juggling or walking a tightrope; one wrong move can spell disaster.
- *Conflict is a bargaining table.* Conflict brings people together for a collective purpose.
- *Conflict is a tide.* Conflict ebbs and flows; on the basis of experience, we can predict when it is likely to occur.
- *Conflict is a dance.* Partners learn how to "move" with each other through their conflict episodes.
- *Conflict is a garden.* Experiences of conflict represent seeds for the future; if cared for, they will result in a worthwhile harvest.

Two parties can be engaged in the same conflict but might frame the conflict quite differently. Do you think of conflict as a trial? As an animal behavior? As a dance? As a balancing act? As a war? As a game?

As you can see, those metaphors represent a wide variety of ideas. Some images are inherently negative, but others could be considered neutral or even positive. Can you imagine how the way you think about conflict might affect your experience of it? For instance, if you think of conflict as a game, a dance, or a garden, might you experience it differently than if you think of it as a war, a struggle, or a mess?

Researchers have found that the way we interpret or "frame" a conflict can greatly affect the way we experience it and the communication choices we make to manage it.[3] While arguing with his co-worker Madison over use of the company car, for instance, Russell suddenly realized that Madison was smiling in the midst of their heated discussion. Her smiling made him even angrier, because he felt she wasn't taking him seriously. The angrier he got, however, the more she smiled. Only during a conversation weeks later did they learn that they frame conflict quite differently: Russell frames conflict as a war, but Madison frames it as a game.

One result of that difference is that Madison probably experienced less stress over the conflict than Russell did. Because Madison sees conflict as a fun competition rather than as a battle between winners and losers, she didn't necessarily feel threatened or distressed by what Russell said. Instead, she interpreted his comments as challenges that tested her interpersonal skills. In contrast, because Russell frames conflict as a war, he interpreted every statement from Madison as an attempt to defeat him. As a result, he finds interpersonal conflict to be stressful and threatening in a way that Madison does not.

Because the way we frame a conflict can influence our experience of it, many therapists encourage people to reframe their conflicts. *Reframing* means changing the way you think about an interpersonal situation so that you adopt a more useful frame.[4] For instance, a therapist or a counselor could help Russell reframe his conflicts with his co-workers so that he sees them as an adventure, a balancing act, or a dance instead of as a war.

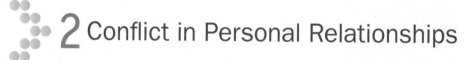

LEARN IT What are the essential elements of interpersonal conflict? What does it mean to reframe a conflict?

APPLY IT For a period of time (say, three to five days), make note of every conflict you observe, whether it includes you or not. Note what each conflict was about, who was involved in it, and how (if at all) it was resolved. For each conflict, identify the expressed struggle, the interdependent parties, the incompatible goals, the scarce resources, and the interference that made it an interpersonal conflict.

REFLECT ON IT With whom do you have conflict most frequently? Which metaphors for conflict seem the most accurate to you?

2 Conflict in Personal Relationships

Conflict occurs at many social levels. Communities, organizations, and certainly nations have conflict with one another. Interpersonal conflict, however, often affects our lives more directly and more intimately than conflicts at those broader levels. In this section, we will examine several characteristics of interpersonal conflict and identify topics most likely to spur conflict in our personal relationships. Next, we will survey the ways that gender and culture influence conflict. We will conclude by considering why conflict seems to be especially common when we're communicating online.

Characteristics of Interpersonal Conflict

Although we have conflicts over different issues with different people, we can make some general observations that apply to all interpersonal conflict. In this section, we'll look at five basic characteristics of conflict in personal relationships.

CONFLICT IS NATURAL. Most of us would be hard-pressed to think of a single important relationship in which we don't have conflict from time to time. Conflict is a normal, natural part of relating to others. Maybe you enjoy listening to music at night, whereas your housemates prefer quiet. Perhaps you feel you've earned a raise at work, but your boss disagrees. Almost every significant relationship—especially those with close friends, relatives, and romantic partners—is bound to experience conflict once in a while.

Having conflict with someone doesn't necessarily mean your relationship is unhealthy or distressed. Indeed, the presence of conflict indicates you have an interdependent relationship. It means you affect each other; if you didn't, you'd have no need for conflict in the first place. So, conflict itself isn't a bad thing. In fact, as we'll see later in this chapter, if we handle conflict productively, it can produce positive outcomes. What matters is how people handle their conflicts. Later in this chapter, we'll explore useful strategies for managing conflict.

CONFLICT HAS CONTENT, RELATIONAL, AND PROCEDURAL DIMENSIONS.
In personal relationships, conflicts often focus on a specific point of contention, but on a deeper level they also have broader implications for the relationship itself. To illustrate that point, let's suppose Marc finds out Amber, his teenage daughter, has been stealing his credit card out of his wallet to participate in online gambling. When Marc confronts Amber about the situation, they argue about the dishonesty of stealing and the risks of gambling. Those are the *content dimensions* of the conflict, the specific topics from which the conflict arose.

Even when Amber promises to change her behaviors, however, Marc doesn't feel completely satisfied with the outcome of their argument. The reason is that there are

also *relational dimensions* to the conflict, which are the implications the conflict has for the relationship. Marc feels that Amber has shown disrespect by stealing from him and that he can no longer trust her. That dimension of the conflict is not so much about the content of their argument (Amber shouldn't steal or gamble) as it is about the nature of their relationship. Although Marc may be successful in changing Amber's behavior, repairing the damage to their mutual respect and trust may require much more time and a much greater effort.

Conflict also has *procedural dimensions,* which are the rules or expectations individuals follow for how to engage in conflict. Suppose Marc believes conflict should be dealt with straightforwardly through open and honest discussion, whereas Amber prefers to avoid conflict, hoping that disagreements will resolve themselves. Marc and Amber may have a difficult time managing their conflict if they adopt such contrasting procedures. In essence, they are attempting to play the same game by completely different rules.

metaconflict Conflict about conflict.

When people adopt dramatically different procedures for managing conflict, they often wind up engaging in **metaconflict,** which is conflict about conflict itself. "You always run away from disagreements," Marc might say to Amber. She might respond, "Well, you want to have a fight about every little issue—sometimes you just have to let things go!" Notice here that Marc and Amber are no longer arguing about Amber's stealing and gambling but about *how they engage in conflict* in the first place. Their metaconflict is the result of approaching conflict with dramatically different expectations or rules. An illustration of the content, relational, and procedural dimensions of conflict appears in Figure 11.1.

CONFLICT CAN BE DIRECT OR INDIRECT. In many instances, people deal with their conflicts directly and openly. When Maria and Sofie disagree on where to spend the holidays, for example, they have a series of arguments in which each one tries to persuade the other to adopt her point of view. When Rosemary grounds her son for using drugs, they argue openly about the seriousness of his behavior and the severity of his punishment.

FIGURE 11.1 The Three Distinct Dimensions of Interpersonal Conflict

People can also express conflict indirectly. Instead of dealing with their conflicts openly, for instance, individuals may behave in ways that are hurtful or vengeful toward others. Jade is upset with her boyfriend, so she deliberately flirts with other men in front of him. Tamir is angry at his wife for inviting her parents to dinner, so he spends the whole evening playing solitaire on his computer. Those behaviors express conflict, but in an indirect way that prevents the conflict from being resolved.

When you are experiencing conflict with another person, which is better: to deal with the conflict openly and directly, or to deal with it indirectly? That's a complex question, and the answer is that neither approach is better in every situation. Handling conflict directly can lead to quicker resolution, but it may also cause the conflict to escalate and become even more serious. Conversely, dealing with conflict indirectly may be easier and more comfortable, but it can also leave the conflict unresolved for a longer period of time. Which approach is better depends on the situation, what your goals are, with whom you're having the conflict, and how important the outcome of the conflict is to you. Later in this chapter, we'll discuss several strategies for engaging in conflict when you experience it.

CONFLICT CAN BE HARMFUL. Experiencing conflict doesn't usually feel good, so it may not surprise you to learn that conflict can be harmful to your well-being when you don't manage it properly. In one study, for instance, psychologists videotaped 150 healthy married couples discussing a contentious topic for six minutes. Two days later, they took a CT scan of each spouse's chest. They found that husbands who had been overly controlling and wives who had been overly hostile during the conflict episode exhibited a greater degree of hardening of the arteries than husbands and wives who didn't display those behaviors.[5]

Other studies have demonstrated that engaging in conflict often causes the body to produce a stress response by increasing the level of stress hormones[6] and natural killer cells[7] in the bloodstream. As one experiment illustrated, the stress created by conflict can even cause wounds to heal more slowly than they otherwise would, especially if the people in conflict behave in a negative, hostile way toward each other.[8] As these and other investigations show, the ways that people handle conflicts, particularly in their romantic relationships, have far-reaching implications for their health.[9]

Conflict is particularly harmful to personal well-being when it escalates into aggression and violence.[10] Researchers estimate that over the past two decades, as many as half of all marital, cohabiting, and dating relationships have involved some combination of verbal, physical, and/or sexual aggression.[11] One study found that 12 percent of women and 11 percent of men had committed at least one violent act—such as slapping, kicking, or punching—against their romantic partner during a conflict episode within the previous year.[12]

communication dark side

THE ROLE OF ALCOHOL USE IN RELATIONSHIP CONFLICT

Managing conflict can be challenging under the best of circumstances, but it appears to be even more problematic when one partner is under the influence of alcohol. Research has shown that excessive alcohol use leads to more aggressive behaviors and elevates the chances of violence within close relationships. It is also a major public health risk. In fact, excessive use of alcohol is the third-leading preventable cause of death in the United States, after tobacco use and malnutrition. Alcohol consumption, then, not only can make conflict more likely but also can intensify existing conflicts. Can it also affect how people respond to conflict?

To answer that question, researchers in one study had participants recall a recent conflict from one of their personal relationships. They then served alcohol to half of the participants until they reached a point of legal intoxication. Finally, they asked all the participants to reflect on the conflict they had described and to indicate the following: (1) how negative their own feelings were, (2) how negative they thought their partners' feelings were, and (3) how much they blamed their partners for the conflict. Compared with their sober counterparts, the intoxicated participants rated their feelings and their perceptions of their partners' feelings as more negative. In addition, intoxicated participants who had low self-esteem were more likely than others to blame their partners for the conflict.

Those findings don't imply that drinking *causes* conflict. They do, however, suggest that alcohol use makes existing conflicts more negative and perhaps more difficult to handle.

ASK YOURSELF

■ Why do you think alcohol affects people's experiences with conflict?

■ If you've ever been engaged in a conflict with an intoxicated person, how did you handle it? Which strategies for handling the conflict were more successful or less successful?

In Crazy Heart *(2009), Jeff Bridges plays country superstar Bad Blake (right), an alcoholic whose relationships are ravaged by conflict.*

Sources: MacDonald, G., Zanna, M. P., & Holmes, J. G. (2000). An experimental test of the role of alcohol in relationship conflict. *Journal of Experimental Social Psychology, 36,* 182–193; Mokdad, A. H., Marks, J. S., Stroup, D. F., & Gerberding, J. L. (2004). Actual causes of death in the United States, 2000. *Journal of the American Medical Association, 291,* 1238–1245.

In such relationships, aggression is often the result of one person's attempts to dominate an argument—and, by extension, to dominate the partner.[13] Although the victims of relational aggression are most likely to be women, men are also victimized, by both male and female romantic partners.[14] Research shows that violence during conflict is approximately as common in gay and lesbian relationships as in heterosexual ones.[15] Certain situations appear to give rise to aggression more often than others, such as when one partner is intoxicated; see the "Communication: Dark Side" box.

One of the most surprising findings concerning aggression is that it doesn't always lead to dissatisfaction in relationships.[16] In fact, people in abusive relationships often see their partners' physical aggression as a sign of love, and they are frequently quick to forgive their partners' aggressive behaviors or even to blame themselves.[17] That statement isn't suggesting that aggression is good for relationships. On the contrary, over time aggression frequently leads to an erosion of trust, happiness, and self-esteem among its victims.[18] Recipients of aggression, however, aren't always quick to end their relationships with the aggressors. Rather, they sometimes report relational satisfaction despite the aggression.[19]

CONFLICT CAN BE BENEFICIAL. It's relatively easy to identify the negative features of conflict: It's stressful, it can damage health, and it can lead to aggression and violence. When conflict is managed well, however, it can have certain benefits. Working through a conflict in a positive, constructive manner can help two people learn more about each other and their relationship.[20] It may also lead them to a more satisfactory solution to the problem than either could have come up with alone. Those benefits may depend on whether only one party in an interpersonal conflict—or both parties—has the skills to manage it well.

Managing conflict constructively can also help to prevent small problems from escalating into larger ones. Let's say your co-worker complains to you constantly about his girlfriend while you're trying to get your work done. Instead of addressing the problem, however, you just let it annoy you day after day until you finally explode at him, yelling, causing a scene, and eventually being reprimanded by your boss. Simply addressing the situation when it first arose would likely have alleviated much of your frustration and prevented that small annoyance from turning into a conflict with your co-worker.

Over time, the ability to handle conflicts positively may give people more confidence in their communication skills and in the strength of their interpersonal relationships. Research on married couples has shown that spouses who engage in constructive conflict behaviors—such as avoiding criticizing their spouses and being responsive to each other's concerns—are happier with their relationships[21] and more satisfied with the outcomes of their conflicts than spouses who don't.[22] It may be that handling conflict constructively makes couples satisfied, or that satisfied couples handle conflict in a constructive manner. In either case, relationship satisfaction and constructive conflict management are strongly connected.

Successful resolution of conflicts can be very beneficial, but can every conflict be resolved? Take a look at the "Fact or Fiction?" box to find out.

The Most Common Sources of Conflict

Like relationships themselves, conflicts come in all shapes and sizes. What are some of the most typical issues people fight about? In one study, communication scholar Larry Erbert asked spouses to report the most common sources of conflict in their marriage.[23] You might be surprised to learn that men and women identified the same three leading sources of conflict. The most common was *personal criticisms,* or spouses' complaints or criticisms of each other's undesirable behaviors or bad habits (such as smoking or excessive drinking). Almost 20 percent of the couples Erbert interviewed mentioned personal criticisms as a common source of conflict.

The second-most-frequent answer, at 13 percent, was *finances,* or conflicts about money. It's not uncommon for spouses to disagree about how their money should be spent, saved, or invested. Further, because money is a scarce resource for many people, conflicts over finances can be particularly difficult.

Although victims of relational violence are most likely to be women, men are also victimized, by both male and female romantic partners.

IF YOU TRY HARD ENOUGH, YOU CAN RESOLVE ANY CONFLICT

Conflict is a natural part of relationships, and there are multiple ways to manage it. The latter observation might lead you to believe that if you have the right skills and try hard enough, you can eventually resolve any conflict you encounter. It would be great if that were true, but it isn't.

The truth is that some conflicts are simply unsolvable. Let's say, for instance, that Juna and her brother Tom are arguing about abortion. As a conservative with strong religious beliefs, Juna cannot support a woman's right to choose abortion under any circumstances. Tom, whose political orientation is more liberal, feels that every woman has the right to choose whether to have a child or to terminate the pregnancy. In other words, Juna's and Tom's positions are diametrically opposed, meaning they share no common ground. As long as they hold those positions, Juna and Tom can argue forever, but they will never resolve their conflict.

When two positions are diametrically opposed, and when the people or groups holding those positions are unwilling or unable to change their positions in any way, the only real options are to avoid the conflict, to agree to disagree, and to try to minimize the effects of the conflict on other aspects of the relationship.

Third on the list was *household chores,* or conflicts over the division of labor. Spouses have to negotiate how to divide up tasks such as cleaning, cooking, gardening, and car maintenance, and many couples find it easy to disagree about who should take on which responsibilities. Conflict can also emerge when spouses fail to meet their responsibilities, because both spouses suffer when the laundry doesn't get washed or the lawn doesn't get mowed.

In his study, Erbert found that personal criticisms, finances, and household chores together accounted for approximately 42 percent of all the conflict topics mentioned. Other common sources of conflict for married couples were their children, employment, in-laws, sex, how they should spend holidays and vacations, how they should spend their time in general, and how they communicate with each other.[24] Studies have also shown that the major topics of conflict are nearly identical for gay, lesbian, and heterosexual couples.[25]

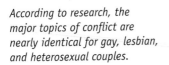

According to research, the major topics of conflict are nearly identical for gay, lesbian, and heterosexual couples.

Many studies have focused on conflict in romantic relationships because of the high degree of interdependence that characterizes those relationships. We experience conflict in a host of relationships, however. Many of us routinely have conflict with superiors or subordinates, neighbors, parents or children, co-workers, instructors, and other people with whom we are interdependent. Like conflicts with romantic partners, many of those conflicts center on issues of power, respect, and the distribution of resources such as money and time.[26] We will look specifically at the central role of power in the next section.

How Sex and Gender Affect Conflict

It's almost cliché to say that sex and gender play an important role in conflict. Indeed, television shows such as *Modern Family* and *How I Met Your Mother* and movies such as *Life as We Know It* and *Scott Pilgrim vs. the World* base their humor on the idea that women and men have difficulty understanding each other—a problem that creates situation after situation that is ripe for conflict. Although differences in their behaviors and ways of thinking can certainly be sources of conflict, women and men often have the added challenge of dealing with conflict in systematically different ways.

Sitcoms such as How I Met Your Mother *base much of their humor on the idea that men and women have trouble understanding each other.*

As we saw in Chapter 2, traditional gender socialization conflates sex and gender by teaching men to adopt masculine traits and behaviors and women to adopt feminine traits and behaviors. At least in North American societies, traditional gender socialization has encouraged women to "play nice" by avoiding conflict and sacrificing their own goals in order to accommodate the goals of others. Conversely, men are often encouraged to engage in conflict directly, using competitive or even aggressive behaviors to achieve victory. At the same time, however, men are often taught not to hurt women.[27]

Those messages about gender can create challenges for both women and men when it comes to managing conflict. Some women may feel that engaging in conflict overtly is contrary to the feminine gender role, so they adopt less direct tactics to achieve their goals. One such tactic is **passive aggression,** in which individuals hide their aggression in seemingly innocent behaviors.

passive aggression A pattern of behaving vengefully while denying that one has aggressive feelings.

Consider the case of Chelsea, who becomes irritated when her boyfriend answers his cell phone whenever it rings, even while they're out to dinner. Instead of telling him how she feels, Chelsea expresses her irritation passively by sometimes failing to answer the phone when he calls. She then calls him back later and claims she hadn't heard the phone ring. In this way, Chelsea avoids overt conflict by behaving aggressively (ignoring her boyfriend's calls) but in a seemingly innocent manner (claiming she didn't hear the phone). As we'll see later in the chapter, however, women may also believe that they must fight for whatever resources are available to them, particularly when they feel they are in a less-powerful position than men.

Society's messages to men about conflict may encourage them to engage in conflict overtly—possibly aggressively—even in situations when a subtler, less direct approach could be just as effective. Because men are taught to engage in conflict directly but also not to hurt women, they may feel particularly conflicted about how to act during conflict episodes with women. Men often resolve that quandary by disengaging, thereby leaving the conflict unresolved. Psychologist John Gottman uses the term *stonewalling* to describe that pattern of withdrawal. As we'll consider later in this chapter, stonewalling can be a particularly problematic behavior for couples.

In opposite-sex romantic relationships, traditional gender messages often encourage partners to adopt a **demand–withdraw pattern,** in which one partner (typically the woman) makes demands ("We need to talk about the problems in our relationship"), and the other partner (usually the man) responds by withdrawing ("I don't want to talk about it").[28] Even though this pattern of behavior largely conforms to typical North American gender roles, research indicates that those gender-related behavior differences are especially common in dissatisfied, distressed relationships.[29] One possible reason that demand–withdrawal is particularly common in distressed relationships is that if one partner usually withdraws from the conversation, then the conflict is unlikely to be resolved. Over time unresolved conflict can lead to dissatisfaction.

demand–withdraw pattern A pattern of behavior in which one party makes demands and the other party withdraws from the conversation.

How you handle conflict may depend partly on your sex. Research shows that men are more likely than women to engage in direct conflict behaviors, which sometimes include being physically aggressive. Women are more likely than men to engage in passive-aggressive behaviors, such as running up the balance on a family member's credit card.

Women and men appear to deal with conflict in much the same ways, whether they are heterosexual or homosexual. Research has found that lesbian and gay couples use strategies similar to those used by heterosexuals to deal with conflict.[30] As family communication researchers John Caughlin and Anita Vangelisti have suggested, however, gay and lesbian couples are also likely to experience potential sources of conflict that seldom afflict straight couples.[31] For one, lesbian and gay partners may have conflict over whom to tell, and how much to tell, about their sexual orientation.[32] If one partner is "out" to family and friends while the other partner conceals his or her sexual orientation, that discrepancy can lead to conflicts related to a couple's social relationships and their long-term plans. Gay and lesbian adults may also encounter discrimination and prejudice from their families, co-workers, or neighbors, which can cause considerable distress and make routine conflicts about other matters seem more substantial than they are.[33]

How Culture Affects Conflict

Just as gender messages encourage people to handle conflicts in particular ways, so do cultural messages. That is, the values and norms individuals learn from their culture can shape the way they respond to conflict with members of their own culture.

Some scholars believe the most important cultural factor is whether one's culture is individualistic or collectivistic.[34] As you'll recall from Chapter 2, people raised in individualistic cultures are taught to value the rights, needs, and goals of the individual. They learn that it is acceptable to disagree with others, and they are encouraged to stand up for themselves in the face of conflict.[35] In contrast, people raised in collectivistic cultures are taught that the group's priorities take precedence over the individual's and that maintaining group harmony takes precedence over pursuing individual success. Thus, they are more likely to manage conflict through avoiding the disagreement, yielding to the other person's wishes, or asking a neutral party to mediate the conflict, because those strategies can help preserve harmony.[36] They would

Individualistic cultures teach people to stand up for themselves in the face of conflict. In contrast, collectivistic cultures teach people to maintain harmony by avoiding conflict.

probably consider the direct, overt behaviors that people in individualistic cultures often use to manage conflict to be insensitive or rude.

A second cultural dimension that influences how people manage conflict is whether the culture is low context or high context.[37] People in low-context cultures (such as the United States) value communication that is explicit, direct, and literal. When they engage in conflict with one another, they therefore expect all parties to be clear about the source of the disagreement and up front about their suggestions for resolution. In comparison, people in high-context cultures (such as Japan) value subtlety, deriving much of the meaning in their conversations from social conventions and nonverbal expressions. When they experience conflict with one another, they place a premium on saving face and not embarrassing the other party. As a result, they tend to discuss disagreements indirectly, without direct accusations or direct requests for action.[38]

Clearly, then, those cultural dimensions—individualism versus collectivism and high context versus low context—lead people to resolve conflicts in different ways. Those differences are often magnified when conflicts arise between people from different cultures. Suppose that Gerry, who was raised in an individualistic culture, is having conflict with Kenan, who was raised in a collectivistic culture. Kenan will likely try to manage the conflict in a way that preserves harmony in the relationships and avoids offending or embarrassing Gerry. He may therefore be distraught if Gerry approaches the conflict in the direct, adversarial way that is common in his culture. Conversely, Gerry may feel that Kenan's more indirect way of engaging in conflict implies that Kenan doesn't care about the conflict or its outcome.

When two people approach a conflict with dramatically different values and norms, they are likely to misunderstand each other's behaviors, and that misunderstanding can exacerbate the conflict.[39] By learning about the norms and behaviors of other cultures and interacting with people from different cultural backgrounds, however, individuals can improve their ability to handle intercultural conflict in constructive ways.

Conflict Online

Conflict is common in face-to-face settings, but it can seem especially frequent when people communicate online. One reason is that computer-mediated communication has a **disinhibition effect,** meaning that it removes constraints and thus invites people to say or do things that they wouldn't in person.[40] Let's suppose Saika gets an e-mail from her supervisor saying that he is rejecting her vacation request for next month. Saika feels angry, particularly because she worked overtime last month while her supervisor was on vacation. Because Saika reads her supervisor's words online

disinhibition effect The tendency to say or do things in one environment (such as online) that one would not say or do in most other environments.

assess your SKILLS

AVOID ONLINE DISINHIBITION

Computer-mediated communication can contribute to conflict because of disinhibition. When you receive an e-mail message, a text message, a Facebook post, or a tweet that makes you angry, consult this checklist before you write back to the person.

I . . .   ✓

. . . realize that I may be misinterpreting the person's words.   _____

. . . bear in mind that I cannot see the person's facial expressions or hear the person's
    tone of voice.   _____

. . . will wait for at least an hour before writing a response.   _____

. . . will read the person's message again before writing a response, and consider whether
    I am misinterpreting it.   _____

. . . will write a response but not send or post it right away.   _____

. . . will wait for at least a few more hours—if not a day or two—before sending or posting
    my response.   _____

. . . will reread my response before sending or posting it, and consider revising it.   _____

. . . realize that the other person may misinterpret my words as well.   _____

FROM ME TO YOU

It takes a great deal of patience not to respond immediately to a message that angers you. Your instinct may be to strike back by making statements in the heat of the moment that you will later regret. Although doing so may feel satisfying in the short term, it often makes a bad situation even worse. A better approach is to gain control over the situation by following the checklist provided here.

Online conflict frequently leads to flaming, which is the exchange of hostile and insulting messages.

instead of hearing them in person, she feels less inhibited about expressing her anger. As a result of her disinhibition, she sends her supervisor an e-mail reply filled with angry, inflammatory statements that she would never make to him in person. Saika's behavior causes her supervisor great distress—and thus intensifies their conflict.

Researchers suggest several strategies for handling potential conflicts in online contexts. First, *don't respond right away.* Instead, give yourself several hours to calm down and collect your thoughts. (Of course, that advice often applies to conflicts that occur in person as well.) Because e-mail puts your words in print right in front of another person, however, you may feel compelled to reply immediately, when instead you should take time to cool down first.

Second, *clarify anything that might be misunderstood* instead of assuming that you know what the other person meant by his or her statements. Third, *put yourself in the other person's shoes,* and think about how he or she would react to your response. Finally, *use emoticons to express your tone,* if it's appropriate, so that your reader knows when you're upset, when you're surprised, and when you're kidding.[41]

Check out "Assess Your Skills" on the preceding page for additional recommendations on avoiding the pitfalls of disinhibition.

LEARN IT In what ways can conflict be harmful? In what ways can it be beneficial? What are the most common topics of conflict in marital relationships? How do messages about gender affect us when we engage in conflict? Which cultural dimensions influence conflict behavior? What is the disinhibition effect?

APPLY IT The next time you receive an e-mail that's negative or aggressive, write a response right away, but then save it instead of sending it. Write a second response 24 hours later, and then compare it with the first response. Do you notice differences in your tone? Is your second response less aggressive and inflammatory? Which response would you choose to send? If it's the second one, then remember this lesson when you receive similar e-mails in the future.

REFLECT ON IT Why might you choose to engage in conflict indirectly rather than directly? When are you most likely to have conflict online?

3 Power and Conflict

We have defined conflict as an expressed struggle between interdependent parties who perceive their goals as incompatible. Just because two parties are interdependent, however, doesn't mean that they are equally powerful. Indeed, conflict often occurs in relationships in which one person—say, a parent or a supervisor—has more power than the other—say, a child or an employee. Conflict often involves a struggle for power between two parties, with each party trying to exercise as much influence or control over the situation as possible. Power and conflict are thus inextricably linked.

In this section, we will define power and examine some of its characteristics, particularly as they relate to the experience of conflict. We will also consider various forms of power and probe how gender and culture influence the expression of power in personal relationships.

Characteristics of Power

Power is the ability to manipulate, influence, or control other people or events.[42] Certain people have more power than others. Nevertheless, we all possess some power, and we exercise it whenever we find ourselves in conflict with others. Let's look at five characteristics of power that will help us understand its relationship to conflict.

power The ability to manipulate, influence, or control other people or events.

POWER IS CONTEXT-SPECIFIC. Most forms of power are relevant only in specific situations. Your boss has power over you at work, for instance, but he doesn't have the right to tell you what to do when you're at home. His influence over you is confined to the work environment. Similarly, your doctor has the power to give you medical advice and prescribe medical treatments, but she doesn't have the right to advise you on your finances, education, or religious beliefs, because those areas are outside her sphere of influence. As such examples illustrate, power is almost always confined to certain realms or contexts.

POWER IS ALWAYS PRESENT.   Even though power is context-specific, some form of power is relevant to every interpersonal interaction. When two people have roughly equal power in their relationship, such as friends, they have a **symmetrical relationship.** Conversely, when one person has more power than the other, such as a teacher and a student, the parties have a **complementary relationship.** The way two people interact with each other depends, in part, on whether their relationship is symmetrical or complementary. For instance, you might say or do things with a friend that you wouldn't say or do with a teacher. Keep in mind, though, that the power balance of a relationship can change over time. Parents and children usually have complementary relationships when the children are young, for example, but as the children become adults, their relationships often become more symmetrical.

POWER INFLUENCES COMMUNICATION.   The symmetrical or complementary nature of relationships often influences the way people communicate. Many years ago, communication researchers Philip Ericson and L. Edna Rogers proposed that relational power is reflected in three specific types of verbal messages people use (Figure 11.2).[43] A **one-up message** expresses dominance and an attempt to control the relationship. One-up messages often take the form of commands, such as "Do the dishes," "E-mail me your report," or "Stop making so much noise." A **one-down message** communicates submission to or acceptance of another person's decision-making ability. Examples include questions such as "Where would you like to go for dinner?" and statements of assent such as "Whatever you'd like is fine with me."

symmetrical relationship
A relationship between parties of equal power.

complementary relationship A relationship between parties of unequal power.

one-up message A verbal message through which the speaker attempts to exert dominance or gain control over the listener.

one-down message
A verbal message that reflects acceptance of, or submission to, another person's power.

One-up message

Stop making so much noise!

One-down message

Do you have any suggestions for what I should wear tonight?

One-across message

Dad needs a new lawn mower.

FIGURE 11.2 Relational Power and Verbal Messages One-up messages convey dominance and control. One-down messages express submission or resignation. One-across messages communicate a desire to neutralize relational power.

[ONE-ACROSS MESSAGES]

Maintain balanced power relations with one-across messages.

WHAT?

Learn to use one-across messages.

WHY?

To help neutralize relational power and control.

HOW?

1. Avoid statements that assert control over a situation, such as "I think we should see a movie tonight."

2. Similarly, avoid statements that concede control over a situation to another person, such as "I'm open to whatever you want to do."

3. Use statements that recognize facts affecting you both, such as "We have several options for something to do tonight."

TRY!

1. Role-play a conversation with a sibling or friend in which you discuss what gift to buy for your father's retirement. Let the other person begin the conversation.

2. Respond with a one-across message to as many of your partner's statements as you can, regardless of their form. Try to come to agreement on a gift selection. Afterward, switch roles and repeat the conversation.

CONSIDER: *How did using one-across messages neutralize power in your conversations?*

Finally, a **one-across message** is neither dominant nor submissive and conveys a desire to neutralize relational control. One-across messages often take the form of statements of fact, such as "Dad needs a new lawn mower" and "There are many brands to choose from."

People in symmetrical relationships often communicate using the same types of messages.[44] They might both use one-up messages ("Put away the groceries." "I'll put them away when I feel like it"). They might both use one-down messages ("Do you have any suggestions for what to wear tonight?" "I'm sure whatever you choose will look great"). Finally, they might both use one-across messages ("There are so many good movies showing in town right now." "And several good plays as well"). In each case, their communication reflects the fact that neither party exercises power over the other. Check out "Got Skills?" for practice with one-across messages.

In contrast, people in complementary relationships frequently communicate using different types of statements. One person might use a one-up message ("Try searching for airfares online"), and the other might respond with a one-down message ("That's a great idea; thanks for the suggestion"). Alternatively, one partner might express a one-down message ("What should we get Grandma for her birthday?"), and the other might reply with a one-up message ("Let's get her some new DVDs"). In complementary relationships, one-up or one-down messages can also precede one-across messages. In response to a one-up message, for instance ("I think we should have pasta for dinner"), a partner might respond with a one-across message ("That's one option"). That move can signal that the partner doesn't wish to be dominated or controlled.

POWER CAN BE POSITIVE OR NEGATIVE.   There's nothing inherently good or bad about power. Rather, as with conflict, the way people handle power makes it positive or negative. Even complementary relationships in which there is a large difference in power can be highly satisfying if they meet two conditions. First, the two parties must agree on the power arrangement. If the less-powerful person begins to question

one-across message
A verbal message that seeks to neutralize relational control and power.

or challenge the other person's power (as when adolescents assert their independence from their parents), the relationship can become dissatisfying. Second, the powerful person should exercise his or her power ethically and responsibly, in ways that benefit both parties. When one party in a relationship abuses power by serving only personal needs or desires or improving his or her situation at the other party's expense, resentment and dissatisfaction can arise.

POWER AND CONFLICT INFLUENCE EACH OTHER.   At their core, many conflicts are struggles for power. Siblings who fight over control of the television remote, neighbors who fight over their property boundaries, and drivers fighting for the few remaining spaces in a parking lot are all clashing over power: Who has the right to control resources?

Just as power influences conflict, conflict can also influence the balance and exercise of power. Let's say that after Shawn turns 15, he has conflict with his parents over household rules. As a result, his parents give him a later curfew and greater flexibility in deciding where he goes and with whom. That development—which was the direct result of Shawn's conflict with his parents—changed the balance of power in the parent–child relationship, with Shawn acquiring more control over his own life.

So far, we've talked about power as if it were a singular entity. In fact, power comes in many forms, as we'll see next.

Forms of Power

People exercise influence or control over others in many ways. In a now-classic study, social psychologists John French and Bertram Raven classified power into five specific forms: reward, coercive, referent, legitimate, and expert power.[45] As we take a closer look at those forms, remember that they aren't mutually exclusive; rather, one person may exercise multiple forms of power in a given situation.

reward power Power that derives from the ability to reward.

REWARD POWER.   As its name implies, **reward power** operates when one party has the ability to reward the other in some way. Your supervisor has power over you, for instance, because she pays you and can promote you for doing what she says. In that case, your pay and the possibility for advancement are the rewards. Similarly, judges on talent shows such as *Dancing with the Stars* and *American Idol* have reward power because they determine who will advance in those contests.

coercive power Power based on the ability to punish.

COERCIVE POWER.   The opposite of reward power is **coercive power,** or power that derives from the ability to punish. When you go to court, for example, the judge has power over you because he can punish you with fines or imprisonment for not doing as he says. Parents and employers often have both reward power and coercive power over their children or their employees; they can provide rewards for good behavior and issue punishments for bad behavior.

referent power Power that derives from one's attraction to or admiration for another.

REFERENT POWER.   French and Raven used the term **referent power** to refer to the power of attraction, noting that people tend to comply with requests made by those whom they like, admire, or find attractive in some way. For instance, you might recognize that you work harder for instructors you like than for those you dislike. Similarly, you may be persuaded to buy products if they are endorsed by celebrities you admire. Perhaps you prefer Revlon cosmetics because you like Halle Berry or you're partial to Subway sandwiches because you admire Michael Phelps. Those examples involve complementary relationships. Referent power can also operate in symmetrical relationships, however. For instance, you might comply with requests from your friends because you like them and want to please them.

LEGITIMATE POWER.   People exercise **legitimate power** when their status or position gives them the right to make requests with which others must comply. If a police officer signals you to pull your car over, you comply because you perceive that the officer has a legitimate right to make you do so. When you travel by air, you follow the instructions of the airport screeners, flight attendants, and pilots because you perceive that their positions give them certain authorities over you in that context.

Many of us tend to comply with requests and pitches made by people whom we like, admire, or find attractive. That is what French and Raven referred to as referent power.

EXPERT POWER.   The last form on French and Raven's list is **expert power,** which operates when we comply with the directions of people we perceive to be experts in a particular area. We follow the advice of a doctor, a professor, a stockbroker, or an electrician because we recognize that their training and experience give them expertise we ourselves don't have. In the film *The King's Speech* (2010), speech therapist Lionel Logue (played by Geoffrey Rush) exercised expert power when helping Britain's King George VI (played by Colin Firth) overcome his debilitating stammer. Like other forms of power, expert power is context-specific. You consult your stockbroker for financial advice, for example, but you wouldn't ask him how to fix your sink, because that goes beyond his expertise.

> **legitimate power** Power based on one's legitimate status or position.

> **expert power** Power that derives from one's expertise, talent, training, specialized knowledge, or experience.

As we considered earlier, different forms of power often operate together. We've seen that parents have both reward and coercive power over their children, for instance, but they often have other forms of power as well. They have referent power if their children obey them out of respect or admiration. They have legitimate power when they exercise

Lionel Logue exercised expert power when helping Britain's King George VI overcome his stutter in The King's Speech *(2010).*

FRENCH AND RAVEN'S FORMS OF RELATIONAL POWER

Reward	Power based on the ability to reward for compliance
Coercive	Power based on the ability to punish for noncompliance
Referent	Power based on liking, admiring, and being attracted to the powerful party
Legitimate	Power based on rightfully granted status or position
Expert	Power based on special knowledge, training, experience, and/or expertise

control on the basis of their position ("Because I'm your mother, that's why!"). Finally, they have expert power when they teach their children how to drive or balance a checkbook. The "At a Glance" box provides a quick reference to help you remember French and Raven's five forms of power.

Sex, Gender, and Power

Few factors influence the experience of power more than sex and gender. Across cultures and time periods, societies have defined male–female relationships largely in terms of men's power over women. The virtually universal practice of *patriarchy,* which structures social units such as families and communities so that men control the resources, has allowed men throughout history to exercise political, religious, and economic power over women.[46] As a result, women historically have experienced more limited access to education, lower-quality health care, fewer economic opportunities, and more limited political involvement.[47]

Those inequities persist in many parts of the world, including the United States. According to the United Nations, only 16.8 percent of elected political representatives in the United States are women. Worldwide, the number is only slightly higher: 18.4 percent.[48] Women and men have equal employment rates in fewer than half the world's countries, and they have equal literacy rates in only a third of the countries. Finally, in a large majority of countries, women earn less than 70 percent of what men in comparable jobs earn.[49]

Traditional gender roles reinforce the inequitable division of power between women and men. As we saw in Chapter 2, stereotypical femininity emphasizes characteristics such as passivity, submissiveness, and accommodation, whereas stereotypical masculinity prizes strength, control, and dominance. To the extent that men and women identify strongly with masculine and feminine gender roles, the inequitable distribution of power may be reflected in their interpersonal behavior. For instance, men may take for granted that what they say at work or at home will matter to those around them. They may also express dominance through verbal aggression, using words to attack or demean people around them.[50] In contrast, if women have less power than men or perceive they do, they may be less likely to assume that other people will take their words or ideas seriously.[51] They may also be inclined to exercise power in more covert ways, such as through passive-aggressive behavior.

As women gain positions of power and influence, gender inequities in power may be eroded. As of 2011, several nations had a female head of state, including Liberia, Germany, Iceland, Costa Rica, and Brazil (Table 11.1). In the U.S. government, women

TABLE 11.1

Countries with Female Heads of State

Country	Head of State	Title
Argentina	Christina Fernández de Kirchner	President
Brazil	Dilma Vana Linhares Rousseff	President
Costa Rica	Laura Chinchilla Miranda	President
Finland	Tarja Halonen	President
Germany	Angela Merkel	Chancellor
Iceland	Jóhanna Sigurðardóttir	Prime Minister
India	Pratibha Patil	President
Ireland	Mary McAleese	President
Kyrgyzstan	Roza Otunbayeva	President
Liberia	Ellen Johnson-Sirleaf	President
Lithuania	Dalia Grybauskaitė	President
Switzerland	Micheline Calmy-Rey	President of Swiss Confederation

Note: This table includes elected and appointed heads of state but excludes monarchs. Information is current as of January 2011.

have assumed unprecedented positions of power in the past three decades, including Secretary of State (Condoleeza Rice, Hillary Clinton), Speaker of the House of Representatives (Nancy Pelosi), and Secretary of Homeland Security (Janet Napolitano).

People who have studied the association between conflict and health have concluded that power affects women and men differently. In one study, a team of researchers led by human ecology professor Timothy Loving took a novel approach to measuring power relations in married couples.[52] The researchers selected 72 couples and instructed each spouse to complete measures indicating how much he or she loved the other. They then checked how closely each person's response matched that of his or her spouse. To determine the spouses' relative power, the researchers applied the *principle of least interest*. That principle states that the partner who is less invested in the relationship is the more powerful partner, because he or she has less to lose by leaving the relationship.[53]

In their study, the researchers used love as the measure of investment. If the wife and husband reported relatively equal love scores, the researchers considered them to have equal power. When the husband's love score was significantly higher than his wife's, the researchers concluded that the wife had more power. Conversely, when the wife's love score was significantly higher than her husband's, then the husband was more powerful.

The researchers then instructed each couple to engage in a conflict conversation while they monitored the stress hormone levels of all the participants. The results indicated that being in a power-balanced marriage benefited women and men by protecting them against an increase in the stress hormone ACTH. The same pattern was observed in marriages in which the wife was deemed more powerful. In marriages in which the husband was deemed more powerful, however, women's ACTH levels

g@t connected

SOCIAL POWER, TWITTER STYLE

College students in the United Kingdom—upset about massive tuition increases—decided to exercise the power of protest. In late 2010, several thousand students took to the streets of London and other British cities to make their voices heard. Realizing that their exercise of power required organization, the students exploited social-networking technology to coordinate their efforts. Here's how:

- *Facebook helped them recruit.* Student leaders advertised protest marches and occupations of university buildings on Facebook to reach widespread audiences.

- *Twitter helped them disseminate information.* Participants used Twitter to update information about marches and occupations on a minute-to-minute basis.

- *Google maps helped them evade police.* During a London march in December 2010, volunteers created a live Google map of police activity to help protesters steer clear of authorities.

Social-networking technologies provide an unprecedented ability to communicate with large numbers of individuals in real time. Taking advantage of that ability allowed the British college students to exercise their power in an organized, efficient way.

rose significantly, indicating increased stress. Among the same group, however, men's ACTH levels dropped significantly, indicating reduced stress.

In sum, then, men experienced no increase in stress as a result of marital conflict under any circumstances. Moreover, when men argued with less-powerful wives, their stress actually decreased. One possible explanation for those results is that because men historically have enjoyed power in social affairs and relationships, they may subconsciously not perceive marital conflict to be threatening and stressful, even when they have less power in the relationship.

Like men, women didn't experience increased stress as a result of conflict when they had equal power with or more power than their spouse. Unlike men, however, they did react stressfully to conflict when they had less power. Because of their less-powerful position, the wives in the study may have felt more threatened and insecure as a result of conflict, causing their stress to elevate. ACTH is only one hormone that reacts to stress, however, so the results might have been different had the researchers utilized other indicators of stress.

Culture and Power

Cultural practices and beliefs also affect the ways in which people exercise power in personal relationships. Remember from Chapter 2 that one dimension along which cultures differ is their power distance. High-power-distance cultures are characterized by an uneven distribution of power. In those cultures, certain social groups—such as royalty, the upper class, and the ruling political party—have considerably more power than the average citizen. Moreover, people in high-power-distance cultures are socialized to view the unequal distribution of power as normal or even desirable. Upper-class citizens are treated with respect and privilege, whereas citizens of lesser status are taught to behave humbly.[54] In particular, lower-status citizens are not expected to question or challenge the decisions, opinions, or directions of the ruling class. When all social groups accept that arrangement, then the society can avoid many potential conflicts.[55] One example of that type of power division is India's caste system, in which people are born into social groups, or *castes*, that largely dictate with whom they can associate.

In contrast, low-power-distance cultures exhibit a more equal distribution of power among social groups. Although some social groups may have somewhat more power than others, the prevailing belief among citizens is that all people are inherently equal and that power differences between groups should be small. One result of that cultural belief is that people from low-power-distance cultures are more likely than their counterparts in high-power-distance cultures to question authority and to engage in conflict with teachers, supervisors, politicians, and others who exercise power over them.

Another difference is that people in low-power-distance cultures often believe they have greater control over the course of their life. Whereas people in high-power-distance cultures are often raised to believe their social class determines their life course, many people in low-power-distance cultures are socialized to believe they can achieve whatever they set their minds to. In the United States, for instance, there are many examples of people, such as Bill Clinton and Oprah Winfrey, who have risen from humble beginnings to positions of great power and influence. As politician Adlai Stevenson, former U.S. ambassador to the United Nations, once noted, "In America, anyone can become president."

To the extent they believe their social class doesn't dictate their lives, people in low-power-distance cultures may be more likely than their counterparts in high-power-distance cultures to engage in conflict with anyone they perceive to be oppressive. As the "Get Connected" box on the preceding page describes, college students in the United Kingdom did just that in 2010 when they used social-networking technology to organize protests against the government.

In India's caste system, people are born into social groups that largely dictate with whom they can associate.

LEARN IT What is the difference between a symmetrical relationship and a complementary relationship? What are French and Raven's five forms of power? What is patriarchy? How do cultural messages influence the exercise of power?

APPLY IT Conflicts that seem to be about one thing, such as what to watch on TV, are often really about power, as in who gets to decide what is watched on TV. The next time you're in conflict with someone, analyze the conflict to identify the power struggle, if any, it involves. As you make decisions about how to communicate during the conflict, try to recognize the underlying power struggle and not just the obvious topic of the disagreement. Also, notice how the power struggle may be different in a symmetrical relationship as opposed to a complementary one. Document your findings in a journal entry.

REFLECT ON IT When do you view the exercise of power as positive? Who has referent power over you?

4 Managing Interpersonal Conflict

There are almost as many ways to handle conflict as there are topics about which to disagree. When you experience conflict in your personal relationships, you need to decide how to manage and resolve them. Sometimes you choose your behaviors wisely, and sometimes you choose poorly, but your actions almost always have an effect on your relationships. We'll begin this section by looking at some particularly problematic conflict behaviors. We'll then examine five general strategies you can use to manage conflict successfully.

Problematic Behaviors During Conflict

Earlier in this chapter, we learned that it isn't conflict itself that is necessarily damaging to our relationships; rather, it's the way we handle conflict that matters. Whereas some relational partners manage conflict maturely and constructively, others deal with it so poorly that it jeopardizes the relationship itself. Which behaviors are the problematic ones?

To find out, psychologist John Gottman has spent years studying how spouses and partners interact with each other during conflict episodes. Conventional wisdom might suggest that couples who fight frequently are most likely to split up. In fact, Gottman's research has found otherwise. According to Gottman, *how couples argue,* and not how frequently they argue, predicts their chances for staying together.[56] Gottman's work has identified four specific behaviors that are warning signs for separation or divorce: criticism, contempt, defensiveness, and stonewalling. Gottman refers to those behaviors as the "Four Horsemen of the Apocalypse" to indicate that they signal distress.[57] Let's take a closer look at each of those problematic behaviors.

criticism The expression of complaints about another party.

CRITICISM. According to Gottman, the first warning sign occurs when partners engage in **criticism** or complaints about each other. Criticism isn't always bad, but it becomes counterproductive when it focuses on people's personality or character rather than on their behavior. Statements such as "You always have to be right" and "You never listen" focus on attacking the person and assigning blame.

Criticisms also tend to be global statements about a person's value or virtue instead of specific critiques about the topic of the conflict. Instead of saying "You should be more attentive when I describe my feelings to you," for instance, a distressed partner might say "You never think of anyone but yourself." Because criticisms so often come across as personal attacks instead of as accurate descriptions of the sources of conflict, they tend to inflame conflict situations. At that point, criticism becomes a sign of a distressed relationship.

Criticism can also be counterproductive when partners engage in *gunnysacking—* that is, privately "saving up" their past grievances and then bringing them up all at once.[58] When Enrique criticized his wife Sonja for spending too much money on their children's school clothes, for example, Sonja responded by criticizing Enrique for past offenses she had not previously discussed with him. "You think *I'm* wasteful?" she replied. "What about all the money you wasted on that stupid fishing trip last year? And while we're on the subject, don't think I didn't notice that money you transferred out of our savings account last month without asking me. What'd you waste that on?

Another piece of overpriced art for your office? You expect me to be careful with money while you've been wasting it ever since we got married!"

Each of Sonja's grievances may have merit. Nevertheless, her response to Enrique's criticism is unproductive. By bringing up all her criticisms at once, Sonja is deflecting attention from their current conflict, with the likely result that the current conflict will remain unresolved.

Expressing contempt is one of the negative behaviors relational partners can perform during conflict.

CONTEMPT. A second warning sign occurs when partners show **contempt** for each other by insulting each other and attacking each other's self-worth. That behavior can include calling each other names ("You stupid idiot"), using sarcasm or mockery to make fun of the other person, and using nonverbal behaviors that suggest a low opinion of the other person, such as eye rolling and sneering. It can also include ridiculing the person in front of others and encouraging others to do the same.

Regardless of its form, contempt functions to put down and degrade the other person. Research indicates that responding to conflict with this type of hostile behavior often increases physical stress in the partners, which can impair their health.[59]

contempt The expression of insults and attacks on another's self-worth.

DEFENSIVENESS. A third danger sign is that partners become defensive during their conflict. **Defensiveness** means seeing oneself as a victim and denying responsibility for one's own behaviors. Instead of listening to their partners' concerns and acknowledging that they need to change certain behaviors, defensive people whine ("It's not fair"), make excuses ("It's not my fault"), and respond to complaints with complaints ("Maybe I spend too much money, but you never make time for the kids and me"). People are particularly prone to feel defensive about criticisms when they recognize that the criticisms have merit but they don't want to accept the responsibility for changing their behaviors.

defensiveness The tendency to deny the validity of criticisms directed at the self.

STONEWALLING. The last of Gottman's "Four Horsemen" is **stonewalling,** or withdrawing from a conversation or an interaction. People who stonewall will often act as though they are "shutting down"; that is, they stop looking at their partners, they stop speaking, and they stop responding to what their partners are saying. In some cases, they even physically leave the room to end the conversation. The reason for

stonewalling Withdrawing from a conversation or an interaction.

Gottman has found that people stonewall when they feel emotionally and psychologically flooded.

[COMPROMISING]

Compromising gives both parties in a conflict something they value.

WHAT?

Learn to compromise when managing conflict.

WHY?

To help both parties in a conflict—such as a conflict over the selling price of a car—gain something of value.

HOW?

1. If it appears that neither party is going to "win" the conflict outright, say "Let's come up with a compromise."

2. Identify what's most important to you in the conflict ("I really need to sell this car for at least $6,500") and then ask the other party to do the same ("I want to get the best deal possible").

3. Propose solutions to the conflict that address each party's most pressing needs ("If you buy the car for $6,500, I'll throw in a mobile GPS unit and a year of satellite radio service").

TRY!

1. With a classmate pretending to be your roommate, practice a conversation in which you address his or her criticisms of your study habits or housecleaning practices at home.

2. Rather than accepting your partner's suggestions for change outright, identify what's most important to you and ask your partner to do the same.

3. Propose a solution that will give each of you something that you want. Continue proposing compromises until your partner accepts.

CONSIDER: *How does thinking about compromise force you to consider your partner's needs as well as your own?*

got **SKILLS** ?

FIVE APPROACHES TO CONFLICT

Carla and Ben, sister and brother, have each saved $1,500 to put toward a car. Their parents can add only enough money to buy one car, not two, so Carla is in conflict with Ben over who should get that money. Here are examples of five different approaches Carla might take when engaging this conflict:

Competing	Carla tries to get her parents to give all their saved-up money to her and none of it to Ben.
Avoiding	Carla doesn't bring up the conflict, hoping her parents will figure out a way to resolve it on their own.
Accommodating	Carla encourages her parents to give their saved-up money to Ben instead of to her.
Compromising	Carla suggests that she and Ben pool their money with their parents' money and buy one car that they will share.
Collaborating	Carla works with Ben and their parents to try to figure out how she and Ben can each get a car.

Laura to enroll in online courses so at least one of them would be home every day. The money they saved in day care made up for the income they lost because of Mick's reduced hours. Moreover, both Laura and Mick felt better because they were able to care for their child themselves.

Collaborating probably sounds like the ideal way to handle conflict—and in many situations, it is. It can also require a great deal of energy, patience, and imagination. Although it might seem like the best approach, it can also be the most difficult.

How might each of those strategies operate in real life? The "At a Glance" box (on page 375) highlights one conflict—two siblings fighting over who is going to get a new car—and illustrates how each of those approaches can be employed when engaging in the conflict.

LEARN IT How are criticism and contempt different? When might avoidance be a better conflict management strategy than accommodating?

APPLY IT Pair up with a classmate and watch an episode of your favorite reality TV show. Whenever conflict is portrayed in the program, help each other identify examples of any of Gottman's "Four Horsemen of the Apocalypse."

REFLECT ON IT How do you feel when someone stonewalls during a conflict with you? When do you find collaborating a challenge?

MASTER the chapter

1 The Nature of Interpersonal Conflict (p. 350)

- Conflict is an expressed struggle between two or more interdependent parties who perceive incompatible goals, scarce resources, and interference.
- People often think about conflict using a variety of metaphors such as a trial, a game, a balancing act, and a garden.

2 Conflict in Personal Relationships (p. 353)

- Conflict is natural. It has content, relational, and procedural dimensions, and it can be direct or indirect. Conflict can be harmful, and it can also be beneficial.

- People have conflict about a range of issues. Some issues—such as personal criticism, finances, and household chores—are especially common in interpersonal relationships.
- Conflict is influenced by sex and gender role orientations, encouraging men to be competitive and women to be accommodating.
- How people manage conflict is affected by whether their culture is individualistic or collectivistic and also by whether it is high context or low context.
- Conflict is especially prevalent in online settings because of the disinhibition effect.

3 Power and Conflict (p. 363)

- Power is the ability to manipulate, influence, or control other people or events.

- Power is context-specific but always present. It can be positive or negative, depending on how it is exercised. Power and conflict influence each other.
- People exercise five general forms of power: reward, coercive, referent, legitimate, and expert.
- Power is influenced by sex and gender roles.
- The way people think about power is affected by whether they come from a high-power-distance culture or a low-power-distance culture.

4 Managing Interpersonal Conflict (p. 372)

- In romantic relationships, four conflict behaviors are reliable predictors of relationship dissolution: criticism, contempt, defensiveness, and stonewalling.
- People use five general strategies for managing conflict: competing, avoiding, accommodating, collaborating, and compromising. Which conflict management strategy is best depends on the situation and on the goals of the participants.

KEY TERMS

accommodating (p. 375)

avoiding (p. 375)

coercive power (p. 366)

collaborating (p. 375)

competing (p. 374)

complementary relationship (p. 364)

compromising (p. 375)

contempt (p. 373)

criticism (p. 372)

defensiveness (p. 373)

demand–withdraw pattern (p. 359)

disinhibition effect (p. 361)

expert power (p. 367)

interpersonal conflict (p. 350)

legitimate power (p. 367)

metaconflict (p. 354)

one-across message (p. 365)

one-down message (p. 364)

one-up message (p. 364)

passive aggression (p. 359)

power (p. 363)

referent power (p. 366)

reward power (p. 366)

stonewalling (p. 373)

symmetrical relationship (p. 364)

DISCUSSION QUESTIONS

1. With whom do you have the most troublesome conflicts? What are your conflicts with these parties about?
2. What have you noticed about the different ways in which men and women engage in conflict?
3. What are some examples of the positive use of power? The negative use?
4. Which of Gottman's "Four Horsemen" would you find the most distressing if enacted in your own relationships? Why?

PRACTICE QUIZ

MULTIPLE CHOICE

1. **According to research by Larry Erbert, the three most common sources of marital conflict, in order, are**
   a. finances, household chores, personal criticism
   b. household chores, personal criticism, finances
   c. personal criticism, finances, household chores
   d. money, sex, in-laws

2. **An imbalance of power, in which one person in a relationship has more power than the other, is known as**
   a. a symmetrical relationship
   b. a complementary relationship
   c. an equitable relationship
   d. none of the above

3. **The term used to describe the power of attraction—in which people tend to comply with requests made by those they like, admire, or find attractive—is**
   a. reward power
   b. coercive power
   c. referent power
   d. legitimate power

4. **Seeing yourself as a victim and denying responsibility for your own behavior are characteristics of**
   a. defensiveness
   b. stonewalling
   c. contempt
   d. complaining

5. **The approach to conflict that is characterized by a moderate concern for others' needs is**
   a. competing
   b. avoiding
   c. collaborating
   d. compromising

FILL IN THE BLANK

6. The _____ dimension of conflict relates to the specific topics that the conflict is about.

7. The _____ pattern of conflict occurs when one partner makes requests and the other partner pulls away.

8. People raised in _____ cultures are taught to consider the group's priorities and maintain group harmony, making them likely to manage conflict through avoidance.

9. In computer-mediated communication, the _____ effect invites people to say or do things they would not do in person.

10. Because of their status or position, individuals with _____ power have the right to make requests with which others must comply.

ANSWERS

RESEARCH LIBRARY

MOVIES

Doubt (drama; 2008; PG-13)
This story, set in 1964 at a Catholic school in the Bronx, New York, focuses on a nun (played by Meryl Streep) who accuses a priest (played by Philip Seymour Hoffman) of abusing a 12-year-old African American male student. The movie portrays both interpersonal and intrapersonal conflict as all of the principal parties confront their doubt in themselves and in each other.

The Social Network (drama; 2010; PG-13)
This movie is about the founding of the social-networking website Facebook. It highlights the multiple conflicts between Mark Zuckerberg, Eduardo Saverin, Cameron and Tyler Winklevoss, and Divya Narendra, each of whom claimed some credit for creating Facebook. The film includes several interpersonal conflicts as well as structured legal conflicts resulting from lawsuits.

BOOKS AND JOURNAL ARTICLES

Erbert, L. A. (2000). Conflict and dialectics: Perceptions of dialectical contradictions in marital conflict. *Journal of Social and Personal Relationships, 17*, 638–659.

Kiecolt-Glaser, J. K., Malarkey, W. B., Chee, M., Newton, T., Cacioppo, J. T., Mao, H.-Y., & Glaser, R. (1993). Negative behavior during marital conflict is associated with immunological down-regulation. *Psychosomatic Medicine, 55*, 395–409.

Oetzel, J. H., & Ting-Toomey, S. (Eds.). (2006). *The Sage handbook of conflict communication: Integrating theory, research, and practice.* Thousand Oaks, CA: Sage.

Wilmot, W., & Hocker, J. (2010). *Interpersonal conflict* (8th ed.). New York: McGraw-Hill.

WEBSITES

www.gottman.com
   This is the home page for the Gottman Relationship Institute, which offers workshops, home study materials, and other resources for partners and family members dealing with conflict.
www.iacm-conflict.org
   This page, sponsored by the International Association for Conflict Management, offers links to several online resources relevant to conflict and conflict management.

12 Deceptive Communication

FEELING THE PAIN OF DISHONESTY

Amanda Broadband had always harbored suspicions about her husband Stuart's past. He claimed to have been faithful during their 15-year relationship, but in 2008 Amanda discovered—in a very public and humiliating way—that he had been lying. The spouses were contestants on Jerry Springer's British television game show *Nothing But the Truth*, in which participants are hooked up to a lie detector and asked a series of personal questions on the air. Those who answer every question truthfully can win the equivalent of $100,000, but one lie and all the money is lost. Faced with the chance to pocket significant cash, Stuart responded to a question about his marital fidelity by revealing that he had carried on a brief affair several years earlier. Although relieved to know the truth, Amanda felt betrayed and deeply embarrassed—all the more so because her husband's deception had been exposed on national television.

N o one likes being lied to. When we find out someone has deceived us, we feel angry and taken advantage of. Although those feelings of betrayal and violation can occur in all relationships, they can be particularly strong—and painful—when the deception occurs in the context of a close relationship, as it did for Amanda and Stuart. Deception hurts us emotionally, and it erodes our trust in others, as the "Communication: Dark Side" box explains.[1]

Yet are you completely honest *all* the time? Do you ever pretend you're happy to see someone, just to avoid hurting that person's feelings? How about those times you say "Sorry, I have plans" when you don't really have plans, but you want to get out of something you don't want to do? Most of us would have to admit we don't always tell "the truth, the whole truth, and nothing but the truth." But being polite, tactful, or discreet isn't really the same thing as lying. Is it?

1 The Nature of Interpersonal Deception

You don't have to look far to find high-profile examples of deception. In 2009, New York Yankees infielder Alex Rodriguez became the most prominent baseball player yet to admit to using performance-enhancing drugs, a charge he had squarely denied before that time. The previous year, track star Marion Jones was sentenced to six months in prison for lying to investigators about using steroids, a confession that also cost Jones her five Olympic medals. From politicians to advertisers to professional athletes, it seems that many people in our world attempt to benefit personally by deceiving others.

Whatever our personal feelings may be about the value of honesty, the reality is that most people conceal the truth on a regular basis.[2] To respect the privacy of a co-worker who is in treatment for alcohol addiction, for instance, you may tell her clients that she's away from work on a "special assignment." By the same token, you may tell your 12-year-old nephew that he did a "wonderful job" performing in his school musical, even though he can barely carry a tune, because you want to encourage him. Sometimes, in fact, we even reprimand people for telling the truth. When children make straightforward comments about other people ("You smell funny," "Your teeth are really yellow"), we usually teach them it is impolite to say such things, even though they are expressing honest opinions.

We might agree that lying is wrong if we do it to hurt someone, but what if we do it to *avoid* hurting someone?[3] We may choose not to think of politeness or discretion as examples of lying, because words such as *lying* and *deception* have negative connotations. However, even when their intentions are admirable, people often misrepresent the truth to achieve them.[4] When we think of lying as a misrepresentation of the truth—no matter what the intention—we realize that deception is often a part of everyday social interaction.

HURTING THE ONES WE LOVE:
DECEPTION CAN DESTROY TRUST

When Kendra Craig first met her husband Andy, he was heavily in debt. Over the next six years, she helped him restructure his finances and pay off all his credit card balances. He then admitted that he owed almost $13,000 on an additional credit card that she didn't know about. Kendra refinanced their house to pay off that debt, but she informed Andy in no uncertain terms that if he ever lied to her again about his debts, she would leave him. Eight months later, Kendra found a credit card statement with a balance of over $6,000 under the passenger's seat in Andy's car. She felt completely betrayed. It was bad enough that Andy was jeopardizing their family's financial health by continuing to accrue debt. The fact that he was also lying to Kendra about it made her feel as though he had completely violated her trust.

Kendra's painful experience is not unique. As you have seen in this course, close personal relationships require the ability to trust. When you learn that someone you care about has lied to you, particularly about a matter of importance, that discovery often makes you less willing to believe other statements that person makes. In other words, it erodes your trust in the individual. When trust is compromised in a close relationship, it may never fully recover, even if you forgive the person for lying. If you find yourself the victim of violated trust, think honestly about how that episode has affected your trust in that person.

ASK YOURSELF

- Where does trust come from? What makes you trust others?
- Has deception ever ruined your trust in another person? If so, how did your willingness to trust that person change over time, if at all?

Throughout this chapter, it's important to keep an open mind and think of deception as just one of many communication processes you're learning about in this class. That doesn't mean you should check your morals or beliefs at the door. On the contrary, how you think about the value of honesty, reliability, and integrity helps to define who you are as a human being. Many people believe that honesty is truly the best policy. Nearly all the major world religions promote the virtue of honesty and condemn deceptive behavior.

Remember, though, that *studying* something isn't the same as *condoning* it. Whether or not you are ethically or morally opposed to lying, understanding deception helps you to become a better communicator.[5] In fact, the more you know about deception, the better you may become at detecting it.

Most of us would probably define deception as "making statements that aren't true," and we might associate it with actions such as fibbing, misleading, exaggerating,

The Girl Scout Law
*I will do my best to be
honest and fair,
friendly and helpful,
considerate and caring,
courageous and strong, and
responsible for what I say and do,
and to
respect myself and others,
respect authority,
use resources wisely,
make the world a better place, and
be a sister to every Girl Scout.*

stretching the truth, concealing the truth, and telling white lies. None of those types of deception, however, represents a fully adequate definition. After all, people can be deceptive by leaving out parts of a story or by giving vague, ambiguous answers to questions. Neither of those scenarios requires saying anything that technically isn't true.

Defining Deception

deception The knowing and intentional transmission of information to create a false belief in the hearer.

According to communication researchers, **deception** occurs when a speaker transmits information knowingly and intentionally for the purpose of creating a false belief in the receiver. In other words, if you communicate in a way that is meant to make someone believe a fact or form an impression you know to be untrue, then you are engaging in deception.

We can think of deceptive acts as falling along a continuum from high-stakes lies to low-stakes lies. *High-stakes lies* are those for which the penalties for getting caught are severe.[6] Many high-stakes lies are forms of *fraud,* which means they are misrepresentations of facts for the sake of material gain. Some types of fraudulent lies are (1) misrepresenting your identity by forging someone else's signature on checks or other documents; (2) impersonating a physician, a police officer, or some other licensed professional; (3) engaging in insider trading by using privileged information to make stock sales or purchases; (4) underreporting your income on your tax returns; and (5) filing false insurance claims. Each of those actions is a high-stakes lie because the penalty for getting caught can include steep fines and imprisonment. The same can be said for *perjury,* or lying under oath, which constitutes a felony.

In addition to carrying legal penalties, high-stakes lies can also carry significant personal penalties. For example, lying to your spouse to cover up an affair or lying to your boss about a substantial mistake you made would also qualify as a high-stakes lie because you could destroy your marriage or lose your job if your lie were to be revealed.[7]

On the other end of the continuum are *low-stakes lies,* for which the penalties for getting caught are comparatively mild. Those lies, sometimes called "white lies," often serve to avoid embarrassing people and hurting their feelings. Some examples of low-stakes lies are (1) telling a friend you "love the graduation gift" she gave you when you actually don't like it; (2) assuring your brother and sister-in-law that helping them move "is no problem," even though it's inconvenient for you; (3) claiming that you arrived late to your haircut appointment because you "ran into heavy traffic on the way" when in fact you left your house late; and (4) saying "nice to meet you" to your newest co-worker even though he makes a bad first impression on you.

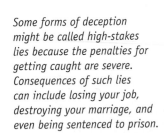

Some forms of deception might be called high-stakes lies because the penalties for getting caught are severe. Consequences of such lies can include losing your job, destroying your marriage, and even being sentenced to prison.

In many cases, the only real penalty for being caught in a low-stakes lie is emotional discomfort. If your hairdresser discovers you actually weren't late for your appointment because of traffic, for instance, you'll probably feel slightly guilty for having told the lie and slightly embarrassed at being discovered. Those emotions will probably be temporary, though, and it's unlikely that more serious consequences will follow.

Many other deceptive acts fall somewhere along the continuum between high-stakes and low-stakes lies. Suppose, for instance, that while taking the midterm exam in your marketing class, you notice your friend Soren cheating on the test. After reading Soren's exam, the professor suspects him of cheating but doesn't have direct proof. She contacts several students—including you—to ask if you witnessed anyone cheating on the test. Because Soren is your friend, you say no. What penalties do you suffer if you are caught in that lie? Perhaps the professor gives you a failing grade on the exam, making it impossible for you to earn a grade higher than *C* in the class. That penalty is certainly more severe than just feeling guilty or embarrassed, but it isn't as severe as losing your job, your marriage, or your freedom. Lies of that sort might therefore be considered *middle-stakes lies.*

The Elements of Deception

In summary, to qualify as deception, a communicative act must have three basic elements:

- The sender must know the information is false.
- The sender must be transmitting the information on purpose.
- The sender must be attempting to make the receiver believe the information.

Importantly, a behavior must exhibit all three characteristics to be considered deceptive.

Our definition of deception excludes certain situations, which we now consider. You probably encounter such situations from time to time in your social interactions.

YOU AREN'T LYING IF YOU BELIEVE THAT WHAT YOU'RE SAYING IS TRUE. Suppose you ask me how long a nautical mile is, and I tell you it's 1,920 meters. That answer reflects what I honestly think. It's also untrue—a nautical mile is actually 1,852 meters. (You should know better than to ask a communication professor such questions.) So, I gave you false information. Did I transmit the information on purpose? Yes: You asked and I answered. Did I intend for you to believe the information? Of course. Nevertheless, according to our definition I wasn't being deceptive because I didn't know the information was false.

YOU AREN'T LYING IF YOU DON'T INTEND FOR OTHERS TO BELIEVE WHAT YOU'RE SAYING. Quite often, you make statements you don't mean for other people to take literally, such as "I'm so hungry I could eat a horse" and "I'm so tired I could sleep 'til Tuesday." You've probably never actually been that hungry or that tired—and if you say something like that, most people who hear you will understand that you don't literally mean what you're saying. If you say "It's raining cats and dogs," you know that felines and canines aren't actually falling from the sky; thus, the literal information is false. Nevertheless, you aren't being deceptive in that situation, because when you use such idioms you're not trying to make others believe the false information. Many forms of teasing and sarcasm also are not meant to be taken literally. We can usually tell by people's facial expressions or tone of voice when they are joking and don't expect us to believe them.

YOU CANNOT LIE TO YOURSELF. From time to time, you may try to make yourself believe facts or ideas that you know aren't true. When you realize such attempts didn't work, you may say, "I was just deceiving myself." According to our definition, however, it is *impossible* for people to deceive themselves. You certainly attempt to change your opinions or beliefs on various issues; sometimes you're successful and sometimes not. Recall, however, that for a communicative act to qualify as deception, the sender—knowing the information is false—must attempt to make the receiver believe it is true.

Snapshots

Tall, Dark, and Handsome chats with Buxom Blonde.

Striking examples of online deception occur on dating websites, where subscribers post personal information with the hope of attracting potential romantic partners. Profiles on dating sites typically ask for information about the subscriber's height, weight, personal appearance, profession, education, hobbies, interests, and preferences in a prospective partner. Perhaps not surprisingly, deception is common on those sites. In fact, research has found that as many as 20 percent of online daters admit to lying about some aspect of their personal profile. When people are asked *how many other people* they believe are being deceptive, however, that figure jumps to nearly 90 percent.[14]

What do online daters lie about? For women, the major areas of deception are age, weight, and physical appearance. For men, they are educational level, income, height, age, and even marital status. (Research suggests that at least 13 percent of men on dating websites are married.)[15] Why is such lying so common? The answer is that online daters are looking for a partner, and so they want their profile to be as attractive as possible, even if it isn't entirely accurate. Unfortunately, their belief that being completely truthful would hurt their chances may be justified. At least one study found that the more honest people were in describing themselves, the less success they had in finding dates online.[16]

Why, exactly, might someone choose to lie, either online or in person? We'll take a look at some of the most common reasons for deception in the next section.

LEARN IT What is deception? Why can't people lie to themselves? What does it mean to call deception a "social lubricant"?

APPLY IT For two days, keep a journal in which you note every time you are deceptive with another person, no matter how or for what reason. Even deception done in the service of routine politeness should be recorded. For each entry, write down what you were deceptive about and what your intention was for deceiving.

REFLECT ON IT While keeping the deception diary, how did you feel when you caught yourself being deceptive to others? How do you feel when you think others are deceiving you, even if it's to spare your feelings?

2 The Diversity of Deceptive Acts

We've seen that lying can't occur by accident. Whenever people attempt to deceive others, they therefore must have a reason. In the examples we have considered thus far, people practiced deception for a number of reasons. Communication research confirms that people have many motivations for lying. You may view some of those motivations to be reprehensible—for example, lying to hurt someone. You may find others to be acceptable under some circumstances—for example, lying to avoid hurting someone.[17]

Some Reasons Why People Deceive

Let's consider some of the most common reasons why people engage in deception, and look at a brief example of each. Can you think of any other motives to add to this list?[18]

- *Some lies benefit the hearer.* To make your friend feel good, you say you like her new haircut even though you don't because it doesn't match her overall style.[19]
- *Some lies help you get to know someone.* You invent an excuse to interact with someone just so that you can get to know the person.
- *Some lies protect your privacy.* Your co-worker asks how you are, and even though you're having problems at home, you say "fine" because you don't want to discuss your domestic situation with her.
- *Some lies help you avoid conflict.* Your romantic partner asks if you want to go with him to a party and you say that you do—even though you don't—to avoid a fight.
- *Some lies make you look better.* At your class reunion, you exaggerate facts about your education and income level to appear more successful than you are.[20]
- *Some lies help you avoid punishment.* You are stopped for speeding and tell the officer you didn't know what the speed limit was—when you actually did—hoping you won't get a ticket.
- *Some lies help you protect yourself from distress.* When your aunt invites you to Thanksgiving dinner, you make up a story about having other plans so that you don't have to listen to your uncle's inevitable criticisms of you.
- *Some lies help you get revenge on someone.* To get back at a former romantic partner for cheating on you, you spread false rumors about that person to his or her friends.
- *Some lies help you hurt someone for no reason.* Out of boredom one night, you make up a rumor about one of your classmates and begin posting it on various class listservs.
- *Some lies protect you or your livelihood.* Out of fear of social rejection or employment discrimination, you deny having a mental illness, even though you are currently being treated for one.
- *Some lies amuse you.* During a conversation with the person sitting next to you on a long flight, you tell her completely made-up stories about yourself.[21]

Whatever people's motives for lying, there are many ways to deceive beyond simply making up information that is entirely untrue. For instance, telling your dentist you have been flossing regularly when in fact you haven't is one way to lie, but there are others as well. In fact, deceptive acts fall into two categories: acts of simulation and acts of dissimulation. Let's take a closer look at each.

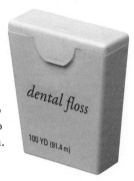

One of the many reasons people deceive is to make themselves look better in front of others. Are you ever less than honest with your dentist about how often you floss? If so, why?

Some Deceptive Acts Are Acts of Simulation

When people provide information that isn't true, they are engaging in **acts of simulation.** Making up an excuse to break a date, telling a potential employer that you have a master's degree when you don't, and telling a friend you like his new car when you really think it's quite unattractive are all acts of simulation. In each of those examples,

acts of simulation Forms of deception that involve fabricating information or exaggerating facts for the purpose of misleading others.

Job candidates sometimes exaggerate the details of their work history to appear more desirable to prospective employers. Research shows that exaggeration is a fairly common form of deception.

you're conveying a message you know isn't true for the purpose of getting your listener to believe it. People can engage in simulation through two different kinds of behaviors: falsification and exaggeration.

PEOPLE CAN LIE THROUGH FALSIFICATION. **Falsification** is outright lying—in other words, communicating false information as though it were true. Suppose, for example, that Ramón is applying for an apartment and he indicates on his application that he has rented before, when in fact he never has. In that case, Ramón has falsified his application; he has presented information that he knows to be false as though it were true. Similarly, if Sarah tells Annette that she is excited about the concert to which she is taking Annette for her birthday when she is actually dreading it, she is also falsifying. Even though Sarah has lied to benefit Annette—whereas Ramón has lied to benefit himself—they have both used falsification.

Studies have shown that falsification is one of the most common ways that people deceive others. In a diary study, for instance, communication scientist Sandra Metts found that people used falsification in almost half (48 percent) of their deception attempts.[22]

PEOPLE CAN LIE THROUGH EXAGGERATION. Another act of simulation is **exaggeration,** in which a person takes a fact that is true in principle and overstates it. Suppose, for example, you're interviewing for a job, and you exaggerate the level of responsibility you had at your last job to make it seem as though you're more qualified than you are. You may give completely true statements about what your responsibilities were, but you may overstate the level of those responsibilities to create a more favorable impression.[23] You might be tempted to think exaggeration isn't a form of deception. In fact, it does intentionally mislead others, so it is deceptive.

Some Deceptive Acts Are Acts of Dissimulation

When we engage in acts of simulation, we make statements or convey ideas that aren't true. In contrast, in **acts of dissimulation** we fail to convey information that, if known, would change the nature of our story. People can engage in dissimulation in two ways: through omission and through equivocation.

> **falsification** A form of deception that involves presenting false, fabricated information as though it were true.

> **exaggeration** A form of deception that involves inflating or overstating facts.

> **acts of dissimulation** Forms of deception that involve omitting certain details that would change the nature of the story if they were known.

PEOPLE CAN LIE THROUGH OMISSION.

Omission simply means leaving out particular details of a story to create a false impression. Suppose Lukas is a salesperson who is attempting to sell a used car to Martha, an elderly woman living on a fixed income. While going over the details of the sale, Lukas tells Martha that "this car has 11,425 miles on it, it comes with a one-year limited warranty, and your car payment will be $185." He then indicates where she should sign to accept the agreement. Martha signs and takes the car home, only to discover later that her car payment is $185 *every two weeks*. When Lukas said her payment would be $185, she assumed that meant per month. Martha quickly realized she could not afford to keep the car, and she felt angry with Lukas for deceiving her.

Strictly speaking, everything Lukas told Martha was true—the car payment was, in fact, $185. Therefore, was Lukas being deceptive? Absolutely, because in all likelihood he knew Martha would assume that he was quoting the amount of her monthly payment

Is it best to lie through omission to people if the truth would hurt them? That was the question facing Vince Vaughn's character in The Dilemma *(2011).*

and not her biweekly payment. Therefore, he knowingly created a false impression in Martha's mind, not by what he said but by what he did not say. Lukas may have told the truth, but he did not tell the *whole* truth, and the end effect was deceptive.

PEOPLE CAN LIE THROUGH EQUIVOCATION.

Equivocation means expressing information that is so vague or ambiguous that it creates the impression it has communicated a message it hasn't actually conveyed. Suppose Rena asks her waiter whether he thinks the pasta primavera is a good choice for dinner, and the waiter says, "It's one of our most popular dishes." Rena interprets that response to mean he thinks the pasta dish is a good choice. In fact, he never actually said that, did he?

Instead of answering Rena's question directly, her waiter gave an ambiguous response that he knew she would interpret as positive. That is an example of equivocation. Just like omission, equivocation deliberately creates a false impression, so it qualifies as a form of deception.

A brief review of the four primary forms of deception appears in the "At a Glance" box. Check out the "Got Skills?" box on the following page to practice your ability to identify those forms of deception in a conversation.

omission A form of deception that involves leaving consequential details out of one's story.

equivocation A form of deception that involves giving vague, ambiguous answers to a question to create the false impression that one has answered it.

AT A GLANCE

FORMS OF DECEPTION

Falsification	Passing off false or fabricated statements as though they were true
Exaggeration	Inflating or overstating information that is true in principle
Omission	Leaving out consequential pieces of information in one's story
Equivocation	Giving vague or ambiguous information to create a false impression

[IDENTIFYING DECEPTIVE FORMS]

Practice crafting each form of deceptive message.

WHAT?

Learn to generate the same deceptive message in multiple forms.

WHY?

To identify the differences and similarities among forms of deception.

HOW?

1. Review the four primary forms of deception (falsification, exaggeration, omission, and equivocation).

2. For each form of deception, write out a question and then an answer that reflects that form. Identify the specific information you are including and excluding to make each answer deceptive.

TRY!

1. Role-play a conversation with a classmate you don't know well, in which he or she asks you six to eight questions about your childhood.

2. Respond to each question deceptively, using one of the four forms of deception. Use each form of deception at least once.

3. After the conversation, ask your classmate to identify which form of deception was reflected in which answer, and correct any wrong responses. Repeat the process with you serving as questioner.

CONSIDER: *How accurately could each of you identify the forms of deception your partner used?*

Finding out that you've been lied to can be distressing. You may feel as though the offender has violated your trust and irreparably harmed your relationship. You may also feel angry at being lied to—and perhaps even embarrassed that you believed the lie. Those negative feelings are probably magnified when the deceiver is someone to whom you are emotionally close, such as a family member, a good friend, or a romantic partner.

The distress generated by discovering they have been lied to makes many people eager to learn how to detect deception in others. Can *you* tell when you're being lied to? What are the best behaviors to look for as clues to deception? What makes certain people better liars than others? Let's explore each of those key questions.

LEARN IT What are some common reasons why people deceive? How is exaggeration an act of simulation? What is the difference between omission and equivocation?

APPLY IT Revisit the list of reasons why people deceive that was presented at the beginning of this section. Select one reason, and then recall a situation when you used deception for that purpose. Write a short description of how you deceived the other person. Then write a description of how you may have served the same purpose *without* being deceptive.

REFLECT ON IT What motives for lying would you add to the list in this section? Whom do you most often notice exaggerating or equivocating?

3 Communication Behaviors and Deception

The Fox television series *Lie to Me* depicts a psychologist who assists government agencies and law enforcement officials in separating deception from truth. Although the psychologist on the show—Dr. Cal Lightman—is fictional, his character is based on the real-life psychologist Dr. Paul Ekman, whose research has identified many of the verbal and nonverbal communication behaviors that are common in deceptive acts. As dramatized in the show, detecting deception successfully requires knowing what clues to look and listen for.

How good are *you* at distinguishing truth from deception? Before you answer, consider the following experiment. I put two average students, Machiko and Jody, in separate rooms. I go into the first room and tell Machiko how I spent my summer vacation. Meanwhile, Jody is alone in another room, doing nothing. Afterward, we all come back together, and I ask both Machiko and Jody whether I'm lying about my summer vacation.

Machiko could hear everything I said, listen to my tone of voice, and watch my body language to evaluate the believability of my story. Jody, however, was in another room and has no idea what I have said. Who will be more accurate in determining whether I have lied? Machiko, right? After all, Jody has no clue as to what I said and might as well flip a coin—at least that would provide a 50 percent chance of being right.

The truth is that Machiko would be more accurate, but not by much. Whereas Jody had a 50 percent chance of being right just by flipping a coin, Machiko's chance of being right—even after being in the room, hearing my story, and watching my body language—is only 55 percent, *just slightly better than if Machiko hadn't been there at all*. Research has shown that under normal conditions, the average person can detect deception about 55 percent of the time.[24] Even police interrogators, psychiatrists,

On the television show Lie to Me, *Dr. Cal Lightman helps government and law enforcement officials separate deception from truth.*

One reason many of us aren't that good at detecting deception is that we want to believe that others are being honest with us. Unless we have a specific reason not to, we tend to believe most of what other people tell us.

truth bias The tendency to believe what someone says, in the absence of a reason not to.

customs officials, and polygraph examiners, whom you might expect to be good at detecting deception, typically do little better than the average person.[25]

Detecting Deception Is Difficult

Why don't we do any better than chance at detecting deception? One reason is that we often look for the wrong clues. How many times have you heard, for instance, that a lack of eye contact is the surest sign you're being lied to? In fact, that idea isn't true, as we'll see shortly. Obviously, the more attention we focus on the wrong clues to deception, the less we focus on the *right clues.* Paying attention to the wrong clues will keep us from being accurate much of the time.[26]

A second reason we're not very good lie detectors is that most of us want to believe most of what we hear. Unless we have a reason not to, we tend to believe what other people tell us. Researchers call that tendency the **truth bias.**[27] Why is the truth bias our default position? One reason is that we generally expect our communication with others to be pleasant, and being lied to can be very unpleasant.[28] Another reason is that it takes a great deal of mental energy to question everything we hear, so it's much easier for us to believe what we're told, unless we have a specific reason not to.[29]

Even though the average ability to detect deception is around 55 percent, we might do better if we know what to look for and what not to look for in people's behaviors. What are the clues that best indicate someone is lying?

Some Behaviors Are Common During Acts of Deception

For a long time, scientists in various disciplines tried to discover a foolproof method for detecting lies. So far, research has identified only a small number of behaviors that show any consistent relationship with deception, and none of them characterizes every lie or every liar.[30] Let's now take a look at some of the verbal and nonverbal behaviors that show reliable associations with lying, and identify some behaviors that do not.

FALSE INFORMATION IS OFTEN INCONSISTENT. One of the most straightforward clues to deception is inconsistency in the information presented. Let's say you call in sick to work on Friday so that you can leave town early for a weekend beach trip. While you're swimming on Saturday, however, your sunscreen washes off, and your boss sees you back at work on Monday with an obvious sunburn. That situation creates information inconsistency: The visual information provided by your appearance contradicts your story about being sick at home. Moreover, because it's hard to fake a sunburn, your boss correctly infers that you faked your illness.

Sometimes liars betray themselves with information inconsistency, and sometimes other people betray them. In fact, communication scholars Hee Sun Park, Timothy Levine, Steven McCornack, Kelly Morrison, and Merissa Ferrara have discovered that information provided by third parties is one of the most common ways people find out they've been lied to.[31] Referring to our previous example, suppose you didn't get sunburned, but your boss's daughter also happened to be at the beach and later innocently mentioned to her father that she had seen you. Clearly, she wasn't trying to get you into trouble. However, because her information was inconsistent with your story about being sick, the implication was that you did not tell the truth.

DECEIVERS OFTEN COMMIT SPEECH ERRORS.
When people are telling lies, they often make more speech errors than usual. Speech errors include behaviors such as taking excessively long pauses in the middle of a conversation (while thinking up a story), using numerous vocal fillers such as "um" and "uh," starting to speak but then stopping abruptly, and taking an extra long time to respond to people's questions.[32]

Why are deceivers more prone to making those errors? The answer is that people often feel guilty or nervous (or both) when they are lying, and those emotions can cause their speech patterns to become less fluent than normal.[33] The key is knowing how smooth and fluent a person's speech *usually* is, so that you can discern when that person is making more speech errors than he or she typically does.

DECEPTION OFTEN INCREASES VOCAL PITCH.
As discussed in Chapter 6, vocal pitch describes how high or low a person's voice is. Sometimes, such as when you wake up in the morning, your pitch is lower than normal and your voice sounds deeper than usual. When you feel nervous, excited, or agitated, the opposite occurs: Your pitch sounds higher than normal.[34]

Because people often become stressed or nervous when they're being deceptive, their pitch tends to rise.[35] Moreover, because they may not even be aware they are speaking in a higher pitch than normal, increased vocal pitch can be a particularly good clue to deception. A study by communication researchers Joyce Bauchner, Elyse Kaplan, and Gerald Miller found that vocal characteristics such as pitch are more reliable clues to deception than any other nonverbal behavior.[36]

TWO EYE BEHAVIORS ARE ASSOCIATED WITH LYING.
The "Fact or Fiction?" box explores how a lack of eye contact is a very poor clue that someone is lying. Much better indicators of deception are *eye blinking* and *pupil dilation* (or widening). If you are like the average person, you blink about 15 to 20 times per minute to keep a consistent layer of moisture on the surface of the eyes.[37] When you feel nervous or anxious, however—the way you might if you were lying to someone—you blink more often, as a way for your body to expend your nervous energy.[38] In addition, your pupils dilate when you get nervous or aroused.[39] Several studies have demonstrated that when people are telling lies, their pupils dilate more than usual.[40]

LIARS OFTEN USE FALSE SMILES.
On average, people don't smile any more or any less than normal when lying.[41] What tends to change, however, is the *type* of smile people use during deception. Specifically, deceivers are more likely than truth tellers to use a *false smile,* the kind of smile people wear when they want to look happier than they really are.[42] One of the distinctive features of genuine smiles is that they cause

Expressive People Are Better Liars

You probably know people who are very expressive; they tend to be outgoing, uninhibited, and very demonstrative of their emotions. According to several studies, expressive people are more successful at deception than unexpressive people, for at least two reasons.[50] First, expressive people tend to be more aware and in better control of their own communication behaviors than unexpressive people. Therefore, the conversational style they adopt when they are lying may appear to be more fluent and normal.[51]

Second, expressive communicators tend to be more aware of other people's behaviors, so they may be more skilled at anticipating a hearer's suspicion and correcting their behavior to allay those suspicions.[52] That doesn't necessarily mean that expressive people lie more often than unexpressive people.[53] But it does mean that they tend to be better at it when they do lie.

Culture Matters, but Only Sometimes

We've seen that the average person detects deception only about 55 percent of the time. Most studies of detection ability, however, have involved speakers and listeners who share the same cultural background. What if you're listening to someone whose culture is different from yours? Would that difference make it harder to detect deception?

When we can both see and hear a speaker, that speaker's culture makes little difference in our ability to detect deception.

Common sense suggests so, because you may not be familiar with another culture's communication practices. If you're not familiar with the way a person behaves when communicating under normal circumstances, then how can you identify changes in those behaviors when the person is lying? In line with that assumption, an early research study concluded that people are in fact much more accurate at detecting deception *within* cultures than *between* cultures.[54]

In that study, however, participants were required to judge deception solely on the basis of *visual* cues. They watched videos of two people in a conversation but were unable to hear what those people were saying. As a result, they were unable to detect information inconsistency or listen for vocal cues. Rather, they had to base their judgments entirely on the behaviors they could *see.*

The researchers later repeated the study, but this time they allowed the participants to *hear* what the speakers were saying. When they did so, they discovered that the participants were equally able to detect deception by speakers of their own culture and speakers of other cultures.[55] We can likely conclude from those results that cultural differences can affect our ability to detect deception, but only when we have limited access to what the speaker is saying. In normal face-to-face conversation, culture appears to matter less.

Motivation Doesn't Always Help

motivation impairment effect A hypothesis that motivation to succeed in a lie will impair a deceiver's verbal performance, making the lie less likely to be believed.

Suppose you felt that you had to lie but the consequences of getting caught were severe, such as being expelled from school or going to jail. You'd probably be highly motivated to lie successfully—but would that help or hurt you? We often perform better when we're highly motivated. According to social psychologist Bella DePaulo, however, that observation doesn't apply to lying. Her hypothesis, called the **motivation impairment effect,** maintains that when people are engaged in high-stakes lies, their motivation to succeed will backfire by making their nonverbal performance *less* believable than normal.[56]

Why does that happen? The answer is that when the consequences of getting caught in a lie are severe, we experience a great deal of nervous energy, which we have to control if we are to succeed in being deceptive. The harder we try to control our nervous energy, however, the more rigid, insincere, and unnatural we can end up looking and sounding. Put simply, when people tell high-stakes lies, their motivation to succeed ultimately will impair their success.[57] In contrast, because low-stakes lies don't produce the same degree of nervous arousal, DePaulo's theory does not predict that motivation to succeed will backfire when people attempt a low-stakes lie.

Suspicion May Not Improve Detection Ability

When we feel suspicious about what someone is telling us, we tend to scrutinize that person's behavior and message more than usual. Therefore, it seems logical to assume we are better able to detect deception when we're suspicious than when we aren't. That doesn't seem to be the case, however. Research tells us that even though suspicion causes people to think they're being lied to, it doesn't always make them any better at spotting deception.[58] In fact, some studies have shown that suspicion can actually make people *worse* at detecting lies, not better.[59]

One reason why suspicion might impair our detection ability is suggested by *interpersonal deception theory,* proposed by scholars David Buller and Judee Burgoon.[60] Interpersonal deception theory argues that skilled liars can detect when people are suspicious and then adapt their behavior to appear more honest.

Suppose, for instance, that Eliah's new doctor asks him how often he exercises. To make a good impression, Eliah exaggerates, saying he swims at least four times a week. He can immediately tell that his doctor is suspicious of his answer, so he adapts his behavior to make himself appear honest. He makes certain he is speaking with a normal vocal pitch and without committing excessive speech errors. He avoids nervous laughter, false smiles, and excessive blinking. He makes sure that he is moving and gesturing normally. Because he notices his doctor's suspicion, that is, he can make certain that he is communicating in ways that signal honesty rather than deception. As a result, his doctor eventually believes Eliah, even though he is being dishonest.

Another reason why suspicion can reduce our ability to detect deception is what researchers call the *Othello error.* That error occurs when a listener's suspicion makes a truthful speaker appear to be lying even though she or he isn't. Let's say Maggie is explaining to a school nurse that her 6-year-old son bruised the side of his face by falling off his bed. Because the nurse sees physically abused children frequently, she has suspicions about the truthfulness of Maggie's account. Maggie senses the nurse's suspicions and gets nervous and flustered. She begins to fidget, makes speech errors, and uses false smiles. Noticing those behaviors, the nurse concludes that Maggie is lying. Maggie, however, is being completely truthful. She looks and sounds deceptive only because the nurse's obvious suspicion has made her nervous. In that instance, the nurse has been inaccurate in detecting deception—not by believing a lie but by failing to believe the truth.[61]

Noninteractive Contexts Are Best for Detection

Suppose Stan's regional manager directed him to file a report about the company's quarterly earnings with the state auditor's office. He told Stan that the report wasn't due for six weeks but that it needed to be filed by the deadline or the company would

The motivation impairment effect explains that when people attempt high-stakes lies, their motivation to succeed can backfire, causing them to behave nervously and therefore to appear dishonest.

incur financial penalties. With so much time before the deadline, Stan kept putting the assignment aside, focusing on more pressing projects. By the time he remembered it, it was three days overdue.

Fearing that his negligence might cost him his job, Stan chooses to lie to his manager about why the report was late. He has several options for how to deliver his lie: He could do it in person, over the telephone, by leaving a voice mail message, or by sending an e-mail. Which option gives him the best chance for success? On the one hand, we might say that an **interactive context,** such as a face-to-face or telephone conversation, helps Stan the most, because he can watch and listen for signs of suspicion from his manager and then adapt his behavior accordingly. On the other hand, a **noninteractive context,** such as voice mail or e-mail, may be best because it gives Stan the most control over his message.

Communication researchers have found that lies are more likely to succeed in an interactive context than in a noninteractive one—but only when the speaker is lying to a *stranger*.[62] Apparently, interacting directly with speakers makes people more likely to believe what those speakers are saying. One possible explanation for that finding is that interactivity helps create a sense of connection with someone else that is lacking in noninteractive contexts. In addition, when people are engaged in conversations, they pay more attention to their own communication behaviors than to the behaviors of others. Consequently, listeners might be less likely to notice any signs of deception displayed by the speaker.[63]

If, however, the speaker and the hearer are already friends, then the interactivity of the context doesn't seem to matter. In those cases, lies are equally successful in interactive and noninteractive contexts. Perhaps if friends already feel an emotional connection with each other, then communicating in interactive contexts no longer provides an advantage.

interactive context
A context for communicating in which participants can see and/or hear each other and react to each other in real time (for example, face-to-face conversation, telephone conversation).

noninteractive context
A context for communicating in which the participants cannot react to each other in real time (for example, a voice mail message, an e-mail message).

When people communicate with strangers, they are less likely to be caught lying if they're talking face-to-face than if they're exchanging e-mail messages. Interactivity heightens our truth bias, but only with strangers. With friends, the mode of communication doesn't affect the ability to detect lying.

Familiarity, expressiveness, culture, motivation, suspicion, and interactivity certainly aren't the only characteristics that influence our detection skills. Yet each of those factors can play an important role in our ability to detect deception successfully.

Although deception is relatively common in interpersonal communication, it can sometimes cause great distress. When deception is discovered in a personal relationship, it can lead to conflict and to feelings of anger and betrayal. We often find it difficult to forgive people who have lied to us, let alone to trust them again.

In this chapter, you've been introduced to many skills for detecting interpersonal deception, and previous chapters have introduced you to skills for managing conflict and maintaining your interpersonal relationships. Armed with those skills, you may find it easier to respond to the emotional distress of deception and to repair the emotional damage it can cause.

MASTER the chapter

1 The Nature of Interpersonal Deception (p. 382)

- Deception occurs when a speaker knowingly and intentionally transmits false information to create a false belief in the hearer.

- Deceptive acts have three basic elements: the speaker knows the information is false, the speaker transmits the information on purpose, and the speaker tries to make the hearer believe that the information is true.

- Deception is especially common in the service of politeness and in computer-mediated communication.

2 The Diversity of Deceptive Acts (p. 388)

- People have several motives for lying, some of which are benevolent, some of which are malicious, and some of which are benign.

- Some deceptive acts are acts of simulation; these include falsification and exaggeration.

- Some deceptive acts are acts of dissimulation; these include omission and equivocation.

3 Communication Behaviors and Deception (p. 393)

- Detecting deception is often very difficult, partly because people often have a truth bias.

- Behaviors common during deceptive attempts include information inconsistency, speech errors, increased blinking, pupil dilation, false smiles, increased vocal pitch, and decreased body movement.

4 Detecting Lies in Different Contexts (p. 398)

- People are more accurate at detecting deception from strangers than from friends, on average.

- Expressive people are often more successful at lying than are unexpressive people.

- Cultural differences appear to matter only when the hearer has limited access to what the speaker is saying.

- Motivation to succeed at lying doesn't always help, and in the case of high-stakes deception it can actually impair an individual's ability to succeed.

- Suspicion does not necessarily improve a person's deception-detection ability.

- Deception detection is higher in noninteractive contexts than in interactive contexts, but only for strangers.

Glossary

A

accommodating A strategy for managing conflict that involves giving in to the other party's needs and desires while subordinating one's own.

action tendencies Biologically based motives toward specific behavioral responses to emotions.

acts of dissimulation Forms of deception that involve omitting certain details that would change the nature of the story if they were known.

acts of simulation Forms of deception that involve fabricating information or exaggerating facts for the purpose of misleading others.

adaptor A gesture used to satisfy a personal need.

affect display A gesture that communicates emotion.

ambiguous language Language having more than one possible meaning.

amygdala A cluster of neurons in the brain that largely controls the body's fear response.

androgyny A gender role distinguished by a combination of masculine and feminine characteristics.

anger An emotional response to being wronged.

approach behaviors Communication behaviors that signal one's interest in getting to know someone.

artifact An object or a visual feature of an environment with communicative value.

asexuality A sexual orientation characterized by a general lack of interest in sex.

attribution An explanation for an observed behavior.

autonomy face The need to avoid being imposed upon by others.

avoidance behaviors Communication behaviors that signal one's lack of interest in getting to know someone.

avoiding A strategy for managing conflict that involves ignoring or failing to deal with the conflict.

avoiding stage The stage of relationship dissolution when partners create physical and emotional distance between themselves.

B

bisexuality A sexual orientation characterized by sexual interest in both women and men.

bonding stage The stage of relationship development when the partners publicly announce their commitment.

breadth The range of topics about which one person self-discloses to another.

C

channel A pathway through which messages are conveyed.

channel-lean context A communication context involving few channels at once.

channel-rich context A communication context involving many channels at once.

chronemics The use of time.

circumscribing stage The stage of relationship dissolution characterized by decreased quality and quantity of communication between partners.

closed-mindedness The tendency not to listen to anything with which one disagrees.

co-cultures Groups of people who share values, customs, and norms related to mutual interests or characteristics beyond their national citizenship.

coercive power Power based on the ability to punish.

cognitive complexity The ability to understand a given situation in multiple ways.

collaborating A strategy for managing conflict that involves working toward a solution that meets both parties' needs.

collectivistic culture A culture that places greater emphasis on loyalty to the family, workplace, or community than on the needs of the individual.

commitment A desire to stay in a relationship.

communication climate The emotional tone of a relationship.

communication codes Verbal and nonverbal behaviors, such as idioms and gestures, that characterize a culture and distinguish it from other cultures.

communication competence Communicating in ways that are effective and appropriate for a given situation.

communication privacy management (CPM) theory Theory that explains how people manage the tension between privacy and disclosure.

comparison level A person's realistic expectation of what the person wants and thinks he or she deserves from a relationship.

comparison level for alternatives A person's assessment of how good his or her current relationship is, compared with other options.

competence face The need to be respected and viewed as competent and intelligent.

competing A strategy for managing conflict in which one's goal is to win while the other party loses.

competitive interrupting Using interruptions to take control of a conversation.

complementary relationship A relationship between parties of unequal power.

compromising A strategy for managing conflict in which both parties give up something they want so that both can receive something they want.

confirmation bias The tendency to pay attention only to information that supports one's values and beliefs while discounting or ignoring information that doesn't.

confirming messages Behaviors that indicate how much we value another person.

connotative meaning A word's implied or secondary meaning, in addition to its literal meaning.

contempt A feeling of superiority over, and disrespect for, others; the expression of insults and attacks on another's self-worth.

content dimension Literal information that is communicated by a message.

context The physical or psychological environment in which communication occurs.

credibility The extent to which others find someone's words and actions trustworthy.

critical listening Listening with the goal of evaluating or analyzing what one hears.

criticism The expression of complaints about another party.

culture The system of learned and shared symbols, language, values, and norms that distinguish one group of people from another.

D

deception The knowing and intentional transmission of information to create a false belief in the hearer.

decode To interpret or give meaning to a message.

defamation Language that harms a person's reputation or image.

defensiveness Excessive concern with guarding oneself against the threat of criticism; the tendency to deny the validity of criticisms directed at the self.

demand–withdraw pattern A pattern of behavior in which one party makes demands and the other party withdraws from the conversation.

denotative meaning A word's literal meaning or dictionary definition.

depression A physical illness involving excessive fatigue, insomnia, changes in weight, feelings of worthlessness, and/or thoughts of suicide or death.

depth The intimacy of the topics about which one person self-discloses to another.

dialectical tensions Conflicts between two important but opposing needs or desires.

differentiating stage The stage of relationship dissolution when partners begin to see their differences as undesirable or annoying.

disconfirming messages Behaviors that imply a lack of regard for another person.

disgust A feeling of revulsion in reaction to something offensive.

disinhibition effect The tendency to say or do things in one environment (such as online) that one would not say or do in most other environments.

display rules Unwritten codes that govern the ways people manage and express emotions.

divorce The legal discontinuation of a marriage.

dyad A pair of people.

E

egocentric Unable to take another person's perspective.

emblem A gesture with a direct verbal translation.

emoticons Textual representations of facial expressions.

emotion The body's multidimensional response to any event that enhances or inhibits one's goals.

emotional contagion The tendency to mimic the emotional experiences and expressions of others.

emotional intelligence The ability to perceive and understand emotions, use emotions to facilitate thought, and manage emotions constructively.

emotional reappraisal The process of changing how one thinks about the situation that gave rise to a negative emotion so that the effect of the emotion is diminished.

empathic listening Listening in order to experience what another person is thinking or feeling.

empathy The ability to think and feel as others do.

encode To put an idea into language or gesture.

envy The desire for something another person has.

equity theory A theory predicting that a good relationship is one in which a person's ratio of costs and rewards is equal to that of the person's partner.

equivocation A form of deception that involves giving vague, ambiguous answers to a question to create the false impression that one has answered it.

ethics A code of morality or a set of ideas about what is right.

ethnicity An individual's perception of his or her ancestry or heritage.

ethnocentrism Systematic preference for characteristics of one's own culture.

ethos A speaker's respectability, trustworthiness, and moral character.

euphemism A vague, mild expression that symbolizes something more blunt or harsh.

evaluative feedback A reply that offers an assessment of what the speaker has said or done.

exaggeration A form of deception that involves inflating or overstating facts.

experimenting stage The stage of relationship development when individuals have conversations to learn more about each other.

expert power Power that derives from one's expertise, talent, training, specialized knowledge, or experience.

explicit rule A rule about behavior that has been clearly articulated.

expressive talk Verbal communication whose purpose is to express emotions and build relationships.

F

face A person's desired public image.

face needs Components of one's desired public image.

face-threatening act Any behavior that threatens one or more face needs.

facework The behaviors one uses to project one's desired public image to others.

facial display The use of facial expression for communication.

falsification A form of deception that involves presenting false, fabricated information as though it were true.

family of origin The family in which one grows up (often consisting of one's parents and siblings).

family of procreation The family one starts as an adult (often consisting of one's spouse and children).

fear The mind and body's reaction to perceived danger.

feedback Verbal and nonverbal responses to a message.

fellowship face The need to feel liked and accepted by others.

femininity A gender role, typically assigned to women, that emphasizes expressive, nurturing behavior.

fundamental attribution error The tendency to attribute others' behaviors to internal rather than external causes.

G

gender role A set of expectations for appropriate behavior that a culture typically assigns to an individual based on his or her biological sex.

gesticulation The use of arm and hand movements to communicate.

glazing over Daydreaming during the time not spent listening.

gossip The sharing of an individual's personal information with a third party without the individual's consent.

grief The emotional process of dealing with profound loss.

H

halo effect The tendency to attribute positive qualities to physically attractive people.

happiness A state of contentment, joy, pleasure, and cheer.

haptics The study of how people use touch to communicate.

hate speech A form of profanity meant to degrade, intimidate, or dehumanize groups of people.

heterosexuality A sexual orientation characterized by sexual interest in members of the other sex.

high-contact culture A culture in which people touch frequently and maintain little personal distance with one another.

high-context culture A culture in which verbal communication is often ambiguous, and meaning is drawn from contextual cues, such as facial expressions and tone of voice.

high-power-distance culture A culture in which much or most of the power is concentrated in a few people, such as royalty or a ruling political party.

homosexuality A sexual orientation characterized by sexual interest in members of one's own sex.

HURIER model A model of effective listening that involves hearing, understanding, remembering, interpreting, evaluating, and responding.

I

identity See *self-concept.*

illustrator A gesture that enhances or clarifies a verbal message.

image The way one wishes to be seen or perceived by others.

image management The process of projecting one's desired public image.

immediacy behavior Nonverbal behavior that conveys attraction or affiliation.

implicit rule A rule about behavior that has not been clearly articulated but is nonetheless understood.

individualistic culture A culture that emphasizes individuality and responsibility to oneself.

infidelity Having romantic or sexual interaction with someone outside of one's romantic relationship.

information overload The state of being overwhelmed by the amount of information one takes in.

informational listening Listening to learn something.

in-group A group of people with whom one identifies.

initiating stage The stage of relationship development when people meet and interact for the first time.

instrumental needs Practical, everyday needs.

instrumental talk Verbal communication whose purpose is to solve problems and accomplish tasks.

integrating stage The stage of relationship development when a deep commitment has formed, and there is a strong sense that the relationship has its own identity.

intensifying stage The stage of relationship development when individuals move from being acquaintances to being close friends.

interactive context A context for communicating in which participants can see and/or hear each other and react to each other in real time (for example, face-to-face conversation, telephone conversation).

interdependence A state in which each person's behaviors affect everyone else in the relationship.

interpersonal attraction Any force that draws people together to form a relationship.

interpersonal communication Communication that occurs between two people within the context of their relationship and that, as it evolves, helps them to negotiate and define their relationship.

interpersonal conflict An expressed struggle between interdependent parties who perceive incompatible goals, scarce resources, and interference from one another.

interpersonal perception The process of making meaning from the people in our environment and our relationships with them.

interpretation The process of assigning meaning to information that has been selected for attention and organized.

intimacy Significant emotional closeness experienced in a relationship.

intimate distance The distance most people in Western cultures maintain with intimate partners; ranges from 0 to 1½ feet.

intrapersonal communication Communication with oneself.

investment The resources we put into our relationships.

I-statement A statement that claims ownership of one's thoughts or feelings.

J

jealousy The perception that the existence or the quality of an important relationship is being threatened by a third party.

Johari window A visual representation of components of the self

that are known or unknown to the self and to others.

K

kinesics The study of movement.

L

language A structured system of symbols used for communicating meaning.

legitimate power Power based on one's legitimate status or position.

libel A defamatory statement made in print or in some other fixed medium.

liking A positive overall evaluation of another person.

listening The active process of making meaning out of another person's spoken message.

loaded language Terms that carry strongly positive or strongly negative connotations.

logos Listeners' ability to reason.

love The emotion of caring for, feeling attached to, and feeling deeply committed to someone.

low-contact culture A culture in which people touch infrequently and maintain relatively high levels of personal distance with one another.

low-context culture A culture in which verbal communication is expected to be explicit and is often interpreted literally.

low-power-distance culture A culture in which power is not highly concentrated in specific groups of people.

M

masculinity A gender role, typically assigned to men, that emphasizes strength, dominance, competition, and logical thinking.

mass communication Communication from one source to a large audience.

message Verbal and nonverbal elements of communication to which people give meaning.

metacommunication Communication about communication.

metaconflict Conflict about conflict.

meta-emotion An emotion about emotion.

model A formal description of a process.

monochronic A concept that treats time as a finite commodity that can be earned, saved, spent, and wasted.

monogamy Being in only one romantic relationship at a time and avoiding romantic or sexual involvement with others outside the relationship.

mood A feeling, often prolonged, that has no identifiable cause.

motivation impairment effect A hypothesis that motivation to succeed in a lie will impair a deceiver's verbal performance, making the lie less likely to be believed.

N

nationality An individual's status as a citizen of a particular country.

need for affection One's need to give and receive expressions of love and appreciation.

need for control One's need to maintain a degree of influence in one's relationships.

need for inclusion One's need to belong to a social group and be included in the activities of others.

need to belong A hypothesis that says each of us is born with a fundamental drive to seek, form, maintain, and protect strong social relationships.

negativity bias The tendency to focus heavily on a person's negative attributes when forming a perception.

noise Anything that interferes with the encoding or decoding of a message.

non-evaluative feedback A reply that withholds assessment of what the speaker has said or done.

noninteractive context A context for communicating in which the participants cannot react to each other in real time (for example, a voice mail message, an e-mail message).

nonverbal channels The various behavioral forms that nonverbal communication takes.

nonverbal communication Behaviors and characteristics that convey meaning without the use of words.

norm of reciprocity A social expectation that resources and favors provided to one person in

a relationship should be reciprocated by that person.

O

oculesics The study of eye behavior.

olfactics The study of the sense of smell.

omission A form of deception that involves leaving consequential details out of one's story.

one-across message A verbal message that seeks to neutralize relational control and power.

one-down message A verbal message that reflects acceptance of, or submission to, another person's power.

one-up message A verbal message through which the speaker attempts to exert dominance or gain control over the listener.

onomatopoeia A word formed by imitating the sound associated with its meaning.

organization The process of categorizing information that has been selected for attention.

out-group A group of people with whom one does not identify.

overattribution The tendency to attribute a range of behaviors to a single characteristic of a person.

over-benefited The state in which one's relational rewards exceed one's relational costs.

P

paralanguage Vocalic behaviors that go along with verbal behavior to convey meaning.

passion A secondary emotion consisting of joy and surprise, plus experiences of excitement and attraction for another.

passive aggression A pattern of behaving vengefully while denying that one has aggressive feelings.

pathos Listeners' emotions.

peer Someone of similar power or status.

perception The process of making meaning from the things we experience in the environment.

perceptual set A predisposition to perceive only what we want or expect to perceive.

personal distance The distance most people in Western cultures maintain with friends and relatives; ranges from 1½ to 4 feet.

personality The pattern of behaviors and ways of thinking that characterize a person.

physical attraction Attraction to someone's physical appearance.

polychronic A concept that treats time as an infinite resource rather than a finite commodity.

polygamy A practice in which one person is married to two or more spouses at once.

positivity bias The tendency to focus heavily on a person's positive attributes when forming a perception.

power The ability to manipulate, influence, or control other people or events.

predicted outcome value theory A theory predicting that we form relationships when we think the effort will be worth it.

primacy effect The tendency to emphasize the first impression over later impressions when forming a perception.

primary emotions Distinct emotional experiences not consisting of combinations of other emotions.

profanity A form of language considered vulgar, rude, or obscene in the context in which it is used.

proportionality The size of facial features relative to one another.

proxemics The study of spatial use.

pseudolistening Using feedback behaviors to give the false impression that one is listening.

public distance The distance most people in Western cultures maintain with public figures during a performance; ranges from 12 to 25 feet or more.

R

reason To make judgments about the world based on evidence rather than emotion or intuition.

rebuttal tendency The tendency to debate a speaker's point and formulate a reply while the person is still speaking.

receiver The party who interprets a message.

recency effect The tendency to emphasize the most recent impression over earlier impressions when forming a perception.

reference groups The groups of people with whom one compares oneself in the process of social comparison.

referent power Power that derives from one's attraction to or admiration for another.

reflected appraisal The process whereby a person's self-concept is influenced by his or her beliefs concerning what other people think of the person.

regulator A gesture that controls the flow of conversation.

relational dimension Signals about the relationship in which a message is being communicated.

relational maintenance behaviors Behaviors used to maintain and strengthen personal relationships.

reward power Power that derives from the ability to reward.

rituals Repetitive behaviors that have special meaning for a group or relationship.

S

sadness Emotion involving feeling unhappy, sorrowful, and discouraged, usually as a result of some form of loss.

Sapir-Whorf hypothesis The idea that language influences the ways that members of a culture see and think about the world.

secondary emotions Emotions composed of combinations of primary emotions.

selection The process of attending to a stimulus.

selective attention Listening only to what one wants to hear.

self-concept The set of stable ideas a person has about who he or she is; also known as *identity*.

self-disclosure The act of giving others information about oneself that one believes they do not already have.

self-esteem One's subjective evaluation of one's value and worth as a person.

self-fulfilling prophecy An expectation that gives rise to behav-

iors that cause the expectation to come true.

self-monitoring Awareness of one's behavior and how it affects others.

self-serving bias The tendency to attribute one's successes to internal causes and one's failures to external causes.

sexual orientation A characteristic determining the sex or sexes to which someone is sexually attracted.

skepticism The practice of evaluating the evidence for a claim.

slander A defamatory statement made aloud.

slang Informal, unconventional words that are often understood only by others in a particular subculture.

small group communication Communication occurring within small groups of three or more people.

social anxiety Fear of not making a good impression on others.

social attraction Attraction to someone's personality.

social comparison The process of comparing oneself with others.

social distance The distance most people in Western cultures maintain with casual acquaintances; ranges from 4 to 12 feet.

social exchange theory A theory predicting that people seek to form and maintain relationships in which the benefits outweigh the costs.

social penetration theory A theory that predicts that as relationships develop, communication increases in breadth and depth.

society A group of people who share symbols, language, values, and norms.

source The originator of a thought or an idea.

stagnating stage The stage of relationship dissolution when the relationship stops growing and the partners are barely communicating with each other.

stereotypes Generalizations about groups of people that are applied to individual members of those groups.

stigma A characteristic that discredits a person, making him

or her be seen as abnormal or undesirable.

stonewalling Withdrawing from a conversation or an interaction.

supportiveness A person's feeling of assurance that others care about and will protect him or her.

symbol A representation of an idea.

symmetrical relationship A relationship between parties of equal power.

symmetry The similarity between the left and right sides of the face or body.

T

task attraction Attraction to someone's abilities and dependability.

terminating stage The stage of relationship dissolution when the relationship is deemed to be officially over.

truth bias The tendency to believe what someone says, in the absence of a reason not to.

turn-taking signal Nonverbal behavior that indicates when a person's speaking turn begins and ends.

U

uncertainty avoidance The degree to which people try to avoid situations that are unstructured, unclear, or unpredictable.

uncertainty reduction theory A theory suggesting that people are motivated to reduce their uncertainty about others.

under-benefited The state in which one's relational costs exceed one's relational rewards.

V

valence The positivity or negativity of an emotion.

vividness effect The tendency for dramatic, shocking events to distort one's perception of reality.

vocalics Characteristics of the voice.

Y

you-statement A statement that shifts responsibility for one's own thoughts or feelings to the listener.

Endnotes

Chapter 1

1. Andersen, H. S., Sestoft, D., Lillebæk, T., Gabrielsen, G., Hemmingsen, R., & Kramp, P. (2000). A longitudinal study of prisoners on remand: Psychiatric prevalence, incidence, and psychopathology in solitary vs. non-solitary confinement. *Acta Psychiatrica Scandinavica, 102,* 19–25.
2. See, e.g., Ray, E. B. (Ed.). (2005). *Health communication in practice: A case study approach.* Mahwah, NJ: Lawrence Erlbaum Associates.
3. Perry, B. D. (2002). Childhood experience and the expression of genetic potential: What childhood neglect tells us about nature and nurture. *Brain and Mind, 3,* 79–100.
4. Field, T. (2001). *Touch.* Cambridge, MA: MIT Press.
5. Holt-Lunstad, J., Smith, T. B., & Layton, J. B. (2010). Social relationships and mortality risk: A meta-analytic review. *PLoS Med, 7*(7), e1000316. doi: 10.1371/journal.pmed.1000316
6. Kiecolt-Glaser, J. K., Loving, T. J., Stowell, J. R., Malarkey, W. B., Lemeshow, S., Dickinson, S. L., & Glaser, R. (2005). Hostile marital interactions, proinflammatory cytokine production, & wound healing. *Archives of General Psychiatry, 62,* 1377–1384; Cohen, S., Doyle, W. J., Skoner, D. P., Rabin, B. S., & Gwaltney, J. M. (1997). Social ties and susceptibility to the common cold. *Journal of the American Medical Association, 277,* 1940–1944.
7. Segrin, C., & Passalacqua, S. A. (2010). Functions of loneliness, social support, health behaviors, and stress in association with poor health. *Health Communication, 25,* 312–322.
8. Link, B. G., & Phelan, J. C. (2001). Conceptualizing stigma. *Annual Review of Sociology, 27,* 363–385.
9. Parker, R., & Aggleton, P. (2003). HIV and AIDS-related stigma and discrimination: A conceptual framework and implications for action. *Social Science & Medicine, 57,* 13–24.
10. Barbato, C. A., Graham, E. E., & Perse, E. M. (2003). Communicating in the family: An examination of the relationship of family communication climate and interpersonal communication motives. *Journal of Family Communication, 3,* 123–148.
11. Baxter, L. A. (2004). Relationships as dialogues. *Personal Relationships, 11,* 1–22.
12. Chan, D. K–S., & Cheng, G. H–L. (2004). A comparison of offline and online friendship qualities at different stages of relationship development. *Journal of Social and Personal Relationships, 21,* 305–320.
13. See, e.g., Usita, P. M., & Blieszner, R. (2002). Immigrant family strengths: Meeting communication challenges. *Journal of Family Issues, 23,* 266–286.
14. Pickett, C. L., Gardner, W. L., & Knowles, M. (2004). Getting a clue: The need to belong and enhanced sensitivity to social cues. *Personality and Social Psychology Bulletin, 30,* 1096–1107.
15. Diener, E., & Seligman, M. E. P. (2002). Very happy people. *Psychological Science, 13,* 81–84.
16. Mehl, M. R., Vazire, S., Holleran, S. E., & Clark, C. S. (2010). Eavesdropping on happiness: Well-being is related to having less small talk and more substantive conversations. *Psychological Science, 21,* 539–541.
17. Popenoe, D. (2007). *The state of our unions: The social health of marriage in America.* Piscataway, NJ: National Marriage Project; see also Glenn, N. D., & Weaver, C. N. (1981). The contribution of marital happiness to global happiness. *Journal of Marriage and the Family, 43,* 161–168.
18. Mead, D. E. (2002). Marital distress, co-occurring depression, and marital therapy: A review. *Journal of Marital & Family Therapy, 28,* 299–314.
19. Yeung, K–T., & Martin, J. L. (2003). The looking glass self: An empirical test and elaboration. *Social Forces, 81,* 843–879.
20. Astin, A. W., Astin, H. S., & Lindholm, J. A. (2010). *Cultivating the spirit: How college can enhance students' inner lives.* San Francisco: Jossey-Bass.
21. Koltko-Rivera, M. E. (2006). Rediscovering the later version of Maslow's hierarchy of needs: Self-transcendence and opportunities for theory, research, and unification. *Review of General Psychology, 10,* 302–317.
22. Johnson, A. M., & Lederer, A. L. (2005). The effect of communication frequency and channel richness on the convergence between chief executive and chief information officers. *Journal of Management Information Systems, 22,* 227–252.
23. Walther, J. B., & Parks, M. R. (2002). Cues filtered out, cues filtered in: Computer-mediated communication and relationships. In M. L. Knapp & J. A. Daly (Eds.), *Handbook of interpersonal communication* (3rd ed., pp. 529–563). Thousand Oaks, CA: Sage.
24. Allwood, J. (2002). Bodily communication dimensions of expression and content. In B. Granström, D. House, & I. Karlsson (Eds.), *Multimodality in language and speech systems* (pp. 7–26). Dordrecht, The Netherlands: Kluwer Academic.
25. Motley, M. T. (1990). On whether one can(not) communicate: An examination via traditional communication postulates. *Western Journal of Speech Communication, 54,* 1–20.
26. This position is usually attributed to Watzlawick, T., Beavin, J., & Jackson, D. (1967). *The pragmatics of human communication.* New York: Norton.
27. See Motley, 1990.
28. Buck, R., & Van Lear, C. A. (2002). Verbal and nonverbal communication: Distinguishing symbolic, spontaneous and pseudo-spontaneous nonverbal behavior. *Journal of Communication, 52,* 522–541.
29. Kramer, M. W., & Hess, J. A. (2002). Communication rules for the display of emotions in organizational settings. *Management Communication Quarterly, 16,* 66–80.
30. National Communication Association. (1999). *How Americans communicate* [online]. Retrieved April 16, 2006, from http://www.natcom.org/research/Roper/how_americans_communicate.htm
31. Huston, T. L., & Melz, H. (2004). The case for (promoting) marriage: The devil is in the details. *Journal of Marriage and Family, 66,* 943–958.
32. For a classic text, see Katriel, T., & Philipsen, G. (1981). "What we need is communication": "Communication" as a cultural category in some American speech. *Communication Monographs, 48,* 300–317.

and similarities in communication (2nd ed., pp. 3–20). Mahwah, NJ: Lawrence Erlbaum Associates.

68. Canary, D. J., & Hause, K. S. (1993). Is there any reason to research sex differences in communication? *Communication Quarterly, 41,* 129–144; Wright, P. H. (1988). Interpreting gender differences in friendship: A case for moderation and a plea for caution. *Journal of Social and Personal Relationships, 5,* 367–373.

69. Wood, J. T., & Inman, C. C. (1993). In a different mode: Masculine styles of communicating closeness. *Journal of Applied Communication Research, 21,* 279–295.

70. See Wood, J. T. (1998). *But I thought you meant . . . : Misunderstandings in human communication.* Mountain View, CA: Mayfield.

71. Wood, J. T. (2007). *Gendered lives: Communication, gender, and culture* (7th ed.). Belmont, CA: Wadsworth.

72. Neppl, T. K., & Murray, A. D. (1997). Social dominance and play patterns among preschoolers: Gender comparisons. *Sex Roles, 36,* 381–393.

73. See, e.g., Clark, R. A. (1998). A comparison of topics and objectives in a cross section of young men's and women's everyday conversations. In D. J. Canary & K. Dindia (Eds.), *Sex differences and similarities in communication: Critical essays and empirical investigations of sex and gender interaction* (pp. 303–319). Mahwah, NJ: Lawrence Erlbaum Associates; Martin, C., Fabes, R., Evans, S., & Wyman, H. (2000). Social cognition on the playground: Children's beliefs about playing with girls versus boys and their relations to sex segregated play. *Journal of Social and Personal Relationships, 17,* 751–771.

74. Lippa, R. A. (2000). Gender-related traits in gay men, lesbian women, and heterosexual men and women: The virtual identity of homosexual-heterosexual diagnosticity and gender diagnosticity. *Journal of Personality, 68,* 899–926.

75. Henley, N. (1977). *Body politics: Power, sex, and nonverbal communication.* Englewood Cliffs, NJ: Prentice-Hall; Henley, N. (1995). Body politics revisited: What do we know today? In P. Kalbfleisch & M. Cody (Eds.), *Gender, power, and communication in human relationships* (pp. 27–61). Hillsdale, NJ: Lawrence Erlbaum Associates.

76. Kalbfleisch, P. J., & Herold, A. L. (2006). Sex, power, and communication. In K. Dindia & D. J. Canary (Eds.), *Sex differences and similarities in communication* (2nd ed., pp. 299–313). Mahwah, NJ: Lawrence Erlbaum Associates.

77. Athenstaedt, U., Haas, E., & Schwab, S. (2004). Gender role self-concept and gender-typed communication behavior in mixed-sex and same-sex dyads. *Sex Roles, 50,* 37–52; Brownlow, S., Rosamond, J. A., & Parker, J. A. (2003). Gender-linked linguistic behavior in television interviews. *Sex Roles, 49,* 121–132.

78. Mehl, M., & Pennebaker, J. (2002, January). *Mapping students' natural language use in everyday conversations.* Paper presented at the third annual meeting of the Society for Personality and Social Psychology, Savannah, GA; Redeker, G., & Maes, A. (1996). Gender differences in interruptions. In D. Slobin, J. Gerhardt, A. Kyratzis, & J. Guo (Eds.), *Social interaction, social context, and language* (pp. 579–612). Mahwah, NJ: Lawrence Erlbaum Associates.

79. Basow, S., & Rubenfeld, K. (2003). "Trouble talk": Effects of gender and gender-typing. *Sex Roles, 48,* 183–187.

80. House, A., Dallinger, J., & Kilgallen, D. (1998). Androgyny and rhetorical sensitivity: The connection of gender and communication style. *Communication Reports, 11,* 11–20.

81. Gay, W. C. (1999). Linguistic violence. In R. Litke & D. Curtin (Eds.), *Institutional violence* (pp. 13–35). Amsterdam: Rodopi.

82. Gay, W. C. (1997). The reality of linguistic violence against women. In L. O'Toole & J. Schiffman (Eds.), *Gender violence: Interdisciplinary perspectives* (pp. 467–473). New York: New York University Press.

83. Wessler, S. (2005). *Discrimination against gay, lesbian, bisexual, and transgender individuals in Maine.* Portland, ME: The Center for the Prevention of Hate Violence.

84. Mulac, A., Bradac, J. J., & Gibbons, P. (2001). Empirical support for the gender-as-culture hypothesis: An inter-cultural analysis of male/female language differences. *Human Communication Research, 27,* 121–152.

85. Mulac, A. (2006). The gender-linked language effect: Do language differences really make a difference? In K. Dindia & D. J. Canary (Eds.), *Sex differences and similarities in communication* (2nd ed., pp. 219–239). Mahwah, NJ: Lawrence Erlbaum Associates.

86. Lumby, M. E. (1976). Code switching and sexual orientation: A test of Bernstein's sociolinguistic theory. *Journal of Homosexuality, 1,* 383–399.

87. Major, B., Schmidlin, A. M., & Williams, L. (1990). Gesture patterns in social touch: The impact of setting and age. *Journal of Personality and Social Psychology, 58,* 634–643.

88. Leathers, D. G. (1997). *Successful nonverbal communication: Principles and applications* (3rd ed.). Boston: Allyn & Bacon.

89. Eakins, B. W., & Eakins, R. G. (1978). *Sex differences in human communication.* Boston: Houghton Mifflin.

90. Uzzell, D., & Horne, N. (2006). The influence of biological sex, sexuality and gender role on interpersonal distance. *British Journal of Social Psychology, 45,* 579–597.

91. Newport, F. (2001, February 21). Americans see women as emotional and affectionate, men as more aggressive. Retrieved July 23, 2007, from http://www.galluppoll.com/content/?ci=1978&pg=1

92. Burgoon, J. K., & Bacue, A. E. (2003). Nonverbal communication skills. In J. O. Greene & B. R. Burleson (Eds.), *Handbook of communication and social interaction skills* (pp. 179–219). Mahwah, NJ: Lawrence Erlbaum Associates.

93. LaFrance, M., Hecht, M. A., & Levy Paluck, E. (2003). The contingent smile: A meta-analysis of sex differences in smiling. *Psychological Bulletin, 129,* 305–334.

94. Hall, J. A., & Friedman, G. (1999). Status, gender, and nonverbal behavior: A study of structured interactions between employees. *Personality and Social Psychology Bulletin, 25,* 1082–1091; LaFrance, M., & Hecht, M. A. (2000). Gender and smiling: A meta analysis. In A. H. Fischer (Ed.), *Gender and emotion: Social psychological perspective* (pp. 118–142). Cambridge, England: Cambridge University Press.

95. Witmer, D. F., & Katzman, S. (1997). On-line smiles: Does gender make a difference in the use of graphic accents? *Journal of Computer-Mediated Communication, 2*(4). Retrieved June 24, 2006, from http://jcmc.indiana.edu/vol2/issue4/witmer1.html

96. A sex difference in anger expression was reported in Coats, E. J., & Feldman, R. S. (1996). Gender differences in nonverbal correlates of social status. *Personality and Social Psychology Bulletin, 22,* 1014–1022. One study that failed to report such a difference was Burrowes, B. D., & Halberstadt, A. G. (1987). Self- and family-expressiveness styles in the experience and expression of anger. *Journal of Nonverbal Behavior, 11,* 254–268.

97. White, G. L., & Mullen, P. E. (1989). *Jealousy: Theory, research, and clinical strategies.* New York: Guilford.

98. Harris, I. D., & Howard, K. I. (1987). Correlates of depression and anger in adolescence. *Journal of Clinical and Adolescent Psychotherapy, 4,* 199–203; Stapley, J. C., & Haviland, J. M. (1989).

Beyond depression: Gender differences in normal adolescents' emotional experiences. *Sex Roles, 20,* 295–308.

99. Kring, A. M., & Gordon, A. H. (1998). Sex differences in emotion: Expression, experience, and physiology. *Journal of Personality and Social Psychology, 74,* 686–703; see also Gross, J. J., & John, O. P. (1998). Mapping the domain of expressivity: Multimethod evidence for a hierarchical model. *Journal of Personality and Social Psychology, 74,* 170–191.

100. Kring & Gordon, 1998.

101. Gottman, J. M., Levenson, R. W., Gross, J., Frederickson, B. L., McCoy, K., Rosenthal, L., Ruef, A., & Yoshimoto, D. (2003). Correlates of gay and lesbian couples' relationship satisfaction and relationship dissolution. *Journal of Homosexuality, 45,* 23–43.

102. For a review, see Floyd, K. (2006). *Communicating affection: Interpersonal behavior and social context.* Cambridge, England: Cambridge University Press.

103. Floyd, K., & Voloudakis, M. (1999). Affectionate behavior in adult platonic friendships: Interpreting and evaluating expectancy violations. *Human Communication Research, 25,* 341–369; Shuntich, R. J., & Shapiro, R. M. (1991). Explorations of verbal affection and aggression. *Journal of Social Behavior and Personality, 6,* 283–300.

104. Floyd, K. (1997). Knowing when to say "I love you": An expectancy approach to affectionate communication. *Communication Research Reports, 14,* 321–330.

105. Floyd, K., & Morman, M. T. (2000). Reacting to the verbal expression of affection in same-sex interaction. *Southern Communication Journal, 65,* 287–299.

106. See Taylor, S. E., Klein, L. C., Lewis, B. P., Gruenwald, T. L., Guring, R. A. R., & Updegraff, J. A. (2000). Biobehavioral responses to stress in females: Tend-and-befriend, not fight-or-flight. *Psychological Review, 107,* 411–429.

107. Floyd, K., & Morman, M. T. (2000). Affection received from fathers as a predictor of men's affection with their own sons: Tests of the modeling and compensation hypotheses. *Communication Monographs, 67,* 347–361; Floyd, K., & Tusing, K. J. (2002, July). *"At the mention of your name": Affect shifts induced by relationship-specific cognitions.* Paper presented at annual meeting of the International Communication Association, Seoul, South Korea; Morman, M. T., & Floyd, K. (1999). Affectionate communication between fathers and young adult sons: Individual- and relational-level correlates. *Communication Studies, 50,* 294–309.

108. Kurdek, L. A. (2006). Differences between partners from heterosexual, gay, and lesbian cohabiting couples. *Journal of Marriage and Family, 68,* 509–528.

109. Floyd, K. (2001). Human affection exchange: I. Reproductive probability as a predictor of men's affection with their sons. *Journal of Men's Studies, 10,* 39–50; Floyd, K., Sargent, J. E., & Di Corcia, M. (2004). Human affection exchange: VI. Further tests of reproductive probability as a predictor of men's affection with their fathers and their sons. *Journal of Social Psychology, 144,* 191–206.

Chapter 3

1. Luft, J., & Ingham, H. (1955). *The Johari window: A graphic model of interpersonal awareness.* Proceedings of the Western Training Laboratory in Group Development. Los Angeles: UCLA.

2. Reported in Myers, D. G. (1980). *The inflated self.* New York: Seabury.

3. Brown, J. D., & Mankowski, T. A. (1993). Self-esteem, mood, and self-evaluation: Changes in mood and the way you see you. *Journal of Personality and Social Psychology, 64,* 421–430; Campbell, J. D. (1990). Self-esteem and clarity of the self-concept. *Journal of Personality and Social Psychology, 59,* 538–549.

4. Tarlow, E. M., & Haaga, D. A. F. (1996). Negative self-concept: Specificity to depressive symptoms and relation to positive and negative affectivity. *Journal of Research in Personality, 30,* 120–127.

5. Swann, W. B., Rentfrow, P. J., & Guinn, J. S. (2003). Self-verification: The search for coherence. In J. P. Tangney & M. R. Leary (Eds.), *Handbook of self and identity* (pp. 367–383). New York: Guilford.

6. Greenwald, A. G. (1995). Getting (my) self into social psychology. In G. G. Brannigan & M. R. Merrens (Eds.), *The social psychologists: Research adventures* (pp. 3–16). New York: McGraw-Hill.

7. Block, J., & Robins, R. W. (1993). A longitudinal study of consistency and change in self-esteem from early adolescence to early childhood. *Child Development, 64,* 909–923.

8. Woodgate, R. (2005). A different way of being: Adolescents' experiences with cancer. *Cancer Nursing, 28,* 121–128.

9. Van der Meulen, M. (2001). Developments in self-concept theory and research: Affect, context, and variability. In H. A. Bosma & E. S. Kunnen (Eds.), *Identity and emotion: Development through self-organization* (pp. 10–38). New York: Cambridge University Press.

10. Rosenblith, J. F. (1992). *In the beginning: Development from conception to age two.* Newbury Park, CA: Sage.

11. Wright, W. (1998). *Born that way: Genes, behavior, personality.* New York: Knopf.

12. Bouchard, T. J., Lykken, D. T., McGue, M., & Segal, N. L. (1990). Sources of human psychological differences: The Minnesota Study of Twins Reared Apart. *Science* (October 12), 223–228.

13. Schwartz, C. E., Wright, C. I., Shin, L. M., Kagan, J., & Rauch, S. L. (2003). Inhibited and uninhibited infants "grown up": Adult amygdalar response to novelty. *Science* (June 20), 1952–1953.

14. Gudykunst, W. B., & Ting-Toomey, S. (1988). *Culture and interpersonal communication.* Newbury Park, CA: Sage.

15. Holstein, J. A., & Gubrium, J. F. (2000). *The self we live by: Narrative identity in a postmodern world.* New York: Oxford University Press.

16. See McIntyre, L. (2006). *The practical skeptic: Core concepts in sociology.* New York: McGraw-Hill; Yeung, K–T., & Martin, J. L. (2003). The looking-glass self: An empirical test and elaboration. *Social Forces, 81,* 843–879.

17. Hergovitch, A., Sirsch, U., & Felinger, M. (2002). Self-appraisals, actual appraisals and reflected appraisals of pre-adolescent children. *Social Behavior and Personality, 30,* 603–612.

18. See Beatty, M. J., & Dobos, J. A. (1993). Adult males' perceptions of confirmation and relational partner communication apprehension: Indirect effects of fathers on sons' partners. *Communication Quarterly, 41,* 66–76.

19. Han, M. (2003). Body image dissatisfaction and eating disturbance among Korean female college students: Relationships to media exposure, upward comparison, and perceived reality. *Communication Studies, 34,* 65–78.

20. Hamachek, D. (1992). *Encounters with the self* (3rd ed.). Fort Worth, TX: Holt, Rinehart & Winston.

21. Hamachek, 1992.

22. Centers for Disease Control and Prevention. (2007). Prevalence of the autism spectrum disorders in multiple areas of the United States, surveillance years 2000 and 2002. Retrieved August 13, 2007, from http://www.cdc.gov/ncbddd/dd/addmprevalence.htm

101. Suler, J. (1996). *The psychology of cyberspace*. Retrieved from http://www.rider.edu/~suler/psycyber/psychber.html

102. Whittle, D. B. (1997). *Cyberspace: The human dimensions*. New York: Freeman.

Chapter 4

1. See Kenny, D. A. (1994). *Interpersonal perception: A social relations analysis*. New York: Guilford.

2. Schermerhorn, J. R., Hunt, J. H., & Osborn, R. N. (2003). *Organizational behavior* (8th ed.). New York: Wiley.

3. Goldstein, E. B. (2007). *Sensation and perception* (7th ed.). Pacific Grove, CA: Wadsworth.

4. Floyd, K., Ramirez, A., & Burgoon, J. K. (2008). Expectancy violations theory. In L. K. Guerrero, J. A. DeVito, & M. L. Hecht (Eds.), *The nonverbal communication reader: Classic and contemporary readings* (3rd ed., pp. 503–510). Prospect Heights, IL: Waveland.

5. Zajonc, R. B. (2001). Mere exposure: A gateway to the subliminal. *Current Directions in Psychological Science, 10,* 224–228.

6. Goldstein, 2007.

7. Burgoon, J. K., Guerrero, L. K., & Floyd, K. (2010). *Nonverbal communication*. Boston: Pearson/Allyn & Bacon.

8. Sowa, J. F. (2000). *Knowledge representation: Logical, philosophical, and computational foundations*. Pacific Grove, CA: Brooks/Cole.

9. Funder, D. C. (1999). *Personality judgment: A realistic approach to person perception*. San Diego: Academic.

10. Fiske, S. T., & Taylor, S. E. (2008). *Social cognition: From brains to culture*. New York: McGraw-Hill.

11. Kelley, H. H. (1967). Attribution theory in social psychology. In D. Levine (Ed.), *Nebraska symposium on motivation* (Vol. 15, pp. 192–238). Lincoln: University of Nebraska Press.

12. Jones, E. E., & Davis, K. E. (1965). From acts to dispositions: The attribution process in person perception. In L. Berkowitz (Ed.), *Advances in experimental social psychology* (Vol. 2, pp. 219–266). New York: Academic.

13. See, e.g., Manusov, V. (1993). It depends on your perspective: Effects of stance and beliefs about intent on person perception. *Western Journal of Communication, 57,* 27–41.

14. Burgoon, Guerrero, & Floyd, 2010.

15. See, e.g., Bruce, V., Georgeson, M. A., & Green, P. R. (2003). *Visual perception: Physiology, psychology and ecology* (4th ed.). New York: Psychology Press.

16. Miró, E., Cano, M. C., Espinoza Fernández, L., & Beula-Casal, G. (2003). Time estimation during prolonged sleep deprivation and its relation to activation measures. *Human Factors, 45,* 148–159.

17. Alaimo, K., Olson, C. M., & Frongillo, E. A. (2001). Food insufficiency and American school-aged children's cognitive, academic, and psychosocial development. *Pediatrics, 108,* 44–53.

18. See Bartoshuk, L. (1980, September). Separate works of taste. *Psychology Today, 14,* 48–63.

19. Dunlap, J. C., Loros, J. J., & DeCoursey, P. J. (Eds.). (2003). *Chronobiology: Biological timekeeping*. Sunderland, MA: Sinauer Associates.

20. Larson, J. H., Crane, D. R., & Smith, C. W. (1991). Morning and night couples: The effects of wake and sleep patterns on marital adjustment. *Journal of Marital and Family Therapy, 17,* 53–65.

21. Ji, L. K., Peng, K., & Nisbett, R. E. (2000). Culture, control, and perception of relationships in the environment. *Journal of Personality and Social Psychology, 78,* 943–955; Knowles, E. D., Morris, M. W., Chiu, C–Y., & Hong, Y–Y. (2001). Culture and the process of person perception: Evidence for automaticity among East Asians in correcting for situational influences on behavior. *Personality and Social Psychology Bulletin, 27,* 1344–1356.

22. Hall, E. T. (1959). *The silent language*. Garden City, NY: Doubleday.

23. Luszcz, M. A., & Fitzgerald, K. M. (1986). Understanding cohort differences in cross-generational, self, and peer perceptions. *Journal of Gerontology, 41,* 234–240.

24. See Ostrove, J. M., & Cole, E. R. (2003). Privileging class: Toward a critical psychology of social class in the context of education. *Journal of Social Issues, 59,* 677–692.

25. Farwell, L., & Weiner, B. (2000). Bleeding hearts and the heartless: Popular perceptions of liberal and conservative ideologies. *Personality and Social Psychology Bulletin, 26,* 845–852.

26. Edmondson, C. B., & Conger, J. C. (1995). The impact of mode of presentation on gender differences in social perception. *Sex Roles, 32,* 169–183.

27. Maeder, E. M., Wiener, R. L., & Winter, R. (2007). Does a truck driver see what a nurse sees? The effects of occupation type on perceptions of sexual harassment. *Sex Roles, 56,* 801–810; Littrell, M. A., & Berger, E. A. (1986). Perceiver's occupation and client's grooming: Influence on person perception. *Clothing and Textiles Research Journal, 4,* 48–55.

28. Lepore, L., & Brown, R. (1997). Category and stereotype activation: Is prejudice inevitable? *Journal of Personality and Social Psychology, 72,* 275–287.

29. Nelson, T. D. (2005). Ageism: Prejudice against our featured future self. *Journal of Social Issues, 61,* 207–221; Buttney, R. (1997). Reported speech in talking race on campus. *Human Communication Research, 23,* 477–506.

30. See, e.g., Hendrix, K. G. (2002). "Did being black introduce bias into your study?" Attempting to mute the race-related research of black scholars. *Howard Journal of Communication, 13,* 153–171; Hughes, P. C., & Baldwin, J. R. (2002). Communication and stereotypical impressions. *Howard Journal of Communication, 13,* 113–128.

31. Aronson, J., Lustina, M. J., Good, C., & Keough, K. (1999). When white men can't do math: Necessary and sufficient factors in stereotype threat. *Journal of Experimental Social Psychology, 35,* 29–46.

32. Snyder, M., & Uranowitz, S. (1978). Reconstructing the past: Some cognitive consequences of person perception. *Journal of Personality and Social Psychology, 36,* 941–950.

33. Allen, M., & Valde, K. S. (2006). The intersection of methodological and ethical concerns when researching a gendered world. In D. J. Canary & K. Dindia (Eds.), *Handbook of sex differences and similarities in communication* (2nd ed., pp. 97–110). Mahwah, NJ: Lawrence Erlbaum Associates.

34. Fyock, J., & Stangor, C. (1994). The role of memory biases in stereotype maintenance. *British Journal of Social Psychology, 33,* 331–343.

35. Lee, Y–T., Jussim, L. J., & McCauley, C. R. (1996). *Stereotype accuracy: Toward appreciating group differences*. Washington, DC: American Psychological Association.

36. Tetlock, P. E. (1983). Accountability and the perseverance of first impressions. *Social Psychology Quarterly, 46,* 285–292.

37. Asch, S. (1946). Forming impressions of personality. *Journal of Abnormal and Social Psychology, 41,* 258–290.

38. Parsons, C. K., Liden, R. C., & Bauer, T. N. (2001). Personal perception in employment interviews. In M. London (Ed.), *How people evaluate others in organizations* (pp. 67–90). Mahwah, NJ: Lawrence Erlbaum Associates.

39. Luchins, A. (1957). Primacy-recency in impression formation. In C. Hovland (Ed.), *The order of presentation in persuasion* (pp. 33–61). New Haven, CT: Yale University Press.

40. Ybarra, O. (2001). When first impressions don't last: The role of isolation and adaptation processes in the revision of evaluative impressions. *Social Cognition, 19*, 491–520.

41. Davelaar, E. J., Goshen-Gottstein, Y., Ashkenazi, A., Haarmann, H. J., & Usher, M. (2005). The demise of short-term memory revisited: Empirical and computational investigations of recency effects. *Psychological Review, 112*, 3–42.

42. McCann, C. D., Higgins, E. T., & Fondacaro, R. A. (1991). Primacy and recency in communication and self-persuasion: How successive audiences and multiple encodings influence subsequent evaluative judgments. *Social Cognition, 9*, 47–66.

43. Schyns, P. G., & Oliva, A. (1999). Dr. Angry and Mr. Smile: When categorization flexibly modifies the perception of faces in rapid visual presentations. *Cognition, 69*, 243–265.

44. Stern, M., & Karraker, K. H. (1989). Sex stereotyping of infants: A review of gender labeling studies. *Sex Roles, 20*, 501–522.

45. Mondloch, C. J., Lewis, T. L., Budreau, D. R., Maurer, D., Dannemiller, J. L., Stephens, B. R., & Kleiner-Gathercoal, K. A. (1999). Face perception during early infancy. *Psychological Science, 10*, 419–422; Morton, J., & Johnson, M. H. (1991). CONSPEC and CONLERN: A two-process theory of infant face recognition. *Psychological Review, 98,* 164–181.

46. King, D. E., & Bushwick, B. (1994). Beliefs and attitudes of hospital inpatients about faith healing and prayer. *Journal of Family Practice, 39*, 349–352.

47. Floyd, K. (2000). Affectionate same-sex touch: Understanding the influence of homophobia on observers' perceptions. *Journal of Social Psychology, 140*, 774–788.

48. Lapsley, D. K., Milstead, M., Quintana, S. M., Flannery, D., & Buss, R. R. (1986). Adolescent egocentrism and formal operations: Tests of a theoretical assumption. *Developmental Psychology, 22*, 800–807.

49. Piaget, J. (1930). *The child's conception of physical causality.* London: Routledge & Kegan Paul; Piaget, J. (1932). *The moral judgment of the child.* New York: Harcourt, Brace & World.

50. Kelley, C. M. (1996). Adult egocentrism: Subjective experience versus analytic bases for judgment. *Journal of Memory and Language, 35*, 157–175.

51. Cummins, R. A., & Nistico, H. (2002). Maintaining life satisfaction: The role of positive cognitive bias. *Journal of Happiness Studies, 3*, 37–69.

52. Hendrick, C., & Hendrick, S. S. (1988). Lovers wear rose-colored glasses. *Journal of Social and Personal Relationships, 5*, 161–183.

53. Fisher, H. (2004). *Why we love: The nature and chemistry of romantic love.* New York: Henry Holt; see also Murray, S. L., Holmes, J. G., & Griffin, D. W. (1996). The benefits of positive illusions: Idealization and the construction of satisfaction in close relationships. *Journal of Personality and Social Psychology, 70*, 79–98.

54. Lupfer, M. B., Weeks, M., & Dupuis, S. (2000). How pervasive is the negativity bias in judgments based on character appraisal? *Personality and Social Psychology Bulletin, 26*, 1353–1366.

55. Webster, E. (1964). *Decision making in the employment interview.* Montreal, Canada: Industrial Relations Centre, McGill University.

56. Anderson, N. (1981). *Foundations of information integration theory.* New York: Academic.

57. Bradbury, T. N., & Fincham, F. D. (1990). Attributions in marriage: Review and critique. *Psychological Bulletin, 107,* 3–33.

58. Manusov, V., & Harvey, J. H. (Eds.). (2001). *Attribution, communication behavior, and close relationships.* Cambridge, England: Cambridge University Press.

59. Weiner, B. (2000). Intrapersonal and interpersonal theories of motivation from an attributional perspective. *Educational Psychology Review, 12*, 1–14.

60. Pascarella, E. T., Edison, M., Hagedorn, L. S., Nora, A., & Terenzini, P. T. (1996). Influences on students' internal locus of attribution for academic success in the first year of college. *Research in Higher Education, 37,* 731–756.

61. Weiner, B. (1985). An attributional theory of achievement motivation and emotion. *Psychological Review, 92*, 548–573.

62. Hooley, J. M., & Campbell, C. (2002). Control and controllability: Beliefs and behaviour in high and low expressed emotion relatives. *Psychological Medicine, 32*, 1091–1099.

63. Block, J., & Funder, D. C. (1986). Social roles and social perception: Individual differences in attribution and error. *Journal of Personality and Social Psychology, 51*, 1200–1207.

64. Sedikides, C., Campbell, W. K., Reeder, G. D., & Elliott, A. J. (1998). The self-serving bias in relational context. *Journal of Personality and Social Psychology, 74*, 378–386.

65. See, e.g., Bradbury & Fincham, 1990; Sillars, A., Roberts, L. J., Dun, T., & Leonard, K. (2001). Stepping into the stream of thought: Cognition during marital conflict. In V. Manusov & J. H. Harvey (Eds.), *Attribution, communication behavior, and close relationships* (pp. 193–210). Cambridge, England: Cambridge University Press.

66. Trower, P., & Chadwick, P. (1995). Pathways to defense of the self: A theory of two types of paranoia. *Clinical Psychology: Science and Practice, 2,* 263–278.

67. Tetlock, P. E. (1985). Accountability: A social check on the fundamental attribution error. *Social Psychology Quarterly, 48,* 227–236; Ross, L. (1977). The intuitive psychologist and his shortcomings: Distortions in the attribution process. In L. Berkowitz (Ed.), *Advances in experimental social psychology* (Vol. 10, pp. 173–220). New York: Academic.

68. Napolitan, D. A., & Goethals, G. R. (1979). The attribution of friendliness. *Journal of Experimental Social Psychology, 15,* 105–113.

69. Corneille, O., Leyens, J.-P., Yzerbyt, V. Y., & Walther, E. (1999). Judgeability concerns: The interplay of information, applicability, and accountability in the overattribution bias. *Journal of Personality and Social Psychology, 76,* 377–387; Webster, D. M. (1993). Motivated argument and reduction of the overattribution bias. *Journal of Personality and Social Psychology, 65,* 261–271.

70. Leyens, J.-P., Yzerbyt, V. Y., & Corneille, O. (1996). The role of applicability in the emergence of the overattribution bias. *Journal of Personality and Social Psychology, 70,* 219–229.

71. Schweinle, W. E., Ickes, W., & Bernstein, I. H. (2002). Empathic inaccuracy in husband to wife aggression: The overattribution bias. *Personal Relationships, 9,* 141–158.

72. Schweinle, W. E., & Ickes, W. (2007). The role of men's critical/rejecting overattribution bias, affect, and attentional disengagement in marital aggression. *Journal of Social and Clinical Psychology, 26,* 173–198.

73. See, e.g., Alicke, M. D., Zerbst, J. I., & LoSchiavo, F. M. (1996). Personal attitudes, constraint magnitude, and correspondence bias. *Basic and Applied Social Psychology, 18,* 211–228.

74. See Woolfolk, R. L., Doris, J. M., & Darley, J. M. (2006). Identification, situational constraint, and social cognition: Studies in the attribution of moral responsibility. *Cognition, 100,* 283–301.

75. Katz, R. C., Hannon, R., & Whitten, L. (1996). Effects of gender and situation on the perception of sexual harassment. *Sex Roles, 34,* 35–42; Bursik, K. (1992). Perceptions of sexual harassment

12. Wegner, D. M., & Vallacher, R. R. (1977). *Implicit psychology: An introduction to social cognition.* New York: Oxford University Press.

13. See, e.g., Eagley, A. H., Ashmore, R. D., Makhijani, M. G., & Longo, L. C. (1991). What is beautiful is good, but . . . : A meta-analytic review of research on the physical attractiveness stereotype. *Psychological Bulletin, 110,* 109–138.

14. Burgoon, J. K., Buller, D. B., & Woodall, W. G. (1996). *Nonverbal communication: The unspoken dialogue* (2nd ed.). New York: McGraw-Hill.

15. Bavelas, J. B., Coates, L., & Johnson, T. (2002). Listener responses as a collaborative process: The role of gaze. *Journal of Communication, 52,* 566–580.

16. Knapp, M. L., Hart, R. P., Freidrich, G. W., & Shulman, G. M. (1973). The rhetoric of goodbye: Verbal and nonverbal correlates of human leave-taking behavior. *Speech Monographs, 40,* 182–198.

17. Knapp et al., 1973; see also O'Leary, M. J., & Gallois, C. (1985). The last ten turns: Behavior and sequencing in friends' and strangers' conversational findings. *Journal of Nonverbal Behavior, 9,* 8–27.

18. Fridlund, A. J., & Russell, J. A. (2006). The functions of facial expressions: What's in a face? In V. Manusov & M. L. Patterson (Eds.), *The Sage handbook of nonverbal communication* (pp. 299–319). Thousand Oaks, CA: Sage.

19. Sroufe, L. A. (1984). The organization of emotional development. In K. R. Scherer & P. Ekman (Eds.), *Approaches to emotion* (pp. 109–128). Hillsdale, NJ: Lawrence Erlbaum Associates.

20. Fox, N., & Davidson, R. (1988). Patterns of brain electrical activity during facial signs of emotion in 10-month-old infants. *Developmental Psychology, 24,* 230–236.

21. Scherer, K. (1995). Expression of emotion in voice and music. *Journal of Voice, 9,* 235–248.

22. Murray, I. R., & Arnott, J. L. (1993). Toward the simulation of emotion in synthetic speech: A review of the literature on human vocal emotion. *Journal of the Acoustical Society of America, 93,* 1097–1108.

23. Johnson, W. F., Emde, R. N., Scherer, K. R., & Klinnert, M. D. (1986). Recognition of emotion from vocal cues. *Archives of General Psychiatry, 43,* 280–283.

24. Moore, M. M. (1985). Non-verbal courtship patterns in women: Context and consequences. *Ethology and Sociobiology, 6,* 237–247; Moore, M. M. (2002). Courtship communication and perception. *Perceptual and Motor Skills, 94,* 97–105.

25. Givens, D. B. (1978). The nonverbal basis of attraction: Flirtation, courtship, and seduction. *Psychiatry, 41,* 346–359.

26. Floyd, K. (2006). *Communicating affection: Interpersonal behavior and social context.* Cambridge, England: Cambridge University Press.

27. Spain, D. (1992). *Gendered spaces.* Chapel Hill: University of North Carolina Press.

28. Kimble, C. E., Forte, R. A., & Yoshikawa, J. C. (1981). Nonverbal concomitants of enacted emotional intensity and positivity: Visual and vocal behavior. *Journal of Personality, 29,* 271–283; Chapman, A. J. (1975). Eye contact, physical proximity and laughter: A re-examination of the equilibrium model of social intimacy. *Social Behavior and Personality, 3,* 143–155; Siegman, A. W. (1978). The telltale voice: Nonverbal messages of verbal communication. In A. W. Siegman & S. Feldstein (Eds.), *Nonverbal behavior and communication* (pp. 183–243). Hillsdale, NJ: Lawrence Erlbaum Associates.

29. Burgoon, J. K., & Koper, R. J. (1984). Nonverbal and relational communication associated with reticence. *Human Communication Research, 10,* 601–626; Cappella, J. N., & Greene, J. O. (1984). The effects of distance and individual differences in arousability on nonverbal involvement: A test of discrepancy-arousal theory. *Journal of Nonverbal Behavior, 8,* 259–286; Kemper, T. D. (1984). Power, status, and emotions: A sociological contribution to a psychophysiological domain. In K. R. Scherer & P. Ekman (Eds.), *Approaches to emotion* (pp. 369–383). Hillsdale, NJ: Lawrence Erlbaum Associates.

30. Burgoon, J. K., Buller, D. B., Hale, J. L., & deTurck, M. A. (1984). Relational messages associated with nonverbal behaviors. *Human Communication Research, 10,* 351–378; Patterson, J. L., Jordan, A., Hogan, M. B., & Frerker, D. (1981). Effects of nonverbal intimacy on arousal and behavioral adjustment. *Journal of Nonverbal Behavior, 5,* 184–198.

31. American Psychiatric Association. (2000). *Diagnostic and statistical manual of mental disorders* (4th ed. text revision). Washington, DC: Author.

32. Troisi, A., & Moles, A. (1999). Gender differences in depression: An ethological study of nonverbal behavior during interviews. *Journal of Psychiatric Research, 33,* 243–250.

33. Burgoon, J. K., Guerrero, L. K., & Floyd, K. (2010). *Nonverbal communication.* Boston: Allyn & Bacon.

34. Guerrero, L. K., & Floyd, K. (2006). *Nonverbal communication in close relationships.* Mahwah, NJ: Lawrence Erlbaum Associates.

35. McGlone, R. E., & Hollien, H. (1963). Vocal pitch characteristics of aged women. *Journal of Speech and Hearing Research, 6,* 164–170.

36. Schötz, S. (2003). Towards synthesis of speaker age: A perceptual study with natural, synthesized and resynthesized stimuli. *PHONUM, 9,* I–X.

37. Mendoza, E., Valencia, N., Muñoz, J., & Trujillo, H. (1996). Differences in voice quality between men and women: Use of the long-term average spectrum (LTAS). *Journal of Voice, 10,* 59–66.

38. Günzburger, D. (1984). Perception of some male-female voice characteristics. *Progress Report Institute of Phonetics Utrecht, 9,* 15–26.

39. Paek, S. L. (1986). Effect of garment style on the perception of personal traits. *Clothing and Textiles Research, 5,* 10–16.

40. Pratt, M. G., & Rafaeli, A. (2004). Organizational dress as a symbol of multilayered social identities. In M. J. Hatch & M. Schultz (Eds.), *Organizational identity: A reader* (pp. 275–312). New York: Oxford University Press.

41. O'Neal, G. S., & Lapitsky, M. (1991). Effects of clothing as nonverbal communication on credibility of the message source. *Clothing and Textiles Research Journal, 9,* 28–34.

42. Street, R. L., & Brady, R. M. (1982). Speech rate acceptance ranges as a function of evaluative domain, listener speech rate, and communication context. *Communication Monographs, 49,* 290–308.

43. Burgoon, J. K., Birk, T., & Pfau, M. (1990). Nonverbal behaviors, persuasion, and credibility. *Human Communication Research, 17,* 140–169.

44. Linkey, H. E., & Firestone, I. J. (1990). Dyad dominance composition effects, nonverbal behaviors, and influence. *Journal of Research in Personality, 24,* 206–215.

45. See Walker, D., & Dubitsky, T. M. (1994). Why liking matters. *Journal of Advertising Research, 3,* 9–18.

46. Floyd, K., & Burgoon, J. K. (1999). Reacting to nonverbal expressions of liking: A test of interaction adaptation theory. *Communication Monographs, 66,* 219–239.

47. Kleinke, C. L. (1977). Compliance to requests made by gazing and touching experimenters in field settings. *Journal of Experimental Social Psychology, 13,* 218–223; Paulsell, S., & Goldman,

M. (1984). The effect of touching different body areas on pro-social behavior. *Journal of Social Psychology, 122,* 269–273.

48. Burgoon, J. K., Stern, L. A., & Dillman, L. (1995). *Interpersonal adaptation: Dyadic interaction patterns.* New York: Cambridge University Press.

49. Lutz-Zois, C. J., Bradley, A. C., Mihalik, J. L., & Moorman Eavers, E. R. (2006). Perceived similarity and relationship success among dating couples: An idiographic approach. *Journal of Social and Personal Relationships, 23,* 865–880; Morry, M. M. (2007). The attraction-similarity hypothesis among cross-sex friends: Relationship satisfaction, perceived similarities, and self-serving perceptions. *Journal of Social and Personal Relationships, 24,* 117–138.

50. Ekman, P., Friesen, W. V., & O'Sullivan, M. (1997). Smiles when lying. In P. Ekman & E. L. Rosenberg (Eds.), *What the face reveals: Basic and applied studies of spontaneous expression using the facial action coding system (FACS)* (pp. 201–214). New York: Oxford University Press.

51. Ekman, P., Friesen, W. V., & Scherer, K. R. (1976). Body movement and voice pitch in deceptive interaction. *Semiotica, 16,* 23–27.

52. Ekman, P., O'Sullivan, M., Friesen, W. V., & Scherer, K. R. (1991). Face, voice, and body in detecting deceit. *Journal of Nonverbal Behavior, 15,* 125–135.

53. Knapp, M. L. (1978). *Nonverbal communication in human interaction* (2nd ed.). New York: Holt.

54. Ellis, H. D., & Young, A. W. (1989). Are faces special? In A. W. Young & H. D. Ellis (Eds.), *Handbook of research on face processing* (pp. 1–26). Amsterdam: North-Holland.

55. Scheib, J. E., Gangestad, S. W., & Thornhill, R. (1999). Facial attractiveness, symmetry, and cues to good genes. *Proceedings of the Royal Society of London, Series B, 266,* 1913–1917; Grammer, K., & Thornhill, R. (1994). Human (*homo sapiens*) facial attractiveness and sexual selection: The role of symmetry and averageness. *Journal of Comparative Psychology, 108,* 233–242.

56. http://www.aafprs.org/patient/ procedures/rhinoplasty.html

57. Ekman, P., Friesen, W. V., & Ellsworth, P. (1972). *Emotion in the human face: Guidelines for research and an integration of findings.* New York: Pergamon Press.

58. Rosenthal, R., & DePaulo, B. M. (1979). Sex differences in accommodation in nonverbal communication. In R. Rosenthal (Ed.), *Skill in nonverbal communication: Individual differences* (pp. 68–103). Cambridge, MA: Oelgeschlager, Gunn & Hain.

59. Eagly, A. H., & Crowley, M. (1986). Gender and helping behavior: A meta-analytic review of the social psychological literature. *Psychological Bulletin, 100,* 283–308.

60. Akert, R. M., & Panter, A. T. (1988). Extraversion and the ability to decode nonverbal communication. *Personality & Individual Differences, 9,* 965–972.

61. Smith, C., Lentz, E. M., & Mikos, K. (1988). *Signing naturally.* San Diego: DawnSign.

62. Iverson, J. M., Tencer, H. L., Lany, J., & Goldin-Meadow, S. (2000). The relation between gesture and speech in congenitally blind and sighted language-learners. *Journal of Nonverbal Behavior, 24,* 105–130.

63. Floyd, K. (2006). *Communicating affection: Interpersonal behavior and social context.* Cambridge, England: Cambridge University Press.

64. Field, T. M. (Ed.). (1995). *Touch in early development.* Mahwah, NJ: Lawrence Erlbaum Associates.

65. Del Prete, T. (1997). Hands off? A touchy subject. *The Education Digest, 62,* 59–61. Quote is from p. 59.

66. Field, T. (2001). *Touch.* Cambridge: MIT Press. Quote is from p. 5.

67. For review, see Field, 2001.

68. Burgener, S., Bakas, T., Murray, C., Dunahee, J., & Tossey, S. (1998). Effective caregiving approaches for patients with Alzheimer's disease. *Geriatric Nursing, 19,* 121–126; Gadow, S. (1984). Touch and technology: Two paradigms of patient care. *Journal of Religion and Health, 23,* 63–69.

69. See, e.g., Tjaden, P., & Thoennes, N. (1998). *Prevalence, incidence, and consequences of violence against women: Findings from the National Violence Against Women Survey.* Washington, DC: National Institute of Justice, NCJ 172837.

70. For example, see Kneidinger, L. M., Maple, T. L., & Tross, S. A. (2001). Touching behavior in sport: Functional components, analysis of sex differences, and ethological considerations. *Journal of Nonverbal Behavior, 25,* 43–62.

71. Zuckerman, M., & Miyake, K. (1993). The attractive voice: What makes it so? *Journal of Nonverbal Behavior, 17,* 119–135.

72. Wolvin, A., & Coakley, C. (1996). *Listening.* Dubuque, IA: Brown & Benchmark.

73. Burgoon, J. K., Guerrero, L. K., & Floyd, K. (2010). *Nonverbal communication.* Boston: Allyn & Bacon.

74. Williams, K. D., Shore, W. J., & Grahe, J. E. (1998). The silent treatment: Perceptions of its behaviors and associated feelings. *Group Processes and Intergroup Relations, 1,* 117–141.

75. For further discussion, see Kamakura, W. A., Basuroy, S., & Boatwright, P. (2006). Is silence golden? An inquiry into the meaning of silence in professional product evaluations. *Quantitative Marketing and Economics, 4,* 119–141.

76. Hall, E. T. (1959). The silent language. Garden City, NY: Doubleday; Hall, E. T. (1963). System for the notation of proxemic behavior. *American Anthropologist, 65,* 1003–1026.

77. Braithwaite, D. O., & Braithwaite, C. A. (2000). Understanding communication of persons with disabilities as cultural communication. In L. A. Samovar & R. E. Porter (Eds.), *Intercultural communication: A reader* (9th ed., pp. 136–145). Belmont, CA: Wadsworth.

78. Park, J. H., Faulkner, J., & Schaller, M. (2003). Evolved disease-avoidance processes and contemporary anti-social behavior: Prejudicial attitudes and avoidance of people with physical disabilities. *Journal of Nonverbal Behavior, 27,* 65–87.

79. Dion, K. K., Berscheid, E., & Walster, E. (1972). What is beautiful is good. *Journal of Personality and Social Psychology, 24,* 285–290; Eagley, A. E., Ashmore, R. D., Makhijani, M. G., & Longo, L. C. (1991). What is beautiful is good, but . . . : A meta-analytic review of research on the physical attractiveness stereotype. *Psychological Bulletin, 110,* 109–139; Kuhlenschmidt, S., & Conger, J. C. (1988). Behavioral components of social competence in females. *Sex Roles, 18,* 107–112.

80. Curran, J. P., & Lippold, S. (1975). The effects of physical attraction and attitude similarity on attraction in dating dyads. *Journal of Personality, 43,* 528–539; O'Grady, K. E. (1989). Physical attractiveness, need for approval, social self-esteem, and maladjustment. *Journal of Social and Clinical Psychology, 8,* 62–69.

81. Efran, M. G. (1974). The effect of physical appearance on the judgment of guilt, interpersonal attraction, and severity of recommended punishment in a simulated jury task. *Journal of Experimental Research in Personality, 8,* 45–54; Efran, M. G., & Patterson, E. (1974). Voters vote beautiful: The effect of physical appearance on a national debate. *Canadian Journal of Behavioral Science, 6,* 352–356; West, S. G., & Brown, T. J. (1975). Physical

attractiveness, the severity of the emergency and helping: A field experiment and interpersonal simulation. *Journal of Experimental Social Psychology, 11,* 531–538.

82. Pointer, M. R., & Attridge, G. G. (1998). The number of discernible colours. *Color Research and Application, 23,* 52–54.

83. Davidoff, J. (1991). *Cognition through color.* Cambridge: MIT Press.

84. Lüscher, M., & Scott, I. (1969). *The Lüscher Color Test.* New York: Random House.

85. Jandt, F. E. (1995). *Intercultural communication: An introduction.* Thousand Oaks, CA: Sage.

86. Burgoon, J. K., Guerrero, L. K., & Floyd, K. (2010). *Nonverbal communication.* Boston: Allyn & Bacon.

87. Feghali, E. K. (1997). Arab cultural communication patterns. *International Journal of Intercultural Relations, 21,* 345–378.

88. Watson, O. M. (1970). *Proxemic behavior: A cross-cultural study.* The Hague: Mouton.

89. Iizuka, Y. (1994). Gaze during speaking as related to shyness. *Perceptual and Motor Skills, 78,* 1259–1264; Larsen, R. J., & Shackelford, T. K. (1996). Gaze avoidance: Personality and social judgments of people who avoid direct face-to-face contact. *Personality and Individual Differences, 21,* 907–917.

90. Matsumoto, D. (2006). Culture and nonverbal behavior. In V. Manusov & M. L. Patterson (Eds.), *The Sage handbook of nonverbal communication* (pp. 219–236). Thousand Oaks, CA: Sage.

91. Ekman, P (1993). Facial expressions and emotion. *American Psychologist, 48,* 384–392; Ekman, P., & Friesen, W. V. (1986). A new pan-cultural facial expression of emotion. *Motivation and Emotion, 10,* 159–168; Scherer, K. R., & Walbott, H. G. (1994). Evidence for universality and cultural variation of differential emotion response patterning. *Journal of Personality and Social Psychology, 66,* 310–328.

92. Matsumoto, 2006; Matsumoto, D. (1991). Cultural influences on facial expressions of emotion. *Southern Communication Journal, 56,* 128–137.

93. Burgoon et al., 2010.

94. Hall, E. T., & Hall, M. R. (1990). *Understanding cultural differences: Germans, French, and Americans.* Yarmouth, ME: Intercultural.

95. Levine, R., & Wolff, E. (1985, March). Social time: The heartbeat of culture. *Psychology Today,* 28–35.

96. McDaniel, E. R., & Andersen, P. A. (1998). Intercultural variations in tactile communication: A field study. *Journal of Nonverbal Behavior, 22,* 59–75; see also Field, T. (1999). American adolescents touch each other less and are more aggressive toward their peers as compared with French adolescents. *Adolescence, 34,* 753–758.

97. Andersen, P. A. (2008). *Nonverbal communication: Forms and functions* (2nd ed.). Long Grove, IL: Waveland; Andersen, P. A., & Wang, H. (2006). Unraveling cultural cues: Dimensions of nonverbal communication across cultures. In L. A. Samovar, R. E. Porter, & E. R. McDaniel (Eds.), *Intercultural communication: A reader* (pp. 250–266). Belmont, CA: Wadsworth.

98. Kramsch, C. (1998). *Language and culture.* New York: Oxford University Press.

99. Fridlund, A. J. (1994). *Human facial expression: An evolutionary review.* San Diego: Academic.

100. Griesler, D. L., & Kuhl, P. K. (1988). Maternal speech to infants in a tonal language: Support for universal prosodic features in motherese. *Developmental Psychology, 24,* 14–20.

101. Wood, J. T. (2009). *Gendered lives: Communication, culture, and gender* (8th ed.). Belmont, CA: Cengage/Wadsworth.

102. Floyd, K., Mikkelson, A. C., & Hesse, C. (2007). *The biology of human communication* (2nd ed.). Florence, KY: Thomson.

103. Burgoon, J. K., & Bacue, A. (2003). Nonverbal communication skills. In B. R. Burleson & J. O. Greene (Eds.), *Handbook of communication and social interaction skills* (pp. 179–219). Mahwah, NJ: Lawrence Erlbaum Associates.

104. Floyd, K. (2006). *Communicating affection: Interpersonal behavior and social context.* Cambridge, England: Cambridge University Press.

105. Blier, M. J., & Blier-Wilson, L. A. (1989). Gender differences in sex-rated emotional expressiveness. *Sex Roles, 21,* 287–295.

106. Nolen-Hoeksema, S. (1987). Sex differences in unipolar depression: Evidence and theory. *Psychological Bulletin, 101,* 259–282.

107. Coats, E. J., & Feldman, R. S. (1996). Gender differences in nonverbal correlates of social status. *Personality and Social Psychology Bulletin, 22,* 1014–1022.

108. Burrowes, B. D., & Halberstadt, A. G. (1987). Self- and family-expressiveness styles in the experience and expression of anger. *Journal of Nonverbal Behavior, 11,* 254–268.

109. Mulac, A., Studley, L. B., Wiemann, J. W., & Bradac, J. J. (1987). Male/female gaze in same-sex and mixed-sex dyads: Gender-linked differences and mutual influence. *Human Communication Research, 13,* 323–344.

110. Wada, M. (1990). The effects of interpersonal distance change on nonverbal behaviors: Mediating effects of sex and intimacy levels in a dyad. *Japanese Psychological Research, 32,* 86–96.

111. Exline, R. V. (1963). Explorations in the process of person perception: Visual interaction in relation to competition, sex, and the need for affiliation. *Journal of Personality, 31,* 1–20.

112. Mulac et al., 1987.

113. Patterson, M. L., & Schaeffer, R. E. (1997). Effects of size and sex composition on interaction distance, participation, and satisfaction in small groups. *Small Group Behavior, 8,* 433–442.

114. Shaffer, D. R., & Sadowski, C. (1975). This table is mine: Respect for marked barroom tables as a function of gender of spatial marker and desirability of locale. *Sociometry, 38,* 408–419.

115. Marieb, E. N. (2003). *Essentials of human anatomy and physiology* (7th ed.). San Francisco: Benjamin Cummings.

116. Fitzpatrick, M. A., Mulac, A., & Dindia, K. (1994, July). *Convergence and reciprocity in male and female communication patterns in spouse and stranger interaction.* Paper presented at the Fifth International Conference on Language and Social Psychology, Brisbane, Australia.

117. Major, B., Schmidlin, A. M., & Williams, L. (1990). Gesture patterns in social touch: The impact of setting and age. *Journal of Personality and Social Psychology, 58,* 634–643.

118. Ibid.

119. See Dortsch, S. (1997). Women at the cosmetics counter. *American Demographics, 19,* 4.

120. See, e.g., Hall, J. A. (2006). How big are nonverbal sex differences? The case of smiling and nonverbal sensitivity. In K. Dindia & D. J. Canary (Eds.), *Sex differences and similarities in communication* (2nd ed., pp. 59–81). Mahwah, NJ: Lawrence Erlbaum Associates.

121. Ekman, P., & Friesen, W. V. (1982). Felt, false, and miserable smiles. *Journal of Nonverbal Behavior, 6,* 238–252.

122. Riggio, R. E. (2005). The Social Skills Inventory (SSI): Measuring nonverbal and social skills. In V. Manusov (Ed.), *The sourcebook of nonverbal measures: Going beyond words* (pp. 25–34). Mahwah, NJ: Lawrence Erlbaum Associates.

123. Riggio, R. E. (2006). Nonverbal skills and abilities. In V. Manusov & M. L. Patterson (Eds.), *The Sage handbook of nonverbal communication* (pp. 79–96). Thousand Oaks, CA: Sage.

124. Riggio, R. E. (1986). Assessment of basic social skills. *Journal of Personality and Social Psychology, 51,* 649–660.

125. See Friedman, H. S., & Riggio, R. E. (1981). Effects of individual differences in nonverbal expressiveness on transmission of emotion. *Journal of Nonverbal Behavior, 6,* 96–102.

126. Friedman, H. S., Prince, L. M., Riggio, R. E., & DiMatteo, M. R. (1980). Understanding and assessing nonverbal expressiveness: The Affective Communication Test. *Journal of Personality and Social Psychology, 39,* 333–351.

Chapter 7

1. See Spitzberg, B. H. (1994). The dark side of (in)competence. In W. R. Cupach & B. H. Spitzberg (Eds.), *The dark side of interpersonal communication* (pp. 25–50). Hillsdale, NJ: Lawrence Erlbaum Associates.

2. Emmert, P. (1996). President's perspective. *ILA Listening Post, 56,* 2–3.

3. Dindia, K., & Kennedy, B. L. (2004, November). *Communication in everyday life: A descriptive study using mobile electronic data collection.* Paper presented at the annual conference of the National Communication Association, Chicago.

4. Barker, L., Edwards, R., Gaines, C., Gladney, K., & Holley, F. (1980). An investigation of proportional time spent in various communicating activities by college students. *Journal of Applied Communication Research, 8,* 101–109; Hargie, O., Saunders, C., & Dickson, D. (1994). *Social skills in interpersonal communication* (3rd ed.). New York: Routledge.

5. Windsor, J. L., Curtis, D. B., & Stephens, R. D. (1997). National preferences in business and communication education: An update. *Journal of the Association for Communication Administration, 3,* 170–179.

6. Wolvin, A. D. (1984). Meeting the communication needs of the adult learner. *Communication Education, 33,* 267–271.

7. See, e.g., Prager, K. J., & Buhrmester, D. (1998). Intimacy and need fulfillment in couple relationships. *Journal of Social and Personal Relationships, 15,* 435–469.

8. Brownell, J. (1990). Perceptions of effective listeners: A management study. *Journal of Business Communication, 27,* 401–415.

9. Carrell, L. J., & Willmington, S. C. (1996). A comparison of self-report and performance data in assessing speaking and listening competence. *Communication Reports, 9,* 185–191.

10. See Lane, K., Balleweg, B. J., Suler, J. R., Fernald, P. S., & Goldstein, G. S. (2000). Acquiring skills—Undergraduate students. In M. E. Ware & D. E. Johnson (Eds.), *Handbook of demonstrations and activities in the teaching of psychology: Vol. 3. Personality, abnormal, clinical-counseling, and social* (2nd ed., pp. 109–124). Mahwah, NJ: Lawrence Erlbaum Associates.

11. Spinks, N., & Wells, B. (1991). Improving listening power: The payoff. *Bulletin of the Association for Business Communication, 54,* 75–77.

12. Broome, B. J. (1991). Building shared meaning: Implications of a relational approach to empathy for teaching intercultural communication. *Communication Education, 40,* 235–249.

13. Wolvin, A. D. (1987, June). *Culture as a listening variable.* Paper presented at the summer conference of the International Listening Association, Toronto, Ontario.

14. Chen, G–M., & Chung, J. (1997). The "Five Asian Dragons": Management behaviors and organization communication. In L. A. Samovar & R. E. Porter (Eds.), *Intercultural communication: A reader* (pp. 317–328). Belmont, CA: Wadsworth.

15. Anderson, K. J., & Leaper, C. (1998). Meta-analyses of gender effects on conversational interruption: Who, what, when, where, and how. *Sex Roles, 39,* 225–252.

16. Bente, G., Donaghy, W. C., & Suwelack, D. (1998). Sex differences in body movement and visual attention: An integrated analysis of movement and gaze in mixed-sex dyads. *Journal of Nonverbal Behavior, 22,* 31–58.

17. Brownell, J. (2002). *Listening attitudes, principles, and skills* (2nd ed.). Boston: Allyn & Bacon.

18. Macrae, C. N., & Bodenhausen, G. V. (2001). Social cognition: Categorical person perception. *British Journal of Psychology, 92,* 239–255.

19. Thomas, L. T., & Levine, T. R. (1994). Disentangling listening and verbal recall: Separate but related constructs? *Human Communication Research, 21,* 103–127.

20. Benoit, S. S., & Lee, J. W. (1986). Listening: It can be taught. *Journal of Education for Business, 63,* 229–232.

21. Bellezza, F. S., & Buck, D. K. (1988). Expert knowledge as mnemonic cues. *Applied Cognitive Psychology, 2,* 147–162.

22. Duncan, S., & Fiske, D. W. (1977). *Face-to-face interaction: Research, methods, and theory.* New York: Wiley.

23. Egan, G. (1998). *The skilled helper* (6th ed.). Pacific Grove, CA: Brooks/Cole.

24. Kuhn, J. L. (2001). Toward an ecological humanistic psychology. *Journal of Humanistic Psychology, 41,* 9–24.

25. Duan, C., & Hill, C. E. (1996). The current state of empathy research. *Journal of Counseling Psychology, 43,* 261–274.

26. Stiff, J. B., Dillard, J. P., Somera, L., Kim, H., & Sleight, C. (1988). Empathy, communication, and prosocial behavior. *Communication Monographs, 55,* 198–213.

27. See Armstrong, B. G., Boiarsky, G. A., & Mares, M. L. (1991). Background television and reading performance. *Communication Monographs, 58,* 235–253.

28. Haider, M. (1970). Neuro-psychology of attention, expectation, and vigilance. In D. I. Mostofsky (Ed.), *Attention: Contemporary theory and analysis* (pp. 419–432). New York: Appleton-Century-Crofts.

29. Ball, S. A., & Zuckerman, M. (1992). Sensation seeking and selective attention: Focused and divided attention on a dichotic listening task. *Journal of Personality and Social Psychology, 63,* 825–831.

30. Media Dynamics, Inc. (2007, February 15). Our rising ad dosage: It's not as oppressive as some think. *Media Matters, XXI*(3), 1–2.

31. Toffler, A. (1970). *Future shock.* New York: Random House.

32. Keller, E. (2007, July 19). Why you can't get any work done: Workplace distractions cost U.S. business some $650 billion a year. Retrieved November 23, 2007, from http://www.businessweek.com/careers/content/jul2007/ca20070719_880333.htm

33. American Psychiatric Association (1994). *Diagnostic and statistical manual of mental disorders* (4th ed.). Washington, DC: Author.

34. Attention-deficit hyperactivity disorder: ADHD in adults. Retrieved March 8, 2008, from http://www.webmd.com/ add-adhd/guide/adhd-adults

35. Versfeld, N. J., & Dreschler, W. A. (2002). The relationship between the intelligibility of time-compressed speech and speech-in-noise in young and elderly listeners. *Journal of the Acoustical Society of America, 111,* 401–408; Wolvin, A., & Coakley, C. (1996). *Listening.* Dubuque, IA: Brown & Benchmark.

36. Golen, S. (1990). A factor analysis of barriers to effective listening. *Journal of Business Communication, 27,* 25–36.

55. Sapadin, L. A. (1988). Friendship and gender: Perspectives of professional men and women. *Journal of Social and Personal Relationships, 5,* 387–403.

56. Rawlins, W. K. (1992). *Friendship matters: Communication, dialectics, and the life course.* New York: Aldine de Gruyter.

57. Kaplan, D. L., & Keys, C. B. (1997). Sex and relationship variables as predictors of sexual attraction in cross-sex platonic friendships between young heterosexual adults. *Journal of Social and Personal Relationships, 14,* 191–206; Sapadin, L. A. (1988). Friendships and gender perspectives of professional men and women. *Journal of Social and Personal Relationships, 5,* 387–403.

58. Egland, K. I., Spitzberg, B. G., & Zormeier, M. M. (1996). Flirtation and conversational competence in cross-sex platonic and romantic relationships. *Communication Reports, 9,* 105–118.

59. Fuiman, M., Yarab, P., & Sensibaugh, C. (1997, July). *Just friends? An examination of the sexual, physical, and romantic aspects of cross-gender friendships.* Paper presented at the biennial meeting of the International Network on Personal Relationships, Oxford, OH.

60. Afifi, W. A., & Faulkner, S. L. (2000). On being "just friends": The frequency and impact of sexual activity in cross-sex friendships. *Journal of Social and Personal Relationships, 17,* 205–222.

61. Werking, K. J. (1997). *We're just good friends: Women and men in nonromantic relationships.* New York: Guilford.

62. Messman, S. J., Canary, D. J., & Hause, K. S. (2000). Motives to remain platonic, equity, and the use of maintenance strategies in opposite-sex friendships. *Journal of Social and Personal Relationships, 17,* 67–94.

63. Rose, S. M. (1985). Same- and cross-sex friendships and the psychology of homosociality. *Sex Roles, 12,* 63–74.

64. Rawlins, W. K. (1981). Friendship as a communicative achievement: A theory and an interpretive analysis of verbal reports. Unpublished doctoral dissertation, Temple University, Philadelphia.

65. Rose, S. M. (1984). How friendships end: Patterns among young adults. *Journal of Social and Personal Relationships, 1,* 267–277.

66. See Bleske-Rechek, A. L., & Buss, D. M. (2001). Opposite-sex friendship: Sex differences and similarities in initiation, selection, and dissolution. *Personality and Social Psychology Bulletin, 37,* 1310–1323.

67. Rose, 1984.

68. See Feld, S. L. (1997). Structural embeddedness and the stability of interpersonal relations. *Social Networks, 19,* 91–95.

69. Sias, P. M., Krone, K. J., & Jablin, F. M. (2002). An ecological systems perspective on workplace relationships. In M. L. Knapp & J. A. Daly (Eds.), *Handbook of interpersonal communication* (3rd ed., pp. 615–642). Thousand Oaks, CA.

70. Sias, P. M., & Cahill, D. J. (1998). From co-worker to friends: The development of peer friendships in the workplace. *Western Journal of Communication, 62,* 273–300.

71. Marks, S. R. (1994). Intimacy in the public realm: The case of coworkers. *Social Forces, 72,* 843–858.

72. Winstead, B. A., Derlega, V. J., Montgomery, M. J., & Pilkington, C. (1995). The quality of friendships at work and job satisfaction. *Journal of Social and Personal Relationships, 12,* 199–215.

73. Zorn, T. E. (1995). Bosses and buddies: Constructing and performing simultaneously hierarchical and close friendship relationships. In J. T. Wood & S. Duck (Eds.), *Under-studied relationships: Off the beaten track* (pp. 122–147). Thousand Oaks, CA: Sage.

74. Largent, R. N. (1987). The relationship of friendship with a supervisor to job satisfaction and satisfaction with the supervisor. Unpublished master's thesis, University of North Dakota, Grand Forks.

75. See Fiedler, F. E. (1957). A note on leadership theory: The effect of social barriers between leaders and followers. *Sociometry, 20,* 87–94.

76. Zorn, 1995.

77. Adelman, M. B., Ahuvia, A., & Goodwin, C. (1994). Beyond smiling. In R. T. Rust & R. L. Oliver (Eds.), *Service quality: New directions in theory and practice* (pp. 139–171). Thousand Oaks, CA: Sage; Locke, K. (1996). A funny thing happened! The management of consumer emotions in service encounters. *Organizational Science, 7,* 40–59.

78. Gwinner, K. P., Gremler, D. D., & Bitner, M. J. (1998). Relational benefits in service industries: The customer's perspective. *Journal of the Academy of Marketing Science, 26,* 101–114.

79. American College of Physicians. Ethics manual. Retrieved January 2, 2011, from http://www.acponline.org/running_practice/ethics/

Chapter 10

1. Hecht, M. L., Marston, P. J., & Larkey, L. K. (1994). Love ways and relationship quality in heterosexual relationships. *Journal of Social and Personal Relationships, 11,* 25–44.

2. Baxter, L. A., & Montgomery, B. M. (1996). *Relating: Dialogues and dialectics.* New York: Guilford.

3. Peterson, G. W., & Bush, K. R. (1999). Predicting adolescent autonomy from parents: Relationship connectedness and restrictiveness. *Sociological Inquiry, 69,* 431–457.

4. U.S. Census Bureau. (2011). Decennial census data on marriage and divorce. Retrieved January 2, 2011, from http://www.census.gov/hhes/socdemo/marriage/data/census/index.html

5. Kaplan, R. M., & Kronick, R. G. (2006). Marital status and longevity in the United States population. *Journal of Epidemiology and Community Health, 60,* 760–765; Manzoli, M., Villarti, P., Pirone, G. M., & Boccia, A. (2007). Marital status and mortality in the elderly: A systematic review and meta-analysis. *Social Science & Medicine, 64,* 77–94.

6. Macintyre, S. (1992). The effects of family position and status on health. *Social Science & Medicine, 35,* 453–464.

7. Duncan, G., Wilkerson, B., & England, P. (2006). Cleaning up their act: The effects of marriage and cohabitation on licit and illicit drug use. *Demography, 43,* 691–710.

8. Bachman, J. G., Wadsworth, K. N., O'Malley, P. M., Johnston, L. D., & Schulenberg, J. E. (1997). *Smoking, drinking, and drug use in young adulthood: The impacts of new freedoms and new responsibilities.* Mahwah, NJ: Lawrence Erlbaum Associates.

9. Kim, H. K., & McKenry, P. (2002). The relationship between marriage and psychological well-being. *Journal of Family Issues, 23,* 885–911; Lamb, K. A., Lee, G. R., & DeMaris, A. (2003). Union formation and depression: Selection and relationship effects. *Journal of Marriage and Family, 65,* 953–962.

10. See Kiecolt-Glaser, J. K., & Newton, T. L. (2001). Marriage and health: His and hers. *Psychological Bulletin, 127,* 472–503.

11. Waldron, I., Hughes, M. E., & Brooks, T. L. (1996). Marriage protection and marriage selection—Prospective evidence for reciprocal effects of marital status and health. *Social Science & Medicine, 43,* 113–123.

12. Bringle, R. G., & Buunk, B. P. (1991). Extradyadic relationships and sexual jealousy. In K. McKinney & S. Sprecher (Eds.), *Sexuality in close relationships* (pp. 135–153). Mahwah, NJ: Lawrence Erlbaum Associates.

13. Mazur, R. M. (2000). *The new intimacy: Open-ended marriage and alternative lifestyles.* Boston: iUniverse.com Inc.

14. Rust, P. C. (2003). Monogamy and polyamory: Relationship issues for bisexuals. In L. Garnets & D. Kimmel (Eds.), *Psychological perspectives on lesbian, gay, and bisexual experiences* (pp. 475–495). New York: Columbia University Press.

15. Bettinger, M. (2004). Polyamory and gay men: A family systems approach. *Journal of GLBT Family Studies, 1,* 97–116; Blasband, D., & Peplau, L. A. (1985). Sexual exclusivity versus openness in gay male couples. *Archives of Sexual Behavior, 14,* 395–412.

16. Munson, M., & Stelbourn, J. P. (Eds.). (1999). *The lesbian polyamory reader: Open relationships, non-monogamy, and casual sex.* Binghamton, NY: Haworth.

17. Bringle & Buunk, 1991.

18. Priambodo, N. (2006, April 17). Dating trends jump on the technological train. *University of La Verne Campus Times.* Retrieved from http://www.ulv.edu/ctimes/web_exclusives_stories/datingtrends.htm

19. See Uebelacker, L. A., Courtnage, E. S., & Whisman, M. A. (2003). Correlates of depression and marital dissatisfaction: Perceptions of marital communication style. *Journal of Social and Personal Relationships, 20,* 757–769.

20. Previti, D., & Amato, P. R. (2003). Why stay married? Rewards, barriers, and marital stability. *Journal of Marriage and Family, 65,* 561–573.

21. Dion, K. K., & Dion, K. L. (1996). Cultural perspectives on romantic love. *Personal Relationships, 3,* 5–17.

22. Amato, P. R., & Previti, D. (2003). People's reasons for divorcing. *Journal of Family Issues, 24,* 602–626.

23. Smock, P. J., Manning, W. D., & Porter, M. (2005). "Everything's there except money": How money shapes decisions to marry among cohabitors. *Journal of Marriage and Family, 67,* 680–696.

24. Compton, J., & Pollak, R. A. (2007). Why are power couples increasingly concentrated in large metropolitan areas? *Journal of Labor Economics, 25,* 475–512.

25. Levine, R. B. (1993). Is love a luxury? *American Demographics, 15,* 27–28.

26. Hsu, F. L. K. (1981). The self in cross-cultural perspective. In A. J. Marsella, B. De Vos, & F. L. K. Hsu (Eds.), *Culture and self* (pp. 24–55). London: Tavistock. Quote is from p. 50.

27. Coontz, S. (2006). *Marriage, a history: How love conquered marriage.* New York: Penguin.

28. Kurdek, L. A. (2004). Are gay and lesbian cohabiting couples really different from heterosexual married couples? *Journal of Marriage and Family, 66,* 880–900.

29. Kurdek, L. A. (1998). Relationship outcomes and their predictors: Longitudinal evidence from heterosexual married, gay cohabiting, and lesbian cohabiting couples. *Journal of Marriage and the Family, 60,* 553–568.

30. Kurdek, L. A. (1994). Conflict resolution styles in gay, lesbian, heterosexual nonparent, and heterosexual parent couples. *Journal of Marriage and the Family, 56,* 705–722.

31. Kurdek, L. A. (1994). Areas of conflict for gay, lesbian, and heterosexual couples: What couples argue about influences relationship satisfaction. *Journal of Marriage and the Family, 56,* 923–934.

32. Kurdek, L. A., & Schmitt, J. P. (1987). Perceived emotional support from family and friends in members of homosexual, married, and heterosexual cohabiting couples. *Journal of Homosexuality, 14,* 57–68.

33. Kurdek, L. A. (1993). The allocation of household labor in gay, lesbian, and heterosexual married couples. *Journal of Social Issues, 49,* 127–139.

34. Balsam, K. F., Beauchaine, T. P., Rothblum, E. D., & Solomon, S. E. (2008). Three-year follow-up of same-sex couples who had civil unions in Vermont, same-sex couples not in civil unions, and heterosexual married couples. *Developmental Psychology, 44,* 102–116; Roisman, G. I., Clausell, E., Holland, A., Fortuna, K., & Elieff, C. (2008). Adult romantic relationships as contexts of human development: A multimethod comparison of same-sex couples with opposite-sex dating, engaged, and married dyads. *Developmental Psychology, 44,* 91–101.

35. Barker, L. A., & Emery, R. E. (1993). When every relationship is above average: Perceptions and expectations of divorce at the time of marriage. *Law and Human Behavior, 17,* 439–450.

36. United States General Accounting Office. Retrieved from http://www.gao.gov/archive/1997/og97016.pdf

37. Knapp, M. L., & Vangelisti, A. L. (2000). *Interpersonal communication and human relationships* (4th ed.). Boston: Allyn & Bacon; Avtgis, T. A., West, D. V., & Anderson, T. L. (1998). Relationship stages: An inductive analysis identifying cognitive, affective, and behavioral dimensions of Knapp's relational stages model. *Communication Research Reports, 15,* 280–287.

38. Peplau, L. A. (2003). Lesbian and gay relationships. In L. Garnets & D. Kimmel (Eds.), *Psychological perspectives on lesbian, gay, and bisexual experiences* (pp. 395–419). New York: Columbia University Press.

39. Fitzpatrick, M. A. (1988). *Between husbands and wives: Communication in marriage.* Newbury Park, CA: Sage.

40. Fitzpatrick, M. A., Fey, J., Segrin, C., & Schiff, J. L. (1993). Internal working models of relationships and marital communication. *Journal of Language and Social Psychology, 12,* 103–131.

41. Wilmot, W. W., & Hocker, J. L. (2001). *Interpersonal conflict.* New York: McGraw-Hill. Quote is from p. 40.

42. Gottman, J. M., & Levenson, R. W. (1992). Marital processes predictive of later dissolution: Behavior, physiology, and health. *Journal of Personality and Social Psychology, 63,* 221–233.

43. Gottman, J. M. (1994). *What predicts divorce?* Hillsdale, NJ: Lawrence Erlbaum Associates.

44. Holman, T. B., & Jarvis, M. O. (2003). Hostile, volatile, avoiding, and validating couple-conflict types: An investigation of Gottman's couple-conflict types. *Personal Relationships, 10,* 267–282.

45. Petronio, S. (2002). *Boundaries of privacy.* Albany: SUNY Press.

46. See Dindia, K., Fitzpatrick, M. A., & Kenny, D. A. (1997). Self-disclosure in spouse and stranger interaction: A social relations analysis. *Human Communication Research, 23,* 388–412.

47. Cordova, J. V., Gee, C. B., & Warren, L. Z. (2005). Emotional skillfulness in marriage: Intimacy as a mediator of the relationship between emotional skillfulness and marital satisfaction. *Journal of Social and Clinical Psychology, 24,* 218–235.

48. Mirgain, S. A., & Cordova, J. V. (2007). Emotion skills and marital health: The association between observed and self-reported emotion skills, intimacy, and marital satisfaction. *Journal of Social and Clinical Psychology, 26,* 983–1009.

49. Gottman, J. M., & Levenson, R. W. (1986). Assessing the role of emotion in marriage. *Behavioral Assessment, 8,* 31–48.

50. Carstensen, L. L., Gottman, J. M., & Levenson, R. W. (1995). Emotional behavior in long-term marriage. *Psychology and Aging, 10,* 140–149.

51. Gottman, 1994.

52. Ibid.

53. Kluwer, E. S., Heesink, J. A. M., & Van de Vliert, E. (1997). The marital dynamics of conflict over the division of labor. *Journal of Marriage and the Family, 59,* 635–653; Perry-Jenkins, M., & Folk, K. (1994). Class, couples, and conflict: Effects of the division of

inc./Getty Images; p. 279 (bottom left): Department of Defense, photo by Staff Sgt. James L. Harper Jr., U.S. Air Force; p. 279 (right): © AP Images; p. 280: © Newscom; p. 281: Randy Faris/Corbis; p. 282: © Stockdisc/PunchStock; p. 283: Masterfile; p. 284 (left): Lars A. Niki/ The McGraw-Hill Companies; p. 284 (right): © Bruce Bi/Lonely Planet Images; p. 286: © Paramount Images/Photofest; p. 288: © Masterfile; p. 292: Hallmark Cards, Inc.; p. 294: © 20th Century Fox Film Corp. All rights reserved/Courtesy Everett Collection; p. 295: © Masterfile; p. 296: ©NetPhotos/Alamy; p. 298 (left): © Mark Karrass/ Corbis; p. 298 (right): © Purestock/ PunchStock; p. 300: © RF/Corbis; p. 301: © MIXA/Getty Images; p. 303: © Digital Vision/Alamy; p. 307: © BananaStock Ltd.

Chapter 10

p. 312: David James/TM and © Copyright Twentieth Century Fox Film Corporation. All rights reserved/Courtesy Everett Collection; p. 315: © AP Images; p. 316: © Image Source/Getty Images; p. 317: © Leland Bobbe/Getty Images; p. 320 (top, left to right): © Thomas Cockrem/Alamy; Steve Raymer/Jupiterimages; Maria Teijeiro/agefotostock; p. 320 (bottom): © CBS/Photofest; p. 321: © Jupiterimages; p. 322: © Jim Wilson/The New York Times/ Redux; p. 323: © Jupiterimages; p. 325: © AP Images; p. 326: image100/Alamy; p. 327: © Thinkstock; p. 330 (top): moodboard/ Corbis; p. 330 (bottom): © RF/ Corbis; p. 331: Source: glasbergen .com Copyright 1997 Randy Glasbergen; p. 333: Blend Images/Getty Images; p. 335: © H. Armstrong Roberts/ClassicStock/Corbis; p. 337: © Jean Mahaux/The Image Bank/Getty Images; p. 339: © Paul Burns/Tetra Images/photolibrary; p. 340 (top): © Ocean/Corbis; p. 340 (bottom): Rubberball/Getty

Images; p. 343: Ariel Skelley/Blend Images/Getty Images

Chapter 11

p. 348: Jeremy Woodhouse/Blend Images/Getty Images; p. 350: © Rob Wilkinson/Alamy; p. 352: Comstock Images/Alamy; p. 354: © BananaStock/PunchStock; p. 356: © Copyright Fox Searchlight Pictures. All rights reserved/ Courtesy Everett Collection; p. 357: Brad Wilson/Stone/Getty Images; p. 358: © Queerstock, Inc./Alamy; p. 359: CBS/Monty Brinton/Landov Images; p. 360 (left): © Masterfile; p. 360 (right): Steve Cole/Digital Vision/Getty Images; p. 361 (left): © BananaStock/PunchStock; p. 361 (right): © Jasper James/agefotostock; p. 362: © Veer Incorporated; p. 364 (left to right): Jose Luis Pelaez Inc./ Getty Images; Santa Clara/Photononstop/photolibrary; © Boutet Jean-Pierre/agefotostock; p. 367 (top): Stuart Ramson; p. 367 (bottom): © The Weinstein Company/ Photofest; p. 370: © EPA/Andy Rain/Landov Images; p. 371: Amos Morgan/Getty Images; p. 373 (top): © Eric Audras/Getty Images; p. 373 (bottom): © BananaStock/Jupiterimages; p. 374: Robert Michael/ Corbis

Chapter 12

p. 380: Photo by Marco Di Lauro/ Getty Images; p. 382: © John Giustina/Getty Images; p. 383 (top): Digital Vision/Alamy; p. 383 (bottom); © Masterfile; p. 384: © Stockbyte/Getty Images; p. 385: Stockbyte/Getty Images; p. 386: Image Source/Getty Images; p. 388: © CartoonStock; p. 389: © RF/ Corbis; p. 390: © SuperStock; p. 391: © Universal/Courtesy Everett Collection; p. 393: © 20th Century Fox Licensing/Merchandising/Courtesy Everett Collection; p. 394: © Simon Jarratt/Corbis; p. 395: © Ian Sanderson/Getty Images; p. 396: Dave and Les Jacobs/Blend Images LLC; p. 400: © AP Images; p. 401:

© Royalty-Free/Corbis; p. 402: Somos/Veer/Getty Images

Text Credits

Chapter 1

p. 29: Items adapted from "A measure of emotional empathy" by A. Mehrabian and N. Epstein in *Journal of Personality* (1972), Vol. 40, pp. 525–543. Reprinted by permission of Wiley-Blackwell/ John Wiley & Sons.

Chapter 2

p. 50: "The development and validation of the intercultural sensitivity scale" by G. M. Chen and W. J. Starosta from *Human Communication* (2000), Vol. 3, pp. 1–14. Reprinted by permission of the author.

Chapter 3

p. 85: "Cross-cultural correlates of life satisfaction and self-esteem" by E. Diener and M. Diener from *Journal of Personality and Social Psychology* (1995), Vol. 68, pp. 653–663. Used by permission of American Psychological Association; p. 91: "HIV-infected persons' attributions for the disclosure and nondisclosure of the seropositive diagnosis to significant others" by V. J. Derlega and B. A. Winstead from *Attribution, communication behavior, and close relationships* ed. by V. Manusov and J. H. Harvey, pp. 266–284. Reprinted by permission of Cambridge University Press.

Chapter 4

p. 137: "A room with a cue: Personality judgements based on offices and bedrooms" by S. D. Gosling, S. J. Ko, T. Mannarelli and M. E. Morris from *Journal of Personality and Social Psychology* (2002), Vol. 82, pp. 379–398. Used by permission of American Psychological Association.

Chapter 6

p. 210: "Assessment of basic social skills" by R. E. Riggio from *Journal*

of Personality and Social Psychology (1986), Vol. 51, pp. 649–660.

Chapter 7

p. 217: "Who are we as we listen? Individual listening profiles in varying contexts" by M. Imhof from *International Journal of Listening* (2004), Vol. 18, pp. 36–45; "The listening styles profile (LSP-16): Development and validation of an instrument to assess four listening styles" by K. W. Watson, L. L. Barker and J. B. Weaver from *International Journal of Listening* (1995), Vol. 9, pp. 1–13; p. 218: "Communication in everyday life: A descriptive study using mobile electronic data collection" by K. Dinidia and B. L. Kennedy. Paper presented at the annual conference of the National Communication Association, Chicago, IL. Reprinted by permission of Kathryn Dindia, Ph.D.; p. 222: "Listening styles: Sex differences in perceptions of self and others" by S. L. Sargent and J. B. Weaver from *International Journal of Listening* (2003), Vol. 17, pp. 5–18. Used by permission of International Listening Association.

Chapter 8

p. 267: "Sex differences in emotion: Expression, experience, and physiology" by A. M. Kring and A. H. Gordon from *Journal of Personality and Social Psychology* (1998), Vol. 74, pp. 686–703. Copyright © 1998, APA. Reprinted by permission.

Chapter 10

p. 316: W. R. Cupach and B. H. Spitzberg, *The dark side of relationship pursuit: From attraction to obsession and stalking* (2004). Mahwah, NJ: Lawrence Erlbaum Associates; "Cyberstalking and the technologies of interpersonal terrorism" by B. H. Spitzberg and G. Hoobler from *New Media & Society* (2004), Vol. 4, pp. 71–92.

Index